A MILTON HANDBOOK

APPLETON-CENTURY-CROFTS

EDUCATIONAL DIVISION

New York   MEREDITH CORPORATION

A Milton Handbook

FIFTH EDITION

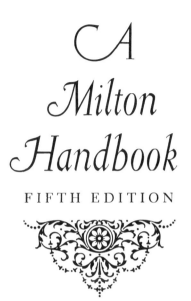

JAMES HOLLY HANFORD & JAMES G. TAAFFE

Endpapers: Pages 1 and 2 of the manuscript, by an unidentified hand, from which the first edition (1667) of *Paradise Lost* was set.

Acknowledgment is made for permission to reprint from the following copy-righted material:

The Complete Prose Works of John Milton, ed. Don M. Wolfe. Volume I, copyright, 1953, Yale University Press. Volume IV, Part I, copyright © 1966 by Yale University.

The Early Lives of Milton, ed. Helen Darbishire, by permission of Constable and Co., Ltd., and Barnes & Noble, Inc.

Private Correspondence and Academic Exercises, Translated from the Latin . . . with an Introduction and Commentary by E. M. W. Tillyard, trans. Phyllis B. Tillyard, by permission of Cambridge University Press.

PREFACE TO THE FIFTH EDITION

It has been impossible to do justice to the "flowery crop of knowledge" about Milton which has sprung up since the publication of this handbook in its original form. Recent works on Milton have dealt extensively with his political and theological ideas, with the cultural backgrounds of the prose and poetry, and many more with close analysis of the texts themselves. Such studies have not always pictured Milton as the representative of Christian humanism in its English manifestation; to A. J. A. Waldock and William Empson, for instance, Milton is a great figure precisely because he questioned the benevolence and justice of the Christian God. He is seen not as putting his stamp on what were indeed the commonplaces of his age but as skeptical of their ultimate value. The challenge to the traditional admirers of Milton thrown out earlier in our century by T. S. Eliot has prompted many to "revaluate" Milton's accomplishments; it has also evoked some brilliant defensive writing, a fine example of which is the answer made by Logan Pearsall Smith. Many recent seventeenth-century studies—ranging from those of Waldock, F. R. Leavis, Empson, J. B. Broadbent, and John Peter to those of Douglas Bush, C. S. Lewis, Joseph Summers, and Christopher Ricks—have a way of taking off from or coming back to the early criticism of Eliot. This is, however, much less characteristic of the studies of Arnold Stein, Isabel MacCaffrey, Rosemond Tuve, and Anne Ferry, who have concentrated upon close textual analysis of the major works. The varied literature of the Milton controversy continues to accumulate annually at a pace which outdistances the most careful and indefatigable bibliographer.

Major contributions to the study of Milton's biography have been made by J. Milton French's monumental five-volume collection of *The Life Records of John Milton* and by Harris Fletcher's still uncompleted *The Intellectual Development of John Milton* (two volumes are now available). The important biography of Milton by William R. Parker was published only a few months before his untimely death. A notable new edition (in progress) of the prose has been launched under the general editorship of Don M. Wolfe, and significant editions of the poems by Merritt Y. Hughes, John T. Shawcross, and Douglas Bush have appeared. While the two-volume index to the Columbia Edition remains one of the more valuable tools for future study, the Columbia Edition will be enhanced by the forthcoming publication of a series of variorum notes to accompany the volumes of poetry.

In the present edition of the *Handbook* a necessary compromise has been made between the old and the new in Milton scholarship. Many articles which elaborate or clarify accepted conclusions or which deal with minor points have been included without comment in the bibliography. Some material deserving of full discussion but not easily incorporated into the present format has been alluded to in the text and notes. Essential corrections have been made, however, and the present trends in research and interpretation have been in one way or another indicated.

In preparing this edition we have had the valuable assistance of John S. Diekhoff and William R. Parker. We also wish to record our thanks to Mrs. Sarah DeVenne, who, as research assistant, performed many of the tasks necessary for this revision.

James Holly Hanford
James G. Taaffe

Note: Professor Hanford's death occurred shortly after the completion of the *Handbook*.

JGT

PREFACE TO THE FIRST EDITION

This volume aims to supply in brief compass a body of materials which will be useful in the scholarly study of the poet Milton. Life is too short to permit many men to master the detail embodied in David Masson's seven-volume biography, not to speak of the additions which have been made to Miltonic lore since Masson's time. It is too short, even, to exhaust the data contained in Milton's own voluminous works. The need of a "ready and easy way" is witnessed by the numerous brief lives and by the annotated school editions of the poems and selections from the prose. Something more comprehensive seems, however, desirable. The mature student will wish to survey Milton's entire literary activity, to be in possession of the essential facts regarding the origin, dates, and circumstances of his individual works, and to have, at least in brief, the assured or reasonably assured results of learned activity on the many other issues and points of interest about him. It is only thus that his significance in English literature can be understood or his greatness properly estimated.

Oddly enough no companion to Milton studies, comparable in scope to the available Shakespeare and Chaucer handbooks, has ever been written. In undertaking to supply the deficiency I have tried to select from the vast mass of material available what seemed most relevant and useful, giving in the footnotes a running bibliography (indexed at the end of the volume) which will enable the student to pursue the subject further at any point. I have necessarily left to the editors and to the various special dictionaries of

Milton's language and allusions (listed in the general bibliography) the task of supplying a detailed interpretation of the texts. Discussion of purely critical problems is also omitted, though the general course of Miltonic opinion is sketched in the final chapter. The first process in the study of Milton should be interpretation rather than judgment, and it is to this end that the materials given in the present volume are aimed. In view, finally, of the ready accessibility in cyclopedias and elsewhere of summary statements of the outward events of Milton's life, and because I am convinced of the superior value of the documents themselves over any modern digest of them, I have substituted for the usual biography the statements of Milton himself and those who knew him, arranged according to the accepted periods of his career.

Of the inadequacy of this handbook to represent the field in which it enters, I am well aware. Miltonic scholarship and interpretation, in distinction from purely aesthetic criticism, have made great strides of late. The discussions are complex and their full results as yet unmeasured. But it is quite certain that the present generation, in discarding many traditional presuppositions and prejudices, and in bringing to bear new data of importance, is in the way of attaining a sounder conception of Milton's essential quality and significance. Interest in him has been wider in the past, but it was never more vital than it is today. The glory of his utterance is as highly valued as ever, the power of his poetic and philosophic thought, as contrasted with the dogmatic aspects of his inherited theology, much more so. His personality, seen in the light of modern psychological knowledge, is no longer to be envisaged, whether with enthusiasm or dislike, in the simple terms of Puritanism, but rather as a complex of emotions and restraints which constitutes one of the most curious phenomena in the annals of poetic genius.

The present volume deals with these matters all too briefly. It will, however, at least guide the reader to the most important of them and it will be justified if it assists him to see Milton in clearer focus as the great figure in whom the intellectual and aesthetic enthusiasms of the Renaissance, the moral forces of the Reformation, and the fervor of a patriotic love of liberty met at their height and dwelt together for a moment, not inharmoniously.

My obligations to authorities, particularly to the more recent ones, are pretty well indicated in the footnotes. But I have omitted specific references to the authority to whom I owe the most— David Masson. His work is thoroughly indexed, and it may be assumed to be my general source for all biographical and historical data where no other is mentioned.

James Holly Hanford

CONTENTS

xi

A MILTON HANDBOOK

Chapter 1

MATERIALS FOR MILTON'S BIOGRAPHY

THE PRELIMINARY MATERIALS

THE LIFE OF MILTON IS KNOWN TO US IN FAR MORE FULLNESS OF detail than that of any other major English poet before the eighteenth century. The reasons for this fact are various. In the first place, he was in his own time a public figure, concerned in political events of a sensational character. His pamphlets in defense of liberty made his name one of which, to use his own extravagant but not wholly unjustifiable praise, "all Europe talked from side to side." His service as Latin Secretary to the Council of State for eleven momentous years entitled him to the attention, favorable and unfavorable, which was accorded to the other members of the Commonwealth government. Then, too, he was a scholar in the days when scholarship was still held in high esteem. As such he was in communication with many distinguished men at home and on the Continent and was noticed as he never would have been in the capacity of a mere man of letters. Although the seventeenth century possessed no such curiosity in literary biography as we have today, the modern interest in such matters was beginning to develop, and before the generation of those who had known Milton personally passed away it was thought worthwhile to set down regarding him many of those intimate details of personality and habit which we wish for in vain in the case of Chaucer, Spenser, or Shakespeare.

Finally, and this perhaps is most important of all, Milton was intensely concerned to have his own image stand in the public eye as he himself conceived it. He inherited the Renaissance thirst for enduring fame, and he combined with this desire an enthusiasm for self-portraiture akin to that of the Romantic poets. He often had occasion to justify himself in his controversial writings against attacks upon his private life, and he did so with the greatest gusto. Like many other humanists he preserved and published a number of his private letters. Carrying, finally, the same conscious inferest in his own personality into the field of creative art, he made his poetry as well as his prose an intimate though dignified record of his own experience.

We have, then, the material for a life of Milton as abundant in its detail of his outward career as it is vital in its human interest. There remain, of course, problems of interpretation. Everyone agrees that Milton was no ordinary person, but the judgments that have been passed on his personality and character have varied with the political sympathy, the moral attitude, and the personal temperament of each biographer. Every age—indeed every individual—will in a measure have his own Milton; and since this is so, it is desirable to have before us the actual materials, the words of Milton himself and of those who knew him, on which our estimates are based. The most important of these are given as fully as possible in the ensuing pages.

Of the individual documents from which citation has been made, Milton's *A Second Defence of the English People* contains the fullest statement he ever made of the facts of his private and public career. The general credibility of this and other utterances about himself cannot be questioned. It has been argued[1] that his remark in *Areopagitica* about visiting Galileo in Italy must be a fabrication, since Galileo was at that time sick and forbidden all communication with foreigners by the Inquisition. But the evidence is too inconclusive to stand against Milton's express statement.

With the interpretation of motive, on the other hand, the case is different. Milton was not able to see himself with dispassionate objectivity, and the reasons he gives for doing thus and thus are

[1] S. B. Liljegren, *Studies in Milton*, pp. 17 ff.

often questionable, though it would be a bold man who would undertake to determine the exact degree to which, in any given instance, he deceived himself. Was Milton really reluctant to exchange the "quiet and still air of delightful studies" for the stormy life of public service? Did he care as little as he pretends for the wide acclaim of his contemporaries? Did he abandon his intention of entering the church because of ecclesiastical tyranny? Did he plan his major prose works beforehand as systematic contributions to the cause of liberty in its various aspects? In general, the answer to these questions is that human motives are always mixed, and that Milton was as adept as any man in rationalizing his actions. It will not do to take his interpretation of his own personality at its face value; neither will it do to reject it, for John Milton was nothing if not sincere. We must also remember that Milton intended his life to be edifying. The personal passages were designed to exhibit the works of God in John Milton—to proclaim the fruits of faith, "his own faith not another's," in order that believers everywhere might be strengthened. The writing of this sort of spiritual autobiography, widely practiced among the Puritans, was the obligation of every man who felt conviction within himself, though ordinarily the record is less complicated by the secular and humanistic factors which were so strong in Milton. This motivation, while it does nothing to authenticate the poet's self-portraiture as an objective and complete analysis like the essays of Montaigne, at least explains and justifies its bias.[2]

The most complete of the contemporary biographies is that of Edward Phillips, first printed as an introduction to a translation of Milton's *State Letters* in 1694.[3] Phillips was Milton's nephew and pupil. As an actual intimate of his uncle's household during his

---

[2] On the subject of Milton's spiritual autobiography, see William O. Haller, *The Rise of Puritanism*, pp. 249–87. Haller has gone further than any previous scholar in the elucidation of Milton's relationship to the Puritan tradition, as represented by the voluminous body of sermons, personal testimonies, doctrinal expositions, and manuals of behavior, now unread, but then an inescapable heritage of every person of Milton's temperament and upbringing. Haller points out that humanistic learning is a strong ingredient in the writing of such Puritans as John Goodwin. With the more ardent sectaries—Lilburne, the Quakers, and later Bunyan—it is, of course, much less so. Milton himself gives as his reasons for entering the controversy the fact that the ministers were unable to compete with the prelates in erudition.

[3] "The Life of Mr. John Milton," Darbishire, *Early Lives*, pp. 49–82.

boyhood and a frequent visitor till Milton's death, his opportunity for knowing the circumstances of his public and domestic life was practically unlimited. Yet we must remember in reading, for example, his detailed account of Milton's first marriage, that he was a boy of twelve when this event took place. He was, moreover, obviously a person of smaller mold, proud of Milton but incapable of comprehending his greatness, and he was rather inclined to gossip. In spite of occasional romancing, however, his narrative is authentic.

Almost equally valuable is the so-called *Anonymous Biography* rediscovered in 1889 among the papers of Anthony Wood and first published by Parsons in 1902 under the title of *The Earliest Life of Milton*.[4] It may have been the work of Cyriack Skinner,[5] but whoever the author is, he writes from an intimate and sympathetic understanding, sharing or at least fully understanding Milton's political and religious ideas and seeming particularly well informed about such matters as his literary habits and his use of amanuenses. The exactness with which he describes Milton's disease of the eyes and the scene of his deathbed shows that he must have been very close to him. This biography, which was not used by Masson, supplies comparatively few facts unknown from other sources; but it is important in furnishing a systematic account of Milton parallel to and independent of that of Edward Phillips.

Still more firsthand material is given by John Aubrey in the notes (1681)[6] which he collected for Anthony Wood's use in his *Athenae* and *Fasti Oxonienses*. Aubrey had not only known Milton himself but inquired diligently about him from his widow, from his brother Christopher Milton, from Edward Phillips, and from others. In many cases he gives the sources of his information. Though much of it is gossip, it is just such gossip as we wish to have, and it appears to be, on the whole, trustworthy. His notes on Milton were published by William Godwin in his *Lives of Edward and John Phillips* (1815) and subsequently by Andrew Clark in his

---

[4] *Ibid.*, pp. 17–34; Darbishire argues for John Phillips as the author.

[5] For the controversy over the authorship, see R. W. Hunt's letter (*TLS*, Oct. 11, 1957, p. 609) in reply to W. R. Parker's case for Cyriack Skinner (*ibid.*, Sept. 13, 1957, p. 547). Hunt's note was answered by Maurice Kelley (*ibid.*, Dec. 27, 1957, p. 787).

[6] "Minutes of the Life of Mr. John Milton," Darbishire, *Early Lives*, pp. 1–15.

edition of Aubrey's *Brief Lives*. Anthony Wood himself based his "Life of Milton" in the *Fasti Oxonienses* (1691–92) chiefly on the material furnished by Aubrey and on the manuscript of the anonymous biographer; therefore, he does not rank as a firsthand witness.

Of the later biographers, two—John Toland (1698) and Jonathan Richardson (1734)—contribute some new items. With them, except for a few recollections of Milton's granddaughter recorded by Birch (1738, 1753) and Newton (1749), the direct tradition ends. There remain, however, the various records—entries of the births, marriages, and deaths of the Milton family; transfers of property; minutes of the Council of State, etc.—which give documentary information on the essential points. Much of this was brought to light in the eighteenth century and is contained in Todd's edition, but the great nineteenth-century work collecting and weighing it was David Masson's *Life of Milton*. The materials discovered since, however, are considerable, and they have been assembled in J. Milton French's monumental *The Life Records of John Milton* and evaluated and discussed in the exhaustive *The Intellectual Development of John Milton* by Harris Fletcher. There is finally a good amount of manuscript in Milton's hand or in those of his amanuenses; this includes, besides the text of his minor poems, a commonplace book made up of citations from his reading, his literary plans, marginalia in books from his library, a few of his letters, etc.

Since Milton and his early biographers are often incomplete and sometimes inaccurate in their statements, it will be well to give here a chronological summary of the most important facts of his outward life and of the chief historical events by which he was affected. Fuller detail regarding the composition, publication, and reception of his works will be found in later chapters, and three passages of importance as revelations of his inner life and thoughts about himself are quoted in Appendix B.

1608	December 9 John Milton born
1618–20?	Tutored by Thomas Young
1620?	Entered St. Paul's School

1625	February 12 Enrolled as a lesser pensioner of Christ's College, Cambridge.
	[March Charles I acceded to the throne.]
	April 9 Matriculated and probably took up residence at Cambridge
1626	Spring Rustication
1628	[The Petition of Right]
1629	March 26 Took B.A. degree.
	December 25 *Nativity Ode*
1632	July 3 Took M.A. degree.
	Settled at Hammersmith with parents
1633	[Laud became Primate]
1634	September 29 *Comus* performed
1635–38?	At Horton
1637	November *Lycidas*
1638–39	Continental tour: Paris, Florence, Rome, Naples, Geneva; August, 1639 returned to England. Took lodgings in St. Bride's Churchyard, London, but soon removed to Aldersgate St.
1639–40	Began to teach his two nephews, John and Edward Phillips
	[March War with Scotland (First Bishops' War).
	Short Parliament.
	Second Bishops' War.
	Long Parliament summoned.
	Laud and Strafford impeached]

1641–42	Anti-prelatical pamphlets
1641	[Execution of Strafford. Irish Rebellion. Grand Remonstrance]
1642	Married Mary Powell, of Cavalier background, who left him shortly. Took more pupils into his household. [Attempted impeachment of the Five Members of Parliament. Preparations for civil war. September 2 London theaters closed. October 23 Edgehill]
1643–45	Divorce tracts
1644	June *Of Education.* November *Areopagitica.* [Battles of Marston Moor and Newbury]
1645	[June 14 Battle of Naseby; victory of Cromwell and his New Model Army.] July or August Reconciliation with wife. Moved to larger house in Barbican
1645–46	First volume of poems published
1646	July 29 First child, Anne, born. [Surrender of Oxford.] Powell family took refuge with the Miltons for a short time
1647	March 13? John Milton, Sr., died. Gave up teaching and moved to a smaller house in High Holborn. [November Charles' flight to Carisbrooke. Army occupied London]

1648	October 25 Second child, Mary, born
1649–53	[The Commonwealth]
1649	[January Execution of Charles I.] February *Of the Tenure of Kings and Magistrates.* March Appointed Latin Secretary to Council of State at an annual salary of £289 14s 4½d.; allowed chambers in Whitehall
1651	February *Pro Populo Anglicano Defensio.* March 16 Third child, John, born. Deprived of (or abandoned) Whitehall lodgings; moved to a house in Petty France, Westminster. Total blindness; granted assistance in office
1652	May 2 Daughter, Deborah, born. May 5? Mary Powell Milton died. June 16? Son, John, died
1653–58	[Cromwell's coup d'etat; the Protectorate]
1654	*Defensio Secunda*
1655	*Defensio pro Se.* Salary reduced
1656	November 12 Married Katherine Woodcock
1657	October 19 Daughter, Katherine, born
1658	February and March Katherine Woodcock Milton and infant daughter died. [September Cromwell died]

1659	Two tracts against church establishment. [Abdication of Richard Cromwell; May Rump restored]
1660	March *The Ready and Easy Way to Establish a Free Commonwealth*. [May The Restoration. Act of Oblivion.] Dismissed from office; took refuge in Bartholomew Close. Arrested, but released on payment of fees
1663	February 24 Married Elizabeth Minshull. Moved to a house in Artillery Walk, Bunhill Fields
1665	Resided at Chalfont St. Giles, Buckinghamshire, for a short time during the plague
1666	[Great Fire of London]
1667	*Paradise Lost* published
1671	*Paradise Regained* and *Samson Agonistes* published
1673	Enlarged and second edition of early poems issued. *Private Letters* and *Academic Prolusions* published
1674	Second edition of *Paradise Lost* published. November 8? Milton died of gout; buried in St. Giles, Cripplegate, London Milton's three daughters and his widow survived him, the latter dying in 1727. The last of his known descendants, Elizabeth Foster, daughter of Deborah Milton, died in 1754

HOME ENVIRONMENT AND EARLY SCHOOLING (1608–25)

MILTON'S STATEMENT

Who I am, then, and whence I come, I shall now disclose. I was born in London, of an honorable family. My father was a man of supreme integrity, my mother a woman of purest reputation, celebrated throughout the neighborhood for her acts of charity. My father destined me in early childhood for the study of literature, for which I had so keen an appetite that from my twelfth year scarcely ever did I leave my studies for my bed before the hour of midnight. This was the first cause of injury to my eyes, whose natural weakness was augmented by frequent headaches. Since none of these defects slackened my assault upon knowledge, my father took care that I should be instructed daily both in school and under other masters at home. When I had thus become proficient in various languages and had tasted by no means superficially the sweetness of philosophy, he sent me to Cambridge . . . (A *Second Defence of the English People*).[7]

EDWARD PHILLIPS' ACCOUNT

He was born in London, in a house in Bread Street, the lease whereof, as I take it—but for certain it was a house in Bread Street—became in time part of his estate, in the year of our Lord 1606.[8] His father, John Milton, an honest, worthy, and substantial citizen of London, by profession a scrivener;[9] to which profession he voluntarily

---

[7] Ed. with preface and notes by Donald A. Roberts, Yale, *Milton*, IV, i, 612–13.

[8] Error for 1608. The tenement was marked by the sign of the spread eagle; Milton's family seal bore the same device.

[9] Scriveners were originally writers of any kind of document. Later they combined the functions of attorney and law stationer. John Milton, Sr., was admitted to the Company of Scriveners in 1600. In 1634 he was chosen master but declined. His fortune was made largely by moneylending. A clear picture of

betook himself, by the advice and assistance of an intimate friend of his, eminent in that calling, upon his being cast out by his father, a bigotted Roman Catholic, for embracing, when young, the protestant faith, and abjuring the popish tenets. For he is said to have been descended of an ancient family of the Miltons, of Milton near Abingdon in Oxfordshire,[10] where they had been a long time seated, as appears by the monuments still to be seen in Milton church; till one of the family having taken the wrong side, in the contests between the Houses of York and Lancaster, was sequestered of all his estate, but what he held by his wife. However, certain it is, that this vocation he followed for many years, at his said house in Bread Street, with success suitable to his industry and prudent conduct of his affairs. Yet he did not so far quit his own generous and ingenious inclinations, as to make himself wholly a slave to the world; for he sometimes found vacant hours to the study (which he made his recreation) of the noble science of music, in which he advanced to that perfection, that as I have been told, and as I take it, by our author himself, he composed an *In Nomine* of forty parts; for which he was rewarded with a gold medal and chain by a Polish prince, to whom he presented it. However, this is a truth not to be denied, that for several songs of his composition, after the way of these times (three or four of which are still to be seen in old Wilby's set of *Airs*, besides some compositions of his in Ravencroft's *Psalms*),[11] he gained the reputation of a considerable master in this most charming of all the liberal sciences. Yet all this while, he managed his grand affair of this world with such prudence and diligence, that by the assistance of divine Providence favoring his honest endeavors, he gained a competent estate, whereby he was en-

---

his activities as a broker will be found in J. Milton French, *Milton in Chancery*, and W. R. Parker, "John Milton, Scrivener: 1590–1632." See also Parker's checklist of the elder Milton's business affairs in *Milton*, II, 689–93.

[10] Milton's immediate ancestors lived at Stanton St. John, Oxfordshire.

[11] For a comprehensive survey of the musical activities of Milton's father, see Ernest Brennecke, Jr., *John Milton the Elder and His Music*. The list of his extant compositions (twenty-one in all), begins with his contribution to *The Triumphs of Oriana* in 1601, the only secular composition, and ends with "Three Fantasias for 5 Viols" in 1621. Nothing is known of any work for Wilby, but the editorship of the *Triumphs*, really Morley's, was often spoken of as Wilby's. The Polish prince was probably Albertus Alasco, who was honored at Oxford in 1583 when the elder Milton was twenty years old.

abled to make a handsome provision both for the education and
maintenance of his children; for three he had, and no more, all by
one wife, Sarah, of the family of the Castons,[12] derived originally
from Wales, a woman of incomparable virtue and goodness: John
the eldest, the subject of our present work; Christopher; and an only
daughter Ann. . . .[13]

But to hasten back to our matter in hand. John, our author,
who was destined to be the ornament and glory of his country, was
sent, together with his brother, to Paul's school, whereof Dr. Gill[14]
the elder was then chief master; where he was entered into the
first rudiments of learning, and advanced therein with that admirable success, not more by the discipline of the school and good
instructions of his masters (for that he had another master, possibly
at his father's house, appears by the *Fourth Elegy* of his Latin
poems written in his 18th year to Thomas Young, pastor of the
English Company of Merchants at Hamburg, wherein he owns and
styles him his master), than by his own happy genius, prompt wit
and apprehension, and insuperable industry: for he generally sat
up half the night, as well in voluntary improvements of his own
choice, as the exact perfecting of his school exercises. So that at the
age of 15 he was full ripe for academic learning, and accordingly
was sent to the University of Cambridge. . . .[15]

CAMBRIDGE (1625–32)

MILTON'S STATEMENT

. . . For seven years I devoted myself to the traditional disciplines
and liberal arts, until I had attained the degree of Master, as it is
called, *cum laude*. Then, far from fleeing to Italy, as that filthy rascal

12 Her last name was probably Jeffreys.
13 Anne was actually the eldest child. Christopher was seven years younger
than John.
14 Alexander Gill (1564–1635), author of *Logonomia Anglica* (1619), a
book of English grammar, rhetoric, and poetics.
15 Darbishire, *Early Lives*, pp. 50–52, 53–54 (modernized).

[Du Moulin] alleges, of my own free will I returned home, to the regret of most of the fellows of the college, who bestowed on me no little honor (*A Second Defence of the English People*).[16]

ITEMS FROM AUBREY

And was a very hard student in the university, and performed all his exercises there with very good applause. His first tutor there was Mr. Chapell,[17] from whom receiving some unkindness [whipped him], he was afterwards (though it seemed opposite to the rules of the college), transferred to the tuition of one Mr. Tovell [Tovey], who died parson of Lutterworth.[18]

MILTON'S ATTITUDES TOWARD THE UNIVERSITY AND HIS STUDIES

I am in the city which the Thames washes with its tidal waters and I am willingly detained in my dear native place. At present I feel no concern about returning to the sedgy Cam and I am troubled by no nostalgia for my forbidden quarters there. The bare fields, so niggardly of pleasant shade, have no charm for me. How wretchedly suited that place is to the worshippers of Phoebus! It is disgusting to be constantly subjected to the threats of a rough tutor and to other indignities which my spirit cannot endure. But if this be exile, to have returned to the paternal home and to be carefree to enjoy a delightful leisure, then I have no objection to the name or to the lot of a fugitive and I am glad to take advantage of my banishment (Elegy I).[19]

At any rate, so far as I know, there are but one or two among us who do not take their flight to theology before ever they are fledged, almost untrained and uninitiated in literature and philosophy alike. And even of theology they are content with a mere smattering, if it be but enough to enable them to piece together

[16] Yale, *Milton*, IV, i, 613.
[17] William Chappell (1582–1649), a well-known tutor, distinguished for his skill as a logician.
[18] Darbishire, *Early Lives*, p. 10 (modernized).
[19] *Complete Poems and Major Prose*, p. 8, ll. 8–20.

after a fashion some little homily and patch it up as it were out of scraps of other men's rags. So much so, that there is a serious risk of our clergy gradually falling into the popish ignorance of former ages.

As for myself, since I find here hardly any congenial fellow-students, I should turn my eyes straightway back to London, if I were not planning this Long Vacation to bury myself deep in literary retirement, and so to speak take cover in the precincts of the Muses (Letter to Alexander Gill,[20] July 2, 1628).[21]

So provocative of animosity, even in the home of learning, is the rivalry of those who pursue different studies or whose opinions differ concerning the studies they pursue in common. . . .

Yet to prevent complete despair, I see here and there, if I do not mistake, some who without a word show clearly by their looks how well they wish me. The approval of these, few though they be, is more precious to me than that of the countless hosts of the ignorant, who lack all intelligence, reasoning power, and sound judgment, and who pride themselves on the ridiculous effervescing froth of their verbiage. Stripped of their covering of patches borrowed from new-fangled authors, they will prove to have no more in them than a serpent's slough, and once they have come to the end of their stock of phrases you will find them unable to utter so much as a syllable, for all the world like dumb men . . . (*First Academic Exercise*).[22]

Then Aristotle, the rival and constant detractor of Pythagoras and Plato, wishing to construct a road to fame on the ruins of these great masters' theories, foisted on Pythagoras the literal doctrine of the unheard symphony of heaven and of the melody of the spheres. But if only fate or chance had allowed your soul, O Father Pytha-

---

[20] This is the younger Gill (1597–1644?), who was tutor at St. Paul's under his father. Eleven years older than Milton, he had distinguished himself in the writting of Greek and Latin verse. Three months after the date of this letter Gill was censured in the Court of Star Chamber for drinking the health of Fenton, assassin of the Duke of Buckingham, and barely escaped more serious consequences. It seems reasonable to suppose that his personal influence was strong in determining Milton's attitudes.

[21] P. B. Tillyard, *Private Correspondence*, p. 8.

[22] *Ibid.*, pp. 53–54.

goras, to transmigrate into my body, you would not have lacked a champion to deliver you without difficulty, under however heavy a burden of obloquy you might be labouring!

After all, we may well ask, why should not the heavenly bodies give forth musical tones in their annual revolutions? Does it not seem reasonable to you, Aristotle? Why, I can hardly believe that those Intelligences of yours could have endured through so many centuries the sedentary toil of making the heavens rotate, if the ineffable music of the stars had not prevented them from leaving their posts, and the melody, by its enchantments, persuaded them to stay. If you rob the heavens of this music, you devote those wonderful minds and subordinate gods of yours to a life of drudgery, and condemn them to the treadmill. . . .

But if our souls were pure, chaste, and white as snow, as was Pythagoras' of old, then indeed our ears would ring and be filled with that exquisite music of the stars in their orbits; then would all things turn back to the Age of Gold, and we ourselves, free from every grief, would pass our lives in a blessed peace which even the gods might envy (*Second Academic Exercise*).[23]

I shall attain the height of my ambition for the present if I can induce you who hear me to turn less assiduously the pages of those vast and ponderous tomes of our professors of so-called exactitude, and to be less zealous in your study of the crabbed arguments of wiseacres. . . .

Many a time, when the duty of tracing out these petty subtleties for a while has been laid upon me, when my mind has been dulled and my sight blurred by continual reading—many a time, I say, I have paused to take breath, and have sought some slight relief from my boredom in looking to see how much yet remained of my task. When, as always happened, I found that more remained to be done than I had as yet got through, how often have I wished that instead of having those fooleries forced upon me I had been set to clean out the stable of Augeas again, and I have envied Hercules his luck in having been spared such labours as these by a kindly Juno.

[23] *Ibid.*, pp. 65–66, 67.

And then this dull and feeble subject-matter, which as it were crawls along the ground, is never raised or elevated by the ornaments of style. . . .

I cannot believe that there was ever a place for them on Parnassus unless it were some waste corner at the very foot of the mountain, some spot with naught to commend it, tangled and matted with thorns and brambles, overgrown with thistles and nettles, remote from the dances and company of the goddesses, where no laurels grow nor flowers bloom, and to which the sound of Apollo's lyre can never penetrate. . . .

Now there are, as I have remarked, two things which most enrich and adorn our country: eloquent speech and noble action. But this contentious duel of words has no power either to teach eloquence or to inculcate wisdom or to incite to noble acts. . . .

But how much better were it, gentlemen, and how much more consonant with your dignity, now to let your eyes wander as it were over all the lands depicted on the map, and to behold the places trodden by the heroes of old, to range over the regions made famous by wars, by triumphs, and even by the tales of poets of renown, now to traverse the stormy Adriatic, now to climb unharmed the slopes of fiery Etna, then to spy out the customs of mankind and those states which are well-ordered; next to seek out and explore the nature of all living creatures, and after that to turn your attention to the secret virtues of stones and herbs. And do not shrink from taking your flight into the skies and gazing upon the manifold shapes of the clouds, the mighty piles of snow, and the source of the dews of morning; then inspect the coffers wherein the hail is stored and examine the arsenals of the thunderbolts. And do not let the intent of Jupiter or of Nature elude you, when a huge and fearful comet threatens to set the heavens aflame, nor let the smallest star escape you of all the myriads which are scattered and strewn between the poles: yes, even follow close upon the sun in all his journeys, and ask account of time itself and demand the reckoning of its eternal passage.

But let not your mind rest content to be bounded and cabined by the limits which encompass the earth, but let it wander beyond the confines of the world, and at the last attain the summit of all human wisdom and learn to know itself, and therewith those holy

minds and intelligences whose company it must hereafter join
(*Third Academic Exercise*).[24]

On my return from that city which is the chief of all cities,
Members of the University, filled (I had almost said "to repletion")
with all the good things which are to be found there in such abundance, I looked forward once more to enjoying a spell of cultured
leisure, a mode of life in which, it is my belief, even the souls of
the blessed find delight. I fully intended at last to bury myself in
learning and to devote myself day and night to the charms of philosophy; for the alternation of toil and pleasure usually has the
effect of annihilating the boredom brought about by satiety and of
making us the more eager to resume our interrupted tasks. Just as
I was warming to my work there came a sudden summons and I
was dragged away by the yearly celebration of our ancient custom,
and commanded to transfer that zeal, which I had intended to devote to the acquisition of knowledge, to foolery and the invention
of new jests—as if the world were not already full of fools, as if
that famous Ship of Fools, renowned in song like the Argo herself,
had been wrecked, or finally as if there were not matter enough
already to make even Democritus laugh. . . .

Some of late called me "the Lady." But why do I seem to
them too little of a man? Have they no regard for Priscian? Do
these bungling grammarians attribute to the feminine gender what
is proper to the masculine, like this? It is, I suppose, because I have
never brought myself to toss off great bumpers like a prize-fighter,
or because my hand has never grown horny with driving the plough,
or because I was never a farm hand at seven or laid myself down
full length in the midday sun; or last perhaps because I never
showed my virility in the way these brothellers do. But I wish they
could leave playing the ass as readily as I the woman.

But see how stupid and ill-advised they are to reproach me
with a thing upon which I can most justly pride myself. For Demosthenes himself was said to be too little of a man by his rivals
and opponents. Hortensius also, the most eminent orator after
Cicero, was called by Torquatus a Dionysiac singing-woman (*Sixth
Academic Exercise*).[25]

[24] *Ibid.*, pp. 68–69, 71–72.
[25] *Ibid.*, pp. 85–86, 98–99.

HAMMERSMITH–HORTON (1632–38)

MILTON'S STATEMENT

At my father's country place, whither he had retired to spend his declining years, I devoted myself entirely to the study of Greek and Latin writers, completely at leisure, not, however, without sometimes exchanging the country for the city, either to purchase books or to become acquainted with some new discovery in mathematics or music, in which I then took the keenest pleasure.

When I had occupied five years in this fashion I became desirous, my mother having died, of seeing foreign parts . . . (A *Second Defence of the English People*).[26]

FROM A LETTER TO AN UNKNOWN FRIEND[27]

Sir, (besides that in sundry respects I must acknowledge me to profit by you when ever we meet), you are often to me and were yesterday especially as a good watch man to admonish that the hours of the night pass on (for so I call my life as yet obscure & unserviceable to mankind) and that the day is at hand wherein Christ commands all to labor while there is light. Which because I am persuaded you do to no other purpose than out of a true desire that God should be honored in every one, I am ever ready, you

---

[26] Yale, *Milton*, IV, i, 613–14.

[27] This letter, which was evidently written not long after Milton's retirement at Hammersmith in 1632, was not published in the poet's lifetime; but two drafts of it exist in his handwriting in the Cambridge Manuscript. It shows him taking the occasion of some older friend's remonstrance at his apparent idleness to search his own motives and satisfy himself and others that his course of life is not a violation of his serious sense of responsibility. The conclusion, which contains the sonnet *How soon hath Time*, seems to imply that Milton is hesitating regarding his earlier intention to enter the Church; it has been omitted here. Parker thinks that Milton's unknown friend was Thomas Young (*Biography*, II, 783).

know, when occasion is, to give you account, as I ought though unasked, of my tardy moving according to the precept of my conscience, which I firmly trust is not without God. Yet now I will not strain for any set apology, but only refer myself to what my mind shall have at any time to declare herself at her best ease. Yet if you think, as you said, that too much love of learning is in fault, and that I have given up myself to dream away my years in the arms of studious retirement, like Endymion with the Moon on Latmus hill, yet consider that if it were no more but this to overcome this, there is on the other side both ill more bewitchful, to entice away, and natural cares more swaying and good more available, to withdraw to that which you wish me as first all the fond hopes which forward youth and vanity are fledge with, none of which can sort with this Pluto's helmet, as Homer calls it, of obscurity and would soon cause me to throw it off if there were nothing else in it but an affected and fruitless curiosity of knowing, and then a natural desire of honor and repute, which I think possesses the breast of every scholar as well of him that shall as of him that never shall obtain it (if this be altogether bad) which would quickly over sway this phlegm and melancholy of bashfullness, or that other humor, and prevail with me to prefer a life that had at least some credit in it, some place given it before a manner of living much disregarded, and discountenanced, there is besides this, as all well know, about this time of a man's life a strong inclination, be it good or no, to build up a house and family of his own in the best manner he may, to which nothing is more helpful than the early entering into some credible employment, and nothing more cross than my way, which my wasting youth would presently bethink her of and kill one love with another, if that were all; but what delight or what peculiar conceit, may you in charity think, could hold out against the long knowledge of a contrary command from above, and the terrible seizure of him that hid his talent, therefore commit grace or nature to nature, there will be found on the other way more obvious temptations to bad as gain, preferment, ambition, more winning presentments of good, and more prone affections of nature to incline and dispose not counting outward causes as expectations and murmurs of friends' scandals taken and such like, than the bare love of notions could resist, so that if it be that which you suppose, it had by

this been round about begirt, and overmastered whether it had proceeded from virtue, vice, or nature in me, yet that you may see that
I am sometime suspicious of myself, and do take notice of a certain
belatedness in me, I am the bolder to send you some of my nightward thoughts some while since since they come in fitly made up
in a Petrarchan stanza [Sonnet VII, *How soon hath Time*, fol-
lows].[28]

I waited long for a letter from you, according to our agreement; but in spite of having received none up to the present, I have
not on that account, believe me, allowed my old good-will toward
you to cool in the least; for I felt sure that you would put forward
the same plea in defence of your dilatoriness as you did at the beginning of our correspondence, one which you have every right to
make use of, and which the friendly relations between us fully justify. For I would not have true friendship tried by the test of letters
and good wishes, which may all be feigned; but its roots and the
source of its strength should go deep into the mind, and it should
spring from a pure origin, so that, even were all tokens of mutual
regard to cease, yet it should endure throughout life, untainted by
suspicion or recrimination. . . .

So, now that you have entered the despotic stronghold of Medicine, pray do not terrify me with your threats or reckon up the

[28] Patterson, *Works*, XII, 320–22 (modernized). This edition will hereafter be cited *CM*.
[29] Milton's friendship with Charles Diodati, a youth of Protestant-Italian
parentage, dates from their association at St. Paul's, where, though the two
boys were of the same age, Diodati was two years ahead of him and evidently
acted as his mentor. Milton wrote affectionate verse letters to him in his early
Cambridge years (Diodati had gone to Oxford) and addressed him in the
Italian love sonnets and in Elegy VI. The two letters of 1637 quoted here
suggest that Milton had been more eager to maintain the relationship than
Diodati and that he had made his absent friend the symbol of his own ideals.
This important emotional episode of Milton's youth closed with the *Epitaph
of Damon* in 1640(?), in which Diodati has evidently been fashioned by
Milton's imagination into a very different kind of human being from what he
actually was. For details about the Diodatis, see Donald Dorian, *The English
Diodatis*.

account in detail and demand of me the repayment in full of all those thousand good healths, should ever I prove a traitor to friendship, which God forbid. But remove that formidable embargo which you have put upon my freedom, forbidding me to be sick without your kind permission. To avert your threats, I assure you that it is impossible for me not to love such men as yourself, for though I know not God's intent toward me in other respects, yet of this I am sure, that he has imbued me especially with a mighty position for Beauty. Ceres never sought her daughter Proserpine (as the legend tells) with greater ardor than I do this Idea of Beauty, like some image of loveliness; ever pursuing it, by day and by night, in every shape and form ("for many forms there are of things divine") and following close in its footprints as it leads. And so, whensoever I find one who spurns the base opinions of common men, and dares to be, in thought and word and deed, that which the wisest minds throughout the ages have approved; whensoever, I say, I find such a man, to him I find myself impelled forthwith to cleave. . . .

To change the subject, I know it is time to satisfy your curiosity. You make many eager enquiries, even asking about my thoughts. I will tell you, Diodati, but let me whisper it in your ear, to spare my blushes, and allow me for a moment to speak to you in a boastful strain. What am I thinking about? you ask. So help me God, of immortality. What am I doing? Growing wings and learning to fly; but my Pegasus can only rise on tender pinions as yet, so let my new wisdom be humble.

To be serious, my plan is to take rooms in one of the Inns of Court, where I hope to find a pleasant and shady spot in which to stroll, and which may afford a more convenient dwelling-place, among congenial companions, when I wish to stay at home, and a more suitable point d'appui if I prefer to roam abroad; here my life is, as you know, obscure and cramped.

Of my studies too I will tell you. My study of Greek history has brought me, by steady work, to the point at which they ceased to be Greeks. I have spent much time on the obscure history of Italy under the Lombards, Franks, and Germans, down to the time when it was set free by Rudolf, King of Germany. What follows, the history of each independent state, will be best studied separately. . . .

Meanwhile, if it is not troubling you too much, please send me Giustiniani's History of Venice. . . .[30]

FROM A LETTER OF SIR HENRY WOTTON TO MILTON, APRIL 13, 1638[31]

Sir, It was a special favor, when you lately bestowed upon me here, the first taste of your acquaintance, though no longer than to make me know that I wanted more time to value it, and to enjoy it rightly; and in truth, if I could then have imagined your farther stay in these parts, which I understood afterwards by Mr. *H.,* I would have been bold in our vulgar phrase to mend my draught (for you left me with an extreme thirst) and to have begged your conversation again, jointly with your said learned friend, at a poor meal or two, that we might have banded together some good authors of the ancient time: among which, I observed you to have been familiar.

Since your going, you have charged me with new obligations, both for a very kind letter from you dated the sixth of this month, and for a dainty piece of entertainment which came therewith. Wherein I should much commend the tragical part, if the lyrical did not ravish me with a certain Doric delicacy in your songs and odes, whereunto I must plainly confess to have seen yet nothing parallel in our language: *Ipsa mollities.* But I must not omit to tell you, that I now only owe you thanks for intimating unto me (how modestly soever) the true artificer. For the work itself, I had viewed some good while before, with singular delight, having received it from our common friend Mr. *R.* in the very close of the late *R.'s* poems, printed at *Oxford,* whereunto it was added (as I now suppose) that

---

[30] P. B. Tillyard, *Private Correspondence,* pp. 13–15.

[31] Sir Henry Wotton (1568–1639), after a long life spent in ambassadorial service abroad, was now retired as Provost of Eton College. He was a distinguished man of broad culture and ripe experience, and his letter is the first recognition of Milton's merits. It was published in the 1645 edition of the *Poems* and refers to the 1637 edition of *Comus,* a copy of which Milton had sent to his new friend. "Mr. H." is probably John Hales (1584–1656) of Eton. "The late R." may have been Thomas Randolph (1605–35), though no copy of his poems bound with *Comus* is known; John Rouse (1574–1652), Robert Randolph (1613–71), or Humphrey Robinson are also likely possibilities.

the accessory might help out the principal, according to the art of stationers, and to leave the reader *Con la bocca dolce.*[32]

ITALY (1638–39)

MILTON'S STATEMENT

When I had occupied five years in this fashion, I became desirous, my mother having died, of seeing foreign parts, especially Italy, and with my father's consent I set forth, accompanied by a single attendant. On my departure Henry Wotton, a most distinguished gentleman, who had long served as King James' ambassador to the Venetians, gave signal proof of his esteem for me, writing a graceful letter which contained good wishes and precepts of no little value to one going abroad. On the recommendation of others I was warmly received in Paris by the noble Thomas Scudamore, Viscount Sligo, legate of King Charles. He on his own initiative introduced me, in company with several of his suite, to Hugo Grotius, a most learned man (then ambassador from the Queen of Sweden to the King of France) whom I ardently desired to meet. When I set out for Italy some days thereafter, Scudamore gave me letters to English merchants along my projected route, that they might assist me as they could. Sailing from Nice, I reached Genoa, then Leghorn and Pisa, and after that Florence. In that city, which I have always admired above all others because of the elegance, not just of its tongue, but also of its wit, I lingered for about two months. There I at once became the friend of many gentlemen eminent in rank and learning, whose private academies I frequented[33]—a Florentine institution which deserves great praise not only for promoting humane studies but also for encouraging friendly intercourse. Time will never destroy my recollection—ever welcome and delightful—of

[32] *CM,* I, ii, 476 (modernized).
[33] A note in the minutes of the Academy of the Svogliati records Milton's reading of a Latin poem at their meeting of Sept. 16, 1638 (French, *Life Records,* I, 389).

you, Jacopo Gaddi, Carlo Dati,[34] Frescobaldi, Coltellini, Buonmattei,[35] Chimentelli, Francini, and many others.[36]

From Florence I traveled to Siena and thence to Rome.[37] When the antiquity and venerable repute of that city had detained me for almost two months and I had been graciously entertained there by Lukas Holste[38] and other men endowed with both learning and wit, I proceeded to Naples. Here I was introduced by a certain Eremite Friar, with whom I had made the journey from Rome, to Giovanni Battista Manso,[39] Marquis of Villa, a man of high rank and influence, to whom the famous Italian poet, Torquato Tasso, dedicated his work on friendship. As long as I was there I found him a very true friend. He personally conducted me through the various quarters of the city and Viceregal Court, and more than once came to my lodgings to call. When I was leaving he gravely apologized because even though he had especially wished to show me many more attentions, he could not do so in that city, since I was unwilling to be circumspect in regard to religion. Although I desired also to cross to Sicily and Greece, the sad tidings of civil war from England summoned me back. For I thought it base that

[34] Carlo Dati, a young man of nineteen at the time of Milton's visit, was perhaps the poet's closest friend among the Florentine intelligentsia. He corresponded with him as late as 1647 (*ibid.*, II, 24–25).

[35] One of Milton's earliest acts in Florence was to write a letter to Benedetto Bonmattei, exhorting him to finish a work on the Italian language which he was writing and expressing his own enthusiasm for the Italian writer (*ibid.*, I, 382–89).

[36] These men represented the intellectual elite of Italy; for an account of them, see Yale, *Milton*, IV, i, 614–18. Milton fails to mention by name Antonio Malatesti, who dedicated a volume of sonnets to him, and he also omits to record his visit to Galileo (mentioned in *Areopagitica*).

[37] The travelers' book of the English Jesuit college in Rome records the presence of Milton and his servant there for dinner, Oct. 30, 1638 (French, *Life Records*, I, 393).

[38] Lukas Holste (1596–1661), a Roman scholar of German birth, was a protégé of the Barberini family. Through his courtesy Milton was shown the manuscript treasures of the Vatican and invited to a musical entertainment at the Barberini palace.

[39] The visit to Manso (1561–1647?) was evidently the high point of Milton's Italian journey. The old nobleman presented him with copies of his poems and his philosophical dialogue on love and received in exchange the only considerable poem written by Milton in Italy—*Mansus* (see Michele de Filippis, "Milton and Manso: Cups or Books?" *PMLA*, LI [1936], 745–56). Manso was actually something of a bigot, and Milton may have exaggerated the warmth of his hospitality.

I should travel abroad at my ease for the cultivation of my mind, while my fellow-citizens at home were fighting for liberty.[40] As I was on the point of returning to Rome, I was warned by merchants that they had learned through letters of plots laid against me by the English Jesuits, should I return to Rome,[41] because of the freedom with which I had spoken about religion. For I had determined within myself that in those parts I would not indeed begin a conversation about religion, but if questioned about my faith would hide nothing, whatever the consequences. And so, I nonetheless returned to Rome. What I was, if any man inquired, I concealed from no one. For almost two months, in the very stronghold of the Pope, if anyone attacked the orthodox religion, I openly, as before, defended it. Thus, by the will of God, I returned again in safety to Florence, revisiting friends who were as anxious to see me as if it were my native land to which I had returned. After gladly lingering there for as many months as before (except for an excursion of a few days to Lucca [the Diodati ancestral home]) I crossed the Apennines and hastened to Venice by way of Bologna and Ferrara. When I had spent one month exploring that city and had seen to the shipping of the books which I had acquired throughout Italy, I proceeded to Geneva by way of Verona, Milan, and the Pennine Alps, and then along Lake Leman. Geneva, since it reminds me of the slanderer More, impels me once again to call God to witness that in all these places, where so much licence exists, I lived free and untouched by the slightest sin or reproach, reflecting constantly that although I might hide from the gaze of men, I could not elude the sight of God. In Geneva I conversed daily with John Diodati,[42]

[40] This would be in Dec., 1638. The civil war had not actually broken out in England, but the significance of the Scottish rebellion against Charles I would have been clear enough to Milton. Some biographers have objected to Milton's representation of himself as answering the call of duty, in view of the leisurely character of his return north.

[41] Milton was apparently in Rome till the end of Feb., 1639. He wrote to Lukas Holste from Florence, March 30, 1639. There are three more records of attendance at meetings of the Svogliati.

[42] Giovanni Diodati (1576–1649), an uncle of Milton's English friend, Charles, was distinguished as a translator of the Bible into Italian. He entertained young men of rank from various parts of Europe as pupils in his house. On June 10, 1639, Milton wrote in the visitors' album of the Cardogni, an Italian Protestant family at Geneva, his name, a Latin motto, and the last two lines of *Comus* (French, *Life Records*, I, 419).

the learned professor of theology. Then by the same route as before, through France, I returned home after a year and three months, more or less, at almost the same time as Charles broke the peace and renewed the war with the Scots, which is known as the second Bishops' War.

The royalist troops were routed in the first engagement of this war, and Charles, when he perceived that all the English, as well as the Scots, were extremely—and justly—ill-disposed towards him, soon convened Parliament, not of his own free will but compelled by disaster (*A Second Defence of the English People*).[43]

But much latelier in the privat Academies of *Italy*, whither I was favor'd to resort, perceiving that some trifles which I had in memory, compos'd at under twenty or thereabout (for the manner is that every one must give some proof of his wit and reading there) met with acceptance above what was lookt for, and other things which I had shifted in scarsity of books and conveniences to patch up amongst them, were receiv'd with written Encomiums, which the Italian is not forward to bestow on men of this side the *Alps*, I began thus farre to assent both to them and divers of my friends here at home, and not lesse to an inward prompting which now grew daily upon me, that by labour and intent study (which I take to be my portion in this life) joyn'd with the strong propensity of nature, I might perhaps leave something so written to aftertimes, as they should not willingly let it die (*The Reason of Church-Government*).[44]

ENGLAND (1640-49)

SCHOOL TEACHING—EDWARD PHILLIPS' ACCOUNT

Soon after his return, and visits paid to his father and other friends, he took him a lodging in St. Bride's Churchyard, at the house of one Russel, a tailor, where he first undertook the education and in-

[43] Yale, *Milton*, IV, i, 614–21.
[44] *Ibid.*, I, 809–810.

struction of his sister's two sons, the younger whereof had been wholly committed to his charge and care.

And here by the way, I judge it not impertinent to mention the many authors both of the Latin and Greek, which through his excellent judgment and way of teaching, far above the pedantry of common public schools (where such authors are scarce ever heard of) were run over within no greater compass of time, than from ten to fifteen or sixteen years of age. Of the Latin, the four grand authors *De Re Rustica*, Cato, Varro, Columella and Palladius; Cornelius Celsus, an ancient physician of the Romans; a great part of Pliny's *Natural History*; Vitruvius his *Architecture*; Frontinus his *Stratagems*; with the two egregious poets, Lucretius and Manilius. Of the Greek, Hesiod, a poet equal with Homer; Aratus his *Phaenomena* and *Diosemeia*; Dionysius Afer *De Situ Orbis*; Oppian's *Cynegetics* and *Halieutics*; Quintus Calaber his *Poem of the Trojan War* continued from Homer; Apollonius Rhodius his *Argonautics*; and in prose, Plutarch's *Placita Philosophorum*, and περὶ παιδῶν ᾿Αγωγίας; Geminus's *Astronomy*; Xenophon's Cyri *Institutio* and *Anabasis*; Aelian's *Tactics*; and Polyaenus his *Warlike Stratagems*. Thus by teaching, he in some measure increased his own knowledge, having the reading of all these authors as it were by proxy; and all this might possibly have conduced to the preserving of his eyesight, had he not, moreover, been perpetually busied in his own laborious undertakings of the book or pen.

Nor did the time thus studiously employed in conquering the Greek and Latin tongues hinder the attaining to the chief oriental languages, *viz.*, the Hebrew, Chaldee, and Syriac, so far as to go through the *Pentateuch*, or Five Books of Moses in Hebrew, to make a good entrance into the *Targum*, or Chaldee Paraphrase, and to understand several chapters of St. Matthew in the Syriac Testament: besides an introduction into several arts and sciences, by reading Urstisius his *Arithmetic*, Riff's *Geometry*, Petiscus his *Trigonometry*, Joannes de Sacrobosco *De Sphaera*; and into the Italian and French tongues, by reading in Italian Giovan Villani's *History of the Transactions Between Several Petty States of Italy*; and in the French a great part of Pierre Davity, the famous geographer of France in his time.

The Sunday's work was, for the most part, the reading each

day a chapter of the Greek Testament, and hearing his learned exposition upon the same (and how this savored of atheism in him, I leave to the courteous backbiter to judge). The next work after this, was the writing from his own dictation, some part, from time to time, of a tractate which he thought fit to collect from the ablest of divines who had written of that subject: Amesius, Wollebius, &c., *viz.*, *A Perfect System of Divinity*, of which more hereafter.[45]

MARRIAGE—EDWARD PHILLIPS' ACCOUNT

During the time also of his continuance in this house [in Aldersgate Street], there fell out several occasions of the increasing of his family. His father, who till the taking of Reading by the Earl of Essex his forces, had lived with his other son at his house there, was upon that son's dissettlement necessitated to betake himself to this his eldest son, with whom he lived for some years, even to his dying day. In the next place he had an addition of some scholars; to which may be added, his entering into matrimony; but he had his wife's company so small a time, that he may well be said to have become a single man again soon after.

About Whitsuntide it was, or a little after, that he took a journey into the country; nobody about him certainly knowing the reason, or that it was any more than a journey of recreation; after a month's stay, home he returns a married man, that went out a bachelor; his wife being Mary, the eldest daughter of Mr. Richard Powell, then a justice of the peace, of Forest Hill, near Shotover in Oxfordshire; some few of her nearest relations accompanying the bride to her new habitation; which by reason the father nor any body else were yet come, was able to receive them; where the feasting held for some days in celebration of the nuptials, and for entertainment of the bride's friends. At length they took their leave, and returning to Forest Hill, left the sister behind; probably not much to her satisfaction, as appeared by the sequel. By that time she had for a month or thereabout led a philosophical life (after having been used to a great house, and much company and joviality). Her

45 Darbishire, *Early Lives*, pp. 60–61 (modernized).

friends, possibly incited by her own desire, made earnest suit by letter, to have her company the remaining part of the summer, which was granted, on condition of her return at the time appointed, Michaelmas, or thereabout. In the meantime came his father, and some of the forementioned disciples.

And now the studies went on with so much the more vigor, as there were more hands and heads employed; the old gentleman living wholly retired to his rest and devotion, without the least trouble imaginable. Our author, now as it were a single man again, made it his chief diversion now and then in an evening, to visit the lady Margaret Lee, daughter to the —— Lee, Earl of Marlborough, Lord High Treasurer of England, and President of the Privy Council, to King James the First. This lady being a woman of great wit and ingenuity, had a particular honor for him, and took much delight in his company, as likewise her husband Captain Hobson, a very accomplished gentleman; and what esteem he at the same time had for her, appears by a sonnet he made in praise of her, to be seen among his other sonnets in his extant poems.

Michaelmas being come, and no news of his wife's return, he sent for her by letter; and receiving no answer, sent several other letters, which were also unanswered; so that at last he dispatched down a foot messenger with a letter, desiring her return. But the messenger came back not only without an answer, at least a satisfactory one, but to the best of my remembrance, reported that he was dismissed with some sort of contempt. This proceeding, in all probability, was grounded upon no other cause but this, namely, that the family being generally addicted to the cavalier party, as they called it, and some of them possibly engaged in the King's service, who by this time had his headquarters at Oxford, and was in some prospect of success, they began to repent them of having matched the eldest daughter of the family to a person so contrary to them in opinion; and thought it would be a blot in their escutcheon, whenever that court should come to flourish again.

However, it so incensed our author, that he thought it would be dishonorable ever to receive her again, after such a repulse; so that he forthwith prepared to fortify himself with arguments for such a resolution, and accordingly wrote two treatises, by which he undertook to maintain, that it was against reason, and the enjoin-

ment of it not provable by Scripture, for any married couple dis-
agreeable in humor and temper, or having an aversion to each other,
to be forced to live yoked together all their days. The first was, his
Doctrine and Discipline of Divorce; of which there was printed a
second edition, with some additions. The other, in prosecution of
the first, was styled *Tetrachordon.* Then the better to confirm his
own opinion by the attestation of others, he set out a piece called
The Judgment of Martin Bucer, a protestant minister, being a translation, out of that reverend divine, of some part of his works, exactly agreeing with him in sentiment. Lastly, he wrote in answer to
a pragmatical clerk, who would needs give himself the honor of
writing against so great a man, his *Colasterion,* or *Rod of Correction for a Sawcy Impertinent.*

Not very long after the setting forth of these treatises, having
application made to him by several gentlemen of his acquaintance
for the education of their sons, as understanding haply the progress
he had infixed by his first undertakings of that nature, he laid out
for a larger house, and soon found it out.

But in the interim before he removed, there fell out a passage,
which though it altered not the whole course he was going to steer,
yet it put a stop or rather an end to a grand affair, which was more
than probably thought to be then in agitation; it was indeed a design of marrying one of Dr. Davis's daughters, a very handsome and
witty gentlewoman, but averse, as it is said, to this motion. However, the intelligence hereof, and the then declining state of the
King's cause, and consequently of the circumstances of Justice
Powell's family, caused them to set all engines on work, to restore
the late married woman to the station wherein they a little before
had planted her. At last this device was pitched upon. There dwelt
in the lane of St. Martin's-le-Grand, which was hard by, a relation
of our author's, one Blackborough, whom it was known he often
visited, and upon this occasion the visits were the more narrowly
observed and possibly there might be a combination between both
parties; the friends on both sides concentring in the same action,
though on different behalfs. One time above the rest, he making
his usual visit, the wife was ready in another room, and on a sudden he was surprised to see one whom he thought to have never
seen more, making submission and begging pardon on her knees

before him. He might probably at first make some show of aversion and rejection; but partly his own generous nature, more inclinable to reconciliation than to perseverance in anger and revenge, and partly the strong intercession of friends on both sides, soon brought him to an act of oblivion, and a firm league of peace for the future; and it was at length concluded, that she should remain at a friend's house, till such time as he was settled in his new house at Barbican, and all things for her reception in order; the place agreed on for her present abode, was the widow Webber's house in St. Clement's Church-yard, whose second daughter had been married to the other brother many years before. The first fruits of her return to her husband was a brave girl, born within a year after; though, whether by ill constitution or want of care, she grew more and more decrepit.

But it was not only by children that she increased the number of the family; for in no very long time after her coming, she had a great resort of her kindred with her in the house, *viz.* her father and mother, and several of her brothers and sisters, which were in all pretty numerous; who upon his father's sickening and dying soon after, went away.[46]

THE ANONYMOUS LIFE

In this while, his manner of settlement fitting him for the reception of a wife, he in a month's time (according to his practice of not wasting that precious talent) courted, married, and brought home from Forresthall [i. e., Forest Hill], near Oxford, a daughter of Mr. Powell. But she, that was very young, and had been bred in a family of plenty and freedom, being not well pleased with his reserved manner of life, within a few days left him, and went back into the country with her mother. Nor though he sent several pressing invitations could he prevail with her to return, till about four years after, when Oxford was surrendered (the nighness of her father's house to that garrison having for the most part of the meantime hindered any communication between them), she of her own accord came, and submitted to him, pleading that her mother had

[46] *Ibid.*, pp. 63–67.

been the inciter of her to that frowardness. He, in this interval, who had entered into that state for the end designed by God and nature, and was then in the full vigor of his manhood, could ill bear the disappointment he met with by her obstinate absenting; and, therefore, thought upon a divorce, that he might be free to marry another; concerning which he was also in treaty. The lawfulness and expedience of this, duly regulate in order to all those purposes for which marriage was at first instituted, had upon full consideration and reading good authors been formerly his opinion; and the necessity of justifying himself now concurring with the opportunity, acceptable to him, of instructing others in a point of so great concern to the peace and preservation of families, and so likely to prevent temptations as well as mischiefs, he first writ *The Doctrine and Discipline of Divorce*, then *Colasterion*, and after *Tetrachordon*. In these he taught the right use and design of marriage; then the original and practice of divorces amongst the Jews, and showed that our Saviour, in those four places of the Evangelists, meant not the abrogating but rectifying the abuses of it; rendering to that purpose another sense of the word fornication (and which is also the opinion amongst others of Mr. Selden in his *Uxor Hebraea*) than what is commonly received. Martin Bucer's *Judgment* in this matter he likewise translated into English. The Assembly of Divines then sitting at Westminster, though formerly obliged by his learned pen in the defense of Smectymnuus, and other their controversies with the bishops, now impatient of having the clergies' jurisdiction, as they reckoned it, invaded, instead of answering, or disproving what those books had asserted, caused him to be summoned for them before the Lords. But that house, whether approving the doctrine, or not favoring his accusers, soon dismissed him.[47]

LITERARY ACTIVITY—MILTON'S STATEMENT

I myself, seeking a place to become established, could I but find one anywhere in such upset and tumultuous times, rented a house in town, sufficiently commodious for myself and my books,

---

[47] *Ibid.*, pp. 22–24.

and there, blissfully enough, devoted myself to my interrupted studies, willingly leaving the outcome of these events, first of all to God, and then to those whom the people had entrusted with this office. Meanwhile, as Parliament acted with vigor, the haughtiness of the bishops began to deflate. As soon as freedom of speech (at the very least) became possible, all mouths were opened against them. Some complained of the personal defects of the bishops, others of the defectiveness of the episcopal rank itself. It was wrong, they said, that their church alone should differ from all other reformed churches. It was proper for the church to be governed by the example of the brethren, but first of all by the word of God. Now, thoroughly aroused to these concerns, I perceived that men were following the true path to liberty and that from these beginnings, these first steps, they were making the most direct progress towards the liberation of all human life from slavery—provided that the discipline arising from religion should overflow into the morals and institutions of the state. Since, moreover, I had so practiced myself from youth that I was above all things unable to disregard the laws of God and man, and since I had asked myself whether I should be of any future use if I now failed my country (or rather the church and so many of my brothers who were exposing themselves to danger for the sake of the Gospel) I decided, although at that time occupied with certain other matters, to devote to this conflict all my talents and all my active powers.

First, therefore, I addressed to a certain friend two books on the reformation of the English church. Then, since two bishops of particularly high repute were asserting their prerogatives against certain eminent ministers, and I concluded that on those subjects which I had mastered solely for love of truth and out of regard for Christian duty, I could express myself at least as well as those who were wrangling for their own profit and unjust authority, I replied to one of the bishops in two books, of which the first was entitled *Of Prelatical Episcopacy* and the second *The Reason of Church-Government,* while to the other bishop I made reply in certain *Animadversions* and later in an *Apology.* I brought succor to the ministers, who were, as it was said, scarcely able to withstand the eloquence of this bishop, and from that time onward, if the bishops made any response, I took a hand. When they, having become a target for the weapons of all men, had at last fallen and troubled us no more, I directed my attention elsewhere, asking myself whether I could in any way advance the cause of true and substantial liberty, which must be sought, not without, but within, and which is best achieved, not by the sword, but by a life rightly undertaken and rightly conducted. Since, then, I observed that there are, in all, three varieties of liberty without which civilized life is scarcely possible, namely ecclesiastical liberty, domestic or personal liberty, and civil liberty, and since I had already written about the first, while I saw that the magistrates were vigorously attending to the third, I took as my province the remaining one, the second or domestic kind. This too seemed to be concerned with three problems: the nature of marriage itself, the education of the children, and finally the existence of freedom to express oneself. Hence I set forth my views on marriage, not only its proper contraction, but also, if need be, its dissolution. My explanation was in accordance with divine law, which Christ did not revoke; much less did He give approval in civil life to any other law more weighty than the law of Moses. Concerning the view which should be held on the single exception, that of fornication, I also expressed both my own opinion and that of others. Our distinguished countryman Selden still more fully explained this point in his *Hebrew Wife*, published about two years later. For in vain does he prattle about liberty in assembly and marketplace who at home endures the slavery most unworthy of man, slavery to an inferior. Concerning this matter then I published several books, at the very time when man and wife were often bitter foes, he dwelling at home with their children, she, the mother of the family, in the camp of the enemy, threatening her husband with death and disaster. Next, in one small volume, I discussed the education of children, a brief treatment, to be sure, but sufficient, as I thought, for those who devote to the subject the attention it deserves. For nothing can be more efficacious than education in moulding the minds of men to virtue (whence arises true and internal liberty), in governing the state effectively, and preserving it for the longest possible space of time.

Lastly I wrote, on the model of a genuine speech, the *Areopagitica*, concerning freedom of the press, that the judgment of truth and falsehood, what should be printed and what suppressed, ought not to be in the hands of a few men (and these mostly ignorant and of vulgar discernment) charged with the inspection of books, at whose will or whim virtually everyone is prevented from publishing aught that surpasses the understanding of the mob. Civil liberty, which was the last variety, I had not touched upon, for I saw that it was being adequately dealt with by the magistrates, nor did I write anything about the right of kings, until the king, having been declared an enemy by Parliament and vanquished in the field, was pleading his cause as a prisoner before the judges and was condemned to death. Then at last, when certain Presbyterian ministers, formerly bitter enemies of Charles, but now resentful that the Independent parties were preferred to theirs and carried more weight in Parliament, persisted in attacking the decree which Parliament had passed concerning the king (wroth, not because of the fact, but because their own faction had not performed it) and caused as much tumult as they could, even daring to assert that the doctrines of Protestants and all reformed churches shrank from such an outrageous sentence against kings, I concluded that I must openly oppose so open a lie. Not even then, however, did I write or advise anything concerning Charles, but demonstrated what was in general permissible against tyrants, adducing not a few testimonies from the foremost theologians. And I attacked, almost as if I were haranguing an assembly, the pre-eminent ignorance or insolence of these ministers, who had given promise of better things. This book did not appear until after the death of the king, having been written to reconcile men's minds, rather than to determine anything about Charles (which was not my affair, but that of the magistrates, and which had by then been effected). This service of mine, between private walls, I freely gave, now to the church and now to the state. To me, in return, neither the one nor the other offered more than protection, but the deeds themselves undoubtedly bestowed on me a good conscience, good repute among good men, and this honorable freedom of speech. Other men gained for themselves advantages, other men secured offices at no cost to themselves. As for me, no man has ever seen me seeking office, no man has ever seen me soliciting aught through my friends, clinging with suppliant expression to the doors of Parliament, or loitering in the hallways of the lower assemblies. I kept myself at home for the most part, and from my own revenues, though often they were in large part withheld because of the civil disturbance, I endured the tax—by no means entirely just—that was laid on me and maintained my frugal way of life.

When these works had been completed and I thought that I could look forward to an abundance of leisure, I turned to the task of tracing in unbroken sequence, if I could, the history of my country, from the earliest origins even to the present day. I had already finished four books when the kingdom of Charles was transformed into a republic, and the so-called Council of State, which was then for the first time established by the authority of Parliament, summoned me, though I was expecting no such event, and desired to employ my services, especially in connection with foreign affairs (*A Second Defence of the English People*).[48]

LATIN SECRETARYSHIP (1649-60)

MILTON'S STATEMENT

Not long afterwards there appeared a book attributed to the king, and plainly written with great malice against Parliament. Bidden to reply to this, I opposed to the *Eikon* the *Eikonoklastes*, not, as I am falsely charged, "insulting the departed spirit of the king," but thinking that Queen Truth should be preferred to King Charles. Indeed, since I saw that this slander would be at hand for any calumniator, in the very introduction (and as often as I could elsewhere) I averted this reproach from myself. Then Salmasius appeared. So far were they from spending a long time (as More alleges) seeking one who would reply to him, that all, of their own accord, at once named me, then present in the Council.[49]

48 Yale, *Milton*, V, i, 621–28.
49 *Ibid.*, p. 628.

EDWARD PHILLIPS' ACCOUNT

When (for this his last treatise [*Of the Tenure of Kings and Magistrates*], reviving the fame of other things he had formerly published) being more and more taken notice of for his excellency of style, and depth of judgment, he was courted into the service of this new commonwealth, and at last prevailed with (for he never hunted after preferment, nor affected the tintamar and hurry of public business) to take upon him the office of Latin secretary to the Council of State for all their letters to foreign princes and states; for they stuck to this noble and generous resolution, not to write to any, or receive answers from them, but in a language most proper to maintain a correspondence among the learned of all nations in this part of the world; scorning to carry on their affairs in the wheedling, lisping jargon of the cringing French, especially having a minister of state able to cope with the ablest any prince or state could employ, for the Latin tongue. And so well he acquitted himself in this station, that he gained from abroad both reputation to himself, and credit to the state that employed him.

And it was well the business of his office came not very fast upon him; for he was scarce well warm in his secretaryship before other work flowed in upon him, which took him up for some considerable time. In the first place there came out a book said to have been written by the king, and finished a little before his death, entituled εἰκὼν βασιλική, that is, *The Royal Image*; a book highly cried up for its smooth style and pathetical composure; whereof to obviate the impression it was like to make among the many, he was obliged to write an answer, which he entituled εἰκονοκλάστης or *Image-Breaker*.

And upon the heels of that, out comes in public the great killcow of Christendom, with his *Defensio Regis contra Populum Anglicanum*; a man so famous and cried up for his *Plinian Exercitations*, and other pieces of reputed learning, that there could nowhere have been found a champion that durst lift up the pen against so formidable an adversary, had not our little English David had the courage to undertake this great French Goliath. To whom he gave such a hit in the forehead, that he presently staggered, and soon after fell. For immediately upon the coming out of the answer, entituled, *Defensio Populi Anglicani contra Claudium Anonymum,* &c. he that till then had been chief minister and superintendent in the court of the learned Christina, Queen of Sweden, dwindled in esteem to that degree, that he at last vouchsafed to speak to the meanest servant. In short, he was dismissed with so cold and slighting an adiew, that after a faint dying reply, he was glad to have recourse to death, the remedy of evils, and ender of controversies.

And now I presume our author had some breathing space, but it was not long. For though Salmasius was departed, he left some stings behind; new enemies started up, barkers, though no great biters. Who the first asserter of Salmasius his cause was, is not certainly known, but variously conjectured at, some supposing it to be one Janus, a lawyer of Gray's Inn, some Dr. Bramhal, made by King Charles the Second, after his restoration, Archbishop of Armagh in Ireland; but whoever the author was, the book was thought fit to be taken into correction; and our author not thinking it worth his own undertaking, to the disturbing the progress of whatever more chosen work he had then in hand, committed this task to the youngest of his nephews; but with such exact emendations before it went to press, that it might have very well passed for his, but that he was willing the person that took the pains to prepare it for his examination and polishment, should have the name and credit of being the author; so that it came forth under this title, *Joannis Philippi Angli Defensio pro Populo Anglicano contra,* &c.

During the writing and publishing of this book, he lodged at one Thomson's next door to the Bull-head tavern at Charing-Cross, opening into the Spring-Garden; which seems to have been only a lodging taken till his designed apartment in Scotland-Yard was prepared for him. For hither he soon removed from the aforesaid place; and here his third child, a son, was born, which through the ill usage, or bad constitution, or an ill-chosen nurse, died an infant.

From this apartment, whether he thought it not healthy, or otherwise convenient for his use, or whatever else was the reason, he soon after took a pretty garden-house in Petty-France in Westminster, next door to the Lord Scudamore's, and opening into St. James's Park. Here he remained no less than eight years, namely, from the year 1652, till within a few weeks of King Charles the Second's restoration.

In this house his first wife dying in childbed, he married a second, who after a year's time died in childbed also. This his second marriage was about two or three years after his being wholly deprived of sight, which was just going about the time of his answering Salmasius; whereupon his adversaries gladly take occasion of imputing his blindness as a judgment upon him for his answering the King's book, &c. whereas it is most certainly known, that his sight, what with his continual study, his being subject to the headache, and his perpetual tampering with physic to preserve it, had been decaying for above a dozen years before, and the sight of one [eye] for a long time clearly lost. Here he wrote, by his amanuensis, his two *Answers to Alexander More,* who upon the last answer quitted the field.[50]

FROM THE ANONYMOUS BIOGRAPHER

While he was thus employed his eyesight totally failed him; not through any immediate or sudden judgment, as his adversaries insultingly affirmed, but from a weakness which his hard nightly study in his youth had first occasioned, and which by degrees had for some time before deprived him of the use of one eye. And the issues and seatons, made use of to save or retrieve that, were thought by drawing away the spirits, which should have supplied the optic vessels, to have hastened the loss of the other. He was, indeed, advised by his physicians of the danger, in his condition, attending so great intentness as that work required. But he, who was resolute in going through with what upon good consideration he at any time designed, and to whom the love of truth and his country was dearer than all things, would not for any danger decline their defense.

Nor did his darkness discourage or disable him from prosecuting, with the help of amanuenses, the former design of his calmer studies.[51]

[50] Darbishire, *Early Lives,* pp. 69–72 (modernized).
[51] *Ibid.,* p. 28.

RETIREMENT, THE GREAT POEMS, LAST YEARS
(1660–74)

EDWARD PHILLIPS' ACCOUNT

So that being now quiet from state adversaries and public contests, he had leisure again for his own studies and private designs; which were his foresaid *History of England*; and a new *Thesaurus Linguae Latinae*, according to the manner of Stephanus, a work he had been long since collecting from his own reading, and still went on with it at times, even very near to his dying day; but the papers after his death were so discomposed and deficient that it could not be made fit for the press; however, what there was of it, was made use of for another dictionary.

But the height of his noble fancy and invention began now to be seriously and mainly employed in a subject worthy of such a Muse, *viz.* a heroic poem, intitled, *Paradise Lost*; the noblest in the general esteem of learned and judicious persons, of any yet written by any either ancient or modern. This subject was first designed a tragedy, and in the fourth book of the poem there are ten verses, which several years before the poem was begun, were shown to me and some others, as designed for the very beginning of the said tragedy. The verses are these:

> O thou that with surpassing glory crown'd!
> Look'st from thy sole dominion, like the god
> Of this new world; at whose sight all the stars
> Hide their diminish'd heads; to thee I call,
> But with no friendly voice; and add thy name,
> O Sun! to tell thee how I hate thy beams
> That bring to my remembrance, from what state
> I fell, how glorious once above thy sphere;
> Till pride and worse ambition threw me down,
> Warring in Heaven, against Heaven's glorious King.

There is another very remarkable passage in the composure of this poem, which I have a particular occasion to remember; for whereas I had the perusal of it from the very beginning, for some years, as I went from time to time to visit him, in a parcel of ten, twenty, or thirty verses at a time, which being written by whatever hand came next, might possibly want correction as to the orthography and pointing; having as the summer came on, not been showed any for a considerable while, and, desiring the reason thereof, was answered: that his vein never happily flowed but from the autumnal equinoctial to the vernal, and that whatever he attempted [otherwise] was never to his satisfaction, though he courted his fancy never so much, so that in all the years he was about this poem, he may be said to have spent but half his time therein.

It was but a little before the King's restoration that he wrote and published his book *In Defence of a Commonwealth*; so undaunted he was in declaring his true sentiments to the world; and not long before, his *Power of the Civil Magistrate in Ecclesiastical Affairs,* and his *Treatise against Hirelings,* just upon the King's coming over; having a little before been sequestered from his office of Latin secretary, and the salary thereunto belonging.

He was forced to leave his house also in Petty-France, where all the time of his abode there, which was eight years, as above-mentioned, he was frequently visited by persons of quality, particularly my Lady Ranalagh, whose son for some time he instructed; all learned foreigners of note, who could not part out of the city, without giving a visit to a person so eminent; and lastly, by particular friends that had a high esteem for him, *viz.* Mr. Andrew Marvel, young Lawrence (the son of him that was president of Oliver's council), to whom there is a sonnet among the rest, in his printed *Poems;* Mr. Marchamont Needham, the writer of *Politicus;* but above all, Mr. Cyriack Skinner whom he honored with two sonnets, one long since public among his *Poems,* the other but newly printed.

His next removal was, by the advice of those that wished him well, and had a concern for his preservation, into a place of retirement and abscondence, till such time as the current of affairs for the future should instruct him what farther course to take. It was a friend's house in Bartholomew Close, where he lived till the act of oblivion came forth; which it pleased God, proved as favorable to him as could be hoped or expected, through the intercession of some that stood his friends both in Council and Parliament; particularly in the House of Commons, Mr. Andrew Marvel, a member for Hull, acted vigorously in his behalf, and made a considerable party for him; so that, together with John Goodwin of Coleman Street, he was only so far excepted as not to bear office in the Commonwealth.

Soon after appearing again in public, he took a house in Holborn near Red Lyon Fields; where he stayed not long, before his pardon having passed the seal, he removed to Jewin Street. There he lived when he married his 3d wife, recommended to him by his old friend Dr. Paget in Coleman Street.

But he stayed not long after his new marriage, ere he removed to a house in the Artillery-walk leading to Bunhill Fields. And this was his last stage in this world, but it was of many years continuance, more perhaps than he had had in any other place besides.

Here he finished his noble poem, and published it in the year 1666. The first edition was printed in quarto by one Simons, a printer in Aldersgate Street; the other in a large octavo, by Starky near Temple-Bar, amended, enlarged, and differently disposed as to the number of books by his own hand, that is by his own appointment; the last set forth, many years since his death, in a large folio, with cuts added, by Jacob Tonson.

Here it was also that he finished and published his history of our nation till the Conquest, all complete so far as he went, some passages only excepted; which, being thought too sharp against the clergy, could not pass the hand of the licenser, were in the hands of the late Earl of Anglesey while he lived; where at present is uncertain.

It cannot certainly be concluded when he wrote his excellent tragedy intitled *Samson Agonistes,* but sure enough it is that it came forth after his publication of *Paradise Lost,* together with his other poem called *Paradise Regained,* which doubtless was begun and finished and printed after the other was published, and that in a wonderful short space considering the sublimeness of it; however, it is generally censured to be much inferior to the other, though he could not hear with patience any such thing when related to him.

Possibly the subject may not afford such variety of invention; but it is thought by the most judicious to be little or nothing inferior to the other for style and decorum.

The said Earl of Anglesey, whom he presented with a copy of the unlicensed papers of his history, came often here to visit him, as very much coveting his society and converse; as likewise others of the nobility, and many persons of eminent quality; nor were the visits of foreigners ever more frequent than in this place, almost to his dying day.

His treatise *Of True Religion, Heresy, Schism and Toleration, &c.* was doubtless the last thing of his writing that was published before his death. He had, as I remember, prepared for the press an answer to some little scribing quack in London, who had written a scurrilous libel against him; but whether by the dissuasion of friends, as thinking him a fellow not worth his notice, or for what other cause I know not, this answer was never published.

He died in the year 1673 [i.e., 1674], towards the latter end of the summer, and had a very decent interment according to his quality, in the church of St. Giles, Cripplegate, being attended from his house to the church by several gentlemen then in town, his principal well-wishers and admirers.[52]

FROM A LATIN LETTER TO PETER HEIMBACH

August 15, 1666. So many of my countrymen have perished in this tragic year of plague that I am not at all surprised if, as you say, you believed a particular rumor that I too had been carried off. I cannot be altogether displeased that such a rumor was current among your fellow-countrymen, as it seems to have been, if it sprang from their interest in my welfare. But I am still alive and well, by the grace of God, Who had prepared a refuge for me in the country. And I pray that I may not yet be found altogether useless for any task which still remains for me to perform in this life.

I am delighted to find that you have remembered me after so long a time, although, to judge by your elaborate compliments,

---

[52] *Ibid.*, pp. 72–76.

there seems some reason to suspect that you do not remember me very clearly, since you express your admiration for the union in my person of so many virtues which are incompatible. For my part, I should dread too large a family as the result of so many unions, if it were not common knowledge that virtues grow and flourish best in poverty and hardships. One of those virtues, however, has not requited me very handsomely for my hospitality. For the virtue you call statesmanship (but which I would rather have you call loyalty to my country), after captivating me with her fair-sounding name, has, so to speak, almost left me without a country. However, the chorus of the others makes a fine harmony. One's country is wherever it is well with one.

I will close by begging you to lay the blame for any faults in spelling or lack of punctuation you may notice upon the boy who writes this at my dictation, and who knows no Latin at all. I am obliged, much to my annoyance, to spell out the letters one by one as I dictate.[53]

FROM THOMAS ELLWOOD, THE QUAKER[54]

Some little time before I went to Alesbury Prison I was desired by my quondam Master Milton to take a house for him in the neighborhood where I dwelt, that he might go out of the city, for the safety of himself and his family, the pestilence then growing hot in London. I took a pretty box for him in Giles-Chalfont, a mile from me, of which I gave him notice, and intended to have waited on him, and seen him well settled in it, but was prevented by that imprisonment.

But now being released and returned home, I soon made a visit to him to welcome him into the country.

[53] P. B. Tillyard, *Private Correspondence*, p. 51.
[54] Thomas Ellwood (1639–1713), who had become a Quaker in 1660 through the influence of the Peningtons and had already suffered persecution, was twenty-three at the time of his introduction to Milton. He continued with him for six weeks, left London on account of his health, and returned later in the year only to have his studies again interrupted, this time by imprisonment. From 1663 to 1669 he lived in Chalfont St. Peter's as tutor to the Penington family. Milton was evidently fond of his admirer and showed him great kindness.

After some common discourses had passed between us, he called for a manuscript of his; which being brought he delivered to me, bidding me take it home with me and read it at my leisure and when I had so done, return it to him with my judgment thereupon.

When I came home and had set myself to read it, I found it was that excellent poem which he intitled *Paradise Lost.* After I had, with the best attention, read it through, I made him another visit, and returned him his book with due acknowledgment of the favor he had done me in communicating it to me. He asked me how I liked it and what I thought of it, which I modestly but freely told him; and after some further discourse about it, I pleasantly said to him, ["]Thou hast said much here of *Paradise Lost,* but what hast thou to say of *Paradise Found?*["] He made me no answer, but sat some time in a muse, then brake off that discourse and fell upon another subject.

After the sickness was over and the city well cleansed and become safely habitable again, he returned thither. And when afterwards I went to wait on him there (which I seldom failed of doing whenever my occasions drew me to London) he showed me his second poem, called *Paradise Regained,* and in a pleasant tone said to me, ["]This is owing to you; for you put it into my head by the question you put to me at Chalfont, which before I had not thought of["].[55]

CONTEMPORARY TESTIMONY AS TO MILTON'S PERSONALITY, HABITS, ETC.

ITEMS FROM AUBREY

His harmonical and ingenious soul did lodge in a beautiful and well-proportioned body.

    In toto nusquam corpore menda fuit—Ovid.

He had a very good memory; but I believe that his excellent method of thinking and disposing did much to help his memory. . . .

[55] *The History of the Life of Thomas Ellwood,* ed. S. Graveson (London, 1906), pp. 198–200 (modernized).

Of a very cheerful humor. He would be cheerful even in his gout-fits, and sing.

Seldom took any physic, only sometimes he took manna [a mild drug used as a laxative].

He was very healthy, and free from all diseases, and only toward his later end, he was visited with the gout, spring and fall. . . .

He was an early riser, scil, at 4 o'clock manè, yea, after he lost his sight. He had a man read to him. The first thing he read was the Hebrew Bible, and that was at 4h. manè ½ h. + Then he contemplated. At 7 his man came to him again, and then read to him and wrote till dinner; the writing was as much as the reading. His 2d daughter, Deborah, could read to him Latin, Italian and French, and Greek. [She] married in Dublin to one Mr. Clarke (sells silk etc.); very like her father. The other sister is Mary, more like her mother. After dinner he used to walk 3 or 4 hours at a time (he always had a garden where he lived): went to bed about 9. Temperate man, rarely drank between meals. Extreme pleasant in his conversation, and at dinner, supper, &c. but satirical. He pronounced the letter R very hard (*littera canina*). A certain sign of a satirical wit. From John Dryden.

He had a delicate, tuneable voice, and had good skill. His father instructed him. He had an organ in his house; he played on that most. . . .

He was visited much by learned men, more than he did desire. . . .

As he was severe on one hand, so he was most familiar and free in his conversation to those to whom most severe in his way of education. N. B. He made his nephews songsters, and sing from the time they were with him.[56]

FROM EDWARD PHILLIPS

. . . And those children he had by the first [wife] he made serviceable to him in that very particular in which he most wanted their service, and supplied his want of eyesight by their eyes and

[56] Darbishire, *Early Lives*, pp. 4, 5, 6, 12 (modernized).

tongue. For though he had daily about him one or other to read to him; some persons of man's estate, who of their own accord greedily catched at the opportunity of being his readers, that they might as well reap the benefit of what they read to him, as oblige him by the benefit of their reading; others of younger years sent by their parents to the same end; yet, excusing only the eldest daughter by reason of her bodily infirmity and difficult utterances of speech (which to say truth I doubt was the principal cause of excusing her), the other two were condemned to the performance of reading, and exactly pronouncing of all the languages of whatever book he should at one time or other think fit to peruse; *viz.* the Hebrew (and I think the Syriac), the Greek, the Latin, the Italian, Spanish, and French. All which sorts of books to be confined to read, without understanding one word, must needs be a trial of patience almost beyond endurance; yet it was endured by both for a long time. Yet the irksomeness of this employment could not always be concealed, but broke out more and more into expressions of uneasiness; so that at length they were all (even the eldest also) sent out to learn some curious and ingenious sorts of manufacture, that are proper for women to learn, particularly embroideries in gold or silver. It had been happily indeed, if the daughters of such a person had been made in some measure inheritrixes of their father's learning; but since fate otherwise decreed, the greatest honor that can be ascribed to this now living (and so would have been to the others, had they lived) is to be daughter to a man of his extraordinary character.[57]

FROM THE ANONYMOUS BIOGRAPHER

He had naturally a sharp wit and steady judgment; which helps toward attaining learning he improved by an indefatigable attention to his study; and was supported in that by a temperance, always observed by him, but in his youth even with great nicety. Yet he did not reckon this talent but as entrusted with him; and therefore dedicated all his labors to the glory of God and some public good;

[57] *Ibid.*, pp. 77–78.

neither binding himself to any of the gainful professions, nor having any worldly interest for aim in what he taught. . . .

He was of a moderate stature, and well proportioned, of a ruddy complexion, light brown hair, and handsome features; save that his eyes were none of the quickest. But his blindness, which proceeded from a *gutta serena,* added no further blemish to them. His deportment was sweet and affable; and his gait erect and manly, bespeaking courage and undauntedness (or a *nil conscire*), on which account he wore a sword while he had his sight, and was skilled in using it. He had an excellent ear, and could bear a part both in vocal and instrumental music. . . .

He rendered his studies and various works more easy and pleasant by allotting them their several portions of the day. Of these the time friendly to the Muses fell to his poetry; and he, waking early (as is the use of temperate men), had commonly a good stock of verses ready against his amanuensis came; which if it happened to be later than ordinary, he would complain, saying he wanted to be milked. The evenings he likewise spent in reading some choice poets, by way of refreshment after the day's toil, and to store his fancy against morning. Besides his ordinary lectures out of the Bible and the best commentators on the week day, this was his sole subject on Sundays. And David's Psalms were in esteem with him above all poetry. The youths that he instructed from time to time served him often as amanuenses, and some elderly persons were glad for the benefit of his learned conversation, to perform that office. His first wife died a while after his blindness seized him, leaving him three daughters, that lived to be women. He married two more, whereof one survived him. He died in a fit of the gout, but with so little pain or emotion, that the tide of his expiring was not perceived by those in the room. And though he had been long troubled with that disease, insomuch that his knuckles were all callous, yet was he not ever observed to be very impatient. He had this elegy in common with the patriarchs and kings of Israel, that he was gathered to his people; for he happened to be buried in Cripplegate, where about thirty years before he had by chance also interred his father.[58]

58 *Ibid.,* pp. 29, 32, 33–34.

FROM THOMAS ELLWOOD, THE QUAKER

This person, having filled a public station in the former times, lived now a private and retired life in London; and having wholly lost his sight, kept always a man to read to him, which usually was the son of some gentleman of his acquaintance, whom, in kindness, he took to improve in his learning.

Thus, by the mediation of my friend Isaac Penington with Dr. Paget and of Dr. Paget with John Milton, was I admitted to come to him—not as a servant to him (which at that time he needed not), nor to be in the house with him, but only to have the liberty of coming to his house at certain hours when I would, and to read to him what books he should appoint me, which was all the favor I desired. . . .

He received me courteously, as well for the sake of Dr. Paget, who introduced me, as of Isaac Penington who recommended me, to both whom he bore a good respect. And having enquired divers things of me, with respect to my former progression in learning, he dismissed me to provide myself of such accommodations as might be most suitable to my future studies.

I went therefore and took myself a lodging as near to his house (which was then in Jewen Street) as conveniently as I could, and from thenceforward went every day in the afternoon (except on the first days of the week), and sitting by him in his dining room read to him in such books in the Latin tongue as he pleased to hear me read.

At my first sitting to read to him, observing that I used the English pronunciation, he told me, if I would have the benefit of the Latin tongue not only to read and understand Latin authors but to converse with foreigners either abroad or at home, I must learn the foreign pronunciation. To this I consenting, he instructed me how to sound the vowels, so different from the common pronunciation used by the English, who speak Anglice their Latin, that (with some few other variations in sounding some consonants in particular cases, as "C" before "E" or "I" like "Ch," "Sc" before "I" like "Sh" etc.) the Latin thus spoken seemed as different from that which was delivered as the English generally speak it, as if it were another language. . . .

It was now harder to me to read than it was before to understand when read. But

> *Labor omnia vincit*
> *Improbus.*
>
> Incessant pains
> The end obtains.

And so did I. Which made my reading the more acceptable to my master. He, on the other hand, perceiving with what earnest desire I pursued learning, gave me not only all the encouragement but all the help he could. For having a curious ear, he understood by my tone when I understood what I read and when I did not, and accordingly would stop me, examine me, and open the most difficult passages to me.[59]

FROM JONATHAN RICHARDSON

I have heard many years since that he used to sit in a grey coarse cloth coat at the door of his house, near Bunhill Fields, without Moorgate, in warm, sunny weather, to enjoy the fresh air, and so, as well as in his room, received the visits of people of distinguished parts, as well as quality; and very lately I had the good fortune to have another picture of him from an aged clergyman in Dorsetshire, Dr. Wright. He found him in a small house, he thinks but one room on a floor. In that, up one pair of stairs, which was hung with a rusty green, he found John Milton, sitting in an elbow chair, black clothes, and neat enough, pale but not cadaverous, his hands and fingers gouty and with chalk-stones. Among other discourse he expressed himself to this purpose: that, was he free from the pain this gave him, his blindness would be tolerable. . . .

In relation to his love of music and the effect it had upon his mind I remember a story I had from a friend I was happy in for

---

[59] Graveson, *Ellwood*, pp. 121–22, 123–24 (modernized).

many years, and who loved to talk of Milton as he often did. Milton hearing a lady sing finely, "Now I swear," says he, "this lady is handsome." His ears now were eyes to him. . . .

Milton had a servant who was a very honest silly fellow, and a zealous and constant follower of those teachers [nonconformists]. When he came from the meeting, his master would frequently ask him what he had heard, and divert himself with ridiculing their fooleries, or, it may be, the poor fellow's understanding: both one and t'other probably. However, this was so grievous to the good creature that he left his service upon it. . . .

As we are at a loss as to the particulars of the affair, what I have suggested will, I hope, be sufficient—only let me add, that that daughter, who was certainly one (if there was really more than one) that was thus serviceable to her excellent father in his distress, expressed no uneasiness that I ever heard of when she gave accounts of Milton's affairs to the many inquirers lately; but, on the contrary, spoke of him with great tenderness. Particularly, I have been told, she said he was delightful company, the life of the conversation—and *that* on account of a flow of subject and an unaffected cheerfulness and civility. One instance of her tender remembrance of him I cannot forbear relating. The picture in crayons I have of him was shown her after several others, or which were pretended to be his. When those were shown and she was asked if she could recollect if she had ever seen such a face: "No, no." But when this was produced, in a transport: " 'Tis my father! 'Tis my dear father! I see him! 'Tis him!" And then she put her hands to several parts of her face: " 'Tis the very man! Here, here."

Other stories I have heard concerning the posture he was usually in when he dictated: that he sat leaning backward obliquely in an easy chair, with his leg flung over the elbow of it; that he frequently composed lying in bed in the morning ('twas winter sure then).

One that had often seen him told me he used to come to a house where he lived, and he has also met him in the street, led by Millington (the same who was so famous as an auctioneer of books about the time of the Revolution and since). This man was then a seller of old books in Little Britain, and Milton lodged at his house. This was three or four years before he died. He then wore no sword that my informer remembers, though probably he did—at least 'twas his custom not long before to wear one with a small silver hilt, and in cold weather a grey camblet coat. His band was usually not of the sort as that in the print I have given; that is, as my original is, but like what are in the common prints of him, the band usually worn at that time. To have a more exact idea of his figure, let it be remembered that the fashion of the coat then was not much unlike what the Quakers wear now.[60]

FROM THE COURT PROCEEDINGS RELATIVE TO MILTON'S WILL[61]

That on or about the twentieth day of July, 1674, the day certain he now remembereth not, this deponent being a practicer in the law, and a Bencher in the Inner Temple, but living in vacations at Ipswich, did usually at the end of the term visit John Milton, his this deponent's brother the testator articulate, deceased, before his going home; and so at the end of Midsummer Term last past, he this deponent went to visit his said brother and then found him in his chamber within his own house situated on Bunhill within the parish of St. Giles, Cripplegate, London. And at that time, he the said testator being not well (and this deponent being then going into the country), in a serious manner, with an intent (as he believes), that what he then spoke should then be his will, if he died before his this deponent's coming the next time to London, declared his will in these very words as near as this deponent can now call to mind. Viz. "Brother, the portion due to me from Mr. Powell, my former [first] wife's father, I leave to the unkind children I had by her; but I have received no part of it, and my will and meaning is they shall have no other benefit of my estate, than the said portion and what I have besides done for them; they having been very undutiful to me. And all the residue of my estate I

[60] Darbishire, *Early Lives*, pp. 203–204, 238, 229 (modernized).

[61] This is a modernized version (French, *Life Records*, V, 90–91). Milton's nuncupative or verbal will leaving all his property to his wife was contested by his daughters, Mary, Anne, and Deborah. The citations are from the sworn testimony of Milton's brother and his servant, who appeared as witnesses for the widow. The will was held invalid on technical grounds.

leave to the disposal of Elizabeth my loving wife" [testimony of Christopher Milton].

That this deponent was servant unto Mr. John Milton, the testator in this case, deceased, for about a year before his death, who died upon a Sunday the fifteenth of November[62] last at night, and saith that on a day happening in the month of July last, the time more certainly she remembereth not, this deponent being then in the deceased's lodging chamber, he the said deceased, and the party producent in this cause his wife, being then also in the said chamber at dinner together, and the said Elizabeth Milton the party producent having provided something for the deceased's dinner which he very well liked, he the said deceased then spoke to his said wife these or the like words as near as this deponent can remember, *viz.* "God have mercy Betty, I see thou wilt perform according to thy promise in providing me such dishes as I think fit whilst I live, and when I die thou knowest that I have left thee all," there being nobody present in the said chamber with the said deceased and his wife but this deponent. And the said testator at that time was of perfect mind and memory, and talked and discoursed sensibly and well, but was then indisposed in his body by reason of the distemper of the gout, which he had then upon him. Further this deponent saith that she hath several times heard the said deceased, since the time above deposed of, declare and say that he had made provision for his children in his lifetime and had spent the greatest part of his estate in providing for them, and that he was resolved he would do no more for them living or dying. . . .[63]

That this respondent hath heard the deceased declare his displeasure against the parties ministrant his children, and particularly the deceased declared to this respondent that a little before he was married to Elizabeth Milton his now relict, a former maid servant of his told Mary one of the deceased's daughters and one of his ministrants, that she heard the deceased was to be married, to which the said Mary replied to the said maid servant, that that was no news to hear of his wedding, but if she could hear of his death that was something; and further told this respondent that all his said

[62] An error for Nov. 8.
[63] A modernized version; see French, *Life Records*, V, 220–21.

children did combine together and counsel his maid servant to cheat him the deceased in her marketings, and that his said children had made away some of his books and would have sold the rest of his books to the dunghill women [testimony of Elizabeth Fisher]. . . .[64]

[64] A modernized version; *ibid.*, V, 222.

Chapter 2

THE PROSE WORKS

It was not without reason that David Masson in his great biography of Milton felt compelled to narrate, beside the events of the poet's life, nearly the whole political, ecclesiastical, and literary history of his times. Milton's career was not a private one, and a full understanding of his character and activity demands acquaintance with the entire series of historical events and changes from the beginnings of the great rebellion to the death of the Puritan movement in the Restoration. There are also the religious, cultural, and scholarly aspects of his age to take account of, for Milton, more perhaps than any other English literary man, received into himself the full intellectual inheritance of his own day. The best way to envisage Milton as a public figure, interpreting and molding great events and being profoundly influenced by them in turn, the best way, also, to arrive at a comprehension of his wide-ranging intellectual activity, to follow his developing thought and ideals, to witness the play of his character in action, is to make a careful study of his voluminous prose works.

INTRODUCTION

Milton said that in writing prose he had the use, as it were, only of his left hand. But that left hand was a powerful one, whether he

55

wrote in Latin or in English, and whenever he dealt with matters of more than transitory significance (and it is characteristic of him to interpret particular issues at hand in accordance with large and enduring principles) his writings at their best constitute a vital and permanent contribution to literature and thought. Many passages have in them all the intensity of Milton's personality. The temperamental and passionate qualities which belonged to him as a poet, while they often prevented him from taking a calm and judicious view of his subject, fired his eloquence and made his work a personal record of the highest interest.

One element in the prose that has militated against its acceptability is the endless haggling over Scriptural and other authority. Milton did this because it seemed necessary and because he had not emancipated himself from the habits of his age. But this was, after all, a secondary and relatively insignificant part of his activity as a publicist and intellectual reformer. His initial thinking was independent and the resort to authority largely by way of defense. The workings of his mind in this regard are well illustrated by the first divorce tract, a document which, in its original form, contains a minimum of citation, but which, in the second edition, introduces many authors whom Milton had obviously consulted only after his fundamental argument was complete.

Even more offensive to some critics than Milton's textual quibbling is the savage joy with which he heaps on his opponents the language of ridicule and abuse. It is difficult to remain sympathetic with him when he resorts to personalities, and it will not quite do to say that Milton shares these practices with other controversialists in that bitter and hard-hitting epoch. We expect better things of one whose mood can at times be so serene and dignified. Milton might have won a crown of laurels even in the dust and heat of battle had he imitated the sweet reasonableness of Hooker or of some exceptional pamphleteers of his own day. William Walwyn, for example, can be much more damaging to the enemy than Milton without ever losing the temper of a Christian or the literary manners of a gentleman.[1]

It is, of course, useless to ask Milton for something he could not or did not choose to give. We must rather accept him for what

[1] See, for example, "A Prediction of Mr. Edwards his Conversion," in Haller, *Tracts on Liberty in the Puritan Revolution*, III, ii, 337–48.

he was and envisage him in the fierceness of the open conflict to which his temperament and his sense of duty drove him, as well as in the calm of contemplation which he affirms that he preferred. Even here we feel his versatility and power. Milton was, as Professor French maintains, a witty, effective satirist, not incapable of genuine though sardonic humor. He adopted the method consciously, or at least knew how to justify his employment of it, and to that extent he worked as an artist.[2] "Now that the confutant may also know as he desires," he writes in the *Apology*, "what force of teaching there is sometimes in laughter, I shall returne him in short, that laughter . . . answering *A Foole according to his folly*. . . ."[3] And again, in *Animadversions*, ". . . *it will be nothing disagreeing from Christian meeknesse to handle such a one* [as Bishop Hall] *in a rougher accent, and to send home his haughtinesse well bespurted with his owne holy-water*."[4] He was familiar with the whole tradition of satire from Aristophanes to his own day, and he apparently enjoyed trying to match it at its best and worst. French gives a picturesque list of "words of endearment," many of them vulgar and colloquial, some coined for the purpose, which Milton bestows upon his enemies in one or another of his pamphlets: "Apostate, ague-cake, Babylonish merchants of souls, mammoc, quillets, scantling, slugs, hell-pestering rabble, Ephesian beasts, riff-raff of Sarum, hip-shot grammarian, hoyden, brain-worm, phlegmy clod," etc., etc. He can do equally well in Latin. There are passages of irony, denunciation, or comic exaggeration in the prose as unforgettable as the parallel outbursts which occasionally found their way into the poetry.

It remains true, however, that the controversial writing is most valuable when it deals least with personalities. And we may well doubt whether an earnest reformer can be called successful when he allows the savage joy of combat to get the better of his constructive purposes. Milton was, after all, born for higher things than to bandy epithets on the level of Martin Marprelate. But his description in *Areopagitica* of ". . . 5 *Imprimaturs* . . . dialoguewise in the Piatza

[2] J. Milton French, "Milton as Satirist," 414–29, and George W. Whiting, "The Satire in *Eikonoklastes*," 435–38.

[3] Ed. with preface and notes by Frederick Lovett Taft, Yale, *Milton*, I, 903.

[4] Ed. with preface and notes by Rudolph Kirk, assisted by William P. Baker, *ibid.*, p. 662.

of one Title page, complementing and ducking each to other with
their shav'n reverences . . ."[5] is Miltonic in its way and sufficiently
amusing, and as such holds its place beside utterances of another
type: ". . . a good Booke is the pretious life-blood of a master spirit,
imbalm'd and treasur'd up on purpose to a life beyond life,"[6] or
". . . God the Son hath put all other things under his own feet; but
his Commandments he hath left all under the feet of charity."[7]

One invaluable thing grew out of the personal emotions excited in Milton by opposition: the prose works are interlarded with
passages in which he pauses to take the reader into his confidence
regarding his inmost thought. He offers his own past life, his ideals,
his hopes of future achievement as the best defense he can make
against those who violate his convictions and impugn his personality.
These appeals for acceptance are touching and eloquent in themselves, and they constitute, as we have seen, an autobiographical
record of great importance. Because Milton was first of all a man
and a poet, they are the most permanently valuable portions of his
prose.

ACADEMIC EXERCISES AND CORRESPONDENCE (1625–66)

Milton's various rhetorical exercises, written in Latin for delivery on
stated occasions in the college or university as a regular requirement
of academic discipline, were preserved by him and published along
with his personal Latin letters by Brabazon Aylmer in 1674 under
the title *Joannis Miltonii . . . Prolusiones Quaedam Oratoriae*.[8]
These disputations or orations deal with such topics as "Whether
day or night be the more excellent," "That occasional sportive exercises are not obstructive to philosophical studies," "That art is
more conducive to human happiness than ignorance." They cover
the entire period of Milton's residence at Cambridge from his soph-
omore year and constitute, in spite of their purely rhetorical char-

[5] Ed. with preface and notes by Ernest Sirluck, *ibid.*, II, 504.
[6] *Ibid.*, p. 493.
[7] *The Doctrine and Discipline of Divorce*, ed. with preface and notes by
Lowell W. Coolidge, *ibid.*, p. 356.
[8] See P. B. Tillyard, *Private Correspondence*; see also Yale, *Milton*, I,
211–306.

acter, an interesting record of a part of his intellectual activity as a student.[9] In the first place, they show that Milton was skilled beyond his fellows in the elegance and ingenuity of his performance of these duties, being already a master of literary expression in the Latin tongue. They are full of a sportive but not always felicitous humor; they reveal also a strong consciousness of superiority and the tendency, so characteristic of the later Milton, to make his own personality an issue in the controversy in which he is engaged. In the sixth exercise he alludes to the epithet "Lady"[10] which had been applied to him and defends his ascetic way of life against the implications of his detractors, answering scorn for scorn. He shows himself already an adherent to the more progressive way of thought represented by Bacon and the humanists generally against the larger and more conservative group which still moved in the ruts of medieval scholasticism. This comes out in the second Prolusion, where Plato is exalted above Aristotle, and in the third, which contains an attack on the evils of scholastic philosophy. It is equally evident in two academic pieces included among Milton's Latin poems. In one of these, *De Idea Platonica quemadmodum Aristotles intellexit*, Milton delicately satirizes the hardheaded attitude which denies the real existence of ideas because they cannot be seen and touched. His sympathies are evidently on the side of the more imaginative Platonic mode of thought. The other, entitled *Naturam non pati Senium*,[11] a defense of the continued vigor of the physical world in opposition to the discomforting idea that it is degenerating toward senility, reveals the hopeful philosophic position that Milton had already allied himself with and which he was never wholly to abandon even after the discouragements of his later life. The issue regarding the decay of nature was but one point in a broad controversy fundamental to the thought of the seventeenth century. This controversy had been brought to a head by the publication of George Hakewill's important *An Apologie or Declaration of the Power and Providence of God in the Government of the*

[9] See David Masson, *Life*, I, 140 ff., 272 ff., for a discussion of the academic requirements under which the exercises were composed and for an attempt to date them. See also Harris Fletcher, *The Intellectual Development of John Milton*, II, 391–552, *passim*.

[10] Quoted above, see p. 17.

[11] For background discussion, see E. L. Tuveson, *Millennium and Utopia: A Study in the Background of the Idea of Progress* (Berkeley, 1949).

World (1627), which denies not only the physical decline of nature but also the general thesis that modern civilization can never hope to rival that of the early world. Milton's verses were written for a Cambridge disputation on the subject of Hakewill's book, and Milton must have been thoroughly conversant with the whole argument. His ardent, reforming temperament forbade him to be anything but a modern, and despite his theological presuppositions and his reverence for antiquity he instinctively championed the point of view which lent encouragement to human effort.[12]

Milton's personal letters (*Epistolae Familiares*), thirty-one in number, date from 1625 to 1666.[13] The earlier ones are addressed to his two tutors, Young and Gill, and to his friend, Charles Diodati. Most of those written after the Hammersmith-Horton period were sent to various Continental correspondents, with some of whom he had become acquainted on his Italian journey. Milton took pains to make these letters models of Latin epistolary art and published them as works of literature. In this respect he was following a tradition of the Renaissance humanists, who endeavored in their correspondence to imitate the elegance of Cicero's letters to Atticus and the members of his own family. They contain, however, valuable personal data and are sometimes the expressions of his most intimate thought and feeling. Epistle VII gives full scope to the Platonic exaltation of his friendship with Diodati. A letter to the Athenian Philaras sets forth very minutely the symptoms of his blindness. Others tell of his sickness and domestic distresses. Throughout the series there is much interesting talk of books and book-buying. In tone the letters are often light and bantering. There is in them a somewhat affected urbanity and a tendency toward self-depreciation which is hardly in accord with Milton's deep satisfaction with his own gifts and achievements. On the other hand, he addresses his friends in terms of admiration sometimes approximating flattery. All this and the occasional note of complaint find precedent in humanistic correspondence generally, particularly in the letters of Erasmus.

[12] See Richard F. Jones, *The Background of the Battle of the Books, Washington State University Humanistic Series*, no. 2, VII (1920), 107 ff.

[13] See P. B. Tillyard, *Private Correspondence*, pp. 5–52; see also Yale, *Milton*, I, 307–36.

In addition to this selection of personal letters published by Milton himself, there exists in manuscript a considerable correspondence with his friends and political associates, all of which is collected in Volumes XII and XVIII of the Columbia *Milton*. There are, first of all, two interesting letters in Greek by Diodati (c. 1626), the first making an appointment for a holiday excursion, the second expressing longing for Milton's company in Cheshire and pleasantly chaffing him for his over-seriousness.[14] Carlo Dati, the Florentine, writes at length (November 1, 1647) in Italian asking Milton to honor a dead poet with some verses, discussing a passage in Catullus, and thanking him in flattering terms for copies of his poems. Leo van Aizema, who, as ambassador from the Hanse towns, had had official dealings with Milton, proposes to translate *The Doctrine and Discipline of Divorce* into Dutch; Peter Heimbach felicitates the poet in 1666 on his release from public affairs. There are also business letters in English from Milton to Whitlock and Bradshaw, a letter from Moses Wall in 1659, and a fragment of a letter from Milton to his brother Christopher recommending an investment. Finally, there is an extensive exchange (twenty-one letters extant) between Milton and Herman Mylius, the agent of the Count of Oldenburg, who was endeavoring to secure Milton's support with the Council in the arrangement of a treaty of amity between the Commonwealth and his own government. Mylius carefully filed this correspondence in the Archives of Oldenburg, where it is today. The German interlards his requests for help with flattery and a display of classical learning well calculated to win favorable notice from a man of Milton's tastes.[15]

THE EARLY ANTI-EPISCOPAL PAMPHLETS (1641–42)

From the spring of 1641 to the spring of 1642 Milton was actively engaged in public controversy on the question of church government, a subject which at that moment held the foreground in the

[14] B. M. *Add. MS.* 5016.
[15] Patterson, *Works*, XII, 338–79. This edition will hereafter be cited CM.

debates of the Long Parliament and was engaging the attention of the entire nation. He composed in quick succession five pamphlets in the interests of the abolition of the episcopal system, each becoming more heated and personal as he himself was attacked by controversialists of the opposing party.

The Long Parliament, summoned in 1640, having taken measures toward the redress of the civil grievances of the nation and disposed of Charles I's tyrannical minister, Strafford, proceeded, in 1641, to the question of church reform. Various bills were introduced in response to public petitions, including the so-called Root and Branch Bill of June, 1641, which provided for the utter abolition of archbishops and other ecclesiastical officers. The intention was to establish a synodical or Presbyterian form of church government analogous to that in Scotland. There was opposition by both the high and broad church parties, and a more moderate bill curtailing the powers of the bishops but preserving the traditional system was proposed in the House of Lords.

The struggle in Parliament was prepared for and attended by a series of pamphlets on both sides of the question, the protagonist of the principle of episcopacy being Bishop Joseph Hall, who published a tract entitled *Episcopacy by Divine Right* in 1640 and another, *An Humble Remonstrance to the High Court of Parliament*, in January, 1641. In reply to this latter work, besides various tracts by Scottish Presbyterians in London, there appeared in March, 1641, a pamphlet entitled *An Answer to a Booke Entitled 'An Humble Remonstrance' in which the Originall of Liturgy and Episcopacy is Discussed*. This was written by a group of English Puritan ministers who signed themselves "Smectymnuus," a word made up of the initials of their various names.[16] The leader of this group was Thomas Young, Milton's former tutor, and it is assumed by Masson that the poet himself may have assisted in its composition. The Smectymnuus pamphlet was followed in April by a reply from Bishop Hall and in May by one from the learned James Ussher, Bishop of Armagh. It was at about this point, probably in May, that Milton, putting aside his literary plans, intervened with his

---

[16] See Frederick L. Taft and Ashur Baizer, "The Legion of Smec," Yale, *Milton*, I, 1001–08.

first ecclesiastical document, *Of Reformation touching Church-Discipline in England and the Causes that hitherto have hindered it*, published anonymously.[17]

This pamphlet begins as a rather temperate and carefully reasoned historical discussion, revealing close study of the progress of the English church from the time of Henry VIII. Milton endeavors first to show the reasons why a compromise with Catholicism rather than a complete Protestant reform came to be adopted in the Anglican church under Henry, Edward, and Elizabeth. He then refutes the arguments of those who contend for episcopacy on grounds of antiquity,[18] showing that the system represented a corruption of primitive Christianity. But primitive Christianity is, in any case, he claims, not a model for later times since there is in the writings of the fathers and historians of the church abundant evidence of depravity and worldliness in the early centuries. Furthermore, the ancient fathers disclaimed authority in the matter of church government and deferred to Scripture. At this point Milton eloquently contrasts the transparent simplicity of truth as one finds it in the Gospel with the tangled forest of theological argument and interpretation. In a second book he assails the defense of an episcopal regime as a form of church government naturally agreeing with monarchy and necessarily implied by it. Finally, he denounces with vehemence the corruptions into which the clergy have fallen, closing with a wonderful prayer for the deliverance of the nation from this un-English tyranny and the completion of God's glorious work of religious reform.

In this work Milton's position is essentially that of Calvinism. He is primarily interested in getting rid of bishops and he does not elaborate a system of church government; by suggesting that the English church should be "brought into unity with our neighbor reformed sister churches" he implies that he has Scotch Presbyterianism in mind as his model. Later, in *The Reason of Church-Government* (1642), he comes out openly in favor of that system.

[17] Ed. with preface and notes by Don M. Wolfe and William Alfred, Yale, *Milton*, I, 514–617. It is impossible to date the pamphlet exactly (*ibid.*, pp. 514–16, and J. Milton French, *Life Records*, II, 32–33).

[18] George W. Whiting, "Milton's Reply to Lord Digby," *RES*, XI (1935), 430–38, has shown that Milton's arguments are directed against a speech of Lord Digby's (1640), which, however, is not mentioned by name.

It is rather ironical that Milton should have been so blind to the possibility of a Presbyterian tyranny over free conscience that he actually mentions and brushes aside the argument of the "libertines" who claimed that the Presbyterian discipline would be more strict than that of Episcopacy and would establish "a Pope in every parish." Within a few years Milton was to feel the truth of this and rage against it. The fact is that he was already writing as a crusading propagandist rather than as a philosopher. His policies and specific points of view were formed in the heat of debate and therefore were subject to modification as the situation changed. Politically he is still, with the majority of his countrymen, conservative, assuming the monarchical form of government as that to which the nation is permanently committed. But to say all this is not to deny that the fundamental trend of his inner thought was already set in the direction of individualism. He had made entries in the Commonplace Book indicating interest in the more radical ideas of the Reformation, and he was already a republican at heart. In only two places in this pamphlet does Milton show his deeper and more personal passion. At the beginning of the second book he describes in a glow of eloquence the ideal aim of the science of government, ". . . to train up a Nation in true wisdom and vertue, and that which springs from thence magnanimity," and he decries the "masterpiece of a modern politician, how to qualifie, and mould the sufferance and subjection of the people to the length of that foot that is to tread on their necks. . . ."[19] At the end, in describing the hymns and hallelujahs which will greet the triumph of the church, he speaks of himself as one who may perhaps be heard among the others ". . . offering at high *strains* in new and lofty Measures. . . ."[20]

The second tract is entitled *Of Prelatical Episcopacy, and whether it may be deduced from the Apostolical Times by vertue of those testimonies which are alleged to that purpose in some late Treatises; one whereof goes under the name of James, Archbishop of Armagh.*[21] This pamphlet, which appeared without Milton's

[19] Yale, *Milton*, I, 571.
[20] *Ibid.*, p. 616.
[21] Ed. with preface and notes by J. Max Patrick, *ibid.*, pp. 618–52. Milton was answering Bishop Hall's *Episcopacy* and may have been answering Peloni Almoni's *A Compendious Discourse* as well. Since the dating of Milton's

name in June or July, 1641, is a brief point-by-point refutation of the patristic authorities employed by Ussher in *The Judgment of Dr. Rainoldes Touching the Originall of Episcopacy* to prove that the order of bishops, superior to that of presbyters, was an institution of the primitive church. Milton shows that the authorities alleged either do not justify the inferences or are themselves untrustworthy. In so doing he exhibits an intimate acquaintance with the church fathers, an acquaintance the foundations of which we know to have been laid by a systematic study of their writings in the Hammersmith period. That study was, to a certain extent at least, impartial and discriminating, and Milton undoubtedly derived important materials for his own thought from the ancient writers of the church; but here, as in the other ecclesiastical pamphlets, his use of them is purely controversial and his attitude is in general disparaging. "Whatsoever time, or the heedlesse hand of blind chance, hath drawne down from of old to this present, in her huge dragnet, whether Fish, or Sea-weed, Shells, or Shrubbs, unpickt, unchosen, those are the Fathers."[22] In the course of the argument Milton condemns Tertullian for making the Son a derivation from and therefore inferior to the Father, precisely the point of view he was himself later to adopt. He ridicules the superstitious acceptance of such marvels as that of the seven sleepers of Cologne. In one passage he refers to the occasional necessity in state affairs of a strong leader, a Brutus or Pericles, taking on the functions of a king, though without thereby acquiring ". . . at any time [more] then a Temporary, and elective sway, which was in the will of the people when to abrogate."[23] This is the earliest intimation of Milton's doctrine of popular sovereignty, his ideas being evidently based on the constitutions of Greece and Rome. He was evidently well prepared in mind for both the Commonwealth and the Protectorate. Some months later the arguments employed in Milton's pamphlet

---

pamphlet is at best a guess, one may accept the contention of George W. Whiting (*Milton's Literary Milieu*, pp. 293–94) that Milton preceded Almoni, or William R. Parker's contention (*Milton's Contemporary Reputation*, p. 15, n 3) that Milton was answering Almoni.

[22] Yale, *Milton*, I, 626.

[23] *Ibid.*, p. 640.

were of considerable influence in shaping Lord Brooke's more famous discourse against Episcopacy referred to in *Areopagitica*.[24]

The third tract, published almost simultaneously with the first and second, is directed against Bishop Hall, whose *A Defence of the Humble Remonstrance against the frivolous and false exceptions of Smectymnuus* had, as we have seen, appeared April 12, 1641. Milton evidently believed in the principle "divide and conquer." His first tract had been a treatise setting forth the historical aspects of the problem; his second and third dealt severally with the two chief defenders of the bishops. The title of the third pamphlet is *Animadversions upon the Remonstrants Defence against Smectymnuus*.[25] Like the others it was anonymous.

Milton's tone toward Hall is much more flippant, satirical, and fierce than that which he had adopted in the refutation of Ussher. He reveals as yet no personal bitterness nor does he resort to slander, but he does everything he can to throw ridicule and scorn upon his opponent's arguments. A reason for this is that Hall himself had made use of similar weapons in dealing with the Smectymnuuans. Besides this, Milton found Hall a cleverer and more popular controversialist, whose sallies naturally provoked rhetoric and satire rather than scholarship. His method is to quote verbatim Hall's more questionable statements and to append some sarcastic comment on each. He alludes to Hall's "toothless satires" in verse and makes merry with his satirical fiction *Mundus Alter et Idem*. Little material which is not already contained in the earlier tracts is added to the discussion except for one section concerning a matter on which Milton had deep and permanent convictions—the question of the true nature of the office of minister of the gospel. To Milton the ministry is an inward calling, a labor of charity ". . . next to that love which dwels in God to save soules. . . ."[26] Ordination is a mere outward symbol which creates nothing and confers nothing. Those who enter the church for material reward of place or profit

[24] See George W. Whiting, "A Pseudononymous Reply to Milton's *Of Prelatical Episcopacy*," PMLA, LI (1936), 430–35. Hezekiah Woodward, who wrote nine pamphlets against episcopacy between 1643 and 1644, seems to owe a general debt to Milton's early tracts (George W. Whiting, "Woodward's Debt to Milton in 1644," SP, XXXIII [1936], 228–35).

[25] Yale, *Milton*, I, 653–735.

[26] *Ibid.*, p. 715.

are no true ministers, and it is unnecessary and harmful to hold out such rewards as is done in the Episcopal system. Neither here nor elsewhere does Milton meet the practical problem of how the unpaid clergy is to be recruited and to live, except to suggest that ". . . rich Fathers will bestow exquisite education upon their Children, and so dedicate them to the service of the Gospell . . . ," and that a true pastor, for greatest labors and greatest merits in the church, ". . . requires either nothing, if he could so subsist, or a very common and reasonable supply of humane necessaries. . . ."[27] The conclusion is that we may leave this care to God. Milton's citation of a passage against hireling ministers from Spenser's *Shepherd's Calendar* reveals one of the sources in his youthful reading of these convictions of his heart.

A period of some eight months elapsed between the publication of the third and the fourth and fifth tracts. During that interval the country was drifting rapidly toward civil war. Charles had been forced to yield on the church question and had signed the Bishops' Exclusion Bill in February, but the paper controversy over Episcopacy continued furiously, the cause of the bishops being again championed in a collection of tracts—*Certaine Briefe Treatises*—by various important divines. Milton's new work was an elaborately written treatise in two books entitled *The Reason of Church-Government urg'd against Prelaty*, published, with the author's name, in January or February, 1642.[28] This is the longest and most interesting of Milton's ecclesiastical tracts. Though pausing occasionally to refute specific arguments in the collective volume above-mentioned, he proceeds on the whole in a more philosophical and considerably less savage manner. He argues systematically that the Presbyterian rather than the Episcopal system is the one prescribed in the gospel and that prelacy, in its external lordliness, in its prediliction for rites, symbolisms, and vestments, and in its reliance on temporal authority in matters which should be purely moral and spiritual, is foreign to the spirit of Christianity. The last point, implying as it does the separation of church and state, represents Milton's profound conviction and is a principle from which he never receded. He becomes eloquent also in opposition to the idea

[27] *Ibid.*, p. 721.
[28] Ed. with preface and notes by Ralph A. Haug, *ibid.*, pp. 736–861.

of enforcing uniformity of belief. The multiplication of sects and schisms, instead of frightening him as it did others, is in his thought a wholesome sign that the living work of the Reformation is going on. Diversity of doctrine, even the wildest, is better than a stagnant uniformity secured by the forcible suppression of free thought. The point of view looks forward to that of the *Areopagitica* which would be composed a year and a half later. Underlying all is the essentially Protestant and Puritan feeling that religion is an affair of the individual. No priest can mediate between the soul and God; faith is not real until it is discovered anew in personal experience; the private conscience is the sole judge of man's moral and spiritual duties. Masson[29] quotes from the fourth pamphlet a noble passage praising the self-confidence of the righteous man who has learned to revere himself and is, therefore, indifferent to the approval or disapproval of others. How, Milton asks, can a man best be led to this "hill-top of sanctity and goodness"? By being thought that he is himself appointed and ordained by God to a sacred calling as a member of the church. The Episcopal system excludes ". . . Christ's people from the offices of the holy discipline . . ." and causes them ". . . to have an unworthy and abject opinion of themselves; to approach to holy duties with a slavish fear, and to unholy doings with a familiar boldness."[30] The logic of this position, as Milton afterward found, leads through Presbyterianism to Independency and finally to pure individualism. But however far in this direction his real opinions may already have gone, he allies himself in these pamphlets with the orthodox Presbyterian cause, and he still speaks of the Scots in terms of friendly admiration. Particularly interesting and important is the long personal digression which forms the introduction to Book II.[31] Milton has kept still about himself long enough. He expatiates upon the idealistic motives which have led him to abandon more pleasing tasks for the duty of playing a man's part in the work of purifying religion from its corruptions, and at the same time he confides to the reader his personal ambition to write a lofty poem which the world will not

[29] *Milton*, II, 374.
[30] Yale, *Milton*, I, 843.
[31] *Ibid.*, pp. 801–23.

willingly let die.[32] The concluding chapter is a denunciation of the mischief that prelacy does in the state, another expanded prose rendering of the invective against the clergy in *Lycidas*.

The general trend of Milton's argument in this, as in his other pamphlets, is toward liberty; but liberty with him was never license, and he introduces his discussion with a philosophic discourse on discipline which contains ideas that he never, in his hottest denunciations of external restraints imposed by man-made laws, rescinded, and which anticipates in a most interesting way some of the basic principles to be embodied in *Paradise Lost*. "For there is," he says, "not that thing in the world of more grave and urgent importance throughout the whole life of man, then is discipline." The flourishing of all civil societies moves upon its axis. It holds with its musical chords all the parts of this life together:

> And certainly discipline is not only the removall of disorder, but if any visible shape can be given to divine things, the very visible shape and image of vertue, whereby she is not only seene in the regular gestures and motions of her heavenly paces as she walkes, but also makes the harmony of her voice audible to mortall eares. Yea the Angels themselves, in whom no disorder is fear'd, as the Apostle that saw them in his rapture describes, are distinguisht and quaterniond into their celestiall Princedomes, and Satrapies, according as God himselfe hath writ his imperiall decrees through the great provinces of heav'n.[33]

One wishes that Milton's controversial position had oftener allowed him thus to deploy his prose eloquence in the praise of order. The passage is worthy to stand beside the best of Hooker. It belongs with that cited above from *Of Reformation* regarding the science of government in indicating how deeply in accord Milton was with one of the central interests of the Renaissance. We learn from the Commonplace Book that Milton had studied Machiavelli, and with admiration, in spite of the divergence between their creeds.

In the last tract, *An Apology against a Pamphlet Call'd A*

[32] See Appendix B.
[33] Yale, *Milton*, I, 751–52.

Modest Confutation of the Animadversions Upon the Remonstrant against Smectymnuus, etc.,[34] issued early in the year (April?) 1642, Milton again returns to the pettier and more personal phases of the controversy. Bishop Hall, aided by his son, had at last swung his battery against Milton himself in the pamphlet to which Milton alludes in his title. Goaded by the scorn of Milton's third tract, the *Animadversions*, the Halls, besides endeavoring to confute his reasons item by item, had launched all manner of scurrilous and irresponsible charges against him in his private life. Milton takes these quite seriously and attends at length to the congenial work of self-vindication. He describes his honorable career at the University, from which the Halls had said he was "vomited" forth. He tells in what employments he actually spends the morning and afternoon hours which he was charged with giving to debauchery, and, finally, replying to the accusation of unchastity, he communicates to the reader his "inmost thoughts," tracing through his early life the growth of an exceptionally idealistic attitude on this very subject.[35] These personal digressions Milton justifies as necessary. He also defends the violence of his invective and the use of undignified, even indecent language, by adverting to the example of Luther and of Christ himself. Having satisfied his readers, or at least himself, on these issues, he returns to the onslaught against the remonstrances point by point. There is little sober reasoning, and Milton is more than once led in the heat of controversy to stultify his better judgment, as when he refuses to see any beauty or excellence in the English liturgy; but the object of leaving no word of his opponents without his retort and of holding the Halls personally up to ridicule is successfully achieved. They are, to use a phase of Masson's, "gored and mangled" on every page. The pamphlet marks something of a turning point in Milton's history as a controversialist. Up to this time he has been simply a vigorous crusader for what seems to him the cause of truth and righteousness and an incidental pleader for attention to his own capacity for another and higher form of service when these disputes are at an end. Now that his own personality is at issue he becomes more deeply concerned. Henceforth the cause, whatever it may be, and

[34] *Ibid.*, pp. 862–953.
[35] *Ibid.*, pp. 889–93.

the man, are one. We may expect as a consequence an intenser intellectual effort and a willingness to resort to baser weapons, also a profounder conviction, and at times the attainment of a loftier and more passionate eloquence.

THE DIVORCE TRACTS (1643–45)

Milton's crusade against the divorce laws of his country followed almost immediately upon the conclusion of the ecclesiastical controversy and continued to occupy him for almost two years. *The Doctrine and Discipline of Divorce* was published before August 1, 1643.[36] A second edition, much enlarged, appeared in February, 1644; a new pamphlet, *The Judgment of Martin Bucer, concerning Divorce*,[37] was published in July of the same year; and finally *Tetrachordon*[38] and *Colasterion*[39] appeared in March, 1645. Milton's active prosecution of this campaign was punctuated by the composition of the tracts *Of Education* and *Areopagitica*. The divorce treatises form, however, a closely knit series and should be considered as a unit.

The composition of the first divorce pamphlet is associated by all Milton's biographers with his own difficulties in his matrimonial venture with Mary Powell, and much speculation as to the precise nature of his experience has been made. The most authoritative statement appears to be that of the anonymous biographer[40] to the effect that Milton, practically deserted by his wife, was preparing for a second marriage and sought to justify himself by writing his first divorce tract. He adds, however, that the need of a more liberal divorce law "had upon full consideration and [by] reading good authors been formerly his opinion."[41] According to Milton's own statement the divorce campaign was a second, impersonal step

---

36 Ed. with preface and notes by Lowell W. Coolidge, *ibid.*, II, 217–356.
37 Ed. with preface and notes by Arnold Williams, *ibid.*, pp. 416–79.
38 Ed. with preface and notes by Arnold Williams, *ibid.*, pp. 571–718.
39 Ed. with preface and notes by Lowell W. Coolidge, *ibid.*, pp. 719–58.
40 Darbishire, *Early Lives*, pp. 23–24; see above, p. 32.
41 *Ibid.*, p. 23 (modernized).

in the cause of liberty, one which followed upon the successful war against the authority of the bishops. Phillips' account agrees essentially with that of the anonymous biographer, stating that Milton's resentment and the consequent incubation of the first pamphlet followed his wife's failure to return to him at Michaelmas (i.e., September 29). The dating creates a problem, for we know that the tract was written and actually on sale by the date of Mary Powell Milton's return, assuming, as Masson does, that Milton was married in 1643. Although Chilton Powell[42] has argued from this discrepancy that Milton's interest in divorce was entirely independent of his personal situation and desires, there is more reason to believe that the marriage took place in June, 1642, rather than in 1643,[43] in which case we can accept the theory of the anonymous biographer that the poet's thoughts were turned in the direction of divorce by the failure of his wife to live up to her duties and his expectations. It is an open question how much further one can go in tracing the details of Milton's experience in the ostensibly impersonal discussion. Certain phrases sound very much like a reflection of his own bitterness and disillusionment. He says, however, very little about desertion as a ground of divorce, assuming that there would be general agreement on that point, though the canon laws which were still officially in force in England failed to recognize it. His main plea is that incompatibility of temper is a more vital impediment to the higher objects of marriage than any other and that the will of the parties should therefore be admitted as decisive for the continuance or dissolution of the bond. He also contended that the divorce should become a complete dissolution of a marriage, not simply a form of legal separation; furthermore, he maintained the right to remarriage by either of the parties. Under his

[42] *English Domestic Relations: 1487–1653* (New York, 1917), pp. 225–31.

[43] See the articles by B. A. Wright, "Milton's First Marriage." Wright points out that political and military conditions in 1643 were against the probability of Milton's having married Mary Powell in that year. The king had set up his standard in Oxford in Oct., 1642; the place was wild with royalist enthusiasm thereafter; and communication with London was difficult. The fact that an unusually long gap in Milton's pamphleteering activities occurred between April, 1642, and Aug., 1643, adds to the probability that those months were the period of his domestic difficulties and subsequent mental distress.

proposal, divorce would become a matter of private jurisdiction in which neither ecclesiastical nor legal authority would prevail. The function of the magistrate in the matter would be limited to the securing of conditions of divorce equitable for both parties. The principle is in perfect accord with the whole of Milton's philosophy. It was because he thought nobly of marriage as a spiritual rather than a merely physical union that he resented the common idea that it was dissoluble only on physical grounds. The idea of an external compulsion binding two human beings together when mutual love and sympathy had departed was repellent to his reason and excited him to eloquent and passionate denunciation. Milton iterates this fundamental idea again and again, and it furnishes one of the vital elements in the voluminous debate.

The attempt to reconcile Scripture with his views, which occupies him through many pages, has lost most of its significance for the modern reader.[44] His major problem was to reconcile two apparently contradictory attitudes toward divorce: one found in Deuteronomy 24:1–2, the other in Matthew 19:3–9. To these two views Milton added a third: "And the Lord God said, It is not good that the man should be alone; I will make him an help meet for him" (Genesis 2:18). Milton's major weakness in reconciling the two arguments was that his solution restricted Christ's words to a specific group and thus denied their general validity. He explains Christ's answer to the Pharisees—"Moses, because of the hardness of your hearts, suffered you to put away your wives"—as follows: Moses' law was a grave and prudent law, full of moral equity, and Jesus approved of it. But the Pharisees, in interpreting "uncleanness" to mean *every* cause of dissatisfaction, however trivial, have wrested it to suit their own bad purposes. Moses preferred to allow them in the hardness of their hearts so to abuse his doctrine "rather than that good men should lose their just and lawful privilege of remedy." Jesus does not, therefore, intend to rescind the Mosaic law or to limit "uncleanness" to adultery but to administer a rebuke to the hypocritical Pharisees. Milton's third tract, *Tetra-*

---

[44] Milton's views have been cogently presented by William Haller, *Liberty and Reformation in the Puritan Revolution*, pp. 78–99, and by Arthur Barker, *Milton and the Puritan Dilemma*, pp. 63–120.

chordon[45] (1645), strengthens what he must have known was a weak argument and enters into more detail into the interpretation of the Scriptural passages; he must have intended to satisfy those who found his earlier explanations a bit too glib.

It is characteristic of Milton's temper and of his views as to the natural superiority of man to woman that he should speak oftenest of man as the injured party and should put the decision in favor of divorce chiefly in his hands. Yet he admits that the situation may sometimes be reversed, and he appears to make an effort to be just to the woman and to put her interests on an equal footing with those of her husband in the matter. If either party is dissatisfied, incompatibility is established and the marriage *ipso facto* dissolved. It belongs to man as the natural head of the house to discern the situation and pronounce the decree.[46]

In the preface to the second edition of the first tract Milton gives the impression that he had arrived at his views about divorce solely as a result of his own reflection, and he speaks of himself as a pioneer in the attempt to free mankind from domestic fetters. Yet the subject had been in almost continuous agitation since the Reformation, and Milton's ideas, though extreme, were not inconsistent with the general drift of Protestant opinion. Certain observations in the Commonplace Book, moreover, show that Milton had interested himself in the general philosophy of marriage as early as the Hammersmith period,[47] and that his mind was already directed toward liberal thought regarding it. It appears, however, that he was ignorant when he began his tract of the great body of Reformation discussion on divorce, for he refers to none of the outstanding authorities. He must have studied them vigorously in the months immediately following the publication of his work, for the revised edition is interlarded with weighty opinions and reverend names. His greatest discovery in this research was the support lent

---

[45] "Tetrachordon" is a technical term in music, referring to the succession of four notes represented by the strings of the Greek lyre; tetrachordon is the four-stringed lyre itself. Milton's tract deals with the four chief Scriptural passages on divorce.

[46] An odd instance of the literary use of his ideas occurs in Farquhar's *The Beaux' Strategem*, where some of the material of the first pamphlet is reproduced in dialogue.

[47] See Yale, *Milton*, I, 406–10, 414.

to his ideas by the Protestant divine, Martin Bucer, who, in his *De Regno Christi* (1577), written for Edward VI, had argued stoutly in favor of absolute divorce (*a vinculo matrimonii*) in place of the separation from bed and board (*a mensa et thoro*) allowed by canon law, and who had also admitted incompatibility as a ground for the annulment of marriage. Milton excerpted and published the relevant chapters of Bucer's book as a second document in the case under the title *The Judgment of Martin Bucer concerning Divorce*.

In the preface to *Tetrachordon* Milton alludes to the fact that Parliament had "been instigated to a hard censure of that former book,"[48] i.e., *The Doctrine and Discipline*. The reference is to the two petitions of the Stationers' Company for the punishment of Milton among other authors of scandalous volumes; one is addressed to the Commons, another, later one, to the Lords. Milton also inveighs briefly against the hostile mention of his "wicked book" by Herbert Palmer in a sermon before Parliament preached in August, 1644,[49] and by Dr. Daniel Featley in his pamphlet, *The Dippers Dipt* (1645).[50] Ephraim Pagitt in his *Heresiography* (1645) had also alluded with horror to Milton's doctrine. The real work of refuting the opponents who had now sprung up against him and of overwhelming them forever was reserved for his last pamphlet, *Colasterion. A Reply to a Nameles Answer against The Doctrine and Discipline of Divorce, wherein the trivial Author of that Answer is discover'd, the Licencer conferr'd with, and the Opinion which they traduce defended. By the former author, J. M.* The "nameless answer" had been published in November, 1644,[51] with a special note of approval affixed to it by the licenser, Joseph Caryl. Milton had inquired into the origin of the document and had discovered that it was the work of a servingman turned solicitor. This wretch he belabors with personal abuse and insult and pays his compliments incidentally to William Prynne, who had stigmatized the monstrous heresy of "divorce at pleasure" in one of his recent

---

[48] *Ibid.*, II, 578.
[49] *Ibid.*, pp. 102–04, 142, 580–81.
[50] *Ibid.*, p. 583.
[51] The text is printed in Parker, *Milton's Contemporary Reputation*, pp. 170–216.

pamphlets, and to the officious licenser himself. Milton answers the arguments, such as they are, by reiterating his former points, but he evidently relies chiefly on ridicule to dispose of his opponents. Outrageous—even gross—as the language he applies to his victims is, there is no evidence that Milton is really angry. His fate, he says, in providing so silly an antagonist, extracts from him a "talent for sport." He promises on further provocation to deliver his answer in a satiric poem. Unfortunately no such occasion was given, and the divorce issue, so far as Milton was concerned, was closed. He did not change his ideas, for they are restated as a part of the program of Christian belief in the *De Doctrina Christiana* (Book I, Chapter X).

OF EDUCATION (1644)

Milton's little tractate[52] on education was anonymously published in June, 1644, just before the second divorce pamphlet. It is addressed as a letter to Samuel Hartlib, who was a public-spirited reformer interested in educational matters, particularly in the ideas of Comenius, and who had requested Milton to make a statement of his views on the subject. The treatise is the fruit of Milton's thoughtful experience of teaching and represents the program of humanistic education as it was conceived by the man who, of all scholars of his time, perhaps, best understood its meaning. The wisdom and modernity of many of the methods recommended (for example, the supplementing of textbook instruction by contact with men of practical experience and by the observation of actual institutions and activities) have won the admiration of all thinkers on this subject. The goal of the discipline which Milton outlines is the formation of the well-rounded scholarly gentlemen who shall also be well-fitted for public leadership, an ideal inherited from the early Renaissance. This is expressed in the famous definition of a complete and generous education as one which "fits a man to

[52] Ed. with preface and notes by Donald Dorian, Yale, *Milton*, II, 357–415.

perform justly, skillfully and magnanimously all the offices both private and publike of peace and war."[53] The way to this object is through an understanding of the civilization of antiquity, not as a dead or remote thing, but as an experience applicable at every point to modern life.[54] Milton insists that the Greek and Latin languages should be studied not for themselves but as tools for the acquisition of the "solid things in them." The emphasis is from the first on the subject rather than the expression. He is violently opposed to forcing children into the composition of empty rhetorical and scholastic exercises before they have anything to say. The program is a severe one; it includes, besides the reading of representative works in almost the whole range of Greek and Latin literature and the study in them of all the arts and sciences, the acquisition of Italian, Hebrew, and even Syriac, and a full course in military discipline. It is interesting to observe in Milton's program a reflection of the education which he had himself received, partly from schools and tutors, partly by his own independent effort. His model school provides for the entire training of boys from the ages of twelve to twenty-one, after which they may, as he himself did, engage in foreign travel. Attendance at the University, which Milton had found so unsatisfactory,[55] is not contemplated in the plan. On the other hand, the liberal principles embodied in the tractate are those of the more enlightened humanist reformers generally and are ultimately based on the educational thought of the ancients—Cicero, Plato, Quintilian, etc. Milton says he will not specify his indebtedness to these "old renowned authors," nor search ". . . what many modern *Janua's* and *Didactics*, more then ever I shall read, have projected. . . ."[56] This is a disparaging reference to the titles of two of Comenius' works. But Milton certainly owed many suggestions to his contemporaries and predecessors in educational theory. The Spaniard Vives, in his *De Tradendis Disciplinis*, has been mentioned as among the most important influences.[57]

It is also pointed out that *Of Education* does not adequately

[53] *Ibid.*, pp. 378–79.
[54] See J. F. Huntley, "*Proairesis, Synteresis,* and the Ethical Orientation of Milton's *Of Education*," *PQ*, XLIII (1964), 40–46.
[55] See Appendix B.
[56] Yale, *Milton*, II, 364.
[57] See the discussion of sources in *ibid.*, pp. 186–96, 212–16.

represent Milton's thought on education as a matter of public policy. The tractate offers an essentially aristocratic plan, one designed for the training of sons of gentlemen to leadership in war and peace. Elsewhere Milton advocates a system of state-supported instruction as necessary to the safety and welfare of a free commonwealth. No man ever believed in education more passionately than Milton or was himself more essentially a teacher.[58]

Of the practical working of his system as applied by Milton himself we have little evidence. The two Phillips boys, his nephews, who are the only individuals we know to have been subjected to the full weight of the pedagogical influence, proved weak vessels. John, the younger, who was Milton's special charge from boyhood and became his assistant as Latin Secretary, rebelled against the serious and lofty tradition in which he had been nurtured even before the fall of the Commonwealth regime. He paid his compliments to Puritanism in *A Satyr against Hypocrites*, ridiculed Cromwell and his colleagues in a burlesque romance, pandered to the sons of Belial by collaborating in a licentious publication, and ended his days as a Restoration hack writer without principle or purpose. There is no doubt as to his ability, and he did bear witness to his classical training by doing some translation, but Milton's idealism was evidently too much for him. His brother Edward was on the whole a good and dutiful product of Milton's teaching but an uninspired one.[59] He was himself a schoolmaster periodically throughout his life, and he produced a considerable amount of work in literary and philological scholarship, particularly an English dictionary, various lexicographical works on Latin, and a *Theatrum Poetarum*, or index of poets of all countries and ages. The introductory discourse on poetry in the last-mentioned volume and several of the comments on individual writers seem to reflect Milton's own ideas and may well have been directly inspired by

[58] For a discussion of the reflections of Milton's pedagogic interests and philosophy in his poetry, see Murray W. Bundy, "Milton's View of Education in *Paradise Lost*," *JEGP*, XXI (1922), 127–52.

[59] Yet, as William R. Parker has pointed out, Edward Phillips was able to recall much of what he had learned from his uncle some fifty years after he was a student in Milton's house; he was able to remember the titles of 27 of the books they had studied. See Parker's excellent article, "Education: Milton's Ideas and Ours."

him.[60] The Latin dictionary is said by Wood to have been based upon his notes. As Milton's literary executor, Phillips later translated into English the *Letters of State*, prefixing to the translation the biographical memoir from which quotation has been made in the first chapter of this *Handbook*. But this was when it was no longer dangerous to exhibit interest in the heroes of the good old cause. He had previously shown that he was no candidate for martyrdom by writing a Royalist continuation of Baker's chronicle through the Cromwellian period. If Milton ever seriously counted on either Phillips to exemplify the virtues of a "complete and generous education," he must certainly have been disappointed, but one feels that no inference can be drawn from this negative result either against the validity of the system or against Milton's personal ability to make it work.

AREOPAGITICA (1644)

Areopagitica,[61] Milton's great defense of the freedom of the press, was the fourth and last of the prose works to be written and published in the industrious year 1644. It appeared in November. The ordinance of Parliament which occasioned it was an act requiring, among other things, that all books be licensed by an official censor before publication. This act, which had been passed June 14, 1643, reflected the increasing determination of the Presbyterians, now in control of Parliament, to reduce English religious practice and opinion to a new uniformity and to silence political opposition. It was recognized by Milton and other men of independent tendencies as a revival in another form of the tyranny of the Stuart regime and particularly of a decree of the court of Star Chamber concerning printing which had been issued in 1637. This

[60] See E. N. S. Thompson, "Milton's Part in *Theatrum Poetarum*," MLN, XXXVI (1921), 18–21.

[61] Ed. with preface and notes by Ernest Sirluck, Yale, *Milton*, II, 480–570. The principle of a free press had been maintained before *Areopagitica* by other Independents, including Roger Williams in his *Bloody Tenet of Persecution*.

earlier licensing act had fallen in 1640 with the abolition of the
court which made it, and for three years printing had been practically free; during this time a multitude of pamphlets had been
published of every shade of religious and political opinion. To
Milton this diversity of writing was a wholesome sign of free intellectual activity, a promise of progress and reform; to the narrower
Presbyterians it was a menace against orthodox Calvinistic thought
and the stability of the new order. The whole matter had a special
significance for Milton personally, since his own writings on divorce
represented exactly such publications as were likely to be suppressed
by the new law. *The Doctrine and Discipline* had, as we have noted,
been attacked in a sermon before Parliament by Herbert Palmer.
As a consequence, doubtless, of this Presbyterian wrath against it,
the attention of the Stationers' Company had been drawn to the
fact that both this document in its first and second editions and
another heretical work which Palmer had coupled with it were
printed without being licensed under the new act. In reply to a
petition by this organization (whose commercial rights were injured
by unlicensed publication), Parliament ordered the printing committee to inquire out the authors of these works. Though the
matter went no further, Milton must have felt in anticipation the
injuries which he himself was likely to be subjected to by the new
decree. We know, however, from a passage[62] in *The Reason of
Church-Government* (1641), that his opinion regarding the liberty
of the press antedated both this personal incident and the ordinance
of 1643 itself. His convictions in this matter were an essential part
of his general philosophy of freedom and a product of his instincts
as a scholar and a teacher.

The work is addressed to Parliament in the hope of influencing
its members to repeal a decree so inconsistent with their own
history and purposes as the restorers of English liberties. After
adroitly complimenting this body on its past achievements and
excusing himself for venturing in a private capacity on this criticism
of their recent act, Milton reviews the history of licensing from
ancient times, showing that it has always been a concomitant of

---

62 "For me I have determin'd to lay up as the best treasure, and solace
of a good old age, if God voutsafe it me, the honest liberty of free speech
from my youth . . ." (Yale, *Milton*, I, 804).

tyranny and associating its invention in its modern form with the reactionary Catholic Council of Trent. The aim is to prove the practice suspect in its origin and a product of the very forces which Parliament has overthrown. Secondly, Milton enters upon a noble defense of the benefit of books freely used, showing how necessary reading of every sort is to the attainment of knowledge and experience in a world where good and evil grow up indiscriminately together.[63] Next he deals with the impossibility of the attempt to make men virtuous by external restraint. Corrupting influences are present everywhere and can be met only by building up an inner discipline and the power of rational choosing; this is the fundamental tenet of Milton's ethical philosophy. He goes on to argue more specifically that the present law will be ineffective even as applied to publication. Though he does not say so, *Areopagitica* itself, being published in defiance of the law, is an instance of the impossibility of enforcing it. Finally, Milton attacks the order as a discouragement to intellectual activity and a hindrance to the cause of truth. The plea here is one of the resolute faith in the competence of human nature, and particularly of English nature, to work out its own intellectual salvation and in the divine property of Truth itself, which is sure to prevail ultimately over error if the two are allowed to grapple. Milton expresses with extraordinary forcefulness the resentment of the mature mind at being kept under watch and ward and vividly displays the results of such a policy— spiritual stagnation and "a starched conformity of opinion." The very spirit of the English Protestant speaks through him, but his principles are as vital and his warnings as necessary today as they ever were.

Milton's plea for liberty failed in its purpose of bringing about an immediate repeal of the licensing act, but it was employed when the issue was raised again in 1679 and 1693;[64] it furnished Mirabeau with the substance of a pamphlet on the freedom of the press in

[63] In *The Reason of Church-Government* (*ibid.*, pp. 818–19), however, Milton did argue that the magistrates exercise their power to prevent young men from being influenced by "libidinous and ignorant Poetasters."

[64] A *Just Vindication of Learning or an Humble Address to the High Court of Parliament in behalf of Liberty of the Press* (London, 1679), and *Reasons humbly offered for the Liberty of Unlicensed Printing* (London, 1693). Both works are abridgements of *Areopagitica.*

1788, and it has armed the minds of individuals in all times against the ever-recurring attempt to silence thought.

In form the *Areopagitica* is a majestic example of the classical oration. The title is that of a written speech of Isocrates, and the "oration" conforms to all the principles of oratory laid down by Quintilian and embodied in Demosthenes and Cicero. The speeches of the fallen angels in the second book of *Paradise Lost*, the description of Satan's address to Eve (*PL*, IX, 670 ff.), and the characterization of the Athenian orators who "wielded at will that fierce Democraty" in the days of a noble eloquence "since mute" (*PR*, IV, 268 ff.) show how deeply Milton had studied and admired this branch of ancient literature.

OF THE TENURE OF KINGS AND MAGISTRATES (1649)

A period of four years' respite from public controversy followed the publication of the last of the divorce tracts in March, 1645. Near the beginning of this interval Milton issued the first edition of his poems. Between 1645 and 1648 he composed six sonnets and translated eight Psalms. He also carried on his work of teaching, adding several pupils to the two Phillips boys who had been with him since 1642. The bulk of his time must, however, have been devoted to study in preparation for projected works, particularly *The History of Britain* and the treatise *Of Christian Doctrine*. It seems likely, also, that the composition of one or both of these works was actually begun in this period. Meanwhile he was silently watching public events, and the movement of his mind regarding them may be clearly traced in the six sonnets above-mentioned. The reception of his divorce pamphlets had completed the work of turning him against the Presbyterian party and of aligning him with the Independents, who, in 1647, finally triumphed in Parliament and took possession of the government. In company with the rest of this group, he must also have become increasingly republican in sentiment as the impossibility of a compromise with Charles became more and more apparent. We know from an early entry in the Commonplace Book that he had long since privately nourished such thoughts even before the civil war began, but he allowed them to find no place in any of his published utterances thus far. By the time the second civil war was successfully concluded and the captive king brought to trial, Milton was quite ready to adhere to the republic and to join the cry for the king's deposition and death.

The document in which he did so, the treatise *Of the Tenure of Kings and Magistrates*,[65] was, like his first contribution to the episcopal controversy, unsolicited. It was probably composed during the king's trial, certainly before his execution on January 30, 1649, and was designed to silence the opposition of the Presbyterians and others against extreme measures and also to reconcile the public mind to the event itself. The pamphlet appeared two weeks after Charles' death. In it Milton makes no indictment of Charles; he does not, in fact, even mention him by name. His carefully reasoned argument[66] is the abstract one that men are by nature free and that their relation to their governors is one of voluntary contract which may be terminated at will. He assembles the authority of the Greeks and Romans, of the church fathers, of modern political theorists, of the Reformation divines, and of Scripture itself to show that men have a right to depose a tyrant and even to put him to death. He cites many instances from history of the exercise of this right. More specifically, he inveighs against the Presbyterian ministers, who, having in the beginning fostered the rebellion, now refuse to accept the logical consequences of their own action. Merritt Hughes has pointed out[67] that the *Tenure* was in direct rebuttal to Presbyterian propaganda like that contained in the ministers' tract, *Representation*.

The underlying philosophy of the tract is in line with the main development of liberal political theory throughout the Middle Ages

[65] Ed. with preface and notes by Merritt Y. Hughes, Yale, *Milton*, III, 184–258.

[66] See the section divisions made by Wilbur E. Gilman, *Milton's Rhetoric: Studies in His Defense of Liberty*. As an example of deliberative rhetoric, *Of the Tenure of Kings and Magistrates* contains an introduction, proposition, discussion, and conclusion.

[67] Yale, *Milton*, III, 107.

and the Renaissance, and Milton says nothing that had not been said a hundred times.[68] In plain and unimpassioned prose Milton argues the great difference between tyranny and kingship, citing Aristotle as one of the chief precedents of his argument. He takes the momentous step of writing himself regicide without the usual accompaniment of enthusiastic eloquence inspired by the contemplation of his own personality and his cause.

WORK FOR THE COUNCIL OF STATE: *ARTICLES OF PEACE* AND *EIKONOKLASTES* (1649)

As a result of the zeal for the Commonwealth displayed in *The Tenure of Kings and Magistrates*, Milton received in March, 1649, an appointment to the office of Secretary for Foreign Tongues to the Council of State. He was immediately called to the performance of a series of exacting literary duties which took precedence over all other work and occupied him continuously for nearly ten years. These duties consisted in the translation of such documents in foreign tongues as were referred to him by the Council, the drafting of the Latin correspondence of state with foreign powers, and finally the composition to order of replies—whether in Latin or in English— to various attacks leveled against the Commonwealth.

Milton's official correspondence or *Letters of State* are usually published among his works, and they constitute an interesting and important record of his public activity. There are 156 such letters in all; about a third of them are from the years 1649 to 1652 and bear the signatures of the Speaker of Parliament, the President of the Council, or some other official of the Commonwealth; the remainder are from the period of the Protectorate (1653–59) under the name of Oliver Cromwell. Milton himself kept copies which were inherited and transcribed after his death by Daniel Skinner. This manuscript, which Skinner was prevented from publishing, was delivered to the Secretary of State and is now in the Public Records Office. In 1676

---

[68] See the discussion of Milton's sources (*ibid.*, pp. 110–25).

a bookseller issued an incomplete edition, which he had obtained surreptitiously, under the title *Literae Pseudo-Senatus Anglicani*. There was a better one in 1690 and an English translation by Edward Phillips in 1694. The Columbia Edition prints the complete series;[69] Masson gives a careful analysis of their contents, with quotations.[70]

Though these letters are not Milton's in substance they are so in expression, and the greatest of them bear unmistakably the stamp of his literary power. Masson believes that they were often written first in English by Milton after consultation with Cromwell or others, read and approved in that form by Parliament or the Council, then translated into Latin. He also believes that Cromwell used Milton especially for letters which he wanted written nobly and passionately: those, for example, in which the United Provinces of the Netherlands are solemnly warned against quarreling with Sweden to the advantage of the common enemy, or the Protestant cantons of Switzerland heartened in their struggle against the Catholics. But the correspondence deals with every sort of issue which came up in England's vigorous foreign policy at that time. There are protests to France against the reception of English pirates in her ports, demands of redress from Spain for the murder of an English agent, appeals to Venice for the release of a captain imprisoned by the Turks, commendations for a league of the Protestant powers. The dispatches which came closest to Milton personally and which most profoundly inspired his Latin eloquence were undoubtedly the ones addressed to Louis XIV and other foreign sovereigns in protest against the massacre of the Waldensian Protestants by the Duke of Savoy. Milton shared fully the indignation of his country at this crime, and the letters are the equally impassioned prose counterparts of the famous sonnet—*Avenge, O Lord, thy slaughter'd Saints*—which he wrote in his private capacity as poet.

Among the first of the more miscellaneous tasks assigned to him was to attack the peace which had been concluded with the Catholics in Ireland by Charles' representative, the Earl of Ormond, in 1648. In May, 1649, Matthew Simmons printed the articles,

[69] XIII, 4–503.
[70] *Milton*, VI, 814–16.

together with the correspondence between Ormond and the Governor of Dublin and a pronouncement by the Presbyterians of Belfast, appending thereto Milton's original discussion entitled *Observations Upon the Articles of Peace with the Irish Rebels.*[71] In this work Milton denounces the Irish bitterly as enemies to religion, condemns the agreement whereby Ireland is in effect released from fealty to England, and answers the various accusations made by the Belfast Presbyterians against the acts of the republicans. This was Milton's contribution to the Irish question; it prepared the way for the merciless suppression of the rebellion a few months later by Cromwell.[72]

The next commission given to Milton by the Council was far more momentous. It was that of writing a work to counteract the menacing effect on public opinion of the famous *Eikon Basilike* or *King's Book,* which had appeared almost immediately after the king's death (i.e., in February, 1649) and had achieved an enormous circulation.[73] The *Eikon,* or, to employ its subtitle, *The True Portraiture of his Sacred Majesty in his Solitude and Suffering,* purports to be a private record of the self-communings of Charles through the last years—almost the last hours—of his life, revealing him as a model of conscientiousness and piety, tender of his family, solicitous for the good of his people, loyally Protestant, and given to earnest prayer. The book was suspected from the moment of its appearance and is now believed to be a pious fraud, the work not of Charles at all but of one of his adherents, Bishop Gauden, who took this means of winning public sympathy for the king's memory and cause by setting up his image as that of a martyed saint. This object is signally accomplished, and the popularity of the work was rightly felt by the leaders of the Commonwealth to constitute a danger of the first magnitude.

[71] This is an abbreviation of the longer title. The work is edited with preface and notes by Merritt Y. Hughes, Yale, *Milton,* III, 259–334.

[72] See the essay on historical background (*ibid.,* pp. 168–79).

[73] According to F. F. Madan, there were "thirty-five editions in London within one year of its first appearance" and at least "twenty-five more in the same period in Ireland and abroad" (*ibid.,* p. 150). See Madan's *A New Bibliography of the "Eikon Basilike" of King Charles the First* (London, 1950), pp. 2–4.

Milton called his answer *Eikonoklastes*[74] (i.e., the image-breaker). It is a lengthy examination of the *Eikon*, chapter by chapter, as was the manner of seventeenth-century controversy. He deprecates the idea of assailing the memory of one who had paid his debt to nature; but, accepting the necessity of meeting such a challenge, he proceeds to demonstrate the worthlessness of Charles' defense of his conduct at every point. The personal indictment which he had avoided making in *The Tenure of Kings and Magistrates* is now drawn with passion. The pious passages, which constitute the most popular feature of the work, he assails as mere hypocrisy, citing Shakespeare's Richard III as an example of a tyrant who masked his evil purposes with religious cant. The most damaging point in the entire statement is his demonstration that one of the rhetorical prayers had been plagiarized word for word from that "vain and amatorious poem," Sir Philip Sidney's *Arcadia*. It was subsequently charged against Milton that he himself, in collaboration with Bradshaw, had caused this prayer to be inserted in some editions of the *Eikon* for the purpose of discrediting the king's sincerity, and the reliability of this charge has been vigorously maintained in at least one study.[75] The balance of evidence is, however, strongly against it, as Merritt Hughes indicates in his discussion of the matter.[76]

In writing *Eikonoklastes* Milton drew heavily on Thomas May's *History of Parliament*, a work published by order in 1647. He also used various official parliamentary declarations. The comparison of his pamphlet with these documents shows him to have been no mere irresponsible controversialist but, to quote one investigator, "a careful (though a partisan) writer utilizing reputable parliamentary authorities, and striving painstakingly to establish his foundation of fact, on which with the aid of his scorching invective he might overwhelm the king's reputation and so demolish the royalist faction."[77] He may also have been acquainted with the *Eikon*

[74] Ed. with preface and notes by Merritt Y. Hughes, Yale, *Milton*, III, 335–601.
[75] See S. B. Liljegren, *Studies in Milton*, pp. 140–52.
[76] "New Evidence on the Charge that Milton Forged the Pamela Prayer in the *Eikon Basilike*," RES, n.s., III (1952), 130–40.
[77] George W. Whiting, "The Sources of *Eikonoklastes*: A Resurvey."

Alethine, which had appeared anonymously on or before August 26, 1649, and which assailed among other things the genuineness of the royal authorship of the *Eikon Basilike.* It is interesting that Milton should abandon this issue and attack the *Eikon Basilike* on the assumption that he had to deal with the king's own words.

POLITICAL TRACTS AND THE CONTROVERSY WITH SALMASIUS AND MORUS (1651–55)

In 1650, the next year after the publication of *Eikonoklastes,* Milton began the last and greatest battle of his controversial career. Charles II, now in exile in France, had engaged Salmasius (Claude Saumaise),[78] a French scholar resident in Holland, to prepare an elaborate Latin tract addressed to the intellectual leaders of Europe and designed to hold up to execration the men who had voted the death of the king. This work, which appeared in England on May 11, 1649, with the title *Defensio Regia pro Carolo I,*[79] though less insidious within England than the *Eikon Basilike,* was even more dangerous than the latter to the Commonwealth in its international relations. It had the prestige of a great name behind it, for Salmasius was universally recognized as one of the foremost men of learning in an age in which scholarly distinction was still supposed to vouch for the validity of a public utterance of this sort.

Milton, in his official capacity and as the most learned and eloquent controversialist on the republican side, was ordered to compose the answer to this attack.[80] The result was the longest of his prose works hitherto—*The Defence of the English People Against Salmasius (Ioannis Miltoni Angli Pro populo anglicano defensio contra Claudii anonymi, alias Salmasii, Defensionem regiam).* It was published in quarto by the printer Dugard and appeared about

[78] See Katheryn A. McEuen, "Salmasius: Opponent of Milton," Yale, *Milton,* IV, ii, 962–82.
[79] See the summary of this document (*ibid.,* IV, i, 101–07).
[80] "That Mr Milton does prepare something in answer to the Booke of Salmatius, and when hee hath don itt bring itt to the Councell" (French, *Life Records,* II, 286).

February 24, 1651.[81] Since Milton's tract was addressed to a Continental rather than an English audience, it was composed in Latin. Its author inevitably felt the thrill of his first appearance before the wider court of European opinion, and he put into the work his maximum effort. Later he spoke with pride of his "noble task of which all Europe talks from side to side." Yet the *Defensio* can hardly be called today a noble work. It is filled from beginning to end with personalities, assailing in abusive phrase the scholarship, the mercenary motives,[82] and the private character of Salmasius, as if to discredit him as a man and a grammarian were the best means of discrediting the cause which he was pleading. In the tract Salmasius is alternately "a talkative ass sat upon by a woman," a brute, a beast, a liar married to a "barking bitch"; there is also argument in abundance, while Milton, confining himself rather to point-by-point replies to his opponent, demonstrates again and again that the action of the regicides was justified by English law, by ancient and modern learned authority, by the precedent of other peoples, by the tyrannical character of Charles, and by public necessity. The materials of *The Tenure of Kings and Magistrates* and of *Eikonoklastes* are repeated and elaborated. The Presbyterians are scored anew. Such eloquence as the piece can show is the eloquence of scorn. Above all Milton denounces the intrusion of a foreigner into the affairs of his countrymen, and he shows at length the inconsistency of Salmasius' point of view with ideas expressed in his previous writings.

The Defence of the English People made such a stir abroad as Milton could have wished.[83] Salmasius, having left the court of Queen Christina of Sweden where he had been living in great honor, died on September 3, 1653. The rumor that he was discredited and disgraced by Milton's work, which had broken his health, is probably without foundation. The reply to which Salmasius was goaded was written but for some reason withheld from publication until 1660. Meanwhile several minor Continental roy-

[81] Ed. with preface and notes by William J. Grace, trans. Donald C. Mackenzie, Yale, *Milton*, IV, i, 285–537.

[82] Whether Salmasius received the reputed £100 for the tract is not known. See W. McNeill, "Milton and Salmatius: 1649," *EHR*, LXXX (1905), 107–08.

[83] See French, *Life Records*, II, 363–65; III, 46–50.

alists entered the field, leveling their attack at Milton personally. It was not, however, until the appearance in 1652 of an anonymous answer of real power (. . . *Regii Sanguinis Clamor ad Coelum Adversus Paricidas Anglicanos* [*The Cry of the King's Blood to Heaven against the English Parricides*]) that he undertook an answer. This new work, *Pro Populo Anglicano Defensio Secunda . . .* (*A Second Defence of the English People by John Milton, Englishman, in reply to an Infamous Book entitled Cry of the King's Blood*[84]), did not appear until about May 30, 1654, though it had been ordered by the Council long before.[85] Milton was waiting, he said, for the rumored reply of Salmasius. Besides this, he was now blind; the complete ruin of his eyesight had followed in 1652 the composition of the *First Defence*, caused according to Milton's own statement by his unremitting application to that task.

The *Second Defence*, like the first, contains an abundance of virulent and undignified personalities, directed now against Alexander More ("Morus"), a Scottish-French scholar domiciled in Holland and closely associated with Salmasius. The actual author was Peter du Moulin, but the more distinguished More had had a hand in the printing and circulation of the volume and had supplied a preface. He was widely believed in Holland to be its author, and reports to that effect, together with certain scandals regarding his relations with one "Pontia" (Bontia),[86] a serving-maid of Salmasius' wife, had reached Milton through the English press. Though More denied responsibility for the work, and though Milton was officially urged by the Dutch ambassador in London to stay his hand, he remained unconvinced and proceeded to administer chastisement accordingly. He made the most of the Pontia scandal and afterward regretted that he had not been able to include other discreditable stories about More which reached him later.

These elements may perhaps be mitigated by the provocation given by the *Regii Sanguinis Clamor* in its personal abuse of Milton and by the controversial practice of the times; in any case, the *Second Defence* is a much nobler and more interesting book than

<hr>

[84] Ed. with preface and notes by Donald A. Roberts, trans. Helen North, Yale, *Milton*, IV, i, 538–686.

[85] French, *Life Records*, III, 376.

[86] See Yale, *Milton*, IV, i, 568 ff.

the first. It was designed to be not merely a crushing blow to the author of the *Clamor* but also a worthy celebration of the cause of the Commonwealth and its great leaders. In the opinion of E. M. W. Tillyard, it "is the greatest of Milton's prose works and one of the greatest of the world's rhetorical writings."[87] The objective of the work is more nearly in accord with Milton's conception of the public function of the poet as stated in *The Reason of Church-Government* than anything he had hitherto written. It is a genuine fruit of patriotic feeling and reveals an enthusiastic love of liberty. These emotions Milton characteristically associates with his own personality, making himself not only the defender of a cause but also a portion of the cause. Such identification it is that rouses the poet in him and fires his noblest eloquence. Thus the passage which he devotes to an account of his life and services to liberty,[88] written to clear his name from the slanders of his opponents, becomes a piece of artistic self-portraiture akin to the great personal expressions of some of the sonnets. Pitched in an even higher tone are his statements about his blindness, the fact of which had been roughly alluded to by du Moulin as a punishment visited upon him by God for his sins. Milton's own meditations on the subject had resulted in a conviction that his blindness was in part a voluntary sacrifice and that the Deity, proving him by the affliction, had vouchsafed in compensation an inward illumination not shared by other men. Far from being a disgrace, his blindness marked him as a creature set apart for God's peculiar uses and worthy of a special reverence. The passage (quoted in Appendix B) is parallel in idea, even in some of its phraseology, with the famous invocation to light at the beginning of Book III of *Paradise Lost.*

The eloquence produced by this new mood carries over into other passages in the work. It reaches great dignity in the panegyric on Cromwell, an enthusiastic portrait in the manner of antiquity which celebrates his triumphs and his character, likening him to the great statesmen and patriots of Greece and Rome.[89] Proof that we are here close to the sources of Milton's specific poetic inspiration

[87] *Milton*, pp. 192–93.
[88] Yale, *Milton*, IV, i, 612 ff.
[89] *Ibid.*, pp. 666 ff.

is furnished by the identity in mood and idea of the passages with the more concentrated expression in the sonnet to Cromwell. In each case the hero becomes for a moment the vessel of Milton's ethical idealism. His praise is made the occasion for the utterance of a plea for the application of principles in the administration of the state without which the English people will slip back into the slavery from which they have risen.

The sequel of Milton's misdirected castigation in the *Second Defence* was a disclaimer and personal vindication by More himself under the title *Fides Publica* (i.e., *Public Testimony in His Own Behalf*). This work, bound in a single volume with a new edition of Milton's *Second Defence*, was issued at The Hague in 1654 by the printer Vlacq, who was quite willing that his press should speak on both sides of the question so long as sales continued to be good. Besides vigorously denying responsibility for the *Clamor* and carefully documenting his own honorable career in reply to the aspersions of the *Defensio*, More very naturally censures Milton's injustice in attacking him, claiming that the English writer had every opportunity of knowing that he was not the author of the work. With keen instinct he pitches upon the evidences of Milton's excessive self-esteem, denouncing his presumption in taking it upon himself to instruct Cromwell in his duties. The *Fides Publica* was followed by a supplement in 1655. Milton's reply, the *Pro se Defensio*, or, to translate its full title, *The English John Milton's Defence for himself, in reply to Alexander Morus, churchman, rightly called the author of the notorious book entitled 'Cry of the King's Blood'*,[90] appeared in August of the same year. This work attempts to establish, if not the actual authorship, yet at least the full responsibility of More for the *Clamor* and to discredit item by item his published testimonials. The new scandals which had come to him too late for inclusion in the *Second Defence* are now rehearsed at length. The work lacks entirely the higher qualities of the *Second Defence* but contains a curious passage in defense of the use of gross language and a personal vilification against the enemies of righteousness which shows how little at ease Milton really was about his own controversial practices. It is only by convincing himself that, in prosecuting private enmities, he is exposing and correcting public

[90] Ed. with preface and notes by Kester Svendsen, trans. Paul W. Blackford, *ibid.*, IV, ii, 687–825.

delinquencies, that he is enabled to take that satisfaction in his achievement which may have been for him a psychological necessity.

THE HISTORY OF BRITAIN (1646–70)

The turmoil of the Salmasius-More controversy was followed by a period in Milton's career of comparative leisure. He had, since the beginning of his blindness, been progressively less active in the Latin secretaryship. An assistant, Philip Meadows, had been appointed for him in 1653; his salary was reduced and commuted to a life pension in 1655, after which time (though he nominally remained in office till the Restoration, and though his state letters continue until 1659) he must have been comparatively free from official responsibilities. The result was a renewed occupation with three works of scholarship begun before the execution of the king but interrupted by the call to public service. One of these, a Latin dictionary, was never completed and remained unpublished. The others were a *History of Britain*[91] and the Latin theological work, *De Doctrina Christiana*,[92] both of which appear to have been finished between 1655 and 1660.

The History of Britain may be regarded as a sort of commutation of Milton's earlier plan for a drama or an epic on a British legendary theme. He rejected the Arthurian story in favor of the more significant and authentic biblical theme, but his literary and patriotic interest in the materials continued keen and demanded expression.[93] More directly, the *History* is the fruit of the long course of historical reading recorded in the Commonplace Book.

[91] Ed. George Philip Krapp, CM, X, 1–325. See the separate volume of notes prepared by Constance Nicholas, *Introduction to 'Milton's History of Britain.'*

[92] Ed. James Holly Hanford and Waldo Hilary Dunn, trans. Charles R. Sumner, CM, XIV, XV, XVI, XVII.

[93] It has been shown that the historicity of Arthur was a matter of political controversy in the seventeenth century as it had been in the sixteenth. King James had emphasized his descent from Arthur and the fulfillment of the British prophecy. The opponents of divine right were critical and made much of the Anglo-Saxon tradition against the British (Roberta F. Brinkley, *Arthurian Legend in the Seventeenth Century* [Baltimore, 1932], pp. 1–25).

About 1640 or 1641 Milton went carefully through Holinshed, Speed, Camden, and Buchanan, together with a few of the older authorities like Gildas and Bede. His carefully annotated copy of Gildas has survived to show the closeness with which he studied his authorities.[94] His study apparently convinced him that the story of his country had never been worthily recorded. The credulity and garrulousness of men like Holinshed must have contrasted strongly in his mind with the dignity of the Greek and Roman historians. He probably resolved shortly after to do something for the annals of his own people like what Tacitus and Sallust had done for Rome, but the more pressing matters of the ecclesiastical and divorce controversies postponed the beginning of the work until about 1646. By March, 1649, he had, as he himself tells us, completed the first four books, bringing the story up to the union of England under Egbert. His secretaryship apparently interrupted further activity until 1655, when he added Books V and VI, containing the story of the Danish invasions and the Norman Conquest. At this point he stopped, but the fact that the work remained unpublished until 1670 would seem to indicate that he continued to cherish his original idea of bringing it up to his own day. The *History* and the Latin dictionary represent perhaps Milton's only uncompleted projects.

In the composition of the work Milton aimed at veracity, brevity, and readableness. Although Milton declares his intention of including "reputed tales" from the old chroniclers for the benefit of "our English poets who by their art will know how to use them judiciously," he does so, as French points out,[95] only grudgingly and with more evidence of disgust at the credulity which accepts them for truth than enthusiasm for their appeal to the imagination. He inveighs against Geoffrey's materials as "too palpably untrue to be worth rehearsing in the midst of truth," objects to Buchanan's taking on himself to relate the inroads of the Scots and Picts into Britain "as if they had but yesterday happened," calls the later Anglo-Saxon chroniclers "obscure and blockish," and condemns even Malmesbury and Huntington for their ambition

---

[94] J. Milton French, "Milton's Annotated Copy of Gildas," *Harvard Studies and Notes*, XX (1938), 76–80.

[95] "Milton as a Historian," *PMLA*, L (1935), 469–79.

to adorn history with surmises of their own. "Them rather than imitate," he writes, "I shall choose to represent the truth naked, though as lean as a plain Journal."[96]

Though he was influenced by modern writers, particularly Holinshed, Camden, and Buchanan, he went back to the original authorities—the Anglo-Saxon Chronicle and Laws, Bede, the medieval chroniclers, etc.—as no English historian had done before him, and he exhibits a very modern sense of the need of weighing their respective values. His critical and scholarly point of view has won the admiration of such a distinguished historian as Sir Charles Firth, who finds that Masson greatly underestimated the originality of Milton's work.[97]

But Milton, however critical he might be of other chroniclers, could not himself write either history or poetry without a fundamentally ethical and philosophic bias. We accordingly find him emphasizing throughout the *History* the relation between national morality and national prosperity, as when he attributes the ease of the Norman Conquest to the corruption of the English, which had "fitted them . . . for this servitude."[98] He often has his eye on contemporary affairs as he analyzes the causes of failure or success in the past; to him a chief value of the study of history is to be found in the lessons which it holds for the modern statesman. As originally written, Book III of the *History* contained a long digression, apropos of the state of Britain when the Romans left it, on the parallel confusion which attended the close of the civil wars in 1648. This was excised by the censor and separately published in 1681 as *Mr. John Milton's Character of the Long Parliament and the Assembly of Divines in 1641*. Personal and political prejudices are revealed in his description of the warrior queen Boadicea as a "distracted woman with a mad crew at her heels," in his unsympathetic treatment of the evangelization of Britain under Augustine, and in his deliberate refusal to go into the details of ecclesiastical history.[99]

[96] CM, X, 180.
[97] "Milton as an Historian," *Proceedings of the British Academy*, III (1907–08), 227–57.
[98] CM, X, 315.
[99] The original edition of 1670 was reprinted without change in 1677 and and 1695. Toland's text, published in 1698, contained several insertions not

DE DOCTRINA CHRISTIANA (1655-60?)

The details of the composition of Milton's great theological work, *De Doctrina Christiana (The Christian Doctrine)*, are not so clear as they are in the case of *The History of Britain*. The statement of Phillips indicates that he returned to it in 1655; Milton himself describes in the preface the collection of the materials from Scripture of which it is composed and the reading of books of divinity in preparation for it as a work which began in his youth. There is, finally, evidence in the preserved manuscript (see below) that the work was complete about 1661.

The manuscript came to light in 1823, and it was published for the first time in 1825. Its earlier history is most interesting. After Milton's death the document was in the hands of a young Oxford graduate, Daniel Skinner, who had served as the last of the poet's literary and scholarly assistants. Quite possibly Milton had himself delivered it with instructions for its publication. At any rate, Skinner recopied the first half of it and sent the whole to the Dutch publisher Elzevir to be printed. Being warned, however, that his responsibility for the publication of such a work would mean the death of his own political ambitions, Skinner had the document returned to him. It subsequently found its way into the Public Record Office, where it lay forgotten until its discovery by the Keeper, Robert Lemon. The work of deciphering, translating, and editing it was entrusted by the command of George IV to Bishop Charles Sumner. Its appearance occasioned Macaulay's famous essay on Milton in 1825. The second half of the manuscript, which represents the original draft, is in the hand of one of Milton's amanuenses, Jeremie Picard, whose work for the poet can be traced in every dictated document which has been preserved

---

found in the first three editions. He apparently used a copy of the 1670 volume annotated by Milton's hand. See Harry Glicksman, "The Sources of Milton's *History of Britain*," *University of Wisconsin Studies in Language and Literature*, II (1920), 105-44.

from the years 1657 to 1661.[100] He was evidently a trained scribe whom Milton regularly employed until the fall of his fortunes at the Restoration compelled him to do with more casual assistance. This portion of the text contains corrections in various other scribal hands, indicating that Milton kept revising, perhaps until his death. These alterations afford a happy hunting ground for those students who suspect Milton's theological opinions of undergoing change.

It is easy to see why the work remained unpublished in Milton's lifetime. He had conceived it in the enthusiasm of the Commonwealth period, when religious belief was in a state of flux and when there seemed to be a hope that mankind could be united in a program of liberal Christianity such as Milton desired. Propaganda was actually underway in Europe, under the direction of Milton's friend, John Dury, for the bringing of the Protestant sects together in a community of belief and action. The *De Doctrina*, written in Latin so that the leaders of European thought might read it and addressed to Christian churches and Christians everywhere, was perhaps intended to furnish the restored theological basis of this new religious unity. With the Restoration all immediate expectation of the fulfillment of the plan (at least so far as England was concerned) came to an end.

Milton's insistence upon the conditional nature of God's decrees would not, to be sure, have hurt him after the passing of the Presbyterian regime, for Anglican theology had always inclined toward this "Arminian" modification of Calvinistic harshness, but his treatment of the second and third persons of the Trinity implied an attitude which to some was anathema. Recent scholarship has contended to the contrary, however, demonstrating that "the Arian element so hastily detected in *De Doctrina Christiana* is nothing but an extension of the 'subordinationism' upheld by the early Christian writers to the Council of Nicaea and revived by the Cambridge Platonists in Milton's own age."[101] The repudiation,

---

[100] See James Holly Hanford, "The Rosenbach Milton Documents," *PMLA*, XXXXIII (1923), 290–96.

[101] C. A. Patrides, *Christian Tradition*, pp. 15–16; see also William B. Hunter, "Milton's Arianism Reconsidered," *HTR*, LIII (1959), 9–35; and Patrides, "Milton and Arianism," *JHI*, XXV (1964), 423–29. William R. Parker's lucid summary and discussion (*Milton*, I, 481–98) should be required reading.

moreover, of all forms and organizations of worship except those simple ones prescribed by Scripture renewed the Puritan indictment against Anglicanism, now reestablished and enforced as the state religion. As if to offend gratuitously, Milton included a statement in favor of divorce and demonstrated that even polygamy is not prohibited by divine law.

The chief virtue of the work in Milton's eyes was that its principles derived solely from Scripture. Its main bulk consists of quotations and references from the Bible, arranged under appropriate headings, with a generalized statement of the doctrine which each group of them supports. Of course Milton could not have arrived at these formulations without a wide acquaintance with the varieties of Christian thought, and he enters into elaborate discussions of many of the controverted points of theological history.[102] He owes much, moreover, especially in Book II, to a Protestant compendium of theology by Wollebius, who is mentioned, along with Fisher Ames, as his model by Edward Phillips.[103] But his infallible test for the acceptance or rejection of a doctrine is its conformity with God's own word as recorded in his inspired writings of the Old and New Testaments.

The peculiarities of Milton's theological ideas will be treated more fully in the discussion of the intellectual background of *Paradise Lost*. The *De Doctrina* reads like a doctrinal commentary on that work and can be ignored by no thorough student.[104] Milton has, however, deliberately avoided in his poem, especially in the more dangerous issues, the clear and uncompromising precision of his statements in the prose. Or perhaps it was simply that these issues ceased to interest him when the doctrinal controversy became less a matter of public concern. The *De Doctrina* is written in a coldly intellectual style, terse and logical, without the slightest touch of eloquence. The document is the steely framework of Milton's intellectual system, deliberately stripped of all the elements of personality, color, and passion which invested his customary vision of the world. His rigid will and the years of logical training

[102] Patrides, *Christian Tradition*.
[103] See Arthur Sewell, *A Study in Milton's Christian Doctrine*, and Maurice Kelley, *This Great Argument*.
[104] Kelley, *This Great Argument*.

at Cambridge are responsible for his ability to accomplish such a result.

LATER ECCLESIASTICAL PAMPHLETS

The troublous times which followed the death of Cromwell in 1658 brought a renewal of Milton's pamphlet activity. Though he was occupied with calmer scholarly tasks and had already begun the composition of *Paradise Lost*, he could not fail, now that public affairs were again in a state of flux, to endeavor to exert an influence. His method was the old one of memorials to Parliament in his private capacity as citizen.

Politically Milton had been, throughout the Protectorate, a staunch Cromwellian. But he never assented to Cromwell's policy of maintaining a modified church establishment with a committee empowered to settle the compensation of ministers and to solder the various denominations together into an orthodox unity. From this unity the Catholics, the High Church and Arminian Episcopalians, the Quakers, and those sects which denied the divinity of Jesus Christ were excluded, and though Cromwell himself attempted to secure toleration even for Jews, he never became an open champion of that complete religious freedom for which Milton hoped. Under a new Protector and a new Parliament it seemed possible that those abuses might be remedied. Milton's convictions in the matter centered in two points: first, that the civil authorities had no right to exercise any compulsion whatsoever in matters of religious belief; second, that the system of tithes or taxes exacted by law for the support of the clergy was an abuse and should give way to voluntary contributions by individual congregations. He attacked these two problems separately, the first in a brief pamphlet entitled A *Treatise of Civil Power in Ecclesiastical Causes; Shewing that it is not lawful for any power on Earth to compel in matters of Religion*, published in late February or early March, 1659.[105] The

---

[105] Ed. William Haller, *CM*, VI, 1–41.

foundation of the argument is that Scripture alone being the divine rule of belief and the interpretation thereof being an affair of private judgment, "no man or body of men in these times can be the infallible judges or determiners in matters of religion to any other men's consciences but their own."[106] Christ's kingdom, moreover, is purely spiritual, and the attempt to regulate it by external force can do only harm. Milton's plea is, as it was in *Areopagitica*, for universal toleration; Papists only are excepted, because they represent a political power dangerous to the safety of the state. Beyond this there is implied rather than clearly expressed the conviction that religion should be left entirely to itself without even such a tolerant state support as Cromwell wished to give it in his establishment. The argument is largely based on Scripture.

On May 25, 1659, Richard Cromwell was forced to abdicate, and the original Rump Parliament, composed largely of republican members, was restored to power. The question of disestablishment and the abolition of the tithe system was now actually brought before the House, and Milton accordingly launched in August his second pamphlet, *Considerations touching the likeliest means to remove Hirelings out of the Church. Wherein is also discoursed of Tithes, Church Fees, Church Revenues; and whether any maintenance of Ministers can be settled by law.*[107] Milton hails the new Parliament with enthusiastic praise, implying that the true custodians of English liberty have returned to power. His thesis is that the mercenary spirit in the clergy has always been the most mischievous evil in the church and that this spirit is encouraged and promoted by the present system of legally enforced contributions. His ideal is a clergy serving without any material reward at all, but he makes so much concession to the necessities of the case as to allow them compensation from the voluntary offerings of their parishioners. Poor congregations may be served by the occasional visits of missionaries supported by the wealthier parishes or even, if necessary, by subsidies out of public funds. In general, he believes that ministers should be content with scanty salaries, finding true reward in the fulfillment of their spiritual mission as preachers of the Word. He is convinced that if profits are cut off, only such men

[106] *Ibid.*, p. 6.
[107] Ed. William Haller, *ibid.*, pp. 43–100.

as are really worthy will be drawn into the ministry. In his suggestion that preachers may support themselves by other occupations and in his denial of the value of an elaborate education for them, we see Milton inclining toward the idea of a lay ministry; this is the logical consequence of his Protestantism and was in fact already in practice among the Quakers and other radical sects. Milton by no means stood alone in his opinions; but the majority was still against him, and Parliament refused to take the proposed action, which looked toward religious disestablishment.

TRACT OF A FREE COMMONWEALTH (1660)

Except for a brief interruption in 1659, the Rump Parliament continued in office until February, 1660. The burning question of the hour was no longer that of establishment or disestablishment, but what form of government would finally emerge from the anarchy into which England had progressively fallen since the death of Cromwell. There was active discussion, in Parliament and out, of the best plan of establishing a republican government which could meet the menace of the restoration of the monarchy for which the public was beginning to clamor with increasing insistency. At this stage of affairs Milton undertook again to exercise an influence on public opinion and on parliamentary action by making a final plea against bringing back the Stuarts and by recommending a constitutional scheme quite different from any that had been proposed. Before his pamphlet could be published, however, General Monk, in whom the real authority now rested, had turned against the Rump, cancelled the writs which it had issued for a reelection, and reconstituted the Long Parliament by restoring the members who had been secluded from it in 1648. This body promptly issued its own writs for the election of "a full and free Parliament." The likelihood of either the newly reconstituted Long Parliament or the people in their approaching choice of its successor listening to anything Milton had to say was very slim. He, nevertheless, issued the tract which he had composed, and conscious of the fact that the

word of General Monk would decide the future of the Commonwealth, sent it to him, with a letter giving its substance in briefer
form.

The tract, which appeared in February or March, 1660, was
entitled *The Ready and Easy Way to Establish a Free Commonwealth and the Excellence thereof with the Inconveniences and
Dangers of Readmitting Kingship in this Nation.*[108] It opens with
a review of the steps which had led to the establishment of the
Commonwealth and a representation of the evils which would
result from undoing the work of liberty by bringing back Charles'
son. His constructive proposal is that sovereignty should henceforth
be vested in a Grand or General Council chosen by a carefully
sifted electorate and sitting in perpetuity. Such a body, Milton
thinks, will provide a stable government by the best men more
effectively than successive parliaments. As a concession to the views
of Harrington and his followers in the Rota Club, Milton reluctantly
admits the principle of a partial rotation whereby a few members
are retired each year and others chosen (apparently by the Council
itself) to fill their places. To this body he adds a smaller council
for executive action, to be elected by the General Council; he also
proposes a series of representative assemblies in every county which
shall have complete autonomy in local affairs. Milton's scheme is
partly modeled on the government of the Netherlands and partly on
the ideal commonwealth of Plato, with its aristocratic rule by the
guardian class. It expresses his lack of faith in a true democracy and
yet avoids the equal evil of a one-man power.

The Ready and Easy Way was eagerly read, and it provoked
immediate replies from the royalist group, who were becoming more
and more outspoken. The "good old cause" was evidently lost, but
Milton fought till the end. He published in April a brief reply to
an open argument for the Restoration by Charles I's former

[108] Ed. William Haller, *ibid.,* pp. 111–49. Milton wrote still a third
appeal against the threatened restoration, the *Proposals of Certain Expedients
for the Preventing of a Civil War now Feared and the Settling of a Firm
Government* (ed. Thomas O. Mabbott and J. Milton French, CM, XVIII,
3–7). No contemporary issue of this pamphlet is known to exist. The best
single edition of *The Ready and Easy Way* is that of E. M. Clark (New
Haven, 1916).

chaplain, Dr. Griffith,[109] and he reissued *The Ready and Easy Way* in a second, expanded edition less than a month before the newly elected Parliament voted the Restoration. In this revision Milton no longer disguises from himself the fact that the event he dreads is practically inevitable. He intensifies the picture of the ruin and disgrace which will attend it and elaborates the scheme of a Grand Perpetual Council, but he knows that he is "exhorting a torrent." His pamphlet has become a final indulgence in free speech, "a little shroving time first," before the "long lent of servitude," his eloquence "the last words of our expiring liberty."

LAST PAMPHLETS (1673–74)

The Restoration silenced Milton politically for many years. Even he realized the uselessness and the danger of further pleas for liberty when there was none. Besides, he was at last engaged on his great poetic enterprise. Yet it seems likely that he would unhesitatingly have laid *Paradise Lost* aside again and risked his personal safety if an occasion had presented itself in which to strike another real blow for liberty. Meanwhile he must have watched the progress of affairs almost as closely as before, and when the last poems were written, he found opportunity to influence public opinion in a limited way on one of the old issues with which he had been concerned. Charles II's Declaration of Indulgence, granting freedom of worship to the Non-Conformists, was issued in March, 1672. The evident fact that it was mainly intended as a relief for Catholics raised a cry against it from Dissenters and Anglicans alike, and it was rescinded by Parliament in the following year. The Non-Conformists hoped for the passage of an act which without benefitting the Papists would free themselves from their disabilities. Some of them advocated a recomprehension within

---

[109] *Brief Notes Upon a Late Sermon, titl'd "The Fear of God and the King"* . . . *by Matthew Griffith, D.D.* This was answered in April by Roger L'Estrange in *No Blinde Guides.*

the establishment. Milton's tract, published along with many others in 1673, was entitled *Of True Religion, Heresy, Toleration, and the growth of Popery*.[110] It is an attempt to bring the Protestant sects together in mutual charity and to induce them to take a tolerant attitude toward indifferences in the nonessential points of doctrine. Any creed based on the word of God, however variously interpreted, is true religion. Heresy is a religion taken up and believed from the traditions of men. Catholicism, therefore, is the essential heresy, and it alone—though rather because of its political pretensions than because of its doctrinal errors—is not to be allowed. Milton deprecates the exercise of violence even toward the Romanists but is firm in advocating the suppression of their public worship. The pamphlet is, as Masson says, a rather tame one compared with the two ecclesiastical tracts written in the last days of the republic.

One further document remains. In the spring of 1674, Milton wrote and published a translation from the Latin of a Polish manifesto entitled *A Declaration of the Election of this present King of Poland, John the III*[111] (i.e., the national hero Sobieski, who had manfully defended his country against the Turks). Milton's interest in the event was kindled because of the insistence it afforded of the true ideal of monarchy: a man universally acknowledged the strongest and most virtuous is elected king by the sovereign people. The implied contrast between the courageous patriot Sobieski and the traitorous idler Charles II is too sharp to be mistaken. With this final recommendation of right reason to his supine countrymen John Milton laid down his pen.

---

[110] Ed. William Haller, CM, VI, 165–80.
[111] Ed. Frank Allen Patterson, *ibid.*, pp. 273–84.

Chapter 3

THE MINOR POEMS

INTRODUCTION

MILTON'S MINOR POEMS IN ENGLISH, LATIN, AND ITALIAN WERE written during the period from the last year of his attendance at St. Paul's School to the moment at which he undertook the actual composition of *Paradise Lost* (i.e., c. 1655). We are told by Aubrey that he was already a poet at the age of ten, but the earliest verses which have been preserved are two Psalm paraphrases, done when he was fifteen years old.

The total body of this work is not large; to Milton himself, who felt, with his contemporaries, that tragedy and epic were the great literary forms and who deliberately shaped his life toward the highest poetic achievement, this experimental and occasional verse was probably trifling. He cherished it sufficiently, however, to publish the bulk of it in an independent volume in 1645 as evidence of his youthful poetic promise.[1] That marked his thirty-sixth year and, the reconciliation with his wife accomplished, he was about to enter on a new and maturer phase of his life activity.

Though this part of Milton's poetical activity was fairly con-

---

[1] A second edition, which appeared in 1673, contained a few additional early pieces and the subsequently composed translations and sonnets.

tinuous for the period which it covered, we may observe in it some especially prolific years and some rather notable gaps. Thus, in his eighteenth year (his second at the University) Milton gave himself eagerly to the composition of Latin verse, writing not less than six poems in the medium. Again from 1629 to 1631, near the end of his residence in Cambridge, he appears to have begun composing in English with a new enthusiasm. At Hammersmith he wrote *Comus* in 1634, and then, except for *Lycidas* in 1637, nothing until his return from Italy, a period of seven years. The more prolific moments of his later life are 1644 to 1646 (six sonnets), April, 1648 (nine Psalms), 1653 (eight Psalms), and 1655 to 1656 (four sonnets).

In the following discussion the poems are arranged chronologically, except that the two early Psalm paraphrases are considered with the translations, most of which belong to the period after 1640.

THE LATIN POEMS

Milton divided the Latin poems which he published in the 1645 volume into poems in elegiac meter, including eight of his epigrams *(Elegiarum Liber)*, and poems in miscellaneous meters *(Sylvarum Liber)*. In the 1673 edition three epigrams were added to the first group and an ode, *Ad Ioannem Rousium*, to the second. In both editions Milton arranged the pieces in an approximately chronological order and he carefully dated many of them, especially those which belong to his earlier college years. These dates, however, are not wholly to be trusted. Elegies II, III, and the poem, *In Obitum Praesulis Eliensis*, which are headed *anno aetatis* 17, can be shown to have been written in 1626, when Milton was in his eighteenth, not his seventeenth year.[2] It is probable that the poet was

---

[2] The date of Elegy IV, regarding which there has been dispute, is apparently fixed by the allusion to the siege of Hamburg, begun by Wallenstein in 1627. Rumor of this event had evidently just reached him. Two summers, two autumns, and three springs have passed, he says (ll. 33–38), since Young left England; he must then be writing in the summer of 1627, i.e., in his nineteenth year. The poem is, however, headed *anno aetatis* 18.

using the Latin phrase regularly in this sense.[3] There is, however, one case (the poem on the death of Gostlin) where Milton's date is two years out of the way, and the precise chronology of those poems regarding which we have no evidence other than the poet's statement is conjectural. There are, moreover, a number, notably *Ad Patrem* and the *Epitaphium Damonis*, to which as works of greater maturity he assigned no dates.[4]

Even with the uncertainty about the dates of composition, the Latin poems constitute an important part of the year-by-year record of Milton's thoughts, feelings, and literary development. The three elegies (I, V, and VII), in which Milton gives rein to his delight in sensuous beauty and dallies with the thought of love, are perhaps unique. They should be read in connection with the passage in the *Apology*, in which he tells how he was first roused to literary enthusiasm by the amatory poetry of the Roman elegists and inspired to imitate them. In addition to the amatory motive these poems contain suggestions of his personal loyalty to his boyhood tutor, Thomas Young (Elegy IV); his discomfort in the atmosphere of the University and his enthusiasm for the life of cultured and studious leisure (Elegy I); his gratitude to his father for providing him with generous opportunities to indulge such tastes *(Ad Patrem)*; his pride in his association with a famous Italian patron of the arts *(Mansus)*. Such works as the poem on the Gunpowder Plot *(In Quintum Novembris)* and the elegies commemorating the deaths of University dignitaries are impersonal academic exercises, but they reveal a zealous enthusiasm for the art of modern Latin composition and much about Milton's intellectual habits and the sources of his literary culture. *In Quintum Novembris*, the most ambitious of these efforts, is an epic narrative of 226 lines describing the attempt of Satan to punish England for its rebellion to his rule by instigating the Pope to frame the plot against King James. It expresses the violent Protestant patriotism of the Fifth of November

[3] See William R. Parker, "Notes on the Chronology of Milton's Latin Poems," p. 114.

[4] Although E. M. W. Tillyard (*Milton*, p. 384) argues that *Ad Patrem* more plausibly belongs to the period after the publication of *Comus* in 1637, we think it more likely belongs immediately following the performance of *Comus* on Sept. 29, 1634, a moment which may have "had more of an impact on Milton's father than its *anonymous* publication three years later" (Parker, "Notes on the Chronology of Milton's Latin Poems," p. 127). Cf. Douglas Bush's argument for 1631 or 1632 ("The Date of Milton's *Ad Patrem*").

tradition and may have had as its model Phineas Fletcher's *Locustae*, a Latin poem on the same theme.[5] If this poem and the five others (Elegies I, II, III, *In Obitum Praesulis Eliensis*, and *In Obitum Procancellarii Medici*) all belong, as commonly supposed, to Milton's eighteenth year (in the fall of 1626), they constitute evidence of an extraordinary poetic outburst at that time. Since the earliest in the series is the first elegy, which records Milton's banishment from Cambridge as a consequence of his quarrel with Chappell, we may perhaps credit the ambitious impulses of this creative time to some kind of stimulation resulting from his rustication and his change of tutors.

One of the later Latin poems, the *Epitaphium Damonis* (1641), warrants careful comparison with its parallel in English, the elegy for Edward King, *Lycidas* (1637). Their very position— *Epitaphium Damonis* is the last poem in *Sylvarum Liber* in 1645, while *Lycidas* concludes the English section of the volume—places them among the last to be composed and indicates something of the poetic maturity one may expect to discover in them. The tribute to Diodati, with its familiar cry, *"Ite domum impasti, domino iam non vacat, agni"* ("Go home unfed my lambs, your troubled shepherd is not free to tend you") is an exercise in the tradition of Greek pastoral and faithfully observes the many conventions of the mode of Theocritus, Bion, and Moschus. It tells incidentally of the poet's own ambitious poetic flights, now no longer to be shared with the beloved companion of his school and college days, and reminisces about his recent Italian excursion and his visit with Manso. Without raising the questions which result in the ultimate ambiguities of *Lycidas*, the *Epitaphium Damonis* concludes with a grand apotheosis of the chaste Damon, who is envisioned enjoying the song and dance of the heavenly realms. This work is incomparably the best of Milton's Latin poems.[6]

The body of Milton's Latin verse represents the finest achieve-

[5] The dating problem here is interesting, for Fletcher's *Locustae* was not published until 1627; if Milton's poem is to be dated 1626, there could be little likelihood of Fletcher's influence.

[6] Tillyard (*Milton*, pp. 99 ff.) is of a different opinion. He says that the poem reveals a troubled, disunited mind and begins to flag after 1. 124, as if Milton were "recalling with false ardor feelings which he has outgrown and which scarcely concern him now." Rand thinks *Ad Patrem* the finest of the Latin poems.

ment in this medium by an Englishman. Professor E. K. Rand, the great classicist, finds it not unworthy to take a place beside its ancient models. Milton at first followed the ornate and romantic style of Ovid; his later poems have more of the Virgilian dignity and restraint. His work also reflects the Renaissance humanists, particularly George Buchanan, who was widely known as the most elegant Latin poet of the time. In pouring so much of his own poetic energy into an ancient tongue (to the extent that in his earlier University years he scarcely wrote anything in English), Milton was following the learned precedent of his age. He recognized, however, that English was to be his ultimate medium, for there are verses on his mother tongue in the *Vacation Exercise* of 1628. From the point of view of his loftier purposes, he probably regarded Latin composition as a way of disciplining his powers; but the use of a learned language gave him an opportunity to say some things in a more direct personal way and to indulge the sensuous side of his nature more freely than he could have in English.

ENGLISH POEMS WRITTEN AT THE UNIVERSITY

On the Death of a Fair Infant Dying of a Cough

Except for the two Psalm paraphrases which date from his school days, this is evidently the earliest of Milton's English poems. Milton heads it *anno aetatis* 17, i.e., 1626. William R. Parker's research[7] has, however, given good grounds for believing that it belongs to 1628, the year in which Milton wrote his *Vacation Exercise* and turned deliberately from Latin to English verse. The infant, according to Edward Phillips,[8] was the daughter of Milton's sister Anne, who had married Edward Phillips the elder on November 2, 1623. An entry in the Parish Register of St. Martin-in-the-Fields gives the dates of baptism and burial of the first three children of this marriage as follows: John, January 16, 1625—March 15, 1629; Anne,

---

[7] *TLS*, Dec. 17, 1938, p. 802.
[8] "The Life of Mr. John Milton," Darbishire, *Early Lives*, p. 62.

January 12, 1626—January 22, 1628; Elizabeth, April 9, 1628—
February 19, 1631.[9] The first daughter, Anne, would, therefore, be
the subject of Milton's elegy; the second, Elizabeth, may be the
child whose birth he seems to predict in the last stanza. If this is
the case, the elegy was written after January 22, and before April 9,
1628. Milton's failure to include it in the first edition of his poems
seems to show that he thought it immature. Perhaps he unconsciously antedated the poem for the same reason.

In this poem Milton employs the rime royal stanza; perhaps
it is derived from the work of Phineas Fletcher, who uses it commonly (with frequent double rhyme, a practice abandoned by
Milton after the first stanza) in his *Poetical Miscellanies* and in
Eliza. Tillyard says that the poem is rather in the tradition of the
Ovidizing Elizabethans than of the Spenserians and cites the following passages as parallel:

> O fairest flower no sooner blown but blasted,
> Soft silken Primrose fading timelessly. . . .
>
> (11. 1–2)
>
> Sweet Rose, fair flower, untimely pluckt, soon faded,
> Pluckt in the bud, and faded in the spring,
> Bright orient pearl, alack too timely shaded,
> Fair creature killed too soon by Death's sharp sting.[10]

The poem's image patterns and rich mythological allusions have
recently been studied by Jackson I. Cope,[11] who demonstrates how
the physical structure of rising and falling anticipates the pattern in
Paradise Lost. Readers generally agree with Don Cameron Allen[12]
and Hugh Maclean,[13] however, that because of the poet's difficulties
in combining Christian and pagan materials in a complex form, the
poem concludes anticlimactically and is only a qualified success.

---

[9] *The Register of St. Martin-in-the-Fields: 1619–1636*, ed. and trans.
John V. Kitto (London, 1936), pp. 35, 242, 40, 233, 54, 258.

[10] *Milton*, p. 19. The latter four lines are a fragment which appeared in
the anthology *The Passionate Pilgrim* (1599).

[11] "Fortunate Falls as Form in Milton's 'Ode on the Death of a Fair
Infant.' "

[12] *The Harmonious Vision*, pp. 47–52.

[13] "Milton's *Fair Infant*."

At a Vacation Exercise in the College, PART LATIN, PART ENGLISH

The English section of this piece is exactly one hundred lines of heroic couplets (a form used generally according to the practice of such Elizabethans as Ben Jonson) and was dated by Milton in the 1673 edition of the poems, where it first appeared, "*anno aetatis 19.*" The Latin prolusion with which it belongs is the sixth, where Milton appears as official spokesman in one of the periodic revels of the collegians either in the spring or summer recess. Masson ascribes it on the grounds of Milton's heading (assuming as usual that "*anno aetatis 19*" means at the age of nineteen) and upon references in the Latin portion to the year 1628 (the Latin text explains the English section, in which the poet masquerades—near the conclusion—as Ens, or Being, and designates certain of his fellow students as the Aristotelian categories, his sons). At the conclusion of Prolusion VI he had announced his intention "to jump the Statutes of the University like the walls of Romulus, and quit Latin in favor of English," for indeed the chief significance of the *Vacation Exercise* is in the lines which express Milton's patriotic and aesthetic enthusiasm for the English tongue and declare his intention to write worthily in it on some lofty theme. In lines 19 ff. he gives his adverse reaction to the fashionable "late fantasticks" in literature, declaring his allegiance to the older and more richly poetic style of Spenser and the Elizabethans. It has been suggested that George Herbert might have been in Milton's mind as having in the era just before him at Cambridge represented the new modes of expression initiated by John Donne. But there are some outrageous puns in the poem, and in the concluding description of the rivers Milton imitates Spenser and Browne, as he was later to do in the poem on the nativity, in some far-fetched metaphors of the sort he seems to be condemning.

On the Morning of Christ's Nativity

Milton printed the great nativity ode, the first serious work of his genius, as the opening poem in the 1645 edition, dating it 1629.

We learn from the close of Elegy VI that it was begun before
daylight on Christmas morning, "as a birthday gift to Christ":

> *Dona quidem dedimus Christi natalibus illa;*
> *Illa sub auroram lux mihi prima tulit.*

The deeply religious mood in which it was undertaken indicates
not only an attitude appropriate to the season but a decision on
Milton's part to abandon literary trifling and consecrate himself to
a way of life in harmony with the most serious kind of poetic
inspiration. It is to be remembered that he had come of age on
the ninth of December in the same year.

The subject is a common one in sixteenth- and seventeenth-
century English poetry. Among the more important of Milton's
immediate predecessors who had written of the nativity in independent odes are Jonson, Drummond, Beaumont, Southwell, and
Sylvester. The theme also appears in Giles Fletcher's *Christ's
Victory and Triumph* and throughout the religious poetry of the
period. Many features of Milton's treatment of the subject find
abundant precedent in this literature, but Milton's ode is, in several
ways, as atypical as it is traditional. For instance, the manger scene,
in which the beasts and shepherds are strangely silent, is severely
underplayed; so too is the usually central issue of Mary's mother-
hood. The great calm of the opening of the ode contrasts with the
traditional Hebraic expression of animism in which all nature is
seen as joyous and full of melody. Traditional nativity songs also
stressed the enlightenment of pagan deities, not their complete
ruin. The only significant parallel between Milton's poem and
another is with Tasso's *Rime Sacre,* in which the cessation and the
overthrow of the pagan deities of Greece and Egypt are described
in a manner very similar to Milton's. Equally important is the
influence of Virgil's Fourth Eclogue, which prophesies the golden
age which was to follow upon the birth of a son to Pollio and is
universally interpreted as an allegory of the birth of Christ. Milton
appears to have regarded the entire body of his youthful work as
belonging roughly to the pastoral genre; his nativity poem is, as
Professor Rand remarks, an attempt "to match the Pagan's Mes-
sianic prophecy . . . [in] a pastoral Birth Song for the real Messiah,

in which Christian purity and truth dispense with the gaudy trim of Pagan imagery."[14]

Yet Milton does not escape from the Renaissance habit of employing a classical mode to conceive a Christian theme. Christ is for him not the suffering Savior but the mighty Pan, kindly come to dwell among men. The sweetness of the manger scene, so beautifully imaged in Crashaw's nativity ode and in Christmas carols, gives way to the picture of an infant Hercules who "can in his swaddling bands control the damned crew" of Satan. Milton's true theme, however, is the moral significance of Christ, who serves as a symbol of ethical and religious truth which in its pure simplicity banishes the multiformity of error typified in the welter of pagan divinities. Accordingly the poem's three movements—I–VII, VIII–XVIII, XIX–XXVII—are balanced and unified by variations in patterns of the two ancient Christian symbols of Light and Harmony.[15] This strategy emphasizes Milton's interest in the principles of Peace and Harmony and reemphasizes the human aspect of the Incarnation. In short, Milton is adoring an idea rather than a person. His poem is Protestant and humanistic rather than Catholic in feeling.[16]

In both meter and style, the proem to *On the Morning of Christ's Nativity* reflects the use made by Chaucer, Spenser, Giles and Phineas Fletcher, and Shakespeare of the rime royal stanza, while the body of the poem itself echoes two vastly different traditions. On the one hand, the final Alexandrine suggests its ultimate origin in Spenser and his followers, while the scheme $a_6 \ a_6 \ b_{10} \ c_6 \ c_6 \ b_{10}$ suggests the realm of popular song and carol, of the madrigals and canzonets, for instance, of Thomas Morley. These two traditions, along with the deliberately archaic diction and frequent instances of the naive, merge to maintain the chosen decorum of "simple strains" played on "native hemlock pipes."[17] "Decorous" also are the seemingly random shifts in tense which

[14] "Milton in Rustication," p. 129.

[15] Rosemond Tuve, "*The Hymn* on the Morning of Christ's Nativity," pp. 37–72; Arthur Barker, "The Pattern of Milton's Nativity Ode."

[16] Don Cameron Allen, "The Higher Compromise."

[17] Louis L. Martz, "The Rising Poet, 1645," *The Lyric and Dramatic Milton*, ed. Joseph H. Summers (New York, 1965), pp. 21–33.

characterize the verbs of the poem. This alternation of tenses gradually narrows and eventually closes the gap between the speaker's present and Christ's birthday, creating a kind of intensified and heightened present as both moments become one and we participate in the timelessness of the event.[18] Tillyard, in noting certain of these traits in the ode, described its essence quite precisely as a "homeliness, quaintness, and tenderness, harmonized by a pervading youthful candor and ordered by a commanding architectonic grasp."[19] Tillyard's remarks and his further analysis of the complex mood out of which the poem sprang raise interesting critical and psychological questions concerning the unfolding of Milton's genius at this turning point in his career.

The poem also contains important anticipations of motives later to be employed in *Paradise Lost.* Thus the idea suggested in stanzas XIV–XXV that the pagan divinities are in reality demons is the basic principle of the representation of the fallen angels. The conception was a familiar one in patristic writers. The idea of the death of Pan and the cessation of oracles is the subject of a long gloss in Spenser's *Shepherd's Calendar* (May) and of an essay by Plutarch. Milton's knowledge of Egyptian deities comes in part from Eusebius' *Praeparatio Evangelorum,* which is full of interesting material concerning the Phoenician and Egyptian gods. The introduction of personifications—Peace, Justice, Truth, Mercy—shows his familiarity with the allegory of the four daughters of God developed by medieval writers and revived by Giles Fletcher in *Christ's Victory* from which Milton derived it. The material of this allegory, stripped of its metaphorical element, is embodied in the debate in Heaven in Book III of *Paradise Lost.*

The Passion

The Passion immediately follows *On the Morning of Christ's Nativity* in the 1645 edition and apparently belongs to the following Easter, April, 1630. It is bound to the preceding work by allusions

---

[18] Lowry Nelson, Jr., "Milton's 'Nativity Ode,'" *Baroque Lyric Poetry,* pp. 41–52.
[19] "The Nativity Ode," *Milton,* pp. 35–42.

1. Portrait allegedly by Cornelius Janssen and supposedly executed in 1618 when Milton was ten. (Pierpont Morgan Library)

2. Milton around age twenty-one. A copy of the Onslow portrait by Benjamin van der Gucht, dated 1792. The much-copied original, long thought destroyed, may now hang in the National Portrait Gallery. (Milton's Cottage, Chalfont St. Giles, Bucks.; photo Woodmansterne, Ltd.)

3. Pastel portrait by William Faithorne, formerly owned by William Baker of Bayfordbury, Hertfordshire. It was apparently either the direct source of the frontispiece for *The History of Britain* (1670) or the source of the copy from which the frontispiece was engraved. (Princeton University Library)

4. Frontispiece from the first edition of *The History of Britain* (1670). The Latin inscription declares the portrait to have been done from life by William Faithorne. (Rare Book Division, The New York Public Library, Astor, Lenox and Tilden Foundations)

5. Autograph page from Milton's Commonplace Book, section on law, p. 179. This page dates between 1639 and 1641. *Add. ms.* 36354. (Trustees of the British Museum)

6. Autograph song by Henry Lawes for Milton's *Comus*. The song is from Lawes's manuscript of his settings of various poems by various authors. *Add. ms.* 53723. (Trustees of the British Museum)

7. Loggan's engraving of Christ's College in 1688. In the upper left are the hundred mulberry trees planted by James I. All but one were chopped down in the early nineteenth century and this one became known as Milton's mulberry tree. (*The Early History of Christ's College* by A. H. Lloyd, Cambridge University Press, 1934)

1

Gul. Faithorne ad Vivum   Delin. et sculpsit.

Ioannis Miltoni Effigies Ætat: 62.
1670.

Savanaruola essendogli mandato una scommunica da Roma non
di dicendo in sua difesa una bella parabola la quale si pruoua ch
piu tosto ubbedije alla intententibne delle leggi che alle parole. l'i
innouation della chiesa.

Lambard saith that laws were first devis'd to bound and limit the pow
governours, that they might not make lust thire iudge, and might thire min
arcbebion. c.3.

Some say they ought to have reasons added to them. il legislatore che rende ragione d
Concil. Trident. l.5. detto, diminuisce l'autonita sua, pche il suddito s'attacca alla raggio
p. 460.   dotta, e quando crede haverla risoluta pensa d'haver anco lebard la 2
Alfred turnd the old laws into english. J would we liu'd now to nd us of thy norm
Sto. p. 80 gibbrish. the laws of Molmutius. as Holinsh. p. 15. and of Queene Martia.
Shed. in the raigne of Sisilius the son of Quintoline. p. 19. Jnas also of the
Saxons k. made many laws. Holinshed. l. 6. c. 1. and he it was that mad
shamefull, and unworthy law of peeter pence. renew'd also by the m
Offa the Mercian so thinking to expiate his horrid sins. Holinshed. l. 6

De jure naturali, gentit et civili quid statuant jurisperiti. vide Justinian. institut. l. 1. tit. 2.

Edward the Confessor reduc't the laws to fewer, pickt them, and set o
name of the common law. Holinsh. l. 8. c. 4.

Lawyers opinions turn with the times for private ends. Speed. 614. 615. Rich. 2.
thire end is to be considerd. p. 616.

Kings of England sworne to the laws see Rex. at thire crowning. King william
granted also   sworne solemnly the second time in the church of St Albons. which he pres
and confirmd by broke. Holinsh. p. 10. Henry the. 1. Comming to the crowne promiseth
charter. Holinsh. lish the unjust laws of the Normans and to restore the laws of k Ed
181 and 183. Speeb. Holinsh. p. 28. Maud the empresse, the Londoners request in this poin
p. 447. Rich. 1. see thereby the faire forwardnesse she was in, to the crowne. Holinsh. St
Speed at his crowning K. John at his absolution from the Popes curse, and interdiction p
of K. John. vid. the same. Holinsh. p. 180. see also p. 181. wch refusing to pforme cost
Subditus.   all the trouble that succeeded p. 183. c p. 186. Henry the 3d at the
                 him and Lewis swore together with his protector Lew the E. of Pe
                 him that he would restore all the rights and liberties before demand
                 father. Holinsh. p. 205. urg'd about it by the B. of Cantur. p. 204.
                 for the which denyd Lewis the f. k. refuses to restore Normandy
                 demand to Hen. 3. the same k demanded againe thistingly answe
                 and begins to assaile his barons. ibid. upon a fifteen graded Hen
                 confirms by parliament the 2 chayters magna, and de Fores
                 an reg. 9. p. 207. but cancell'd by him most ignobly when he c
                 to age. p. 208. Hubert de Burgh being cheife setter on. p. 209. b
                 being at full age freely of his owne consent an. reg. 21. gra
                 confirm'd these 2 charters. Holinsh. p. 220. also an. reg. 37. wit
                 tence of excommunication against the breakers therof. p. 248. wi
                 ter execration which the K. used against him selfe if he broke the
                 yet afterwords sought to be absolv'd of it by the Pope. and brea
                 sworne to it againe with his son Prince Edward. p. 258. and also h
parliam. Oxf.   E. of Cornwall after his proud denial. p. 261. and curse denount
                 breakers. 262. causes his absolution to be read. 263. accepts ag
Marleborow   ordinances of Oxford. 265. renounces again. ibid. promises again
parl.   prisoner to the Barons. 268. and confirm'd by parl. at Marlebor
                 vide subditus.

Henry Lawes

the 5 songs following were set for a Maske
presented at Ludlow Castle before ye Earle of Bridgwater
Lord president of Wales October 1634.

from ye Heavens now I fly, and those happy Clymes ly ye were day never dyes &c

Eye up in the Broad fields of the sky there I suck ye liquid Ayer all &c

midst the garden faire ... Hesperus & his daughters three that sings about the

Golden Tree. Iris there with humid Bow waters the Odorous banks that blow

flowers of more mingled hew, then her purpled Scarfe can shew

Beds of Hyacinths & roses, where many a Cherub soft reposes.

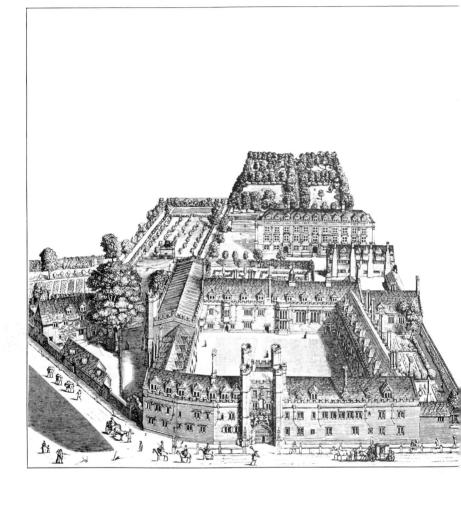

in the opening lines and by the use of a meter identical with that employed in the introductory portions of the other. The poem represents an attempt to continue in the lofty religious vein of the poet's new consecration in 1629. Quite possibly he projected such a series of commemorations of the divine events at their appropriate anniversaries in the church calendar as are to be found among the works of Herbert and Donne. The poem *On the Circumcision* constitutes a third member of the group. *The Passion* contains (1. 26) a specific reference to Marco Girolamo Vida's Latin poem, *Christias*, which with Giles Fletcher's *Christ's Victory* and the religious verse of his brother Phineas and of Sylvester, must be counted among the sources of Milton's devotional poetic mood at this period. *The Passion*, however, remained unfinished, and Milton appended a note to the effect that he found it "above the years he had when he wrote it." The truth is that the crucifixion was not a congenial theme to him at any time. Even this early he seems to have felt instinctively that man's salvation depends upon himself and that he needs Christ as a guide and model perhaps more than as a redeemer. His lack of inspiration in *The Passion* is evident: both the emotion and the style are forced, and Milton seems unable to pass beyond the process of introduction into the theme itself.

Song: On May Morning

The only evidence for the date of this lyric is its position in the 1645 volume among the University poems. Milton had grouped his more serious religious pieces together at the beginning. The lighter verse follows, arranged apparently in chronological order, with this poem at its head. Had it not been composed before the tribute to Shakespeare and the two pieces on the University carrier, we think he would have placed it after them, with *L'Allegro* and *Il Penseroso*. Its simple and graceful lyricism is a result of Milton's writing for the moment in the classic Jonsonian rather than in the Fletcherian tradition. He was evidently at this time and for several years to come an eclectic follower of many masters. Although the return to lighter themes may be a reaction to his failure to complete *The Passion*, it is not surprising that he could not have maintained consistently that mood of high seriousness which he had proclaimed in Elegy VI and illustrated in his poem, *On the Nativity.*

On Shakespeare

This sixteen-line tribute in heroic couplets, Milton's first English publication, was originally printed anonymously among other commendatory verses prefixed to the second folio of Shakespeare's work in 1632. Though it there bore the title *An Epitaph on the Admirable Dramatick Poet W. Shakespear,* Milton's readers would properly have called the poem either an epigram or an epitaph, the latter being generally recognized as a specific type of the former, more general category. Ben Jonson, for instance, had included several epitaphs among the collection he entitled *Epigrammes.* In the 1645 edition Milton dated the poem 1630, suggesting that he may have written it two years before publication, though it is more likely that later he antedated it, as he may have done *On the Death of a Fair Infant.* The poem was reprinted five times during Milton's lifetime—in 1640, in the edition of 1645, again in 1664, and in 1673.

The idea which Milton elaborates is a traditional one; readers would recognize its classical counterpart in Horace's "*Exegi monumentum aere perennius*" (*Carminae,* II, 20) and its contemporary precedent in Ben Jonson's lines on Shakespeare in the dedicatory material of the first folio: "Thou art a monument without a tomb." The conceit that Shakespeare, by turning his readers to stone, creates for himself a monument was perhaps suggested by the second stanza of the elegy of William Browne on the Countess of Pembroke:

> Marble piles let no man raise
> To her name; for after days
> Some kind woman, born as she,
> Reading this, like Niobe,
> Shall turn marble, and become
> Both her mourner and her tomb.

In addition to the phrase "Star-ypointing *Pyramid,*" there are also echoes from the epitaph on Sir Edward Stanley, a poem then generally attributed to Shakespeare:

Not monumentall stones preserves our Fame;
Nor sky-aspiring Piramides our name;
The memory of him for whom this standes
Shall outlive marble and defacers hands
    When all to time consumption shall be given,
    Standly for whom this stands shall stand in Heaven.

Significant verbal parallels have also been pointed out between Milton's poem and two Elizabethan plays: Massinger's *The Fatal Dowry* and Thomkis' *Albumazar*. These indications reveal Milton's close familiarity with the English literature of his own and the preceding age and also his capacity for assimilating the phrase and thought of others. Milton's admiration for Shakespeare was sincere, in spite of the implied reservations of other passages in his works. Like every critic for more than a century after Shakespeare's death, he praises him as a spontaneous genius rather than as a conscious artist (cf. *L'Allegro*, ll. 133–34).

On the University Carrier

The date of composition of the two poems on this subject is fixed by the death of Thomas Hobson, the carrier, January 1, 1631. They belong with the poem *On Shakespeare* metrically; as examples of seventeenth-century punning and the conceited epigram, they seem to have enjoyed some contemporary popularity in University circles. A version of the second was first printed in the sixth edition of *A Banquet of Jests* (1640), and both were printed, anonymously, in *Wit Restor'd* (1658). Milton's attitude, jocose but not unkindly, is similar to that which he had previously taken in the second Latin elegy on the death of the University beadle. It is characteristic of undergraduate feeling toward those minor academic functionaries who are made butts of ridicule during their careers and offices only to have it faintly remembered at their passing that they were human. This is one of the few places in his work where Milton exhibits humor unmixed with moroseness.[20]

---

[20] See the several examples of other Hobson epitaphs gathered by G. Blakemore Evans, "Milton and the Hobson Poems," *MLQ*, IV (1943), 281–90; IX (1948), 10. Willa McClung Evans has discovered a version in song ("Hobson in Comic Song," *PQ*, XXVI [1947], 321–27). See also William R. Parker, "Milton's Hobson Poems: Some Neglected Early Texts."

An Epitaph on the Marchioness of Winchester

The Lady Jane, wife of John Paulet, fifth Marquis of Winchester, died in childbirth, April 15, 1631. Milton may have been
socially acquainted with her family, but in any case the event was
important enough to elicit several University celebrations, including
poems by Jonson and Davenant. Milton's poem is actually more
restrained and unadorned than the ponderous tribute produced by
the current poet laureate, Ben Jonson himself. The opening lines
of the *Epitaph* echo Browne's famous poem on the Countess of
Pembroke, and in its sweet simplicity of manner the poem contrasts
sharply with Milton's earlier and more Spenserian elegy, *On the
Death of a Fair Infant*. The studies of Ants Oras and E. S. Sprott
have revealed the close relationship of the poem's octosyllabic
couplets to those of *L'Allegro* and *Il Penseroso*.[21]

POEMS OF UNCERTAIN DATE (1629-34)

L'Allegro AND *Il Penseroso*

The date of this pair of lyrics remains uncertain. They do not
appear in the Cambridge Manuscript in which Milton set down
practically everything that he wrote from the Hammersmith period
on. Ascribed by Masson (though without "positive certainty") to
the beginning of the Horton period (i.e., Hammersmith, autumn,
1632), the lyrics have been dated by Fletcher and Bateson as early
as 1629. If on the basis of Bateson's argument over the translation
of the Latin noun *cicutis* from Elegy VI (December, 1629), we
accept 1629 as a probable date, then the octosyllabics of *L'Allegro*
and *Il Penseroso* precede those of *An Epitaph on the Marchioness*

[21] "Metre and Chronology in Milton's 'Epitaph on the Marchioness of
Winchester,' 'L'Allegro,' and 'Il Penseroso,'" *N&Q*, CXCVIII (1953), 332–
33; *Milton's Art of Prosody*, pp. 16–20.

of *Winchester.*[22] Ants Oras, however, has suggested that because *L'Allegro* and *Il Penseroso* are far more sophisticated metrically than the *Epitaph*, they were, consequently, written after it.[23] Tillyard and Parker argue for the summer of 1631, a date accepted by Bush in his edition of the poems and by French in the *Life Records.* Tillyard notices their debt to the first Prolusion and thinks they were intended for a university audience, while Parker writes that

> there is a certain amount of hesitation implied in these twin poems which suggests the problem resolved in the Seventh Prolusion (early in 1632), Sonnet VII, and the letter [Elegy VI]. We know from the Seventh Prolusion that in 1631 Milton had spent a happy summer in the country. . . . The mood of one is the mood of On Hobson and On May Morning. Il Penseroso becomes, then, a lyric harbinger of How soon hath time, On Time, and At a Solemn Music.[24]

Parker's argument is the more convincing, but without further evidence the date will remain uncertain; we can establish only that 1629 is a *terminus ad quem* and 1632 a *terminus a quo.*

Whatever the date of composition, the poems belong to the tradition of the Elizabethan lyric, and several definitive poems may be indicated as having almost certainly furnished Milton with suggestions. Chief among these is the piece prefixed to Burton's *Anatomy of Melancholy* and entitled A *Dialogue between Pleasure and Pain.* Here, to be sure, the contrasted objects are the painful (the galenic) and the pleasurable (the Aristotelian) types of melancholy;[25] but some of the detail is so similar to Milton's that it seems plausible that Burton's poem afforded the initial suggestions. The opening of *Il Penseroso* is plainly reminiscent of a song in Beaumont and Fletcher's *Nice Valour,* in which "vain delights" are banished and "lovely melancholy" welcomed in a formula identical with Milton's. One of Nicholas Breton's lyrics has also been mentioned as resembling *L'Allegro* and *Il Penseroso* and

---

[22] *Seventeenth-Century News Letter* (March, 1949), back page.
[23] "Metre and Chronology," pp. 332–33.
[24] "The Chronology of Milton's Early Poems," *RES,* II (1935), 282.
[25] Lawrence Babb, "The Background of *Il Penseroso.*"

appears to have been in the poet's memory as he wrote.[26] All three of the lyrics mentioned use the octosyllabic measure of Milton's poems. There is no precedent, however, for the precision and comprehensiveness with which Milton marshals his details or for the intricate and artful manner in which each detail in one poem is counterpoised in the other. His delight in the visual picturesqueness of his essentially evocative images fixes his twin lyrics at the opposite extreme from Donne's witty extravaganzas, while the tone and strategy of Marvell's *Upon Appleton House* may be said to represent the mean between Donne and Milton.[27]

Traditionally *L'Allegro* and *Il Penseroso* have been viewed biographically as the finest expressions of Milton's joyous and sensitive poetic nature at a moment in his life when he could still indulge a dilettante enthusiasm for beauty in nature and the manifold delights of music, books, society, and self-pleasing reverie without the intrusion either of his moral idealism or of his intense personal passion. We know that he was much given to weighing and considering the choices which lay before him in reference to the fulfillment of his hopes and expectations for himself. In the Sixth Elegy he considers the claims of poetry born of two different inspirations, a gayer and more trivial, on the one hand; a soberer and more purposeful, on the other. He there declares his allegiance to the latter and proposes for himself a severe life of self-denial in preparation for it. This is essentially an ethical resolution; but it implies also a choice of customary aesthetic occupation, and *L'Allegro* and *Il Penseroso* may represent a somewhat lighter balancing of a similar issue. The solitary reflective life of study was certainly more in accord with Milton's idea of his own future activity than the social ideal, and though the gay man is sometimes alone in his enjoyment, he is not generally so. *Il Penseroso*, therefore, may be said to represent Milton's temperamental preference and the program which he expected to adopt, though without completely suppressing the other. Donald C. Dorian,[28] in pleading for the autobiographical significance of the companion poems, points

---

[26] J. L. Lowes, "*L'Allegro* and *The Passionate Shepherd*," MLR, VI (1911), 206–209.

[27] J. B. Leishman, " '*L'Allegro*' and '*Il Penseroso*' in Their Relation to Seventeenth Century Poetry."

[28] "The Question of Autobiographical Significance in *L'Allegro* and *Il Penseroso*," MP, XXXI (1933), 175–82.

out that they describe not merely ideal days but customary occupations and thus represent a kind of summing up of two possible
attitudes toward life.

On the other hand, it has been argued that an exclusively
biographical discussion too severely limits our approach to the
lyrics. The subject of the poems, Rosemond Tuve cautions, is not
Milton's mirth, but Mirth, not Milton's melancholy, but Melancholy.[29] Studies of the poems' progressive emphasis upon sound,
music, and light have revealed their complementary natures and
indicated the way in which the "pealing organ" and "full voic'd
Choir" of *Il Penseroso* culminate a movement begun in *L'Allegro*.
The sensual music of that "Lydian air" is made explicitly Christian
in the concluding lines of *Il Penseroso* and the speaker's merger of
the two worlds—pagan and Christian—is figured in the images of
sound in the two poems. The ecstasy induced at the end of
Il Penseroso is the ecstasy experienced by man when his "song,"
reflective of his own inner harmony, corresponds to the greater
harmony of nature.[30] Milton had considered the experience of man's
music coming into harmony with that of the cosmos in the earlier
On the Morning of Christ's Nativity. Here, however, the experience
of knowing things by their causes and of seeing into the hidden
things of the universe is one of Platonic ascent, and the significant
images are those clustered around Musaeus, Orpheus, "thrice great
Hermes," and Plato. Cleanth Brooks's[31] study of the imagery of the
poem has been extended by later scholarship; the more recent
emphasis is upon how the greater images of the poems act as
figures for traditional conceptions of the intellect as it strives for
the secret knowledge of the universe. Such, surely, is a significant
addition to the various biographical readings of the twin lyrics.

At a Solemn Music, On Time, AND Upon the Circumcision

With these poems we reach the body of material which
Milton set down in the manuscript volume now preserved at

---

[29] Rosemond Tuve, "The Structural Figures of *L'Allegro* and *Il Penseroso*," pp. 15–36.
[30] Kester Svendsen, "Milton's *L'Allegro* and *Il Penseroso*," *Explicator*,
VIII (1950), no. 49.
[31] "The Light Symbolism in 'L'Allegro' and 'Il Penseroso.' "

Trinity College, Cambridge. The order in which the various compositions stand in that document is some indication of their relative dates, though by no means a complete or certain one. We have also the fact that Milton arranged the poems in the 1645 edition with some thought of their chronological order; but here again the situation is not wholly clear, since he occasionally adopted another principle of arrangement. The earlier items in the manuscript are as follows: *Arcades, At a Solemn Music* in three drafts, a prose letter to a friend, *On Time, Upon the Circumcision,* three sonnets of later date (copied on a page which had been left blank), *Comus,* and *Lycidas. Comus* is dated 1634. The prose letter contains the sonnet, *How soon hath Time,* which is described as "my nightward thoughts some time since." The letter itself is apparently a first draft, like *At a Solemn Music. On Time* and *Upon the Circumcision* are clean copies. They stand after *The Passion* and before *At a Solemn Music* in the 1645 edition. *Arcades,* which though much corrected in the autograph, hardly looks like a first attempt; it is grouped in the edition with *Lycidas* and *Comus,* presumably because of its pastoral character. It is safe to say that no one will succeed in dating precisely the pieces which precede *Comus* in the manuscript, but we are on sure enough ground in ascribing them all to the close of Milton's University career or the beginning of his sojourn at Hammersmith.

With regard to the literary quality of the three lyrics little need be said. They are in the form of odes or canzoni with irregular rhyme and line length, a unique experiment for Milton, except the approach toward it in *Lycidas.* In his mind they evidently constituted one group with the poems on Christ's birth and death, a body of sacred or at least solemn verse by which he wished his early earnestness to be judged. Though less successful intrinsically than *On the Morning of Christ's Nativity* they are works of a sincere inspiration, in the best vein of seventeenth-century meditative poetry. *On Time* has the character of an inscription, as its cancelled manuscript title, "Set on a Clock Case," suggests.[32] *At a Solemn Music* bears witness to Milton's enthusiasm for the "Sphere-born harmonious Sisters, Voice and Verse," and its mystical and Christian

---

[32] Cf. O. B. Hardison, Jr., "Milton's 'On Time' and Its Scholastic Background."

interpretation of the Platonic idea of the music of the spheres is characteristic of Milton's thought.[33] Both pieces conclude with the contemplation of heaven and immortality, a theme much in Milton's thoughts throughout his early life. *Upon the Circumcision* is relatively unattractive; Milton seems to be forcing himself to meditate on the significance of an event which has for him little more than a conventional appeal. Here, as in *The Passion*, he shows unconsciously his remoteness from the emotion of religious sorrow.

Arcades

This short masque, consisting of three songs and a recitation in pentameter couplets, follows the ten sonnets in the 1645 edition and is the first item in the Cambridge Manuscript. These facts and the evident connection of the piece with *Comus* are the sole basis for the date of composition, which is given by Masson as 1633 or possibly 1634, but by Grierson as 1630 or 1632. According to Milton's own note in the 1645 edition it was "part of an entertainment presented to the Countess Dowager of Derby at Harefield by some noble persons of her family." These noble persons presumably included the family of Sir John Egerton, Earl of Bridgewater, her stepson, for whom Milton wrote *Comus* in 1634. It is probable that Henry Lawes, then musical tutor in the Egerton family, who later supervised the production of *Comus*, was also the deviser of this masque. Lawes's friendship with Milton is established by the sonnet addressed to him in 1646. No great degree of intimacy between Milton and the distinguished circle of the Countess of Derby is necessarily implied by his having been engaged to furnish the words for these masques; yet Harefield is not a dozen miles from Horton, and some acquaintance may have existed. The Countess of Derby, a daughter of Sir John Spencer of Althorpe, had married Ferdinando Stanley, Lord Strange. To her Edmund Spenser, who counted himself of the same family, had dedicated the *Tears of the Muses* in 1591. By a second marriage in 1600 she had become the wife of Sir Thomas Egerton, Lord-Keeper of the Seal. The Countess was

---

[33] See John Hollander, *The Untuning of the Sky* (Princeton, 1961), pp. 315–31.

already in her seventies when Milton wrote *Arcades,* and her birthday, which possibly occurred on May 4, would have been an appropriate occasion for the masque.

Because Milton's verses present a situation rather than a plot, the masque may be read symbolically "in terms of a pilgrimage from the profane to the religious," in which the Countess is the central symbol of "Heavenly Wisdom."[34] A group of shepherds have been searching for their Arcadian queen; finding her in the person of the great lady in whose honor the entertainment is given, they sing her a song of compliment. The Genius of the Wood, a part probably taken by Lawes, enters and addresses her. The conception of such a figure is a familiar one in the masque and is repeated in the Attendant Spirit in *Comus.* In the beautiful song, "O'er the smooth enamelled green," he brings the Arcadians to the lady. A dance and a concluding lyric follow. One notable passage describes the music of the spheres, an idea which appealed powerfully to Milton's imagination and is employed also in the *Nativity* and in the poem *At a Solemn Music.* The whole is done in the purest and most delicate Elizabethan vein. The tone is that of the Jonsonian masque, but no specific influences are traceable in Milton's work. On the basis of Milton's statement, *Arcades* is usually described as a fragment, but there is nothing in the piece itself to indicate incompleteness. Of the character of the rest of the entertainment we know nothing.

ENGLISH POEMS WRITTEN AT HAMMERSMITH AND HORTON (1632–38)

Comus

The entertainment we know as *Comus* was entitled by Milton simply *A Maske . . . Presented at Ludlow Castle . . . ;* its un-Miltonic title was earlier used by Toland (1698) and Fenton (1725)

---

[34] John M. Wallace, "Milton's *Arcades.*"

and generally popularized by the eighteenth-century poet and divine, John Dalton, whose adaptation, entitled *Comus*, was produced for the stage in 1738.[35] *Comus* is dated 1634 in both the Cambridge Manuscript and in the editions. In 1637 Henry Lawes had the work printed (without Milton's name), claiming it "so lovely, and so much desired, that the often copying of it hath tir'd my Pen to give my several friends satisfaction, and brought me to a necessity of producing it to the publicke view."[36] Except for the poem *On Shakespeare*, which was printed, also anonymously, in 1632, this was Milton's first published work. It reappeared without important change in the 1645 and 1673 editions of the poems, but the presumed stage copy, the Egerton or Bridgewater Manuscript,[37] and the Cambridge Manuscript are significantly shorter than the version Lawes published in 1637. What presently constitutes lines 779–805 does not appear in the printed version of 1637; the other major change is a transferral of several passages from the opening lines of the Attendant Spirit to his concluding speech, with the addition of some fifteen lines.[38] These changes figure as the crux of E. M. W. Tillyard's interpretation; he concludes that the words of the Attendant Spirit provide the Lady a resolution—marriage—between the doctrines of Comus (Acrasia) and Continence (Belphoebe): "The Lady, though but young, will one day be a great Lady. She must take her place in society and do what is expected of her. And by having triumphed as Belphoebe, she is free to proceed to her true part of Amoret."[39]

Of the occasion for which *Comus* was written we have only such information as is given in the 1637 and 1645 editions, viz., that it was performed at Ludlow Castle on Michaelmas night, September 29, 1634. The parts of the Lady and her two brothers were taken by the Earl's three children (who were fifteen, eleven, and nine respectively): the Lady Alice Egerton, Lord Brackley, and Thomas Egerton. The producer was Lawes, who, as we have seen, had been

---

[35] Dalton's version was in its sixth edition by 1741 and saw three editions its first year of publication.

[36] Patterson, *Works*, I, ii, 475. This edition will hereafter be cited *CM*.

[37] Published for the family by Lady Alix Egerton.

[38] See John S. Diekhoff, "The Text of *Comus*"; and C. S. Lewis, "A Note on *Comus*."

[39] "The Action of Comus," *Studies in Milton*, p. 95.

music tutor in the Egerton family and had had experience in masques.[40] He himself took the part of Thyrsis, and he refers to himself as "your Attendant Thyrsis" in the dedication of the 1637 edition to Lord Brackley. In lines 494–496 Milton puts into the mouth of the Elder Brother a graceful compliment to Lawes as the musician

> Whose artful strains have oft delay'd
> The huddling brook to hear his madrigal,
> And sweeten'd every musk rose of the dale.

We know from Sonnet XIII how much Milton admired his compositions, and Lawes's musical settings of several of the *Comus* lyrics have been preserved.[41]

Comus is, in point of time, one of the last representatives of the English masque, a type of courtly entertainment introduced from Italy in simple form as early as the time of Henry VIII and developed to its highest point of elaboration by Ben Jonson and others in the reign of James. The masque is essentially a private entertainment, performed usually by amateurs and depending for its effects on music, pageantry, and dance. The courtly dance is, indeed, the essential and original feature. It had become the custom also to introduce a set of comic or grotesque characters, the parts being more often taken by professionals, and to assign them one or more dances of a burlesque character. This humorous element was known as the antimasque. It is represented in *Comus* by the rout of monsters, men and women who have been transformed by the enchanter; perhaps these same actors assumed the roles of the countrymen who do a rural turn at the close. The subject matter of the masque is almost always a combination of mythology and allegory adapted in the Elizabethan manner to the social occasion for which the masque is written. Although *Comus* illustrates every one of the points made in the above description, there are differences between it and the traditional masque of the period, though some of the variant characteristics are to be found in the masque-

---

[40] He had written the music for Shirley's *The Triumph of Peace* and for Carew's *Coelum Britanicum* in 1633. See Willa McClung Evans, *Henry Lawes: Musician and Friend of Poets* (New York, 1941).

[41] B. M. Add. MS. 11518. See the edition by E. H. Visiak, *The Mask of Comus*.

like plays or "morals" of James Shirley. Enid Welsford's standard work on the masque summarizes what appear to her and others as the difficulties with the genre of *Comus*: Milton's minimizing the element of pageantry and dance, the fact that his outdoor scenes seldom indicate anything of the ordinary setting of the banquet hall (with the exception of Scene II), his expansion of the dialogue far beyond its usual limits, and his injection into it of an earnestness of meaning quite foreign to the tradition. She concludes that Milton's *Comus* is certainly not a masque, at least not in the traditional sense.[42] Confronted with the question of the equivocal genre of *Comus*, Gretchen Finney[43] and Eugene Haun[44] have attempted to clarify the question by discussing *Comus* in relation to the general Italian and English musical drama. A more extreme position than Welsford's is represented by Don Cameron Allen's attitude; he considers *Comus* an artistic failure, a "patchwork of styles." For him, "The poem is not a masque at all." Whereas Welsford complains that "*Comus* is dramatized debate,"[45] Allen has contended that the poem's failure is "further complicated by Milton's unsuccessful attempt to establish a true intellectual conflict in the debate between Comus and the Lady."[46] Rosemond Tuve and John Arthos see no reason to question the genre of the poem that Masson considered Milton's most perfect. To what genre shall we assign *Comus*? Precisely, we think, to the one in which Milton placed it when he gave it its title: *A Maske*. C. L. Barber's recent essay ought to provide us with a welcome beginning:

> The work of criticism, as against the pleasure, is in good part the altering of expectations to suit the thing at hand. My experience with A Mask Presented at Ludlow Castle has been a case in point; it has involved giving up expectations of drama for expectations appropriate to the masque. Invited to consider Milton's masque as comedy, I report back after six months that Milton's masque is a masque![47]

---

[42] *The Court Masque*, pp. 316–23.
[43] "*Comus, Dramma per Musica.*"
[44] "An Inquiry into the Genre of *Comus.*"
[45] *The Court Masque*, p. 318.
[46] "The Higher Compromise," p. 36.
[47] "*A Mask Presented at Ludlow Castle:* The Masque as a Masque," p. 36.

Obviously Milton adapted the genre not only to his own sensibilities, just as he was later to do with the pastoral elegy, but also to the practical necessities of the situation. Our anticipations of dramatic conflict are, as Allen notes, really not fulfilled, but that is because the genre, as Milton conceived of it, is concerned with a presentation and an uncovering of the two great images—the Lady and Comus. We are meant to be variously entertained as we witness something of what the struggle between the Lady— reasonableness, order, and virtue—and Comus—disorder, libertinism, and voluptuousness—is *like*. This is not to say that we observe such a struggle directly but that we are constantly aware of what is suggested within the figures and images before us. "We see," writes Rosemond Tuve, "what things look like; and we see the real not behind the apparent but in the apparent."[48] The poem reveals its meaning quite gradually, and as the image patterns of light and dark slowly complete the greater metaphor, we become more and more aware that, among other things, *Comus* is concerned with the relationship between fiction and reality, between metaphor and "truth." Of course, the way in which the masque moves alternately between the reality of the Ludlow surroundings and the fiction of the pastoral, between the Lady as masquer and her life-role as young Lady Alice Egerton, suggests something of Milton's version of the traditional interrelationship of masquers and audience. Slowly we become aware that the masque speaks to the greater audience of the poem, to readers of *Comus*, of Everyman's confrontation with the subtlety of intemperance masking as the spirit of natural order.

We have, we think, come to recognize the essentially Christian theme of the masque. Regardless of how we interpret the Circe myth (which is the hinge of the entertainment), it had, by Milton's time, been consistently read as Christian allegory.[49] Thus Denis Saurat's comment that "there is nothing Christian about *Comus*"[50] represents an extreme view of a work in which we witness something of the way in which chastity is assisted by the supernatural powers

[48] "Image, Form, and Theme in *A Mask*," p. 143.

[49] Cf. John Arthos who thinks *Comus* is not allegorical (*On "A Mask Presented at Ludlow-Castle"*).

[50] *Man and Thinker*, p. 16. For a reply, see Tuve in "Image, Form, and Theme in *A Mask*," p. 136.

(Haemony) and supernatural figures (Sabrina and Thyrsis) which hasten to defend the chaste soul.[51] Surely A. S. P. Woodhouse is closer to the heart of *Comus* when he argues that the poem's primary concern is with the "translation" of the virtue of chastity into the Christian doctrine of virginity.[52] Postulating two orders in the life of man, those of nature and of grace, he reminds us that the one is apprehended in experience and interpreted by reason, while "to the order of Grace belongs man in his character of supernatural being, with all that concerns his salvation." In the order of nature, the virtues are temperance and continence; on the level of grace is the exclusive doctrine of virginity. Common to both orders is chastity, the central virtue of the poem. *Comus* becomes, then, a masque in which the Lady quests for fulfillment on a divine level; that her arduous and hazardous pilgrimage is successful is signalled by the images of Joy and Youth in the Epilogue. Voluntary obedience to God results in freedom imaged in the enjoyment of those very qualities adversaries say will be denied the virtuous.

In this symbolically Christian masque, Milton has a special role for music and dancing. It is difficult now to accept Welsford's statement that "it is possible to read *Comus* and hardly realise that there are dances; it is possible to act *Comus* without introducing any dances at all."[53] On the contrary, dancing in the masque is indispensable (there are several explicit instructions for it), and it functions significantly in the spectacle. Before Comus reveals himself in speech, we see the nature of him and his crew imaged before us in the dithyrambic Morris dance of the antimasque. Their dance, echoed near the conclusion by the peasant round, is a visual manifestation of the disorder of their souls. In contrast, the Lady's courtly and aristocratic, elegant and sophisticated dance is a perfect reflection of the beauty and proportion of her soul. It is also a way for us to see, rather than to be told, something of the beauty of the Lady's condition. Comus is not confronted with a cold renunciation, but with the positive charms of Order and Temperance imaged in the courtly dance rhythms. One of the favorite Renaissance images

[51] See John Steadman's cogent argument for the allegorical interpretation of Haemony ("Milton's *Haemony:* Etymology and Allegory").
[52] "The Argument of Milton's *Comus*"; see also his "*Comus* Once More."
[53] *The Court Masque,* p. 317.

of order, the dance unites ecstasy with control and its presence suggests the way in which the Lady is in tune with the cosmos. The dance is one of Milton's ways of visualizing for us the Platonic doctrine that the condition of the soul reflects itself in the outward form—creates, indeed, the body which is its temple.[54]

The question of Milton's literary sources in *Comus* is a rewarding one.[55] It so happens that we can trace with more certainty than in the case of *Paradise Lost* the varied elements, ancient and modern, which his extraordinarily assimilative mind converted to its uses. Such a study serves to illustrate Milton's culture and also to throw into relief the highly individual quality which his imagination imparts to his materials. For Milton's borrowings, here and elsewhere, are rarely literal. Even when we are reasonably sure of his indebtedness, the relation is apt to be so distant and intangible that one feels that his recollection must have been unconscious.

The mythological groundwork of Milton's story is, of course, the Circe episode in the *Odyssey* (Book X). Milton had precedent for giving an allegorical interpretation to the myth in the Platonizing mythographer, Heraclides Ponticus, and he is known to have owned a copy of his *Allegoriae in Homeri Fabulas*.[56] A more immediate suggestion came to him, however, from Spenser, whose Bower of Bliss (*FQ*, II, xii, 42 ff.) is presided over by the enchantress Acrasia, a Circe-like figure symbolic of intemperance and surrounded by creatures who have been transformed to beasts.[57] That Milton had paid special attention to the ethical meaning of this passage we know from *Areopagitica*, where he wrote of "our sage and serious poet Spenser . . . a better teacher than Scotus or Aquinas, [who in] describing true temperance under the person of Guyon, brings him in with his palmer through the cave of Mammon and the bower of earthly bliss, that he might see and know, and yet abstain." In addition to these sources, Milton may have known of William

---

[54] See especially 11. 453 ff. See also the recent neo-Platonic reading of *Comus* by Sears Jayne, "The Subject of Milton's Ludlow *Mask*."

[55] See Arthos, *On "A Mask Presented at Ludlow-Castle*," pp. 1–15.

[56] *CM*, XVII, 577. For a discussion of Milton's use of classical myth see Douglas Bush, *Mythology and the Renaissance Tradition*, pp. 277–81, and Tuve, "Image, Form, and Theme in *A Mask*," pp. 130 ff.

[57] See Merritt Y. Hughes, "Spenser's Acrasia and the Circe of the Renaissance," *JHI*, IV (1943), 394–96.

Browne's *Inner Temple Masque*, which had been acted about 1620 and also dealt with Circe and Ulysses; like *Comus* it employs an antimasque using monsters.

Comus himself originates from a personification of the Greek compound noun κῶμος (revelry), which had already taken place in antiquity.[58] But Milton must have been familiar with the conception from more modern sources. In Ben Jonson's masque, *Pleasure Reconciled to Virtue* (1619), Comus appears as a glutton. In a neo-Latin play, the *Comus* (Oxford, 1634) of Erycius Puteanus (Hendrick van der Putten), he is an embodiment of a more refined sensuality and, as with Milton, a magician. The resemblances between Milton's *Comus* and this play are too striking to be the result of an accident.[59] The author sees in vision a riotous banquet in which Comus, an embodiment of intemperate pleasure, has as his guests various personified pleasures and passions. An old man declaims against the various vices and attacks the ideals held by the revelers. Some specific parallels in the speeches of Comus are pointed out by Todd. But whatever precedents Milton may have had for his chief character, he is apparently original in making Comus a son of Circe and Bacchus.

The central fiction of the masque, the abduction and rescue of the Lady, has many analogues. The closest is George Peele's *Old Wives Tale*,[60] where two brothers go in search of their sister, Delia, who has been imprisoned by an "inchanter vile." He gives her a magic potion causing her to forget her brothers and rather feebly endeavors to win her to his lust. The brothers meet an old man who knows the arts of magic and enlist his aid, but they are themselves enthralled and goaded to labor by their enchanted sister. The release of all three comes when the magician's glass is broken by the wife of the old man and his wreath and sword possessed by a dead man, Jack. A dance of harvestmen and an echo dialogue offer slight parallel incidents to events in *Comus*. While the main action of the play is much obscured by the introduction

---

[58] In the Trinity Manuscript Milton wrote at the point of entrance (1. 92) of Comus: *intrant κωμάζοντες.*

[59] See Ralph H. Singleton, "Milton's *Comus* and the *Comus* of Erycius Puteanus," *PMLA*, LXVIII (1943), 948–55.

[60] See E. A. Hall, "*Comus, Old Wives Tale,* and Drury's *Alvredus,*" *Manly Anniversary Studies* (Chicago, 1923), 104–44.

of various unrelated episodes, Milton very probably took the suggestion for his plot from Peele. Here again, however, his elaboration of the plot material was partly determined by his beloved author Spenser. In *The Faerie Queene* (III, xii, 27 ff.) the chaste Amoret is imprisoned by a magician in a castle symbolizing lust. She stands chained before Busyrane, her captor, who endeavors to force her to do his will. Her rescuer, breaking in, compels the enchanter to release her by saying his charms backward. The formula parallels Milton's lines 816–18:

> Without his rod revers't
> And backward mutters of dissevering power,
> We cannot free the Lady that sits here.

Another quite probable influence is Fletcher's *The Faithful Shepherdess*,[61] a pastoral drama with a decidedly masque-like tone. If, however, in molding his drama, Milton is mainly under the sway of the Elizabethans, his classical predilections lead him to make it conform, wherever possible, to ancient precedent. Clear traces are to be found in the Euripidean prologue and in the somewhat riddling dialogue (lines 277–91) in which each speech is exactly a line's length (stichomythia).

When all these elements (and others less tangible might be mentioned) are taken into account, the paramount influence remains that of Spenser. The masque is, as A. S. P. Woodhouse has commented, "in the fullest sense Spenserian allegory, with different levels of meaning."[62] Besides the points already mentioned, there is a clear relation between Spenser's Garden of Adonis (*FQ*, III, vi, 29 ff.) and the description of the paradise of heavenly love at the close of *Comus*. For one episode, that of Sabrina, Milton directly refers to Spenser as his source (*FQ*, II, x, 18–19). His use of the pastoral name Meliboeus is also analogous to Spenser's own praise of Chaucer as Tityrus and suggests that Milton recognized a kindred discipleship. "Milton has acknowledg'd to me," Dryden wrote in 1700, "that *Spencer* was his original." We know from other evidence that his devotion to Spenser was in 1634 a rather recent thing,

---

[61] See W. E. A. Axon, "*Comus* and Fletcher's *Faithful Shepherdess*," *Manchester Quarterly*, VIII (1882), 285–95.
[62] "*Comus* Once More," pp. 222–23.

partly superseding Milton's earlier literary allegiance to the Fletchers and Jonson. It seems quite clear that Spenser was of great value to Milton at this time, as Joan Larsen Klein has demonstrated,[63] in helping him interpret his genius to himself, in fostering his political idealism and his enthusiasm for purity, in teaching him how to give concrete literary embodiment to Platonism, and, specifically, in furnishing him with no small part of the substance of *Comus*.

In the account of his developing personal ideals in the *Apology* (1642), Milton says that the solemn cantos of the fables and romances of knighthood (by which he evidently means chiefly *The Faerie Queene*) taught him the beauty of the virtue of chastity:

> Next (for heare me out now Readers) that I may tell ye whether my younger feet wander'd; I betook me among those lofty Fables and Romances, which recount in solemne canto's the deeds of Knighthood founded by our victorious Kings; & from hence had in renowne over all Christendome. There I read it in the oath of every Knight, that he should defend to the expence of his best blood, or of his life, if it so befell him, the honour and chastity of Virgin or Matron. From whence even then I learnt what a noble virtue chastity sure must be, to the defence of which so many worthies by such a deare adventure of themselves had sworne.[64]

This instructs us to look to Spenser as one of the molding influences upon Milton's experience and a chief inspirer of his poetry in the Hammersmith period and thereafter—and this in spite of the fact that Milton's taste was leading him more and more away from the somewhat exuberant manner of expression which Spenser employed and passed on to his successors. The style of *Comus*, like that of *L'Allegro* and *Il Penseroso*, has affinities with the Elizabethan and Jonsonian lyric and masque; it is not, save in a passage or two, Miltonic in the later sense. Yet, with all its grace and delicacy, it

---

[63] See her fully annotated article, "Some Spenserian Influences on Milton's *Comus.*"

[64] Ed. with preface and notes by Frederick Lovett Taft, Yale, *Milton*, I, 890–91. See Ernest Sirluck's article on Milton's conception of the poet and his attitude toward chastity, "Milton's Idle Right Hand."

has a quality of logical exactness and a condensation which are a fruit of Milton's classical self-discipline. Tillyard has analyzed the mixture of manners in *Comus*, pointing out that the masque begins with a Euripidean prologue, passes into vigorous dramatic dialogue, changes to pure poetry in the Lady's soliloquy, returns to the formulae of Euripidean dialogue in the stichomythy between Comus and the Lady, and changes to the vein of A *Midsummer Night's Dream* in Comus' speech beginning, "I know each lane and every alley green." It is quite possible that Milton practiced different styles throughout the masque, and the success of his verse is unquestionable. Although the motto which appears on the title page of Lawes's edition, and which must have been selected by Milton,

> *Eheu quid misero mihi! floribus austrum Perditus*

> ("Alas, did I propose to my own destruction,
> wretched man that I am, when I let the south
> wind blow upon my flowers")

"has been taken to mean that Milton deprecated any criticism of his masque—that he was reluctant to come out of privacy and run the risks of publication—the quotation, in context, means that the shepherd accuses himself of *neglecting his proper business*. Still," continues William R. Parker, "an ambiguity remains: the pastoral poet who penned the words quoted [i.e., Virgil] was eventually to write an epic."[65]

Lycidas

Following the death of his mother on April 3, 1637, Milton spent much of the latter part of that plague year in London where he must have been angered at the prosecution that summer of Bastwick, Burton, and Prynne, the Puritan pamphleteers. The experience of grief he had at his mother's death was soon to become intensified by the loss of the Cambridge resident who became the subject of *Lycidas*. The date of the composition of *Lycidas* may be inferred from the cancellation in the Cambridge Manuscript,

---

[65] *Milton*, I, 143.

"Novem: 1637." Edward King, the graduate of Christ's College in whose memory the poem was written, was the son of Sir John King of Yorkshire and had been admitted to Cambridge (along with his elder brother) on June 9, 1626, when he was fourteen. Almost four years younger than Milton—and already published— he had taken the B.A. in 1630 and the M.A. in 1633. There is no evidence that he and Milton were intimate friends,[66] though Phillips assumes it, but there is a tradition (though late) that they were rivals for a fellowship. In the summer of 1637 King sailed for Ireland, and when his ship struck a rock, he was drowned in the Irish Sea on August 10 of the same year. *Lycidas* was first printed, with the initials "J. M.," as the last poem in a collection of memorial verses, Latin, Greek, and English, the English section of which is entitled *Obsequies to the Memory of Mr. Edward King, Anno. Dom. 1638*.[67] Milton republished it with minor alterations in his editions of 1645 and 1673. Although variations in these printed versions are chiefly those of spelling and punctuation, the Cambridge Manuscript contains many revisions made during the process of composition, material of the keenest interest to the student of the poetic process. We learn, for example, that the flower passage was an afterthought, and we can trace the phrasing of many another passage through various stages on the way to its final form.[68] Each of four extant copies of the 1638 edition bears corrections made by either Milton himself or his printer. One of these, inserted in Milton's hand, "he well knew" for "he knew" in line 10, provides the specific question for the modern editor of whether to print "he knew himself to sing" or "he well knew himself to sing." Milton had written "he well knew" twice in the manuscript and let it stand; a copy of 1638 with Miltonic corrections inserts a "well" marginally; the 1645 and 1673 editions, which presumably repre-

---

[66] See James G. Taaffe, "Mrs. John Drury: A Sister of Lycidas," *N&Q*, CCVII (1962), 60–61.

[67] The little book has been edited in a facsimile reproduction by Ernest C. Mossner.

[68] Collations from the Cambridge Manuscript with the versions of 1638 and 1645 may be seen in *CM*, I, ii, 459–74; C. A. Patrides reprints the "most significant corrections" in his *Milton's "Lycidas,"* pp. 10–11. See also Henry Hitch Adams, "The Development of the Flower Passage in 'Lycidas,' " *MLN*, LXV (1950), 468–72.

sent Milton's carefully made official version of his work (but contain other errors), reprint "he knew." Plenty of opportunity here for theory! John Diekhoff's is a convincing argument, however, for the authority of the edition over the manuscript,[69] and the consensus of current editors supports that conclusion;[70] but the present editors decide for "he well knew," assuming that Milton overlooked the omission in proofreading the 1645 edition, which was set from the 1638, but not, perhaps, from one of the extant corrected copies. The line, then, stands as a significant metrical variation, indicative of another of Milton's numerous audacities and deliberate refusals to satisfy our expectations in *Lycidas*.[71]

In genre and form, *Lycidas* is a pastoral elegy, embodying a set of conventions[72] which had gradually become fixed in poetic usage from antiquity. Chief among these are the fiction that all nature mourns the dead shepherd's loss; the question "where were ye, Nymphs"; the procession of appropriate mourners, each uttering his grief; the pastoral consolation, or change of tone from sadness to joy in the thought of the dead shepherd's immortality. Most of these features are embodied also in the parallel elegy, *Epitaphium Damonis*. Their ultimate classical origins may be sought in the First and Second Idylls of Theocritus, Moschus' *Lament for Bion*, Bion's own *Lament for Adonis*, and the Fifth and Tenth Eclogues in Virgil's *Bucolics*.[73] To these conventions the Renaissance added the fiction of the poet and his friend as companion shepherds feeding their flocks and the tendency to introduce allegorically (since Christianity also uses pastoral imagery) an attack on the corruption of the church. Milton probably knew, among others, the pastorals of Petrarch, in which this material is prominent.[74] He certainly knew

[69] "*Lycidas*, Line 10," *PQ*, XVI (1937), 408–10.

[70] A random survey indicates that only the edition of Milton's poems by John T. Shawcross follows the manuscript as authority.

[71] A fascinating reading of *Lycidas* by Roy Daniells considers the distortions and corruscating variations in the poem as significant aspects of its total meaning (*Milton, Mannerism and Baroque*).

[72] The standard essay is James Holly Hanford's "The Pastoral Elegy and Milton's 'Lycidas.'"

[73] These (except Theocritus' Second Idyll) appear conveniently in Scott Elledge, *Milton's "Lycidas."*

[74] See Edward S. Le Comte, "'Lycidas,' Petrarch, and the Plague," *MLN*, LXIX (1954), 402–404, for a passage from Petrarch's Eclogue IX as a parallel to l. 217 of *Lycidas*.

The Shepherd's Calendar of Spenser, where, besides much ecclesiastical allegory, there is a meditation on fame which parallels that in *Lycidas*. The November eclogue in *The Shepherd's Calendar* is an elegy, and from it Milton borrowed a turn or two of phrase. He appears also to have been indebted to Castiglione's Latin elegy, *Alcon*.[75] Milton makes no effort to avoid these precedents; indeed, he evidently rejoices in reworking the traditions anew.

But in Milton's hands the elegy becomes an intensely personal utterance. The theme is concerned more with the poet's own ambitions and anxieties than with the accomplishments of his dead friend. Indeed, David Daiches has suggested that the subject of the poem is actually "man in his creative capacity . . . man is always liable to be cut off before making his contribution. . . . In *Lycidas* Milton circles (he is spiralling rather than circling), and he reaches the centre only when he has found a solution. . . ."[76] Thus Milton, in speaking through the bereaved shepherd of *Lycidas*, is, like Shelley in *Adonais*, primarily taking account of the meaning of the experience to himself. King is the prospective poet and priest who has been cut off in the midst of his early promise by the hand of fate. Of what use is high endeavor when life is subject to such accidents? And what can a young man think when he sees those younger than he taken early while the evil remain to prosper? While seeking answers to these questions, the "uncouth swain" reverts again and again to the pastoral artifices which collectively reassure him that order and justice will ultimately prevail. For whether love, benevolence, and harmony are natural principles is precisely the question facing Milton's speaker. While the pastoral mode with all its elaborate fictions may also function as a way of depersonalizing the event, Milton employs these devices metaphorically to create the image of an Eden-like world. Until we come to know "other fields" and "other groves" in paradise, we are to be consoled by the images of a place symbolic of our innocence and youth. At the close of this confession of faith, Milton turns toward the future with a resolution chastened by the truth of Christ's saying, "Blessed are they that mourn, for they shall be comforted." Rosemond Tuve

[75] See Thomas Perrin Harrison, Jr., "The Latin Pastorals of Milton and Castiglione," *PMLA*, L (1935), 480–93.
[76] *Milton*, p. 75.

has written that *"Lycidas* is the most poignant and controlled statement in English poetry of the acceptance of that [mortality] in the human condition which seems to man unacceptable."[77] The poem, writes Don Cameron Allen, "is . . . from the deep heart's core."[78]

Metrically *Lycidas* is a combination of regularity and freedom. The verse is prevailingly iambic pentameter varied occasionally by the introduction of three-foot lines. The rhyme varies from the couplet form to intricate stanzaic arrangements,[79] and there are, daringly enough, ten unrhymed lines.[80] The elegy opens with a fourteen-line stanza which appears to be a variation of the sonnet form,[81] while it concludes with a stanza of *ottava rima.* F. T. Prince has argued that what Masson called Milton's "free rhythmic paragraphs" may be variations upon a traditional Continental form. The Italian *canzone* is composed of several verse paragraphs which follow an intricate and identical rhyme scheme, while the song itself concludes with a shorter unit called the *commiato.* Both Milton's handling of the metrical pauses and his tendency to prolong his cadence through a succession of lines seem to have precedent in the structure of the *canzone* as it was defined by Dante in the *De Vulgari Eloquentia.* It was here in particular that Dante explained the harmony between hendecasyllables and heptasyllables, something of which is apparent in the variations of pentameter and trimeter in *Lycidas.*[82] Spenser's November eclogue, which Milton knew, also variously reflects the *canzone* pattern in its verse form.

As a work of art, *Lycidas,* in spite of the disparagement of Johnson, who was offended by the artificiality of its pastoralism, has received almost universal praise. Isabel G. MacCaffrey echoes modern opinion when she writes that Milton "never exercised his power

[77] "Theme, Pattern, and Imagery in *Lycidas,*" p. 73.

[78] "The Translation of the Myth: The Epicedia and *Lycidas,*" p. 53. The essays by Tuve and Allen, joined by Ruth Wallerstein's "Iusta Edouardo King," are the significant critical statements on the elegy.

[79] See Ants Oras, "Milton's Early Rhyme Schemes and the Structure of *Lycidas.*"

[80] See John Crowe Ransom's contentions in his provocative essay, "A Poem Nearly Anonymous." The essay is reprinted in various places (e.g., the Patrides collection). See also Martin Battestin's rebuttal, "John Crowe Ransom and *Lycidas:* A Reappraisal."

[81] See Keith Rinehart, "A Note on the First Fourteen Lines of Milton's *Lycidas.*"

[82] "Lycidas."

to better effect,"[83] while F. T. Prince regards *Lycidas* as "one of the chief glories of English lyrical verse."[84] Writing during the nineteenth century, William Hazlitt found the poem "perfect art." The style, though ornamental and allusive, varies with the mood; it rises or falls as Milton "somewhat loudly sweeps the string" in moments of exaltation and denunciation or bids his Muse return again to the pastoral strain with its subdued note of tender melancholy. The analogy of music comes again as one considers the masterly way in which Milton has managed these fluctuations. No symphony was ever composed of more varied emotional elements or blended them more skillfully into artistic unity. That unity is formed of three major sections, and Arthur Barker's comments on the three-part structure have come to be regarded as standard:

> The first movement laments Lycidas the poet-shepherd; its problem, the possible frustration of disciplined poetic ambition by early death, is resolved by the assurance, "Of so much fame in heaven expect thy meed." The second laments Lycidas as priest-shepherd; its problem, the frustration of a sincere shepherd in a corrupt church, is resolved by St. Peter's reference to the "two-handed engine" of divine retribution.[85] The third concludes with the apotheosis, a convention introduced by Virgil in Eclogue V but significantly handled by Milton. He sees the poet-priest-shepherd worshipping the Lamb with those saints "in solemn troops" who sing the "unexpressive nuptial song" of the fourteenth chapter of Revelation. The apotheosis thus not only provides the final reassurance but unites the themes of the preceding movements in the ultimate reward of the true poet-priest.[86]

Much modern criticism has centered upon the logical and emotional structure of the elegy, each critic pointing afresh to the

[83] "*Lycidas:* The Poet in a Landscape," p. 65.

[84] "Lycidas," p. 71.

[85] Because the much-discussed "two-handed engine" continues to evoke speculation as to its meaning, W. A. Turner's summary of the prevailing guesses ("Milton's Two-Handed Engine," *JEGP*, XLIX [1950], 562–65) should probably be updated to include the additional commentary since 1950. Probably the "engine" is, as Maurice Kelley has suggested, the great two-handed sword wielded by Michael against God's enemies.

[86] Barker's comment was made in the course of his article, "The Pattern of Milton's *Nativity Ode*," pp. 171–72.

way every detail functions as part of a perfectly conceived whole
and to the manner in which the speaker finds his consolation.
Every account[87] proves again the truth of Edward Phillips' tribute:
"Never was the loss of friend so elegantly lamented."

THE SONNETS

Milton's twenty-three sonnets fall into several chronological groups.
The first of the ten contained in the 1645 edition, *O Nightingale,
that on yon bloomy Spray*, was thought by Smart to be "one of
Milton's earliest works" and has been dated 1629 or 1630. Critics
have pointed out that its tone resembles that of Elegies V and VI.
Since it does not appear in the Cambridge Manuscript, it must
have preceded Milton's earliest entries (1632) there. There is even
less certainty about the date of composition of the five Italian
sonnets with the *canzone*. Either they belong to the period immediately following Sonnet I (i.e., 1630 or early 1631), a position
defended by several scholars,[88] or as Masson and, more recently,
E. A. J. Honigmann[89] contend, they were composed later during
the Italian journey. In them Milton attempted to make the flower
of a foreign speech grow in a climate not its own, and he pictured
himself (Canzone) as surrounded by youths and maidens who
expostulated with him for writing in an alien and unintelligible
tongue. Although the weight of the argument over the dates seems
to rest with those who think these sonnets are a product of Milton's
University years, without new evidence the issue will remain in
doubt. About the remaining four, however, the dates are more
certain. *How soon hath Time* (Sonnet VII) was written on his
twenty-fourth birthday; *Captain or Colonel, or Knight in Arms*

---

[87] See especially Wayne Shumaker, "Flowerets and Sounding Seas"; Cleanth
Brooks and John Edward Hardy, "Essays in Analysis: *Lycidas*," *Poems of Mr.
John Milton* (New York, 1951), pp. 169–86; A. S. P. Woodhouse, "Milton's
Pastoral Monodies"; and Richard P. Adams, "The Archetypal Pattern of Death
and Rebirth in Milton's *Lycidas*."

[88] E.g., Hanford, Woodhouse, Smart, Dorian, and Darbishire; see John
Carey, "The Date of Milton's Italian Poems."

[89] E. A. J. Honigmann, *Milton's Sonnets*, pp. 76–81.

(Sonnet VIII) belongs to the year 1642. *Lady that in the prime of earliest youth* (Sonnet IX) and *Daughter to that good Earl* (Sonnet X) followed in 1644. This whole group was published consecutively in the 1645 edition of the poems.

In the 1673 edition Milton reprinted Sonnets I through X in that order and added nine additional sonnets; four other sonnets (XV, XVI, XVII, XXII)—composed in the period from 1645 to 1658—were probably for political reasons not included in the 1673 edition. They remained unprinted until 1694.[90] Several of these numbered from XI to XXIII had, however, been published before 1673. The tribute to Lawes appeared in Lawes's own *Choice Psalms* in 1648 and the commemorative to Vane in Sikes's *The Life and Death of Sir Henry Vane* in 1662.

The Italian sonnets, whenever they were written, are in honor of an Italian lady, Emilia, whose name is revealed in riddling fashion in Sonnet II. She is a "type of foreign beauty," a singer and "adorned with more languages than one." Presumably she was someone whom he had met in the circles of the Diodati family in London. Milton assumes in declaring his passion for her the extravagant attitude of the sonneteer and makes liberal use of the conventional phraseology of Petrarch. As J. S. Smart and F. T. Prince have demonstrated, however, Milton's stylistic models were more likely Bembo and Della Casa;[91] they offered Milton precedent for intricate and purposefully disarranged syntactic patterns, frequent enjambment, and for his disregard for the definite, distinct division between octave and sestet. The Italian penchant for multiplying antitheses and parallel phrases, a tendency which results in a kind of controlled pleonasm, is also apparent in Milton's sonnets. Prince has argued that these Italian sonnets—and the English examples that follow—are the young poet's conscious exercises in an idiom and style to be employed later in his projected epic poem. It seems also likely, however, that the pieces are a result of Milton's dilettante enthusiasm for the newly discovered delights of the Petrarchan sonnet and a boyishly proud display of his mastery of the tongue best suited to the refinements of poetic love: "*Questa è lingua di cui si vanta Amore.*"

---

[90] *Ibid.*, pp. 59–75.
[91] *The Sonnets of Milton*, pp. 22–39; "Milton's Sonnets."

The first English sonnet on the nightingale constitutes an introduction to the series and belongs with the Italian sonnets in spirit and style. In it, Milton, following the Chaucerian tradition (though his poem is a sonnet in Petrarchan form), writes himself gracefully into the role of unsuccessful lover. The later English sonnets, beginning with the one on his twenty-fourth birthday, reflect a complete change of attitude. The romantic note disappears entirely; the style is plain and direct; there is more of the conventional phraseology which belongs to the tradition. They are the most immediately personal of all Milton's utterances, representing emotional moments in his later life experience which find no adequate expression in the prose writing in which he was then primarily engaged.

Much has been written about Milton's sonnets, and the reader has the advantage of two well-annotated editions. J. S. Smart's *The Sonnets of Milton* has long been the definitive treatment. He has cleared away much error regarding their relation to literary tradition and has explained many obscure details of meaning. He points out that Milton characteristically makes use of the form at a time when its vogue has already passed and that his dedication of the sonnet to themes other than those of love is not an innovation, as it is so often said to be. Tasso, one of Milton's favorite authors, has a category of heroical sonnets on subjects similar to that of Milton's address to Cromwell, and even the Elizabethan tradition, though mainly amatory, is not by any means exclusively so. E. A. J. Honigmann's more recent study is a fine supplementary volume to be consulted along with Smart. Honigmann establishes clearly the occasions which Milton's sonnets commemorate; and, conversely, he emphasizes those topical threads which knit the sonnets together. For instance, Milton's love of freedom, his belief in "voluntary association," is obvious in Sonnets XI, XII, XV–XVII; his impatience with religious intolerance in Sonnets XV–XVIII; his praise of achievement in Sonnets IX, X, XIII, XV–XVII. And apparent throughout all the sonnets is the more inclusive theme of all of Milton's work: the dedication of his talents to the service of God's will.

On the whole Milton's sonnets strike a new note of lofty dignity; they fully justify Wordsworth's description:

In his hands
The thing became a trumpet; whence he blew
Soul-animating strains—alas, too few!

His tribute refers primarily to the group in which Milton touches on great public events and personalities: the sonnets to Cromwell, Vane, and Fairfax, and the great one on the massacre in Piedmont. Those in which he expresses a more personal emotion—the sonnet *How soon hath Time, the subtle thief of youth*, the two poems on his blindness, and the one written in memory of his wife—combine pathos with an earnest ethical and religious idealism. The addresses to Lawes, Skinner, Edward Lawrence, Lady Margaret Ley, to the unidentified virtuous young lady of Sonnet IX, and the elegy for Mrs. Katharine Thomason are pitched in lower key, but they are beautifully expressive of a friendliness and a humane sympathy quite at variance with the common impression of Milton as a harsh and austere Puritan. The two sonnets on the reception of his divorce pamphlets and the twenty-line sonnet (*caudata*) *On the New Forcers of Conscience under the Long Parliament* are a revelation of the poet's capacity for scathing denunciation. The whole group is a complete record of Milton's unique personality in all its varying moods. The workmanship throughout is of the highest quality, and each poem is in its own way a memorable and impressive work. Samuel Johnson's disparagement of the sonnets ("of the best it can only be said that they are not bad") is one of the strangest literary judgments on record. The history of their influence tells a very different story: it was Milton rather than the Elizabethans who set the style of the English sonnet at its revival toward the end of the eighteenth century. The importance of Milton's sonnets as the chief inspiring force and model of those of Wordsworth is well known.

THE PSALMS AND OTHER TRANSLATIONS

The task of reducing the Psalms to regular meters, whether as a literary exercise or for the purpose of adapting them to congregational singing, seems to us now of all literary endeavors the most vain and forbidding. Yet it was little less than a passion for Milton's predecessors and contemporaries. He himself tried his hand at it on three different occasions in his life, each time with a somewhat different motive and result.

In 1624 at the age of fifteen (if one can trust the statement prefixed to the poems in the 1645 edition) he wrote paraphrases on Psalms CXIV and CXXXVI. These compositions have a special interest in that they constitute Milton's earliest preserved poetry of any sort. They may be school exercises, but it seems more likely that they were written under the encouragement of Milton's father, who was interested in the composition of Psalm settings, contributing several to Ravenscroft's Psalter, which was published in 1621. There are traces in their phraseology (e.g., the use of such epithets as "froth-becurled") of Milton's early fondness for Sylvester's translation of Du Bartas' *La Semaine*. Psalm CXIV is in Sylvester's meter and is more closely imitative of his style than Psalm CXXXVI. Tillyard[92] calls attention particularly to the violence of the following lines of Psalm CXIV as thoroughly representative of the manner of Sylvester's rendering:

> That glassy floods from rugged rocks can crush,
> And make soft rills from fiery flint-stones gush.

In several expressions, moreover, he appears to be following Buchanan's versions of the Psalms in Horatian meters, which were much admired for their elegant Latinity and sometimes read in schools.[93] Despite their lack of originality, Milton's renderings have a freedom of rhythm and an elegance of language which marks them as the products of a genuine if immature poetic enthusiasm.

The second set of translations comprising Psalms LXXX to LXXXVIII was first published in the 1673 edition of the poems with the heading, "*Nine of the Psalms done into Meter, wherein all but what is in a different Character, are the very words of the Text, translated from the Original.*" They were translated in April, 1648, and may indicate that Milton was involved in the Scottish

---

[92] *Milton*, pp. 8–9.
[93] See James Holly Hanford, "The Youth of Milton."

revisions of the Psalter which appeared in 1650.[94] These Psalms are more literal and less eloquent than the two youthful ones. Milton's purpose in writing them—if he was not involved with the Scottish revisions—probably was to supply a version at once accurate and doctrinally sound to supplant the old Sternhold and Hopkins Psalter for congregational singing. He accordingly adopted the common service meter (8 + 6). It has been pointed out that Milton's rendering of the Hebrew is sometimes mistaken, and evidence has been adduced to show that he resorted to the Vulgate for assistance.[95] Standard practices, however, called for translators to consult all editions available to them, and Milton probably used the Vulgate in an attempt to come closest to contemporary idiom.[96] It seems likely that he was as competent as anyone in his time in interpreting the originals, and the errors seem, in most cases at least, to be due to the recollection of a phrase from some other version that was familiar to him.

Finally in 1653 he turned Psalms I–VIII into a variety of metrical and stanzaic forms, no two being exactly the same. One surmises that he had resumed this task at this time as a means of amusement and spiritual consolation in the early period of his blindness. The attempt to follow the Hebrew with a minute fidelity was now abandoned; occasional touches reveal the degree to which Milton was reading his own experiences into the psalmist's cry to God out of the anguish of his soul.

A single non-Scriptural translation appeared in the 1673 edition, the remarkably ingenious version of Horace's *Quis multa gracilis,* "rendered almost word for word without Rhyme according to the Latin Measure, as near as the Language will permit." Other fragmentary bits (generally in blank verse) from classic and Italian authors are scattered through the prose.

[94] W. B. Hunter, Jr., "Milton Translates the Psalms."
[95] Edward Chauncey Baldwin, "Milton and the Psalms."
[96] Marian H. Studley's article, "Milton and His Paraphrases of the Psalms," is a necessary supplement to Baldwin.

Chapter 4

PARADISE LOST

COMPOSITION AND DEVELOPMENT

STEPS IN THE DEVELOPMENT OF MILTON'S PLAN

THE STORY OF THE EVOLUTION OF PARADISE LOST IN MILTON'S MIND is an intimate and vital part of his biography for a period of over a quarter of a century. The record of his preliminary meditation of the project is to be found chiefly in his published writings and in his preserved manuscript notes. This record of "long choosing and beginning late" (including his early deliberations over a subject) is here given chronologically.

1628: AT A VACATION EXERCISE Milton expresses his ambition to employ the English language in "some graver subject" comparable to the *Iliad* or the *Odyssey*. Addressing his mother tongue, now employed in the triviality of a mock oration, he voices his more serious poetic purposes (ll. 23–52). There is no suggestion here of the theme of the fall of man, nor indeed of any specific subject. The lines are rather a survey of the whole scene and materials of epic poetry as his imagination conceived them: though the coloring is Greek we have no difficulty in recognizing the

147

Christian and Miltonic substance. Apollo sings "before the thunderous throne" as the angels in *Paradise Lost* hymn the praises of the Almighty; the "deep transported mind" of the poet already wanders in anticipation through "misty Regions of wide air" and explores the mysteries of created nature. In the figure of "green-ey'd Neptune" defiant of Heaven, there is even a hint of the motive of rebellion. The atmosphere and broader scope of Milton's intention are already clear; regarding the specific theme and the person of an epic hero Milton has no very tangible ideas.

DECEMBER, 1629: ELEGY VI   Although the elegy may bear close resemblance to an academic exercise, in it Milton literally dedicates himself to elegiac poetry and prescribes for himself a way of life appropriate to such an ambition.[1] For the later account in the *Apology* of the resolution thus taken on his twenty-first birthday and of the steps which led to it, see Appendix B. The terms in which he describes his proposed subject matter carry us directly back to *At a Vacation Exercise*, but they are considerably more specific and suggest Virgil rather than Homer as a model:

> But the poet who sings of heaven subject now to mature Jove, and of pious heroes and leaders half divine, who sings now of the sacred conferences of the high Gods, now of the abysmal realm where barks a savage dog, that poet should live sparingly as did the Samian teacher and should find in herbs his simple food.

1630: MANUS   He announces the legendary history of Britain as his theme:

> I will someday recall in song the things of my native land, and Arthur, who carried war even into fairyland. Or I shall tell of those greathearted champions bound in the society of the Round Table, and (O may the Spirit be in me!) I shall break the Saxon phalanxes with British war.

That his thoughts should take this direction is not surprising. The precedent of Virgil taught him to seek a national hero; Spenser and

---

[1] See William R. Parker's caution about reading Elegy VI strictly autobiographically in a review in *MLN*, LV (1940), 216–17, and in *Milton*, I, 69–70

the Tudor revival of interest in British origins directed him to Arthur. Obviously, however, this theme provided no scope for the cosmic interests exhibited in *At a Vacation Exercise.*

1639–41 (?): EPITAPHIUM DAMONIS   Milton, through the persona of Thyrsis, implies that he has made a first attempt at the Arthurian epic and describes his proposed subject more fully as embracing the history of the Britons from the landing of Brutus to the times of Arthur (11. 155–78). This is the last we hear of such a poem as being actually in progress or even definitely projected. Milton gives as a reason for abandoning it his sense of the inadequacy of his style, hitherto accustomed only to the simpler themes of pastoral; but other reasons are not far to seek. In the *History of Britain* he deals critically with the sources of historical knowledge about King Arthur, expresses the doubt "whether ever any such reign'd in *Britain,*" and speaks scornfully of those "who can accept of legends for good story."[2] In *Paradise Lost* (IX, 29 ff.) he seems to be congratulating himself on having declined to meddle with a kind of subject which requires the poet

> . . . to dissect
> With long and tedious havoc fabl'd Knights
> In Battles feign'd.

His change from enthusiasm to distaste is remarkable but intelligible. It is to be associated with the general distrust of antiquarianism and the figments of monkish annalists expressed in the early ecclesiastical pamphlets in which Milton was soon to be engaged.[3] The historicity of the Arthurian legend had been challenged as early as Polydore Virgil. When James I revived the Tudor claim of descent from Arthur, new forces of seventeenth-century historical scholarship were brought to bear on the question. The controversy is rightly considered a factor determining Milton's change of attitude.[4]

1642: REASON OF CHURCH-GOVERNMENT   Milton tells of the

[2] Patterson, *Works,* X, 127–28. Hereafter this edition will be cited *CM.*
[3] See Putnam Fennell Jones, "Milton and the Epic Subject from British History," *PMLA,* XLII (1927), 901–09.
[4] See Roberta F. Brinkley, *Arthurian Legend.*

formation of his resolution to write a great English poem and makes an important statement regarding the function and purpose of poetry as he had proposed it for himself—showing, incidentally, that he is undecided both as to the form and substance of his work. The passage is given in full in Appendix B. We may note that his tentative protagonist must be not only one of our victorious kings but "the pattern of a Christian *Heroe*."[5] Arthur's unfitness for such a role must have been increasingly apparent as Milton's sympathies turned more strongly away from the traditions of Catholic and feudal Christianity. His feeling, also, that it is incumbent on him to vindicate literature against the disrepute into which it has fallen leads him naturally back toward a specifically religious subject matter. He mentions Biblical along with classical models, and in the more general description of the poet's office which follows he gives emphasis to his obligation to sing directly of God's almightiness and of "what he works, and what he suffers to be wrought with his providence in his Church."[6] All this moves us on toward *Paradise Lost*.

1640–42: THE CAMBRIDGE MANUSCRIPT   Shortly after his return from Italy Milton set down a list of about a hundred possible literary subjects from Biblical and British history—some of them merely indicated, some already developed into tentative outlines.[7]

---

[5] Ed. with preface and notes by Ralph A. Haug, Yale, *Milton*, I, 813–14.

[6] *Ibid.*, p. 817.

[7] The order of the materials in the manuscript is as follows:

p. 35. The first three outlines for a drama on the Fall, with three additional titles under the head "other Tragedies." Among these are "Adam in Banishment" and 'The Deluge."

p. 36. Numerous Biblical subjects from the Old Testament (including "The Deluge"), a few of them with suggestions for treatment.

pp. 37–38. Thirty-three British subjects from Holinshed, Malmesbury, Speed, etc.

p. 39. Well-developed outlines for "Abraham from Morea," "Baptistes," and "Sodom Burning."

p. 40. A continuation of "Sodom Burning" and the fourth outline for a drama on the Fall, under the heading "Adam Unparadiz'd," the titles of six New Testament subjects.

p. 41. Titles of "Scotch stories," with brief outlines of a 'Phineas" and a "Christus Patiens."

In "The Trinity Manuscript and Milton's Plans for a Tragedy" William R. Parker infers that, after beginning with the project of *Paradise Lost* as drama, Milton was temporarily dissatisfied with it and turned to canvass other possibilities. He thinks quite rightly that Milton's mind probably never reverted to most

All the plans are for dramas, but it is possible that there was a similar list of epic themes which has not been preserved. The subject of the fall of man evidently now holds first place in his thoughts. His successive redraftings of the plan for a drama on this theme constitute the first definite step in the composition of *Paradise Lost*. Phillips reports at this time that he definitely saw a version of Satan's address to the sun (IV, 32–113) as the opening of such a drama. The four outlines in order of composition are as follows:

FIRST DRAFT *(canceled)*	SECOND DRAFT *(canceled)*[8]
The Persons	*The Persons*
Michael	Moses
Heavenly Love	Wisdom, Justice, Mercy
Chorus of Angels	Heavenly Love
	The Evening Star Hesperus
	Chorus of Angels
Lucifer	Lucifer
Adam ⎫	Adam
Eve ⎬ with the serpent	Eve
Conscience ⎭	Conscience
Death	Labour ⎫
Labour ⎫	Sicknesse ⎪
Sicknesse ⎪	Discontent ⎬ Mutes
Discontent ⎬ Mutes	Ignorance ⎪
Ignorance ⎪	Feare ⎪
with others ⎭	Death ⎭
Faith	Faith
Hope	Hope
Charity	Charity

of these ideas. We may fairly suppose, however, that he was projecting more than one drama, the reform of the English stage being at this time uppermost in his thoughts. The Abraham, John the Baptist, and Sodom plays are almost as fully elaborated as the final draft of *Paradise Lost*. He seems even to have made an addition to the Sodom outline after completing "Adam Unparadiz'd." Though he keeps recurring to historical subjects, he elaborates none of these as he does several from Scripture.

8 From the facsimile of the Cambridge Manuscript reproduced in *CM*. Each draft also has various cancellations; see Harris Fletcher, *Milton's Works in Facsimile*, II, 16–29.

THIRD DRAFT

The Persons. Moses προλογίζει recounting how he assum'd his true
bodie, that it corrupts not because of his [being] with god in the
mount declares the like of Enoch and Eliah, besides the purity of
the pl[ace] that certaine pure winds, dues, and clouds praeserve
it from corruption whence he hasts to the sight of god, tells they
cannot se Adam in the state of innocence by reason of thire sin.

Justice ⎫
Mercie ⎬ debating what should become of man if he fall
Wisdome ⎭

Chorus of Angels sing a hymne of the creation

Act 2

Heavenly Love

Evening starre

Chorus sing the mariage song and describe Paradice

Act 3

Lucifer contriving Adams ruine

Chorus feares for Adam and relates Lucifers rebellion and fall

Act 4

Adam ⎫
Eve ⎭ fallen

Conscience cites them to Gods examination

Chorus bewails and tells the good Adam hath lost

Act 5

Adam and Eve, driven out of Paradice praesented by an angel with
Labour griefe hatred Envie warre famine Pestilence

sicknesse ⎫
discontent │ mutes to whom he gives thire names
Ignorance ⎬ likewise winter, heat Tempest etc.
Feare │ entered into the world
Death ⎭

Faith ⎫
Hope ⎬ comfort him and instruct him
Charity ⎭

Chorus briefly concludes

FOURTH DRAFT[9]

Adam Unparadised. [I] The Angel Gabriel, either descending or

[9] Masson's modernized transcript, *Life*, II, 107–08. The act divisions, suggested by those in the third draft, have been supplied by the present editors.

entering—showing, since this globe was created, his frequency as much on Earth as in Heaven—describes Paradise. Next the Chorus, showing the reason of his coming—to keep his watch, after Lucifer's rebellion, by command from God; and withal expressing his desire to see and know more concerning this excellent and new creature, Man. [II] The Angel Gabriel, as by his name signifying a Prince of Power, tracing Paradise with a more free office, passes by the station of the Chorus, and, desired by them, relates what he knew of Man, as the creation of Eve, with their love and marriage.—[III] After this, Lucifer appears, after his overthrow, bemoans himself, seeks revenge on Man. The Chorus prepares resistance at his first approach. At last, after discourse of enmity on either side, he departs; whereat the Chorus sings of the battle and victory in Heaven against him and his accomplices, as before, after the first Act, was sung a hymn of the creation.—[IV] Here again may appear Lucifer, relating and insulting in what he had done to the destruction of Man. Man next and Eve, having by this time been seduced by the Serpent, appears confusedly, covered with leaves. Conscience in a shape accuses him, Justice cites him to the place wither Jehovah called for him. In the meanwhile the Chorus entertains the stage, and is informed by some Angel of the manner of his Fall. Here the Chorus bewails Adam's fall.—[V] Adam then, and Eve, return and accuse one another; but especially Adam lays the blame to his wife—is stubborn in his offence. Justice appears, reasons with him, convinces him. The Chorus admonisheth Adam, and bids him beware Lucifer's example of impenitence.—The Angel is sent to banish them out of Paradise; but, before, causes to pass before his eyes, in shapes, a masque of all the evils of this life and world. He is humbled, relents, despairs. At last appears Mercy, comforts him, promises the Messiah; then calls in Faith, Hope, Charity; instructs him. He repents, gives God the glory, submits to his penalty. The Chorus briefly concludes.—Compare this with the former Draft.

These drafts show that Milton had in mind a play similar in character to the Italian *sacre rappresentazione*, which mingled Biblical story with medieval allegory.[10] They show also that he

---

[10] See Grant McColley, *"Paradise Lost,"* p. 290.

planned to preserve some semblance of classical form, the unities of place and time being strictly maintained and the chorus employed at the end of each episode in the ancient manner. More illuminating is the insight the plans give us into the nature of his thought. Not only is full exposition of the scheme of salvation provided for as in *Paradise Lost* itself, but Milton's favorite early theme of chastity and heavenly love is clearly written in. Thus in the third draft the prologue of Moses indicates the highly Platonic nature of paradise, suggesting the passage with which the Attendant Spirit opens *Comus* and also the famous passage on chastity in the masque. How prominent this element was in Milton's first thoughts on the subject is made clear by his elaboration of the pageant of Love and Hesperus into a whole act. In the fourth draft it is greatly reduced in the interests of the story itself. It is still implicit, however, in Gabriel's prologue, and it survives prominently in the epic. It is possible to recognize every element suggested by the plans in one form or another in *Paradise Lost*.[11] Wisdom, Justice, and Mercy do not actually debate in the poem, but the substance of what they have said is given in the celestial dialogue of Book III. The angels still sing the hymn of creation, and Gabriel narrates its incidents. Adam and Eve sing their own marriage song; death, labor, sickness, and the other consequences of sin are revealed in concrete form by Michael. There are even traces of the original personification, and Adam pronounces the name of Death. The order of events in the epic is on the whole that of the fourth draft, but there are some interesting alterations. Thus, in the poem, freed from the necessity of preserving unity of place, Milton can begin with Satan on the burning lake and introduce the indispensable infernal council. The narrative of creation is likewise made to follow instead of to precede that of the war in heaven, a gain both in effectiveness and significance.[12]

CIRCA 1642   Edward Phillips states that Milton showed him the opening verses of a tragedy: "This Subject was first designed a Tragedy, and in the Fourth Book of the Poem there are Ten Verses

[11] *Ibid.*, pp. 292–93.
[12] See Allan H. Gilbert, *On The Composition of "Paradise Lost,"* pp. 18–23.

[11. 32–41], which several Years before the Poem was begun, were shewn to me, and some others, as designed for the very beginning of the said Tragedy."[13] It is not clear in Phillips' account whether the tragedy he saw was a direct outgrowth or modification of Milton's fourth draft, a part of that fourth draft itself, or part of a fifth draft of which we have no record.

1654 In the *Second Defence of the English People,* Milton makes a statement implying that he has in a sense fulfilled his expressed intention of celebrating the exploits of his own country-men—not the deeds of the early kings but the more thrilling achievements wrought by Cromwell and the people of England in the Great Rebellion:

> *Moreover, just as the epic poet, if he is scrupulous and disinclined to break the rules, undertakes to extol, not the whole life of the hero whom he proposes to celebrate in his verse but usually one event of his life (the exploits of Achilles at Troy, let us say, or the return of Ulysses, or the coming of Aeneas in Italy) and passes over the rest, so let it suffice me too, as my duty or my excuse, to have celebrated at least one heroic achievement of my countrymen. The rest I omit. Who could extol all the achievements of an entire nation?*[14]

This is to some degree a characteristic piece of Miltonic rationalization, for the immediate motivation of the defense was something quite different, but the idea may well have served to free the poet's mind from a self-imposed obligation which might have interfered with his concentration of effort on the Biblical epic.

REASONS FOR THE CHANGE FROM DRAMA TO EPIC

We do not know exactly either when or why Milton abandoned his idea of a drama on the Fall and determined to cast his materials into epic form. It is apparent from the fourth draft that Milton,

[13] Darbishire, *Early Lives,* p. 72.
[14] Ed. with preface and notes by Donald A. Roberts, trans. Helen North, Yale, *Milton,* IV, i, 685.

when he came to visualize the drama more concretely, found himself obliged to sacrifice much of the material which belonged to the larger theme as he had first conceived it. He must have hesitated to treat the subject thus narrowly; yet there is no reason to believe that this fact alone would have deterred him. In 1922 Quiller-Couch, speculating that the closing of the theaters in 1642 determined Milton's change of plan,[15] argued that he had intended his *Adam Unparadised* for actual performance as a revived mystery play in classical form.[16] Milton's own earlier experience with the masque and the fact that religious allegory did not seem as remote from popular interest then as it does today are suggested by Quiller-Couch as reasons for thinking it probable that he "meant to achieve on the actual stage something of the sort that Handel afterwards achieved in oratorio"[17] and that he was deterred by the edict from proceeding. There is evidence, however, that if Milton intended public performance of his work, he was looking for a kind of performance very different from any provided by the traditions, public or private, of the Jacobean stage. In the *Reason of Church-Government* Milton urges the magistrates themselves to take over the problem of providing public sports and pastimes for the people, and he invites them to consider whether even religious instruction may not be given, "not only in Pulpits, but after another persuasive method, at set and solemn Paneguries, in Theaters, porches, or what other place, or way may win most upon the people to receive at once both recreation, and instruction. . . ."[18]

These sentences do, indeed, throw light upon Milton's attitude and perhaps explain the trend of his thought toward drama after his return from Italy. But the official prohibiting of stage plays a few months after the passage was written could hardly have seemed to him decisive against such ceremonies and exhibitions as he here described. One wonders how much Milton would himself have been against the edict. The later restrictions imposed by the regime he certainly disliked, but in the passage cited he talks like a

---

[15] "Milton," *Studies in Literature,* Second Series (New York and Cambridge, Eng., 1922), p. 140.
[16] *Ibid.,* pp. 138–39.
[17] *Ibid.,* p. 140.
[18] Yale, *Milton,* I, 819–20.

Puritan of the corruption which the youth of the nation sucks in "from the writings and interludes of libidinous and ignorant Poetasters," and he expressly disapproves of the pastimes which were "autoriz'd a while since" as provocations of drunkenness and lust.[19]

Milton himself may have offered a reason for his failure to continue either *Adam Unparadised* or any other purely artistic project during the civil war. The accomplishment of such designs, he says, "lies not but in a power above mans to promise." He will pursue them "as farre as life and free leasure will extend." But there is a prior duty, to free the land "from this impertinent yoke of prelaty, under whose inquisitorius and tyrannical duncery no free and splendid wit can flourish."[20]

It seems reasonable to suggest, however, that evidence other than biographical be considered in speculating upon why Milton abandoned the dramatic mode. Confronting him was the matter of securing the proper dramatic effect while having the fall of Adam and Eve reported by an angel; he must have known the weaknesses involved in avoiding the direct scene itself. Of course, if he had presented the seduction on the stage, he faced the delicate problem of the speaking serpent figure as a leading actor in the scene.[21] We may also assume he wished to avoid this. More likely, however, Milton rejected the drama simply because his conception of his work changed in scope as he envisioned his poem containing elements (such as the length and form of Book VII, for example) beyond those possible for drama. Dryden's unsuccessful operatic version of Milton's poem reveals the extent to which the epic as Milton conceived of it depended upon structures and patterns of carefully manipulated *spaces* rather than upon the temporal sequences of drama.[22]

Whatever the reason, Milton thus foresaw in 1640 that he would, until the political issue was settled, make scanty progress with his masterpiece. He did not foresee how long drawn out the struggle would be or how deeply he himself would be involved. It seems likely that he paused from time to time in the intervals of

[19] *Ibid.*, pp. 818–19.
[20] *Ibid.*, p. 820.
[21] See Gilbert, *On the Composition of "Paradise Lost,"* pp. 22–23.
[22] See Isabel G. MacCaffrey, *Paradise Lost as "Myth,"* pp. 49–51.

controversy and official business to remeditate the literary problem. His theme of the fall of man, already preferred before the others, would naturally have come to incorporate within itself more and more of the materials of Milton's experiences and thought, and it must soon have become apparent to him that only the epic form could embrace his purposes in their full maturity.

CONJECTURES ON THE DATES OF COMPOSITION
OF THE POEM

Thus far critics and scholars have been unable to determine the precise time when Milton actually began composition of the poem we know as *Paradise Lost*. He may have begun composition in the period of leisure following the termination of his literary war with More in 1655 or later, following the appointment of Andrew Marvell as Assistant Latin Secretary in 1657. Aubrey, on the oral authority of Edward Phillips, may be correct in stating that the poem was begun about two years before the king came in—i.e., about May, 1658.[23] Phillips in his published life of Milton is less definite. It seems improbable that Milton had progressed far in the work before the stormy and dangerous moment of the Restoration intervened to disturb him again. Masson guesses that Books I and II might have been complete before this event and the poem resumed after Milton had been released from custody and become permanently domiciled in Jewin Street.[24] He points with good reason to a passage (ll. 26–27) in the invocation of Book VII:

> On evil days though fall'n, and evil tongues;
> In darkness, and with dangers compast round,

as clearly reflecting Milton's estimate of his own situation after the Restoration. Tillyard emphasizes the relationship between the *Second Defence* and the earlier books of *Paradise Lost* and argues for a renewal of poetic activity before 1654. The Hymn to Light at the beginning of Book III is, he says, a poetic version of part of

---

[23] See Darbishire, *Early Lives*, p. 13.
[24] *Milton*, VI, 440–44.

the prose passage on Milton's blindness (quoted in Appendix B) and was probably composed about the same time.[25] There is further an analogy between the "characters" of the Devils in Book II and those of Cromwell and his fellows in the *Defence*. It is entirely possible that Milton might have returned to these materials at a later time, but Tillyard's general thesis that the first part of *Paradise Lost* is pervaded by the mood and spirit of Milton's prose work has much to recommend it.

The poem is said by Aubrey to have been finished in 1663. It was certainly complete before the autumn of 1665, when Thomas Ellwood, according to a well-known anecdote recorded in his autobiography, was handed the manuscript by Milton at Chalfont St. Giles.[26] The minimum period probably covered by its composition was, therefore, some five years, with interruptions. For the recorded details of Milton's habits of dictation, etc., see Chapter 1.

PUBLICATION

Paradise Lost was published in 1667. The articles of agreement (now in the British Museum)[27] between Milton and the printer, Samuel Simmons, are dated April 27;[28] the poem is entered in the Stationers' Register August 20.[29] The actual printing of the work

[25] *Milton*, pp. 192–97.

[26] *The History of the Life of Thomas Ellwood*, ed. S. Graveson (London, 1906), p. 199.

[27] B. M. *Add. MS.* 18861.

[28] The articles are transcribed in J. Milton French, *Life Records*, IV, 429–31. The contract is remarkable for the protection it gives the author. Simmons agrees to print not more than 4,500 copies in three impressions of 1,500 copies each, to pay £5 down, a second £5 "at the end of the first impression," a third £5 "at the end of the second impression," and a fourth £5 "at the end of the third impression." The impressions are accounted to end when 1,300 of the possible 1,500 copies are sold. The publisher presumably had the 200 additional copies to dispose of as he saw fit without further payment to Milton. According to the law of that period not more than 1,500 copies of any book could be printed without resetting. The contract calls for a sworn accounting of sales at demand before a Master in Chancery. No provision is made for further impressions or for a new edition. In 1680 Elizabeth Milton gave over all her rights in the copy of the second edition to Simmons for £8. What, if anything, Milton received on the first instance for the copy of the second edition is not known.

[29] *Ibid.*, pp. 433–34.

presumably followed in the autumn. Between thirteen and fifteen hundred copies had been sold by April, 1669, when Milton received the second payment of five pounds due to him according to the agreement. Of this first impression only a part was actually put on sale in 1667. The printer issued subsequent installments from time to time with different title pages.[30] Accordingly, the preserved copies of the first edition bear varying dates—1667, 1668, and 1669. In some cases Milton's name is used; in at least one, simply his initials. For one of the 1668 issues, Milton added to the beginning of the volume the arguments to the various books and the prefatory note on the verse. There are minor variations in the text, especially towards the close of the poem, due to disturbance of the type during the process of printing. The bibliographical problems connected with the first edition are therefore very complicated; Pollard,[31] Fletcher,[32] Darbishire,[33] and Hanford[34] have made significant contributions toward solving these textual problems.

The second edition appeared in 1674, the year of Milton's death. Besides making a few textual changes and distributing the arguments in their proper places throughout the poem, Milton here divided Books VII and X into two each, thereby making an epic of twelve books instead of the original ten.

The original manuscript of *Paradise Lost* is not preserved. There is, however, a fair copy of Book I in the Morgan Library in New York. (The first two pages of the fair copy appear as endpapers in this edition of the *Handbook*.) This transcript was formerly supposed to have been prepared not for the press but for inspection by the licenser,[35] whose imprimatur it bears; but the fact that it has come down to us through Jacob Tonson, who states in a preserved letter that he bought it along with the copyright of *Paradise Lost*,

---

[30] See Fletcher, *Milton's Works in Facsimile*, II, 162–76. Bibliographers give the number variously from six to twelve. It is easy enough to explain the use of title pages bearing new dates, but we can only speculate on why there were issued at least two different title pages bearing the date 1667. Masson's contention that the sale was slow is not a convincing one.

[31] "The Bibliography of Milton," *The Library, Second Series*, X (1909), 23–28.

[32] *Milton's Works in Facsimile*, II, 162–76.

[33] *The Manuscript of "Paradise Lost,"* Book I.

[34] "The Manuscript of *Paradise Lost*," MP, XXV (1928), 313–17.

[35] For the licensing inscription, see French, *Life Records*, IV, 433–34.

the presence in the margins of printer's symbols made in the process of laying off the copy for pagination, and other evidences demonstrate conclusively that the text of the 1667 edition was set from it. A comparison of the printed text with its original, besides throwing additional light on Milton's intentions regarding spelling, makes possible the restoration of some authentic readings in Book I.

EXPOSITORY OUTLINE

BOOK I

Following the practice of Homer and Virgil, Milton invites his Muse to sing first a statement of his theme: Man's first disobedience and the loss of paradise. Consideration of this subject inevitably involves the redemption, the sacrifice of "one greater Man" for the restoration of all men. As the invocation continues, the Heavenly Muse (later identified as Urania)[36] is revealed to be the divine inspiration which unfolded the secrets of creation to Moses on Sinai.[37] The epic speaker pleads for her aid in his creation: the "great Argument" which will maintain the cause of Providence and make apparent the justice of God's dealing with men. The Muse is then asked to sing of first things first, and the poem continues to parallel ancient epic formula in the adoption of the motif "what cause?" and its answer, "th' infernal Serpent," the origin of whose malice, viz., pride and ungrateful rebellion, is here briefly alluded to. These allusions to Satan's rebellion, his defeat, and fall lead to our first view of the fallen angel at the moment when, recovering from the confusion of his grand defeat, he raises his head from the burning lake that is hell.

Surveying with comprehensive sweep the fearful scene about

[36] On Urania see William B. Hunter, Jr., "Milton's Urania." See also Anne Ferry, *Milton's Epic Voice.*

[37] See James Holly Hanford, "That Shepherd Who First Taught the Chosen Seed: A Note on Milton's Mosaic Inspiration," *UTQ*, VIII (1939), 403–19. A fine analysis of ll. 1–26 is made by David Daiches, "The Opening of *Paradise Lost.*"

him, he beholds Beelzebub (literally, god of flies), called the Prince of Devils in Scripture. His address (11. 84–124), couched in language of unrivaled grandeur, is expressive of the situation and of the human passions which dwell with superhuman intensity in his heart. At the root of his sense of the glory of the attempt, and of his determination to persist, is the fundamental perversion of his will. This, in turn, implies a perversion of the intellect, for his language reveals that he has lost his original comprehension of God and has attributed to Him motives and a being like his own. He falls into the heresy of the Manichees, who held the angels to be coexistent with God; attributes his own creation to Fate; and proclaims his independent immortality. He thus manifests himself as the "father of lies," though at first our perception of his true nature is swallowed up in admiration of the heroic "virtue" which he brings with him as mark and seal of his divine origin.

Beelzebub (11. 128–55), though he holds the same fatalistic creed as his lord, is inferior in his ability to face the situation. Satan meets his pessimism (11. 157–91) with a superb expression of resolute opposition to the will of God and proposes the terms of the eternal warfare between good and evil (11. 162–68). His conclusion ironically echoes the terms of the redemption of Adam and Eve; he will, he claims, repair his own loss. Every word reveals him deeper in his own intellectual hell.[38] Satan can be heroic only in hell, and with loss the only situation which makes pride admirable, he reaches his highest glory when, standing at length on the burning shore, he welcomes the appalling region as his future home (11. 214–70), expressing the great (but false) principle of the supremacy of soul over its environment.[39] In the following address to the host (11. 315 ff.) he assumes the role of an inspiring leader rousing his troops from lethargy by stinging words, filling them with his own great spirit.

Descriptions of the landscape of hell[40] and of the personal appearance of Satan and his lieutenants are interspersed throughout

[38] See C. A. Patrides, "Renaissance and Modern Views on Hell," *HTR*, LVII (1964), 217–36.
[39] Don Cameron Allen, "*Paradise Lost*, I, 254–55," *MLN*, LXXI (1956), 324–26.
[40] See J. B. Broadbent, "Milton's Hell," *ELH*, XXI (1954), 161–92.

the action from the beginning (11. 44 ff.). Thus we are given at first the general impression of the fiery gulf in which the devils lie confounded and of the "darkness visible" of the infernal region (11. 50 ff.); then the more specific image of Satan, prone on the flood, with head uplifted; then further details progressively, as the leaders, followed by their legions, rise from the lake and take their places on the burning plain. Elaborate and suggestive similes, more abundant here than in any other portion of the poem, enrich the description at every point.[41]

Having assembled the infernal host, Milton proceeds to an enumeration, following the precedent of Homer's catalogue of ships and heroes in the second book of the *Iliad*.[42] The names are drawn partly from Scripture and partly from Egyptian and Greek mythology, on the theory, already adopted in the poem on the nativity, that the divinities worshipped by the idolaters of Palestine and by the pagans generally were in reality the fallen angels who had subsequently seduced mankind from allegiance to the true God. The marshalling of the multitude in military order is followed by further description of their dread commander and by a more reasoned but not less passionate address, as of a general who knows that his first task in war is to secure by eloquence the devotion of his men to the purposes for which he wishes to employ them. The account of the building of Pandemonium (11. 670 ff.), in form a Doric temple,[43] and of the miracle whereby the chosen representa-

---

[41] See James Whaler, "The Miltonic Simile"; "Compounding and Distribution of Similes in *Paradise Lost*"; "Animal Simile in *Paradise Lost*." Cf. Kingsley Widmer, "The Iconography of Renunciation: The Miltonic Simile."

[42] Grant McColley, "The Epic Catalogue of *Paradise Lost*," ELH, IV (1937), 180–91, notes striking resemblances in Milton's list to the enumeration of pagan deities in Alexander Ross's *Pansebeia, A View of All Religions of the World* (1653), showing that Milton recites the descriptions of Moloch, Chemos, Peor, Baalim, and Astoroth in the reverse order in which they occur in Ross. The title of this work may also have suggested Milton's "Pandemonium." Selden's *De Diis Syriis* (1617) should also be consulted as a basic Miltonic source of knowledge supplementary to the fathers and to Scripture. Whole chapters, freighted with learning, are there devoted to Dagon, Beelzebub, Moloch, and other deities mentioned in *Paradise Lost* and the *Nativity Ode*. Milton refers to other works of Selden and probably knew this one, which had first established its author's fame as an orientalist.

[43] A striking parallel exists between certain features of Milton's description of hell and travelers' accounts of a volcanic region near Naples known as the Phlegraean Fields. The ruins of an amphitheater in the neighborhood, dedicated

tives of the army are transformed to pygmean size that they may be housed within the council chamber (11. 775 ff.)—a wholesale metamorphosis unknown to Ovid—bring the book to a close. Lest, however, the concluding impression should be one of littleness, Milton leaves the great leaders unchanged, presenting us with a final image of their mighty presence seated "far within" and ready for the "great consult."

BOOK II

The narrative and descriptive elements which have bulked large in Book I now give way to a primarily dramatic representation of the infernal council. Milton brings to bear upon the account a lifelong study of statesmanship and oratory in ancient and modern books, supported by the memory of his experience with the leaders of the revolution. His council is a magnified image of those human deliberations on which the fates of nations hang. As often happens in the public affairs of men, the assembly is secretly dominated by a single master will. Individuals may voice their convictions and display their passions, each with a type of eloquence appropriate to his personal character and temper, but the ultimate policy is predetermined. Satan, in the opening of the debate (11. 11 ff.), assumes that all are with him in the purpose of recovery and revenge. The choice which is offered is one of means—open war or covert guile. Moloch, with the characteristic impetuosity and bluntness of the soldier, advises an immediate attack (11. 51 ff.)—an unreasoning counsel of desperation delivered with brevity and force.[44] Belial, the smooth-tongued trimmer, winding his way subtly into the argument, recommends a policy of peace to which his slothful and luxurious temper predisposes him (11. 119 ff.). The two represent contrasting types of public leaders—the jingo with his

---

to Vulcan, suggest Pandemonium, though the architecture of the latter structure bears detailed resemblance to St. Peter's. It seems very likely that here, as in the explicit allusions to Valdarno, Milton is embodying in the poem visual recollections of his sojourn in Italy. See Marjorie Nicolson, "Milton's Hell and the Phlegraean Fields," *UTQ*, VII (1938), 500–13.

[44] See Robert C. Fox, "The Character of Moloc in *Paradise Lost*."

instinctive advocacy of violence and the plausible but cowardly counselor of peace at any price. Mammon, the third speaker, builds upon the sentiments of Belial, which have commended themselves to the audience, still smarting from their recent defeat; his more constructive suggestion is to give up war and make the most of hell—availing themselves of its resources, exploiting its hidden riches, acclimating themselves to an environment which can at least be made to satisfy an impulse to possess and to create (11. 229 ff.). Such advice, from him who afterward became the pagan god of wealth, is greeted with a murmur of approval; public opinion seems to be drifting dangerously in a direction contrary to the intention of Satan. Then Beelzebub, the type of the subservient politician, as responsive to the purposes of his master as badness could desire, rises clad in the aspect of impressive statesmanship to stem the tide (11. 310 ff.). He introduces into the discussion a new fact, craftily held back till the progress of the debate demanded it—the existence of an undefended world peopled by creatures liable to attack—a matchless opportunity for the satisfaction of a revenge as fierce as Moloch's, by means as safe as Belial's, and with a possibility of profit more rich than that contemplated by Mammon. His proposal promptly voted, it remains for Satan to confirm his leadership by offering to undertake the hazardous task of carrying it out. He does so with grand heroic gesture (an infernal parody of the Son's willingness to undertake a merciful mission for men), winning infinite renown in hell. The whole situation is molded to Satan's benefit, and his personal enterprise made, under democratic sanction, to figure as a splendid act of public service. The fact implies a human lesson, teaching us, as Milton points out, to scan with suspicion the specious deeds of men:

> . . . Which glory excites,
> Or close ambition varnisht o'er with zeal.
>
> (11. 484–85)

After the assembly, the devils, like the heroes of the *Aeneid*, engage in epic recreation, the lower sort in physical sports, the higher sort in song and poetry, the noblest of all in philosophical discourse (11. 506 ff.). Still others undertake the geographical exploration of their new abode. As always, their doings are the patterns and types of the varied activities of men. They initiate the chief subjects of speculation and anticipate the main trends of all secular philosophy. As angels their intellectual flights surpass the human; as fallen souls they have lost the key to truth and find "no end, in wand'ring mazes lost" (1. 561).

The narrative now turns to Satan coursing through space and describes his encounter with Sin, his daughter and paramour in heaven, and with Death, their son. The three comprise a grotesque parody of the heavenly Trinity. This allegorical confrontation is a fine example of Milton's macabre humor, as the epic is momentarily deflated from the realm of heroic politics to that of banal domesticity.[45] Loathsome as the episode is, it has its significant place in the economy of the poem, bringing to our attention the real ugliness of evil which has hitherto been masked in the dazzling brightness of its author. It is Sin, who, following her nature, disobeys the injunction of God by opening the gates of hell.

The journey of Satan through Chaos (as the battered voyager swims into the calm and light which radiate from ordered nature) and the description of the realm of the uncreated and of the old anarch who personifies its blind confusion conclude Book II (11. 890 ff.).

BOOK III

The change of scene to heaven is introduced by a new invocation—the much-discussed prayer to Light (11. 1–55).[46] In what need not necessarily be read as Milton's own personal utterance,[47] the epic speaker emphasizes his loss of physical sight, grouping himself with those other prophets of antiquity—Thamyris, Maemonides, Tiresias, and Phineus—who, though "outward blind," saw

---

[45] See Joseph Summers' excellent treatment of this episode in *The Muse's Method*, pp. 39–55.

[46] For detailed discussion, see William B. Hunter, Jr., "The Meaning of 'Holy Light' in *Paradise Lost* III"; and Merritt Y. Hughes, "Milton and the Symbol of Light," *SEL*, IV (1964), 1–33.

[47] Readers will recognize, however, that the pathos of blindness, the consoling love of beauty, the thirst for fame, and the consciousness of inward vision constitute lyric threads interweaving themselves with the objective narrative.

deeply into the secret nature of things. Lamenting "wisdom at one entrance quite shut out" (he is cut off from all the avenues of knowledge open to those who can see), the speaker comes to "see" that his handicap is a kind of advantage, for it has sharpened the brilliance of his "inner light," the insight he has into the ways of the universe. Although he has lost the vision of an orderly and outward paradise, the speaker has, given the terms in which the inner vision is described (e.g., "irradiates," "plant"), learned to see with the inner illumination of those who have realized the paradise within.[48]

The celestial dialogue which follows (11. 56–415) is an exposition, dignified but cold, of the theological scheme. With such purely didactic material, Milton, as a poet, can do little. He is careful to emphasize what God is *not* in this passage; above all, he is not another being as Satan is. He is the total of Moral Law, the Intelligence which creates all things, Reason, and Primal Energy. And heaven is *not* simply the inverse of hell. God is not an orator who needs to persuade; his is simply the voice of Moral Law proclaiming what it is. Irene Samuel has observed that God's voice "has offended readers because they assume that the 'I' who speaks is or should be a person like other persons. The flat statement of fact, past, present, and future, the calm analysis and judgment of deeds and principles—these naturally strike the ear that has heard Satan's ringing utterance as cold and impersonal."[49] What some readers dislike in the flatness of God's pronouncements is exactly right in this situation. It is the Son, however, who supplies the drama in the episode, for it is He who acts as foil for the Father; after God's statements of man's free will, his ultimate fall, His justice, and the necessity of redemption, the Son's love and compassion contrast and are enhanced by the passionlessness of the Father's utterances. Following God's pronouncements and the angelic exaltation as the Son prophesies His triumph over death, Milton turns from the matter of divine decrees to the angelic song of worship (11. 372 ff.), emphasizing the Son's sacrifice as an example of "Love nowhere to be found less than Divine."

As the scene changes to refocus on Satan, alighting on the

---

[48] See Ferry's sensitive reading, *Milton's Epic Voice*, pp. 20–37.
[49] "The Dialogue in Heaven," p. 603.

convex of the world and beholding for the first time the beauties of the earthly garden (11. 416 ff.), the epic signals a definite change in moral direction by employing once again the long Miltonic simile (11. 431–36). The place where Satan finds himself was later to become the traditional Limbo, the Paradise of Fools, peopled by figures who typify the various satanic qualities—viz., "bluster and disguise," pride, vanity, and spiritual emptiness.[50] To be clustered on this windy outer shell of the universe were the progeny of the giants of the world, the builders of the Tower of Babel, and the foolish suicides who thought themselves divine.

At a distance Satan is permitted a vision of angels ascending and descending from the Gate of Heaven via Jacob's Ladder, the stair often identified symbolically as the link which, like the golden chain of Zeus, binds the universe together. Standing on the lowest stair, Satan "looks down with wonder" on the universe beneath him, surveying with one great sweep the beauty of its order and harmony. Sighting the archangel Uriel, Satan hypocritically assumes the role of a good angel, eager to know of God's work and especially desirous of knowing what orb in which the newest creature, man, dwells. Uriel answers honestly, for his is not the power to penetrate Satan's disguise, and after he points out the direction to paradise, Satan, coasting to earth, comes to rest on Niphates' top, the mountain later to be the site of Satan's vain temptation of Christ.

BOOK IV

The opening scene, with Satan standing torn by inward passion on the top of Mount Niphates, brings us again into the realm of drama. The remorseful soliloquy which follows (11. 32 ff.) represents a reaction from the outward confidence which Satan has assumed before his host, a revelation of the hell within his soul.[51] He now experiences the bitterer aspect of the truth of his own principle that "the mind is its own place." The conclusion is a new

[50] See F. L. Huntley, "A Justification of Milton's 'Paradise of Fools,'" *ELH*, XXI (1954), 107–13.
[51] See Ernest Schanzer, "Milton's Hell Revisited," *UTQ*, XXIV (1955), 136–45.

resolve to accept evil for his good. The disfiguring of his countenance, which results from his inward struggle and causes the angel
to recognize him as one of the fallen spirits, is a step in the
progressive change of his appearance carefully marked by Milton
as evidence of the manner in which the soul transforms the body
for better or for worse to its own essence (see *Comus*, ll. 453–75).

Finally Milton comes to describe the Garden of Eden (ll.
208 ff.), a geographical place we as readers have never known and
will never know, and a place and spiritual condition now forever
closed to Satan. Having delayed his description until Book IV and
having preceded it with a vision of hell and a didactic statment of
True Knowledge, Milton now turns to the central level on which
the drama of man will be played. In his description of Eden as this
"heaven on Earth," Milton emphasizes the variety in order characteristic of the place, and brings to bear a wealth of comparison
from his classical and romantic reading. He calls Eden the archetype
on which all future fabled gardens will depend. The picture of our
first parents in their naked majesty and beauty, surrounded by the
abundant delights of paradise, is in accordance with the ornate
traditions of Renaissance literature and art. An instinctive emotion
of admiration and pity—the momentary assertion of his angelic
nature—wells up in Satan, immediately to be checked by the recollection of his cruel purpose (ll. 358 ff.). It is thus that he stultifies
his better impulses and prepares himself to do what else, though
damned, he would abhor.

The first words which we hear Adam speak (ll. 411 ff.) are
appropriately ones of gratitude, the next are to recall the prohibition,
the pledge of their obedience and the symbol of their moral nature.
Eve, in a significant narrative of her first experiences (ll. 440 ff.),
reveals the sweet simplicity and frankness of her soul in innocence
and the intensity of her love. The incident serves not to suggest
Eve's weakness, nor is it a foreshadowing of the Fall; it is in
counterpoint to it as an example of how growth is possible in
paradise. The perfection of Adam and Eve is not a static condition
but a dynamic one. Eve relates her first moments honestly to Adam
(her superior on the scale of being) and indicates that she now
knows the proper moral lesson to be drawn from an incident which
may have been dangerous, but was not:

> How beauty is excell'd by manly grace
> And wisdom, which alone is truly fair.
>
> (11. 490–91)

Faced with the moral choice between her beauty and Adam's wisdom, she chooses correctly. The incident, then, may be seen to strengthen the bond between the couple, not to weaken it.[52]

Satan, who had been listening to the conversation between the two, now speaks again (11. 505 ff.); his dominant impulse is no longer pity but the more ignoble one of envy. He anticipates the arguments of skepticism regarding the command which he is later to use to Eve and which she in turn is to communicate to Adam. The warning by Uriel of the angelic guard is followed by Eve's palinode about how earthly glories are magnified by Adam's relationship to them and to her, and this is followed by Eve's questions about the night, stars, and heavenly economy. Again she directs her query to Adam, and she receives the correct answer; and again the bond between the two is strengthened, not weakened. Adam and Eve then retire to their nuptial bower (11. 610 ff.). It is in accord both with tradition and with the special purpose of motivating the subsequent action of the poem that the pair is represented primarily as lovers. Milton takes the occasion (11. 736 ff.) to exalt the ideal domestic relationship of man and woman in both its physical and its spiritual aspects and to denounce the false conception of chivalric love, which his observation has taught him to be too often the mask of corruption. True love exists only in marriage, and it is founded not in an unsound exaltation of woman but in mutual esteem, with rational recognition of the superior dignity and authority of man. The hard saying, "Hee for God only, shee for God in him," implies a natural hierarchy of existence on earth, corresponding to that which Satan has attempted to break down in heaven. But Eve, like the angels, while looking to her lord for interpretation of God's will and her own duty, has also like them an independent relation to and revelation of the divine. To Milton all this was beautiful and right.

[52] Of course, this view (offered by Stanley Fish in *Surprised by Sin*), directly contradicts the interpretations of Arnold Stein in *Answerable Style*, Millicent Bell in "The Fallacy of the Fall in *Paradise Lost*," and E. M. W. Tillyard in *Studies in Milton*.

The angels now mount guard with military precision (11. 776 ff.) and encounter Satan, "his lustre visibly impair'd" (1. 850). His uneasy shuffling with truth is contrasted with the clear and righteous certainty of the obedient ministers of heaven. The portent of the scales of Justice, adapted from the *Iliad*, affords the usual striking conclusion of the book.

BOOK V

Satan's first approach to Eve is made through her unconscious self in sleep. She wakes still troubled with her dream of sin and receives from Adam a lesson in the accepted psychology of Milton's time (11. 95 ff.).[53] Her comfort is his wise pronouncement that involuntary motions of evil in the mind, when unapproved by the will, leave no spot or blame behind. Like several earlier incidents, the episode of the dream should be read in counterpoint to the Fall, not as a foreshadowing of it. The morning prayer which follows (11. 153 ff.), fervid and spontaneous, needing no set form, no temple, no musical accompaniment, is a magnificent descant on the great theme "The Heavens declare the glory of God." Its "various style," apparent in its irregular movements, is the ideal analogue to the perfection of the singers.[54] This, far more than his metrical paraphrases, is Milton's true poetic version of the Psalms, and it shows how deeply he had entered into the majesty of Hebraic religious feeling. As if in answer to their invocation God sends Raphael (literally, "medicine of God"), the companionable angel, to warn and instruct them in their need. His coming is made the occasion for a discussion of the angelic nature and its relation to the human (11. 404 ff.).[55] The question whether Raphael can partake of human food leads to the explanation that all being is one uniform scale, the higher members differing from the lower only in degree. Thus the angels have, like man, a material body and

[53] See William B. Hunter, Jr., "Prophetic Dreams and Visions in *Paradise Lost*."

[54] See Summers' excellent reading of 11. 153–208, *The Muse's Method*, pp. 75–84.

[55] See Walter Clyde Curry, "Milton's Scale of Nature," *Milton's Ontology*, pp. 158–82.

all functions analogous to his, though more refined. Milton is expressing in this curious passage two profound anti-medieval convictions which constitute the basis of his thought: the metaphysical idea that matter is real and that there is no sharp distinction between spirit and matter, the one passing insensibly into the other; and the ethical inference that the natural functions of the body are not something shameful and unworthy. The angel passes on to a new affirmation of the freedom of the will (11. 519 ff.) and then to his long narrative of the revolt and fall of Lucifer (11. 563 ff.). This discourse, which corresponds in the epic structure to the relation of Odysseus to the king of the Phaeacians and of Aeneas to Dido, besides completing the story, serves to put Adam in possession of all the information necessary for victory in his coming trial. Knowledge, to Milton, is the best weapon against sin. The philosophic assumption which underlies the narrative—and indeed Milton's whole conception of his poem—is given in lines 536–76. Spiritual facts can only so be represented to human sense, but there is also perhaps a real analogy between earth and heaven, the former being, according to the Platonic doctrine of ideas, an imperfect replica of the latter, and this analogy justifies the phrasing of divine events in material terms.[56] Following God's announcement of the Son's elevation, Satan initially defected from the angelic forces. That night, the dazzling figure of Sin, sprung full-grown from Satan's head (an event narrated in Book II), won over one-third of the loyal angels to the side of the apostate angel of the north. One, however, refused to join Satan; the incident of Abdiel (11. 803 ff.), concluded in the next book, reveals Milton's lofty conception of the moral courage which enables the individual to stand alone in his convictions against the world.

BOOK VI

Raphael's narrative continues with the war in heaven, recording that on the first day of battle Satan was struck both by Abdiel and Michael and that the opposing forces fought to a draw. The

---

[56] See William G. Madsen, "Earth the Shadow of Heaven: Typological Symbolism in *Paradise Lost*," PMLA, LXXV (1960), 519–26.

recounting of the second day's battle contains the much maligned episode of the invention and first use of artillery; this should be considered not as an isolated piece of sensationalism but as a necessary completion of the idea of the book. The technical evolutions which attend the firing of the cannon are drawn from military textbooks which Milton had attentively studied and serve to give a representative and contemporary aspect to the whole.[57] That Satan's mind is dominated by and limited to the material—as opposed to the spiritual—should now be obvious. The second day's victory goes, with the aid of gunpowder, to the Satanic forces. Finally, on the third day (11. 628 ff.), Milton converts the conflict into a primitive battle of the Titans; the armies desert their discipline and, abandoning arms, hurl confusedly at each other whatever crude missiles come to hand. He intends to suggest that the last end of war is like its beginning—bestial, anarchic, inconclusive. The utmost refinements of scientific slaughter are but a mask of chaos and can only end in disruption of the orderly civilization of which they are the product. The significance of the account is definitely indicated at the close of the book (11. 680 ff.), when the Almighty, beholding the confusion, declares:

> War wearied hath perform'd what War can do,
> And to disorder'd rage let loose the reins,
> With Mountains as with Weapons arm'd, which makes
> Wild work in Heav'n, and dangerous to the main.
>
> (11. 695–98)

He sends forth the Son in majesty to put an end at once to evil and to strife.

Dr. Johnson's verdict that the "confusion of spirit and matter which pervades the whole narration of the war of Heaven fills it with incongruity"[58] is true, for, as Arnold Stein has pointed out, Satan's basic error may be seen in his particular confusion of spirit and matter, or more precisely, in his attempt to usurp spirit by means of matter.[59] The whole episode, whose flytings often approach

---

[57] See James Holly Hanford, "Milton and the Art of War."

[58] "Milton," *Lives of the Poets*, ed. George Birkbeck Hill (New York, 1957), I, 185.

[59] "Milton's War in Heaven—An Extended Metaphor," *ELH*, XVIII (1951), 201–20.

epic farce, is a burlesque on any materialistic concept of might. Viewed in this way, Satan's invention of gunpowder and artillery is a symbolic act, an achievement of Satan's mastery over the material, the undisciplined act of a mind which recognizes no values outside the self and which asserts materialistic values of might. The punishment he receives is an appropriate one: he and his men descend the scale of being, becoming less spiritual (intellectual) and more material. They are sent to the place which is a direct analogue of their spiritual condition.

BOOK VII

A new invocation to Urania (11. 1–39), possibly containing personal allusions to the poet's isolation in the alien and hostile society of the Restoration,[60] introduces an account of the creation. This theme Milton pursues with eagerness after the general precedent of such independent Biblical poems as Du Bartas' *La Semaine* and Tasso's *Il Mondo Creato*.[61] Adam frames a modest request for the story (11. 70 ff.), and the angel (Raphael), in granting it, suggests the true object of such knowledge

> To glorify the Maker and infer
> Thee also happier,
>
> (11. 116–17)

forewarning him against vain exploration of the secret things of God. It was in such a spirit that Milton himself taught in his school the natural science of the day. The ornate and majestic paraphrase of Genesis which follows is indeed a paean of created nature and its great Author. Many phrases of the Scriptural original

---

[60] See the two arguments over the possible autobiographical references to the Restoration: McColley, *"Paradise Lost": An Account*, pp. 300–01, and J. B. Broadbent, "Links Between Poetry and Prose in Milton," *E&S*, XXXVII (1956), 49–62.

[61] For a discussion of the complex origins of Milton's account of the creation, see below, pp. 186–95. See also George W. Whiting, "The Golden Compasses in *Paradise Lost*," *N&Q*, CLXXII (1937), 294–95; and Arnold Williams, "The Work of the Days," *The Common Expositor* (Chapel Hill, 1948), pp. 40–65.

are preserved intact but a wealth of detail is added. The poet enumerates the tribes of fishes, birds, and animals with an appropriate sense of their marvelous variety. The creation of man himself is more briefly handled. When the six days' labor is completed the angels sing a psalm of gratitude; nor are they silent through the long Sabbath day of rest. The purpose of their song (11. 602 ff) suggests the significance of this book (which comes after the narrative of celestial war) in Milton's larger thought: the active formation of good follows the destruction of evil in the natural order of the universe. God is even greater in His return from this victory over inchoate matter than He was in His triumph after the defeat of the angels.

> . . . To create
> Is greater than created to destroy.
>
> (11. 606–07)

The idea of the superiority of the works of peace is one of Milton's noblest convictions. It lies at the heart not only of this portion of *Paradise Lost* but of the sonnets to Cromwell and Fairfax, and it determined in no small degree the character of his own zealous activity in the Commonwealth.

BOOK VIII

Instructed regarding the origin of evil, warned by an example of the consequences of disobedience, and taught to contemplate the wonders of created nature, Adam now receives further lessons on no less vital points. His questions concerning the construction of the universe (11. 15 ff.), unlike his inquiries hitherto, trespass dangerously near the boundary which divides legitimate curiosity from veritable prying into matters which are no concern of man. The angel perhaps detects in Adam's suggestion that there is a disproportion in God's creation a tendency to pick flaws in—rather than to admire—the scheme of things. He throws out a hint of the Copernican system in partial solution of these human doubts (11. 122 ff.) but quickly turns to draw the lesson:

> Solicit not thy thoughts with matters hid
>
> . . . .
>
> . . . Be lowly wise:
>
> Think only what concerns thee and thy being.
>
> (11. 167, 173–74)

Adam is thus warned against the folly and the danger of random speculation and taught to focus his attention on such studies as have a direct bearing on the practical art of righteous living.

Adam's narrative of his first moments (11. 250 ff.), corresponding to Eve's in Book IV, is exquisite in itself and profound. The quick instinctive motion of his upward spring is the symbol of his aspiration heavenward. His first moment of consciousness is one of physical self-survey. Then he turns to inquire his origin, arriving by natural reason at the idea of a divine author with attributes of goodness and of power. Having gone thus far on his search unaided he is vouchsafed a revelation, and awakening from his trance he receives the prohibition (11. 316 ff.)—a kind of categorical imperative which confirms him as a religious and moral being.

His next instinct (11. 357 ff.) is for some human companionship. By whimsically pretending to argue him out of it, the Deity brings home the lesson that he is a man and not a brute. He then receives God's last best gift, accepted with an outburst of passionate gratitude and a superb flash of insight into the true relations of man and woman (11. 491–99). The recalling of this episode leads Adam to confess his own illusions about Eve and her influence over him. That he has controlled his illusion is obvious in his frequent use of "seems"; that he will probably not allow her to dominate him now that he has "confessed" and recognized the danger from the direction of passion may be the significance of the episode.[62] Adam has turned upward along the scale for information and enlightenment, and the angel, quick to see that Adam's illusion might master him, asserts the supremacy of the will and warns Adam that he must at all costs maintain self-mastery in passion (11. 561 ff.). As Adam reveals that he knows what is right,

[62] See Arnold Stein's discussion, *Answerable Style*, pp. 81 ff.; cf. that of Fish in *Surprised by Sin*, pp. 228 ff.

. . . Yet still free
Approve the best, and follow what I approve
(11. 610–11)

he asks Raphael about love in heaven. Falling again into his more
genial mood, the angel tells (11. 618 ff.) how angels love—a strange
and wonderful exposition similar in philosophic purport to the
account in Book V of the relations of human and angelic activities
in matters of digestion.

BOOK IX

The moment of a great change in the tone of the narrative is
marked by a meditative introduction (11. 1–47) in which the poet
surveys his theme and acclaims it, in its spiritual character, not less
but more heroic than those of the great epics of antiquity which
dealt with wars and outward struggle. Milton has evidently seriously
considered the question whether his subject, with its novelty of an
unhappy outcome, can properly be brought into conformity with
the established epic type. He has also weighed the other assumptions
against him: his four and forty degrees of northern latitude, the
common notion that genius no longer flourishes in a senile world,
his own advancing age. He is confident, however, of the wisdom of
his choice, and he refers all to the aid of his celestial patroness.

The imaginative sweep which comes and goes with Satan prevails again in the description of his sevenfold encircling of the
world (11. 62 ff.). There is more bitterness and more despair in
the soliloquy which precedes his imbruting himself within the serpent, and it is his own word which expounds the symbolism of
the act.

The coming of morning brings a new dialogue between Adam
and Eve. (11. 192 ff.). The latter, with an impulse housewifely but
ultimately unfortunate, proposes a brief separation that they may
work at their gardening without the interruptions of affectionate
discourse. Adam, in his superior wisdom, deprecates such hyper-
conscientiousness and warns her of the danger in exposing herself

unprotected to the assault of the tempter. Such an apparent slighting of her firmness hurts Eve's feelings and brings the first small cloud upon the domestic horizon. It is not quite clear whether the poet intended Adam's attitude throughout this dialogue to be regarded as irreproachable and Eve's alone the cause of trouble. Eve apparently has much the best of the argument. She criticizes, as Milton himself would have done, the naive idea that the mere temptation leaves a stain of dishonor on the soul, and she employs the very language of *Areopagitica* in her denunciation of a fugitive and cloistered virtue unexercised and unbreathed (11. 322–41). The trouble is, of course, that creatures of perfection need not seek trials to purify them, and that in separating herself from Adam she leaves behind a source of wisdom to which she could have turned for enlightenment. There is no clear indication that the division of labor is a step which must precede the Fall; that it is that step does not endow it with particular significance. Adam himself, in his refusal to coerce her will (11. 342 ff.), acts in the spirit of love and trust, reminding her that happiness and freedom depend upon her obedience. With or without the company of Adam, if she remain obedient, she need have no fears.

The parting of Adam and his spouse is full of tender loveliness, and classical mythology is ransacked for images wherewith to express Eve's beauty. Satan, watching her, is like an Iago plotting the ruin of Desdemona or even more exactly like another Lovelace preparing for what is to all intents and purposes a seduction. His crafty approach through the insidious means of flattery is subtly conceived (11. 494 ff.). Eve is deluded in her weakness; but once confronted by the tree of prohibition, she recognizes clearly the guilt involved. This is Milton's modification or interpretation of the Biblical statement, "The woman was deceived." He could not have her sin unconsciously. To overcome her hesitation Satan musters all his eloquence, bursting forth without exordium, like some ancient orator—Cicero, for example, in his first oration against Cataline. He employs all the arguments which skepticism can suggest against God's purposefully arbitrary and irrational-seeming command and, with the cooperating aid of mere physical appetite at the noontide hour, prevails. Eve unconsciously falls into the trap of giving her

Law (i.e., Reason) to God, of attempting to argue the reasonableness of a test of Faith.[63] Her disobedience is followed by an unnatural exhilaration as of wine. She exhibits new and unworthy motives of selfishness and jealousy in thinking what course she shall pursue with Adam, and she appears before him with a lying word upon her lips.

The fall of Adam himself (11. 896 ff.) is motivated by passion; at least it is that which prompts his immediate resolve. His understanding, he thinks, has enabled him to penetrate the deceit, as Eve with her feebler mentality did not. He thinks his alternatives are life with Eve and death, or life without Eve. He too has failed the test of Faith, for in thinking that he understands the situation, he creates a closed argument in which he fails to consider the possibility of throwing himself upon God's mercy at that moment.[64] He soon falls under the influence of a reasoning as false as hers and experiences afterward the same transient delight in sin.

The representation is colored by the Greek idea of hybris—the intoxication of the mind which afflicts the sinner and leads him to fancy himself the equal of the gods. A new element, moreover, has entered his relations with his mate—the element of lust, in contrast with the former innocence and purity of their married love (11. 1034 ff.). Disillusionment promptly follows and bitter recrimination. The fruits of the tree are indeed new knowledge, but a knowledge which is really sophistication leading to self-contempt and shame.

In Milton's treatment of this, the central incident of his poem, there are—besides its dramatic vividness and keen psychology—many essential points of moral and theological doctrine. He explains in the *De Doctrina Christiana* that the fall of our first parents, properly considered, was a transgression of the whole law, all sins being included in the act—unbelief, ingratitude, disobedience, gluttony; in the man, excessive uxoriousness; in the woman, a want of proper regard for her husband, parricide, theft, invasion of the rights of others, sacrilege, deceit, fraud in the means employed to attain the object, pride, and arrogance. The eating of the fruit, therefore,

---

[63] As Stanley Fish has argued, "Eve need not be won by reasons, merely won to reason" (*Surprised by Sin*, p. 254).
[64] *Ibid.*, pp. 261–72.

becomes a type or even a symbol of sin. Adam's act was to Milton in no sense noble or heroic. It was, indeed, less pardonable than Eve's in proportion to his superior intelligence and moral strength. The book, as a whole, displays Milton's unique power of analysis of the ways of evil in the soul.

BOOK X

The account of the judgment (11. 103 ff.) proceeds in strict accord with the Scriptural narrative in Genesis 3, no detail being omitted. The allegory of Sin and Death is completed as the hideous pair ascend to earth and prepare to set their seal of mastery upon created nature (11. 229 ff.). Satan returns to proclaim the triumph of his epic adventure (11. 410 ff.)—a triumph which is turned to bitterness by the metamorphosis of the demons into serpents and of their shout of applause into a hiss, the sign of scorn. This degradation of their forms is the consequence and outward symbol of the degradation of their souls. A similar though less complete alteration is carried out by angels in obedience to divine command in the realm of physical nature, now no longer pure (11. 641 ff.). The passage illustrates the habit of mingling science and theology which Milton inherited from medieval thought.

A more human note is struck in the Job-like lament of Adam (11. 720 ff.), which is reminiscent also of the baffled speculations of Hamlet on life and death. A fine contrast not altogether favorable to the man is drawn between the remorse of Adam and Eve. She is more concerned with his state than with her own. He exhibits the brutality of disillusionment, and Milton resorts to Euripides and Ariosto[65] for bitter reflections on the course of the eternal feminine, but Adam is ultimately won by the helpless pathos of her appeal. She exhibits a fertile but unsound ingenuity in her suggestion of a way to avoid the doom pronounced upon their offspring with an implication of stoic fortitude which wins Adam's admiration (11. 966 ff.). His own courage returns in the attempt to comfort her,

[65] i.e., *Hippolytus*, 11. 616 ff.; and *Orlando Furioso*, XXVII, 117, 119 120.

and the book ends—in contrast to the ending of Book IX—with a cessation of mutual blame and an access of sincere repentance.

BOOK XI

Further celestial dialogue (11. 1–125) prepares for the decree of banishment, to be pronounced, with an accompanying remission of the penalty of immediate death, by Michael, the minister of God's justice.

Adam has a presentiment of some further change through the mute signs of nature (11. 193 ff.). Eve, with pathetic irony, is made to express her willingness to submit to any fate in this beloved home of paradise. At the news that they must leave forthwith, Adam is struck dumb, and it is Eve who utters the first spontaneous lament (11. 268 ff.). Her strong instinctive love of the flowers that she has tended and of the nuptial bower that she has adorned is rudely violated. The angel gently reminds her that her going is not lonely. Then Adam expresses his profounder fear of a break in his communion with the Divine (11. 296 ff.). To reassure him of the continued presence of God with him and his offspring and to discipline his soul in patience, Michael leads him to a lofty hill and begins a visionary revelation of the future of the race. This prophecy (11. 429 ff.), which corresponds to the Sibyl's predictions in the sixth book of the *Aeneid* of the course of Roman history, serves to round out the larger meaning of Milton's epic by displaying the operation of hereditary sin consequent upon Adam's act. At the same time it illustrates the manner in which God's love contends with the waywardness of man until in the process of time His crowning purpose, of humanity's salvation through the sacrifice of Christ, is fulfilled. The passage, which extends through the remainder of Book XI and the greater part of Book XII, is a marvelous condensation of Hebrew story, comprising grave moral lessons. The first part of the exposition appropriately ends with the Flood and the apparition of the rainbow as the first prefiguring symbol of God's restoring and redeeming grace.[66]

---

[66] See Summers' discussion, *The Muse's Method*, pp. 186–208.

BOOK XII

From this point, the beginning of revelation of a second world, with its higher and more mysterious matter, the angel no longer presents the scenes to Adam's eyes but narrates them to his intelligence. As the events in the history of the chosen people shape themselves, Adam sees more and more clearly the operation of a providential plan. Moses and Joshua are indicated to him as types of Christ (11. 238–48, 310–14). The corruption and dissension which follow the return from captivity with the resultant passing of David's scepter to a stranger are said to be permitted so that the

> Anointed King *Messiah* might be born
> Barr'd of his right.
>
> (11. 359–60)

At the angel's mention of the virgin birth of Christ, the meaning of the mysterious words of the Deity is revealed, and Adam bursts forth in joy (11. 375 ff.).

The fuller story of Christ's sacrifice (11. 386 ff.), his resurrection, his triumph over Satan, his restoration of mankind to bliss leaves the listener in doubt whether he should repent him of his sin, or rejoice:[67]

> Much more, that much more good thereof shall spring.

[67] An interesting controversy was started by John Erskine's suggestion that Milton changed his theological attitude toward the Fall and its results before he reached the conclusion of his poem ("The Theme of Death in *Paradise Lost*," *PMLA*, XXXII [1917,] 573–82). That his conception of it as a mingled tragedy and blessing is in perfect accord with Christian tradition was shown by Cecil A. Moore ("The Conclusion of *Paradise Lost*," *PMLA*, XXXVI [1921], 1–34). A. O. Lovejoy ("Milton and the Paradox of the Fortunate Fall") cites Du Bartas, Giles Fletcher, Andreini, patristic writers, and finally a passage in the Roman liturgy for Easter as instances of the recurrent motif, "O felix culpa!" C. A. Patrides ("Adam's 'Happy Fault' and XVIIth Century Apologetics," *Fran S.*, XXIII [1963], 238–43) supplements Lovejoy. St. Augustine gives the paradox a more general form, raising the question whether evil itself may not be a source of good and the Fall therefore a part of God's purpose. The only solution of the intellectual difficulty was, says Lovejoy, to keep the theme of the Fall as a supreme misfortune separate from the theme of its happy consequences through the sacrifice of Christ.

He acknowledges the lesson that man too has his part in the redemption and expresses his resolve to walk henceforth the patient moral way of obedience and slow self-conquest. The angel sets the seal of approval on Adam's new-found wisdom (11. 574 ff.), bidding him add deeds to his knowledge answerable—faith, virtue, patience, temperance, and love, the soul of all the rest. So shall he build a paradise within, far happier than the one he has lost. This is the grand climax of the poem, the spiritual goal of Milton's art.[68] In a brief conclusion (11. 606 ff.) we are brought back again to the specific subject of the loss of Eden. Eve awakes from a gentle dream in which she has received the essential revelation of the great deliverance through her seed. Softened and exalted, she faces a future now no longer terrible. The closing lines describe in terms of mingled hope and sadness the departure of the pair from Eden.

COSMOLOGY AND DOCTRINAL CONTENT

The physical action of *Paradise Lost*, taking place as it does in heaven, earth, hell, and Chaos, obliges Milton to visualize the structure of the universe and to commit himself for imaginative purposes to one of the several astronomical systems which in his day offered themselves as rival explanations of the phenomena. He inevitably adopted the Ptolemaic as it was interpreted in his day—with the earth fixed at the center and the seven planets and the fixed stars revolving in concentric circles about it—as being firmly established in poetic and theological tradition and as better adapted to imaginative representation. With the mathematical detail of this system he was thoroughly familiar, and we know that he taught the elements of astronomical calculation on the Ptolemaic basis in his school, using a revised edition of the medieval textbook by Sacrobosco.[69] But he was familiar also with the principles of the Copernican system and with the discoveries which had followed the invention of the telescope.

---

[68] See Louis Martz, *The Paradise Within*.

[69] Allan H. Gilbert, "Milton's Textbook of Astronomy," *PMLA*, XXXVIII (1923), 297–307.

As a Platonist, a student of mathematics, and a friend of Galileo's, he could not escape being interested in these exciting issues. The astronomical dialogue in Book VIII not only raises the fundamental question of the celestial motions but also suggests the related hypotheses of a plurality of worlds:

> For such vast room in Nature unpossest
> By living Soul . . .
> . . . is obvious to dispute.
>
> (11. 153–54, 158)

The problem of Milton's own attitude and of the sources and extent of his knowledge has been much discussed. The arguments he uses are seventeenth-century commonplaces, many of them being found in Galileo's *Diologus*, which one would think Milton likely to have read. But a strong case has been made by Grant McColley for his direct indebtedness to three English pamphlets of his own time: Bishop Wilkins' *The Discovery of a New World* and the *Discourse That the Earth May Be a Planet*, published together in 1640, and Alexander Ross's *The New Planet No Planet* (1646). Wilkins states the new ideas in language strikingly similar to Milton's own. Ross, in his refutation, apparently suggested some of the material employed by the angel to show Adam the futility of all astronomical hypotheses. The purpose of the dialogue, according to McColley, is simply to present the moot points advanced by Wilkins as England's most vigorous exponent of the "new philosophy" and to evaluate cosmological speculation in general, rather than in any real sense to weigh the rival theories.[70] There is a certain legacy from Bacon in Milton's insistence on the fruitlessness of mere speculation, and the idea that unrestrained curiosity in God's secrets may be a dangerous symptom of irreverence and pride is a traditional one which the poet was bound to incorporate in a story of the fall of man.

The greatest effect of Milton's contact with the new astronomy was the immense stimulus which it gave to his imagination. Marjorie Nicolson[71] believes that it was not books but the actual experience

[70] See Grant McColley, "Milton's Dialogue on Astronomy: The Principal Immediate Sources," *PMLA*, LII (1937), 728–62; and Kester Svendsen, *Milton and Science*.

[71] "Milton and the Telescope," *ELH*, II (1935), 1–32.

of celestial observation which significantly colored his scientific interests and enabled him to move in worlds of space hitherto unrealized. Telescopes were common in Milton's time both in Italy and in England. Milton's references to the Italian "optic glass" and the wonders revealed by it have an unmistakably firsthand character.[72] The poet mentions the four outstanding discoveries of Galileo: sun spots,[73] the true nature of the Milky Way,[74] the topographical features of the moon,[75] and—most important of all—the planets or moons of Jupiter.[76] A "sense of cosmic perspective," writes Nicolson, "is as characteristic of Milton as is the so-called 'Miltonic style'—for which, indeed, it is in part responsible; yet it is also characteristic of his generation. Shakespeare . . . lived in a world of time, Milton in a universe of space. . . ."[77] Space dominates *Paradise Lost:*

> We begin to perceive it first through the eyes of Satan as, astounded and momentarily appalled, he gazes into the Chaos which opens beyond the gates of Hell. . . . We see it through the eyes of God as he "bent down his eye/His own works and their works at once to view," and saw in one glance the sanctities of Heaven close about him, the "Happy Garden" upon earth, "Hell and the Gulf between. . . ." We realize it again in the further voyages of Satan—voyages, one may suspect, which were inherited from and which were to influence that group of "voyages to the moon" in which the seventeenth century delighted.[78]

It is easy to follow Nicolson in her belief that all this owes much to the sudden enlargement of the seventeenth century through the invention of the telescope and that the imaginative interest in the universe, so characteristic of Milton's later as distinguished from his

[72] See *PL*, I, 287–91; III, 588–90; V, 261–63; *PR*, IV, 40–42, 56–57.
[73] *PL*, III, 588–90.
[74] *Ibid.*, VII, 577–81.
[75] *Ibid.*, I, 290–91.
[76] *Ibid.*, VIII, 148–52.
[77] Nicolson, "Milton and the Telescope," pp. 17–21. See also Jackson I. Cope, "Time and Space as Miltonic Symbol," *ELH*, XXVI (1959), 497–513; and the appropriate sections of M. M. Mahood, *Poetry and Humanism*, and MacCaffrey, *Paradise Lost as "Myth."*
[78] "Milton and the Telescope," pp. 21–23.

earlier work, is a heritage of the new astronomy. To this latter learning, however, he refused to commit himself and he rejected it as the cosmological basis for his poem. We must not, however, forget that Dante was able to invest his medieval universe with an equal grandeur.

For the material data which Milton found necessary to his representation of heaven, earth, and hell he resorted to all manner of sources and to his own invention, employing Scriptural suggestions wherever possible and taking pains to add nothing which would be directly contradictory to Holy Writ. It is not to be thought that he offered such details as the causeway from hell to earth, the chain by which the visible universe depended from heaven, or the spheres themselves which encircled the earth and carried the planets and the fixed stars, as obligatory to the understanding. They were simply imaginative representations which have a theological rather than a scientific validity. Sometimes he is deliberately vague, as when he says that heaven is "undertermin'd square or round" (II, 1048. Often his concrete detail or measurement is useful only for the moment and defies adoption into the general scheme, as where he says that the distance from hell to heaven was three times the distance from the center of the earth to the pole of the uttermost encircling sphere (I, 73–74).

For these reasons it is misleading to make a detailed plan for Milton's universe, though many have been offered. The diagram given on page 187 represents only his fundamental conceptions, which are as follows.

Infinite space is thought of as originally divided into two parts: heaven above, also called the Empyraean, and Chaos or uncreated matter beneath. Within this Chaos God "puts forth his virtue" and builds first hell at the bottom, as a receptacle for the falling angels, and then the visible universe, usually referred to as "the World," as a home for man. The latter consists of the fixed earth as a center, with a shell of concentric spheres moving about it at varying rates of speed. Beyond this shell, of course, is Chaos. The spheres themselves are ten in number. The first seven, beginning with the one nearest the earth, carry the planets (including the sun and the moon) and are named from them. This is their order: the moon, Mercury, Venus, the sun, Mars, Jupiter, and Saturn. The eighth,

HEAVEN OR THE EMPYRAEAN

Chaos

Chaos

The Created Universe

EARTH

Sphere of the Moon
Sphere of Mercury
Sphere of Venus
Sphere of the Sun
Sphere of Mars
Sphere of Jupiter
Sphere of Saturn
Sphere of the Fixed Stars
Crystalline Sphere
Primum Mobile

Outside Shell

Chaos

Chaos

HELL

A Diagram of Milton's Universe

properly designated the Coelum Stellatum, carries all the fixed stars. The ninth, the Crystalline, contains no bodies. Outside that shell is an ocean (III, 482). The tenth is the Primum Mobile or, in Milton's expression, "the first moved." Its function is to impart motion to the rest. Milton appears to have thought of the whole apparatus as encased in a hard, opaque, protective shell which was immovable.[79] He uses the term "firmament" for the whole space of "elemental air" between earth and the watery Crystalline heaven; it would comprise all the first eight spheres, which are evidently not spheres in any material sense.

Milton's system, as thus outlined, parallels in general that of Dante, and Milton may be said to have grasped his predecessor's intentions although there are some notable points of divergence.[80] In the first place, Dante locates hell in the center of the earth itself. Milton, in adopting the other alternative provided by theological tradition, remarks (Argument, Book I) that hell is "describ'd here, *not in the Centre* (for Heaven and Earth may be suppos'd as yet not made, certainly not yet accurst) *but in place of utter darkness, fitliest call'd* Chaos." He defends this location also on the same grounds and with reference to the opinion of Chrysostom and Luther in the *De Doctrina Christiana* (Book I, Chapter 33). In *Paradise Lost* (XII, 224), however, he refers casually to a bituminous pit in Babylonia as "the mouth of Hell." Dante, secondly, makes only nine spheres, omitting the Crystalline or identifying it with the Primum Mobile. These are, moreover, with him actual heavens in which the spirits of the blessed appear. His tenth heaven of heavens is the infinite space beyond. In technical astronomical discussions the spheres ranged from nine to eleven in number. Milton, of course, omits all reference to purgatory—with Dante a mountain on the earth opposite to Jerusalem—and he places paradise, which Dante locates on the top of the purgatorial mountain, on the Tigris River in Mesopotamia. At the time of the Flood it was washed away and became a desert island in the Red Sea.

An immense amount of cosmological and other lore is given in *Paradise Lost*; the poem is in this aspect a kind of cyclopedia of

[79] See Allan H. Gilbert, "The Outer Shell of Milton's World," *SP*, XX (1923), 444–47.

[80] For detailed discussion, see Irene Samuel, *Dante and Milton*.

the popular science of Milton's time. The remarkable thing about Milton's comprehensive grasp of human knowledge is the way in which he unifies the whole and subjects it to the service of his philosophy of life. His closest precedent in this respect is Dante, and the general attitude which makes science a part of theology in the broadest sense is medieval.

The following reference (the list might easily be extended) will serve as a guide to Milton's conceptions with regard to the physical construction of the universe:

> hell, II, 570–628
> Chaos, II, 890–967
> the created universe, II, 1034–53; III, 418–735; V, 171–208; VII, 205–547
> heaven, III, 56–79; V, 563–87; VI, *passim*
> the causeway from hell to earth, X, 272–324
> Eden and paradise, IV, 208–87
> physical changes after the Fall, X, 651–714
> the rival astronomical theories, VIII, 15–168
> the scale of nature and the forms of life, V, 469–90; VII, 387–547[81]

Paradise Lost is still more a repository of theological metaphysical, moral, and political doctrine. Milton has himself suggested a classification of this body of ideas and principles in the headings under which he accumulated in his private notebooks the materials of his thought.[82] He has an *Index Theologicus*,[83] an *Index Ethicus*, an *Index Oeconomicus* (i.e., domestic), and an *Index Politicus*. The same fundamental scheme of thought is in his mind when he says in *Areopagitica* that liberty is religious, domestic, and civil. These divisions run into each other, and a completely logical account of the Miltonic system demands some such comprehensive and detailed analysis as is attempted by Denis Saurat in his *Milton: Man and Thinker*. For practical purposes, however, Milton's own simpler

[81] See the numerous articles by McColley, and appropriate sections of the work of Whiting and Curry.

[82] *A Commonplace Book of John Milton*, ed. Alfred J. Horwood (Camden Society, 1876); see also CM, XVIII, 128–227, for the edition by James Holly Hanford, with trans. and notes by Nelson Glenn McCrea.

[83] This portion of Milton's notes is lost.

scheme will serve. Indeed, since he himself endeavored to compre-
hend the whole body of his thinking within the terms of Christianity, his work on the *Christian Doctrine* becomes the best plain
guide to the intellectual fabric of *Paradise Lost* and *Paradise Regained*. It is theological, in that it deals with the nature of God
and his relations to man; it is ethical, economic, and political, in
that it sets forth man's duties in the private, domestic, and civic
spheres—at least in so far as these duties can be formulated from
Holy Writ.

To present here even the main features of Milton's system is
manifestly impossible. It is also unnecessary, as they are stated or
clearly implied in the poem itself. In many instances the doctrinal
expositions in verse follow passages in the *De Doctrina* point by
point.[84] The latter, however, are unmixed with imagery or literary
fiction, and they are elaborate arguments where *Paradise Lost* merely
affirms conclusions. A comparison of the two works is the best
test of what he regarded as matters of faith and what as matters
of the imagination.

Much light is thrown on the degree of literalness with which
the poet took the concrete details of *Paradise Lost* (whether these
details were strictly Biblical or not) by the discussion of the Scriptural representation of God in the *De Doctrina*, Book I, Chapter 2.
He there says that actual knowledge of God passes the comprehension of man; that He is exhibited in Scripture not as He really is
but in such a way as to suit our understandings. It is best, instead
of forming subtle imaginings, to accept His own account of Himself
as if it were the literal truth. "If 'it repented Jehovah that he had
made man,' . . . let us believe that it did repent him, only taking
care to remember that what is called repentance when applied to
God, does not arise from inadvertency, as in men." If He ascribes
to Himself a human image, why should we be afraid to do the
same, understanding thereby "not . . . that God is in fashion like
unto man in all his parts and members, but that as far as we are
concerned to know, he is of that form which he attributes to himself in the sacred writings."[85]

This idea, the so-called theory of accommodation, fitted well with

[84] See the brilliant exposition of Maurice Kelley, *This Great Argument*.
[85] CM, XIV, 33–35, 37.

Milton's Platonism and lent support to his confidence in the authenticity of his own inspiration. He had early conceived of himself as a revealer of truth in the Platonic sense. Poetic myth was the only possible way of representing the ideas to human apprehension, and only the poet-seer who had looked on the face of truth unveiled could so represent them. When Milton undertook to write the epic of the Fall and became thereby a successor—if not a reincarnation—of Moses, he must have taken satisfaction in the thought that the original word itself was but accommodated truth. He could not have missed—and he did not miss—the Platonic suggestions in the Mosaic account of the revelation on the Mount,[86] and he must have made the most of the analogy between that primary revelation and his own experience of immediate inspiration from on high. He, too, had heard the voice of God and was no less than his predecessor the author of divine fictions. His own poetic elaboration of the Biblical story might, therefore, claim a place beside the imagery of Scripture itself as a shadow of reality. But his imagination, however trustworthy, was not free as it would have been on a secular subject. It must only supplement—not contradict—the Biblical data, and it must conform to the framework of a body of reasoned doctrine. We have accordingly in *Paradise Lost* a historical fiction divinely sanctioned, embodying not a fallible philosophy of human origin but the verities of the Christian religion itself.

In its broad features Milton's theology is the historic Catholic system modified by Reformation thinkers, including the fundamental doctrines of the special creation of man, his fall from grace, his salvation through the atoning sacrifice of Christ. The part played by Satan in the temptation, the facts of Christ's incarnation and resurrection, the Last Judgment with the final separation of the

---

[86] For example, Moses' shining face and the veil which he wore when he came before the people. Though Milton nowhere mentions these attributes, he makes Moses speak like a very Plato in the proposed prologue to the drama of the Fall. The connection between the Greek philosopher and the Hebrew prophet was already made in Eusebius' *Praeparatio Evangelorum*, a book which we know Milton to have read. Plato is there said to be a Moses speaking Greek (see Saint-Brisson's translation [Paris, 1846], pp. 129–31). Milton, of course, believed that the Greeks had derived their inklings of Truth from the Hebrews. The whole train of thought which made it possible for him to identify himself imaginatively with Plato, Moses, and whatsoever prophets and bards besides, flowed easily from the philosophy of poetic inspiration embodied in the *Ion*.

damned from the saved—these things are the cornerstones of Milton's religion, as they had been of St. Augustine's and of John Calvin's. He also accepts from traditional theology the idea of the angels as intermediaries between God and man and as appointed guardians of man's welfare. On the other hand, he rejects, along with all the reformed theologians, the special Roman Catholic doctrines of purgatory, the intercession of the saints, the papal authority, besides many practices such as confession. He departs from the Anglican church in abandoning the idea of an ecclesiastical hierarchy and in admitting no prescriptive form of worship.

Less obvious but of equally far-reaching importance are his disagreements with orthodox Calvinism, the accepted theology of the Presbyterian church. The first point is in regard to the doctrine of predestination and free will. Reformation theology generally had always tended to minimize man's part in salvation and to ascribe everything to the grace of God, who had determined from all eternity the role of the damned and the elect. Milton announces with equal vehemence the moral responsibility of the individual. He was enabled to do so by his acceptance of the doctrines of Arminius, who, without abandoning the great Protestant principle that man is dependent in all that concerns his salvation upon the grace of the spirit of God, so modified the rigorous Calvinistic statements regarding predestination, depravity, etc., as to make man responsible for his own damnation.[87] In the Calvinistic theology the decrees of God are absolute; in the Arminian they are conditional. The divine will is still supreme, but its supremacy is moral. God is not more bound to punish than to forgive. He has elected to salvation or reprobation only those whose final faith or disbelief He foresaw. His foreknowledge is certain but it does not necessitate the event. Similarly the atonement, with the Calvinist, was for the elect alone, and for them its working was infallible. It so satisfied divine justice on their behalf that they could not fail to be saved. The Arminian, on the other hand, held that the atonement was universal. It made the salvation of all men possible, the result in each case being conditioned *by faith,* which lay within the will of the individual. So, finally, according to the doctrine of original sin,

----

[87] Patrides, *Christian Tradition,* pp. 191, 194–95.

depravity, for the Calvinist, was complete. It admitted no possibility of spiritual good. Arminianism held that depravity was a bias which left the free will and man responsible for his own destiny through the choice of faith or unbelief. The original and inherited sin is met and neutralized by the free grace of Christ—the second Adam.

That Milton was Arminian rather than Calvinistic may clearly be seen in his definition of all the crucial theological terms which were in controversy. Thus predestination is defined as "the decree whereby God in pity to mankind, through foreseeing that they would fall of their own accord, predestined to eternal salvation those who should believe and continue in the faith." In other words, predestination is conditional upon the will of man.

The principle of moral freedom is central in Milton's theological thought and, as applied to Adam, it is the heart of his justification of the ways of God to man. In the *Areopagitica* Milton complains that those who deny Adam's power of choice between good and evil make him a "mere mechanical Adam" like the figure in the puppet shows; elsewhere in his prose writings he says that to rob a man of his freedom is to impute injustice to God. In addition one of the choruses in *Samson Agonistes* raises the question of God's justice and directly attacks the Calvinist position along the lines held to by Arminius, who contended, as we have seen, that the operation of the divine will was not necessitated from within but conditioned by the belief or unbelief of his creatures:

> Just are the ways of God,
> And justifiable to Men.
>
> . . . .
>
> Yet more there be who doubt his ways not just,
> As to his own edicts, found contradicting.
>
> . . . .
>
> As if they would confine th' interminable,
> And tie him to his own prescript,
> Who made our Laws to bind us, not himself.
>
> (11. 293 ff.)

In *Paradise Lost* the justification of the divine way lies in the representation of Adam as a free agent and in the revelation of the working of God's grace which allows to him and his descendants the opportunity for a new exercise of moral choice and of consequent salvation even after the Fall. Naturally in the poem Milton does not elaborate the theological argument, but he goes out of his way again and again to insist on the fact of Adam's freedom. (See especially *PL*, III, 96 ff., the key passage for an understanding of Milton's theological interpretation of the Fall.) Conversely Milton makes little of the sacrifice of Christ as an atonement for sin. He accepts it as a necessary condition of man's salvation but not as taking the place of man's individual choice of good. Neither personally nor as a part of his system did the idea greatly move or interest him.[88] Thus he was naturally led to treat in *Paradise Regained* of Christ's victory over Satan in the temptation rather than of his crucifixion. Milton underplays the sacrificial value of Christ's example and emphasizes the ethical value of His life.

Closely related to this departure from orthodoxy is his view—expressed in some parts of *Paradise Lost*—of Christ himself as a being divine but distinctly lower than God and of the Holy Ghost as still more inferior in importance. Without entering into intricate theological distinctions we may say that Milton is not an orthodox Trinitarian in the sections where Christ and the Father converse (e.g., Book III). He was a heretic both from the Catholic and from the Calvinistic standpoint; he did not, however, stand alone, for great theologians in this era (e.g., Servetus, Socinus, and Ochino) had advocated similar views. In other places in *Paradise Lost*, however (particularly in Book VII), Milton conceals or modifies his anti-Trinitarian views, portraying Father and Son as inseparable and identical.[89]

One other point remains. It is an essential one in Milton's whole metaphysics. He denied the generally accepted doctrine of creation *ex nihilo:* that God created the world out of nothing. The matter which he reduced to order was as eternal as spirit. It was indeed a part of the substance of God himself. This statement receives explicit expression both in *Paradise Lost* and in the *Chris-*

[88] Maurice Kelley, "The Theological Dogma of *Paradise Lost*, III, 173–202," *PMLA*, LII (1937), 75–79, argues that the doctrinal statements in this passage regarding predestination and its concordance with the mercy, grace, and wisdom of God are precisely in accord with the anti-Calvinistic utterances of *De Doctrina.*

[89] Patrides, *Christian Tradition*, pp. 22 ff.

tian Doctrine. The deep is boundless because God is boundless. It is not, however, vacuous. If it is uncreated it is because God retires from it and puts not forth his virtue, which is free to act or not (*PL*, VII, 168 ff.).[90] Thus Milton obliterates the sharp distinction between matter and spirit and at the same time affirms the reality of both.[91]

We may now turn more specifically to Milton's ethics. His general principles are grounded in the study of ancient ethics, particularly Plato, Aristotle, and the Stoic writers. From them he derived the idea of the conflict of reason and passion in the soul of man and a conviction as to the importance of knowledge as an instrument of virtue. Thus the angel Raphael instructs Adam in all that it is essential for him to know in order to meet temptation successfully. Adam fails when he restricts his intelligence, allowing himself to be blinded to the possibility of divine mercy; his is a false impression of the situation, and he follows the dictates of his own alternatives, which draw him toward Eve. In contrast, Christ, the "better man," foils Satan in *Paradise Regained* by maintaining his faith in God and thus clearly surveying all the enticements which are held out to him, analyzing them Socratically, and detecting their fallaciousness. His discourses are intended as a model for men confronted with a similar series of choices.

If Milton's general conception of man's moral nature is founded on the ethical wisdom of the ancients, it is, however, in Scripture that he finds at once the sanction and the content of human virtue. God is the author of the moral law; duty is the sole daughter of His voice. First given to Adam in the form of an arbitrary command, then to Moses as a set of specific obligations, the law is finally embodied as a spirit in the person of Christ and in that form supplements or supersedes all earlier revelations. It is no longer arbitrary but completely conformable to reason: "God and reason bid the same." It is written not alone in the Book but in the hearts of all believers, and to them is left the problem of its application.

---

[90] Denis Saurat, in his *Man and Thinker*, makes much of this expression as evidence that Milton shared with the Jewish *Zohar* the theory of "creation by retraction." Really the two ideas are quite different. In the *Zohar* God retires from the cosmos, leaving it free; in Milton he retires from Chaos. "Retires," in this case, means merely that he does not exert his power.

[91] See Patrides, *Christian Tradition*, pp. 26–53.

This is what Milton means by the gospel liberty (*De Doctrina Christiana*, Book I, Chapter 28), and it is on this principle of the authority of the individual conscience that he challenges the validity of man-made laws which do not have its sanction.

In the second book of the *De Doctrina* Milton gives a full discussion of the specific duties of man toward God, toward himself, and toward his neighbor, basing his formulation chiefly on the New Testament. Man's duties to himself are temperance, chastity, frugality, industry, fortitude, meekness, veracity, faithfulness, gravity, justice, liberality, gratitude. Chapter XV opens the subject of reciprocal duties, as between parent and child, husband and wife. This includes a discussion of divorce, which falls in Milton's Commonplace Book under the head of *Index Oeconomicus*. There follows a brief chapter on public duties, political and ecclesiastical.

Much of this material reappears, sometimes in the form of doctrinal statement, oftener by implication, in *Paradise Lost*. Especial emphasis is given to the subject of the proper relation of husband and wife, since this is the one primarily involved in the story of Adam and Eve. To Milton the peace and virtue of the home were best assured if the wife remained in a proper state of subjection to her husband. Such subordination to a natural superior was, indeed, the proper law of the whole universe. Thus woman should look up to man, man to angel, inferior angel to superior angel, and all to God. It was the attempted disruption of this order which led alike to the fall of Satan and the fall of man. Milton's criticism of the system of chivalric or courtly love is that it reverses the normal situation by placing woman above man. Hence Satan assumes the role of Petrarchan lover when he makes his initial attack on Eve.

On the question of the sources and affiliations of Milton's thought much has been written.[92] Milton's mind had ranged through the whole realm of speculation. Ancient philosophy, Biblical and patristic thought, Reformation theology in all its varieties, the philosophic movements and religious heterodoxies of his own day—all were familiar to him, and from them he culled the elements of his eclectic system. One distrusts the attribution of his fundamental ideas to the influence of any single source. Here are some of the

[92] *Ibid.*; see also Harris Fletcher's monumental *The Intellectual Development of John Milton.*

men or schools whose intellectual relationship with Milton has been most strongly advocated: Bernardo Ochino,[93] Jakob Boehme,[94] the Cabalists,[95] Henry More and the Cambridge Platonists,[96] Giordano Bruno,[97] Michael Servetus,[98] the Quakers.[99] Not one of these is mentioned in the *De Doctrina Christiana*, which, nevertheless, lists dozens of standard theologians. It is true, however, that Milton would have been likely to suppress the names of the less reputable authorities. He says in the introduction that he had not even read any of the works of heretics, so-called, "when the mistakes of those who are reckoned orthodox first taught me to agree with their opponents whenever these opponents agreed with Scripture."

In spite of all his rationalism, however, Milton never really crosses the line which divides Christian and idealistic thought generally from naturalism in any of its ancient or modern manifestations. He could, for example, have no part in the materialistic conclusions of a Lucretius, however much one side of his intellect may have been allured by it. Accordingly, he banishes to Chaos the operation of mere material forces. In that realm of being, which God neglects, we have the Epicurean atoms clashing blindly against each other according to the laws of chance but powerless to evolve an ordered world without the exercise of the divine will. With regard to the radical and naturalistic thought of the sixteenth and seventeenth centuries, Milton is apparently partly conscious of its menace to the idealist tradition both in the field of abstract speculation and of practical conduct. His opposition to the theological determinism of the Calvinists has behind it an opposition to the more dangerous determinism of the materialists. This is the source, we believe, of

[93] L. A. Wood, *The Form and Origin of Milton's Antitrinitarian Conception* (London, 1911). Wood's thesis, however, seems to have been disproved by Patrides' evidence.

[94] Margaret L. Bailey, *Milton and Jakob Boehme: A Study of German Mysticism in Seventeenth-Century England* (Oxford, 1914).

[95] Saurat, *Man and Thinker*.

[96] Marjorie Nicolson, "The Spirit World of Milton and More," *SP*, XXII (1925), 433–52.

[97] S. B. Liljegren, "La Pensée de Milton et Giordano Bruno," *RLC*, III (1923), 516–40.

[98] Martin A. Larson, "Milton and Servetus: A Study in the Sources of Milton's Theology," *PMLA*, XLI (1926), 891–934.

[99] Alden Sampson, *Studies in Milton and An Essay on Poetry* (New York, 1913).

his distrust of uncontrolled intellectual speculation. The point of view of the Renaissance thinker who philosophized solely in order that he might philosophize had its logical result in the political realism of Machiavelli, in ethical libertinism of free livers like the youthful Donne, and in the realistic naturalism of Hobbes; and to all this Milton was unalterably opposed. As he relegates the unguided action of force and chance to Chaos, so he surrenders the naturalistic point of view in conduct and belief to Satan. It has been suggested that *Paradise Lost* was intended primarily as a reply to Hobbes.[100] *Leviathan* was published in 1651, and whether or not Milton had read it, he must have been aware of the stir of opposition and alarm which it caused in philosophic circles. Both politically and religiously its doctrines would have been anathema to him, and it may well be that in setting out to "justify the ways of God to men" he consciously directed his inspired utterance against this great antagonist of the faith.

Philosophically, then, Milton is a Christian idealist, though he classes himself in theology with the heretics—Arius, Socinus, Arminius, Ochino, Servetus, and who not? His religious as well as his political sympathies were on the side of the independent sects and the individual promoters of spiritual religion in the seventeenth century. In his metaphysics he shares the pantheistic tendencies of his age. His ethical thought, on the other hand, is largely grounded in the study of ancient philosophy. Temperamentally he felt a strong affinity for the Stoic doctrine, as may easily be seen by his references to the teachings of this school in *Paradise Lost* and *Paradise Regained*.[101] But he is equally drawn toward Platonism, whether in its original form or as it came to him through the more fanciful interpretation of the Neo-Platonists and the Cabala.[102] Finally it must be remembered that Milton met many of the speculative and moral ideas which he employs already embodied in imaginative literature and that such applications are likely to have stimulated his poetic mind more powerfully than any abstract

[100] Marjorie Nicolson, "Milton and Hobbes," *SP*, XXIII (1926), 405–33.

[101] *PL*, II, 562–69; *PR*, IV, 300–08. In both passages Stoicism comes last in the list of pagan philosophies condemned and is dwelt upon most fully, as if it were better worth the pain of a refutation.

[102] See Irene Samuel, *Plato and Milton*, and Nicolson, "The Spirit World of Milton and More."

statement could do. The influence of Spenser's cosmic speculation and moral allegory is discussed on pages 215 ff.

Political theory is not explicitly dealt with in *Paradise Lost,* yet the poem reflects in an important way Milton's long study of and experience with the problems of government. The first two books show concretely by what arts leadership is acquired and maintained in the state, how perplexing issues are threshed out in council, how great public enterprises are organized and executed. There is a certain analogy between Satan and Cromwell as political statesmen, though they are, in Milton's thought, exact opposites in their ideals and purposes—the one aiming only at destruction; the other, ultimately, at the nobler victories of peace. The infernal host, when it sends

> From every Band and squared Regiment
> . . . the worthiest
>
> (*PL,* I, 758–59)

to conference in Pandemonium, acts precisely as the Parliamentary Army had acted in the crises of the Great Rebellion. Writing to Henry Oldenburg in 1659, Milton declined to compose a history of the late troubles of England, saying that they required "oblivion rather than commemoration." Yet he has in spite of himself commemorated them.

If the portrait of Satan reflects to this extent the actual phenomena of politics in a sinful and warring world, the accounts of Adam and the patriarchs illustrate that ideal theocracy in human society toward which the thought of the Puritans aspired. Paul Elmer More has observed that the true theme of *Paradise Lost* is paradise itself. The hope of a godly social order, needing no law but the voice of the Lord, as interpreted through his prophets, had long since departed from Milton; his efforts to guide England to a practical solution of its problems ended with *The Ready and Easy Way* in 1659. He turns now to a dream of the early world, addressing himself to the individual rather than to mankind at large. The recovery of the moral "paradise within thee" is the only way to freedom; when that is achieved the problems of politics will settle themselves.

One conviction which always dominated Milton's political

thinking—the idea that there is a natural order of superior and
justice—receives emphasis more than once in *Paradise Lost*. Satan
inferior in the universe, the preservation of which means peace and
and Eve attempt to break this order, with results disastrous to
themselves and to others. The idea is put—like some other partial
truths—in the mouth of Satan (V, 792–93):

> . . . for Orders and Degrees
> Jar not with liberty, but well consist.

But it is Abdiel who voices its full meaning. It is no servitude, he
says, to serve authority ordained by God and nature,

> When he who rules is worthiest, and excels
> Them whom he governs. This is servitude,
> To serve th' unwise. . . .

(VI, 177–79)

This represented Milton's real and final conclusion. The fact is
that he never was by temperament or experience a democrat. He
lived in isolation, knew nothing of the common man, and naturally
distrusted him. In the early ecclesiastical pamphlets, to be sure, he
expresses confidence in the "plain people" to elect ministers of the
church, and in *Areopagitica* he glories in the competent intelligence
of the English nation, but these opinions were formulated in the
course of argument and when Milton still saw no gulf between
the aims of the people and his own. Later he became self-con-
tradictory on the subject. In the *Tenure of Kings and Magistrates*,
for example, he asserts the right of the people against the magistrate,
but always with the reservation that they choose good rather than
ill. Similarly in the *Defence of the English People* he advocates the
theory of popular sovereignty, yet he praises the independent army
for repelling the tumultuous violence of the citizens and mechanics
of London. When finally the nations turned against the good old
cause and hailed the return of the Stuarts, Milton was open in his
denunciation of those who preferred "bondage with ease" to
"strenuous liberty," and he proposed in the *Ready and Easy Way*
what amounts to a self-perpetuating aristocracy as a form of government. This brings him to the political philosophy embodied
in *Paradise Lost*[103] and later in *Samson Agonistes*.

[103] See Don M. Wolfe, *Milton in the Puritan Revolution.*

The book sources of Milton's political thinking are easily traceable. He inherited his interest in the theory of government from the earlier Renaissance and with it his tendency to find the basis of his convictions in the writings of the ancients. Next to Holy Writ, the Greek and Latin historians, orators, poets, and philosophers were to him great textbooks of political wisdom. His own republicanism had its roots in Roman soil. But he had also studied with diligence the records and theories of later ages, following a consistent program, some of the details of which may be gathered from his Commonplace Book. Among the outstanding modern contributors to political theory entered in the list are Jean Bodin, Buchanan, Machiavelli, and Sir Thomas Smith. His controversial activity sent him scurrying to the authorities, as we have seen, but much of his political study antedates this period. For the liberalism of his own conception of government he had, of course, abundant support—as for example in Buchanan—and none of his ideas is new. A good notion of his position in the history of such speculation may be obtained from any account of political theory in the Renaissance.

THE LITERARY SOURCES

The purpose of this section is to indicate in summary fashion the chief authorities and sources which Milton probably knew and may have employed in constructing his version of the story of the Fall. The discussion here involves primarily the myth or outward narrative; the philosophical and theological elements are considered in the preceding section. The two cannot, however, be absolutely separated.

In discussing the sources of the legend, readers should distinguish between various types of material from the point of view of Milton's attitude toward them. The Biblical references he considered as solely authoritative. Other sources had weight in his mind about in proportion to their antiquity, except that Jewish and Christian writers would be preferred to pagan as standing nearer the fountainhead of truth. Such materials had, even when manifestly fictitious, a kind of legendary authenticity, and Milton invariably preferred their detail to his own invention. He also preferred it, when there was a choice, to more modern elaborations. There can, however, be no doubt that he had read more than one literary version of the fall of man and received from them, consciously or unconsciously, suggestions for the artistic handling of his materials.

Obviously no account of the sources of Milton's epic can be considered as exhaustive, for the poem holds in solution the whole of his immense reading. Except for the Biblical and other ancient authorities, we must look not to the works which deal with the identical subject which he treats for the most vital influences, but rather to those great masterpieces of ancient and modern literature, whatever their subject, which most profoundly impressed him and with which he habitually dwelt. In other words, the essential study of the literary origins of *Paradise Lost* is the study of the formation of Milton's genius insofar as it was molded by the minds of other men. We shall attempt to indicate here only such general influences in *Paradise Lost* as can be rather definitely pointed to in connection with some larger feature of the poem.

HEBREW AND PATRISTIC AUTHORITIES

The foundation passage in Scripture for the fall of man is Genesis 2; for the war in heaven and the fall of Satan (the Dragon) it is Revelation 12. But Milton has employed in one place or another every relevant Biblical text, and the student who would examine in full the basis of the legend in its larger outline should consult a concordance under the heads "Adam," "Eve," "Satan," etc.[104] Scripture is also used for the subsidiary elements of the story. Thus the names and characters of the demons in Book I are largely drawn from the Old Testament. The allegory of Sin

---

[104] See the comprehensive account of the literary relations of *Paradise Lost* by Marianna Woodhull, *The Epic of Paradise Lost* (New York, 1907); see also James H. Sims, *The Bible in Milton's Epics*, especially pp. 259–83.

and Death in Book II is an elaboration of James 1:15. The whole account of the creation in Book VII is built upon the first chapter of Genesis. The prophecy of Michael is a resume of Old and New Testament history. Finally Milton is everywhere dependent on the Bible for detail; witness the enormous number of Scriptural references cited in the editions of Todd, Verity, and Hughes. An outstanding example is the description of the chariot of the Paternal Deity in Book VI, 749 ff., a mosaic from the first chapter of Ezekiel. The borrowings are of course intended to be recognized; extending as they do to the minutest turn of phrase, they put one's familiarity with Scripture to a severe test. Milton's poem is, as he doubtless expected it to be, an invitation to read and reread the Bible, and many an Old or New Testament passage which has been perhaps passed by unnoticed acquires force and meaning when we return to it from Milton's poetic interpretation.

Beyond the canonical books of the Bible there was also the Apocrypha, which would have enjoyed in Milton's mind an only slightly diminished prestige. The Book of Enoch contained a statement as to the fall of the angels, and Milton derived from it at least the name of Satan's standard bearer, Azazael.[105] His employment of Raphael as the genial messenger of God to Adam in his innocence was suggested by the Book of Tobit, where this angel is the helpful guide and companion of the hero through his several adventures (cf. *PL*, V, 221–23).

Milton also found in the rabbinical commentaries on the Old Testament narrative many legendary details which proved useful in elaborating and interpreting the myth. The outstanding points of contact between these embellishments of the Scriptural account of Adam and Eve and Milton's handling in *Paradise Lost* may readily be gathered from Louis Ginsberg's scholarly and comprehensive account of the rabbinical materials in his *Legends of the Jews* (Vol. I).[106] It is said, for example, that Satan was envious of

---

[105] The Book of Enoch was inaccessible in Milton's time, but he had met the passage in question in the *Chronographia* of the Byzantine chronicler, Georgius Syncellus; the book was published in Paris in 1657. See Saurat, *Man and Thinker*, p. 209. More extensive claims have been made for the influence of the Book of Enoch by Grant McColley, "The Book of Enoch and *Paradise Lost*," HTR, XXXI (1938), 21–39.

[106] Seven vols. (Philadelphia, n.d.)

man in his conjugal relations (cf. *PL*, IV, 502 ff.); that he offered to Eve as proof of the harmlessness of the forbidden fruit the fact that he himself had eaten it and had not died (cf. *PL*, IX, 687 ff.); that he suggested to her God's jealousy as the real motive of the prohibition (cf. *PL*, IX, 703 ff.).

Of Milton's knowledge of these Talmudic writings there can be no doubt, since he frequently employs them in his prose works.[107] He mentions, for example, in *Tetrachordon* the idea of the originally bisexual nature of Adam, a rabbinical fancy which he made no use of in *Paradise Lost*. Among the later Hebrew sources certainly known to Milton was the work of the medieval rabbi Maimonides. There was also the Jewish history of Josephus and the parallel work of Yosippon, called the Pseudo-Josephus, both of which he explicitly refers to.[108] From the latter he appears to have taken suggestions as to the manner in which Satan approached Eve to tempt her and the motive of jealousy which led her to forestall a possible second marriage of Adam's by giving him the apple. There also he probably found the basic idea for the naive details of the conversation between God and Adam (*PL*, VIII, 403–11), where both speculate on their loneliness. Yosippon writes:

> *Now Adam walked about the Garden of Eden like one of the ministering angels. God said : Just as I am alone in My world, so is Adam; just as I have no companion, neither has Adam. Tomorrow the creatures will say, "He does not propagate, he is surely our creator." It is not good for man to be alone, I will make a helpmeet for him.*[109]

Fletcher has shown that many of the ideas and motives of the Cabala (e.g., those which Saurat claimed attributable to the body of Jewish mystical philosophy known as the *Zohar*) might more plausibly have come to him directly from such rabbinical com-

---

[107] See Harris Fletcher, *Milton's Semitic Studies* (Chicago, 1926) and *Milton's Rabbinical Readings* (Urbana, 1930).

[108] Harris Fletcher, "Milton and Yosippon," *SP*, XXI (1924), 496–501.

[109] T. Gaster, trans. (Oriental Translation Fund, London, 1899), p. 17. Fletcher *(Milton's Rabbinical Readings)* refers to Rashi's commentary on Genesis 2 in Buxtorf's Bible as a basis for Milton's treatment of the episode of Eve's creation. There is, however, in Rashi no such specific parallel as this one from Yosippon, which Fletcher does not mention.

mentary as is to be found in Buxtorf's Hebrew Bible and from the other Hebraic authorities. They were also present in the writings of the Cambridge Platonists.

Equally important and almost equally intangible is Milton's debt to the Greek and Latin writings of the fathers of the church. We know from the Commonplace Book that he had studied them thoroughly, beginning with the Hammersmith period, along with his reading in the early Byzantine historians. They dealt extensively, of course, with questions connected with the Biblical narrative of the Fall and supplied many features which became a permanent part of the legend during the Middle Ages. Some of these details they adopted from Jewish speculations which would not otherwise have been accessible to Milton. Thus the conversion of the fallen angels into demons and their identification with the false gods of the Gentiles is a piece of Jewish tradition perpetuated in the fathers. The parallel between Adam and the Messiah and between Eve and Mary is also patristic.

A very important authority for Milton's interpretation of the fall of man—particularly with reference to the elements of sensuality involved in it—was St. Augustine, and every mature student of *Paradise Lost* should read Book XIV, Chapters 11–28, of the *City of God*, where the matter is dealt with. It will be evident enough that Milton had before him in interpreting the Fall many of the issues raised by this mighty elaborator of Catholic Christianity and that the Protestant poet is influenced even where he is in fundamental disagreement with St. Augustine and is making a point against him. The relation here is primarily philosophical and theological, but there are obvious effects also in the course of the narrative. Still another patristic source of Milton's ideas is Lactantius, from whom he quotes in the Commonplace Book.[110]

It would be useless to go on enumerating the Christian commentators, Hebraists, and theologians from whose works Milton might have taken a turn of thought or even the suggestion for an incident; the list would extend over centuries. Of medieval writers he naturally made little direct use. His angelology, for example, is not that of the standard Catholic authority, the Pseudo-Dionysius,

[110] See Kathleen Hartwell, *Lactantius and Milton* (Cambridge, Mass., 1929).

De Coelesti Hierarchia. Milton may or may not have read this work, but he would in any case have been sufficiently familiar with the system from Dante's *Divine Comedy*. With the works of many Reformation and contemporary scholars he was acquainted, including those of John Selden, who, besides being the greatest legal antiquarian of his time, was also a learned writer on Hebrew antiquities. His *De Diis Syriis* affords many illustrations for Milton's demonology.

FORMATIVE INFLUENCES ON *Paradise Lost* IN GREEK
AND ROMAN LITERATURE

Ancient epic—the *Iliad*, the *Odyssey*, and the *Aeneid*—furnishes Milton with his authoritative model of form and structure as Scripture does of substance and interpretation. The classical epic conventions were, of course, fixed by Renaissance usage and formulated in critical theory; but it is right to assume in regard to Milton's employment of them that his conscious sources are in each case the ancient originals themselves. They are the precedents to which he wishes the reader to revert, recognizing with admiration the manner in which the new material is ingeniously made to conform to the ancient mold. For the larger structural features of *Paradise Lost*, the *Aeneid*, which itself derives both from the *Iliad* and the *Odyssey*, is a sufficient illustration. The principal points of comparison are as follows: 1) the beginning of the poem with the action proper at a midpoint in the larger story of which it is a part; 2) the introduction of this larger story by way of narrative and prophecy in the course of the narrower action; 3) the alternation of scenes on earth with scenes in heaven; 4) the alternation of dramatic dialogue with more or less extensive narrative and descriptive passages. Among the smaller features in *Paradise Lost* which have their precedent in ancient epic may be mentioned: 1) the invocation, repeated at important moments of change in the action; 2) the enumeration of the host of Satan in Book I; 3) the representation of a council of leaders in Book II and of divine personages in Book III; 4) the introduction of an allegorical episode, as that of Sin and Death, Book II; 5) epic games, Book II; 6) descriptions of technical processes—e.g., the building of Pandemonium, Book II, and the casting of cannon, Book VI; 7) a celestial visitant warning and advising a mortal; 8) war, episodes of single combat with challenge and reply, Book VI; 9) historical prophecy divinely inspired, Books XI–XII; 10) dreams, Books V, XII.[111]

Of the other types of ancient literature Greek drama is the most conspicuous in its structural influence on *Paradise Lost*. The way to such influence was opened by the fact that Milton's more particular theme, the fall of man, found closer parallels in classical tragedy than it did in classical epic, and that he had originally planned to cast his materials in dramatic form. In the completed poem the careful motivation of the action and the revelation through dialogue and soliloquy of the inner experience of his characters certainly go back rather to dramatic than to epic precedent. The literary influences in this respect are rather vague, and often they seem more Elizabethan than Greek; but there can be no doubt that in portraying, for example, the unnatural exhilaration of Adam and Eve immediately after their sin Milton is drawing upon the ancient representation of hybris.

The remaining influence of ancient literature is largely a matter of style and allusion. We may note, however, that Milton's infernal council has a precedent in Claudian's *De Raptu Proserpinae* and that in Eve's description of her first experiences (IV, 449 ff.) the poet draws on the myth of Narcissus and falls for a moment into the spirit of pastoral narrative, recollecting such a passage as the pursuit of Daphne by Apollo in the *Metamorphoses* and employing the inevitable *quem fugis* motive adopted by Ovid from Theocritus.

NARRATIVE TREATMENTS OF THE FALL AND RELATED THEMES IN
MEDIEVAL AND RENAISSANCE LITERATURE

Paradise Lost, as a Biblical and didactic epic, belongs to a tradition which reaches back to the early centuries of Christian culture and persists in full vigor through the Renaissance. Among

---

[111] For specific references and discussion of additional points, see the admirable study by Davis P. Harding, *The Club of Hercules: Studies in the Classical Background of "Paradise Lost."*

the earliest of these is St. Avitus' *Poematum: De Mosaicae Historias Gestis* (507 A.D.),[112] which treats of the Fall incidentally in the course of a paraphrase of Bible history and lays down the main lines of the literary elaboration of the material. There are actually several striking parallels between the two works.[113] It is by no means impossible that Milton should have known this work, which was printed before his time and thought well of by the Protestant humanists for its good Latinity. Christian writings of similar types are mentioned among the prescribed studies at St. Paul's School in Colet's original program of instruction.[114]

It has also been said that Milton employed a work of the same type as that of Avitus which develops the story of the fall of man nearly in the plot form which it assumes in *Paradise Lost*. This work is the Anglo-Saxon Genesis, attributed to Caedmon, particularly that portion known as Genesis B.[115] An outline follows.

Satan and his followers revolt and fall. They are banished to a hill of alternate cold and heat. God, to supply their places, creates the world and places Adam and Eve in a garden of beauty and delight. Satan, in a dramatic address to the rebel angels, laments his present situation, complains of God's injustice in creating man, and plots to extend his empire by corrupting Adam and Eve. He sends an emissary to earth who pretends to be a messenger from heaven and tempts Adam in Eve's presence but is repulsed. Turning to Eve, who is thoroughly deceived, he succeeds. Adam also falls, and a revulsion of feeling follows, with bitter lamentation and remorse.

The general parallelism here with *Paradise Lost* of course means nothing, since, as we shall see, many of the later treatments, some of which Milton certainly knew, proceed in essentially the same manner. There are, however, some rather striking similarities of detail in Satan's speeches to his followers, in the account of the journey through the abyss to earth, and in the self-reproaching dialogue of Adam and Eve after the Fall. In both poems Satan contrasts the horrible scene about him with the delights of his

---

[112] See the translation by Watson Kirkconnell, *The Celestial Cycle*, pp. 3–19.

[113] *Ibid.*, p. 506.

[114] Fletcher, *The Intellectual Development of John Milton*; see also D. L. Clark, *John Milton at St. Paul's School*.

[115] Kirkconnell, *The Celestial Cycle*, pp. 19–43, 510–13.

former home. He mentions to his followers the creation of earth and man as a rumor (cf. *PL*, I, 650 ff.). He flatteringly praises Eve's beauty, though not, as in Milton, before her sin. But there is no evidence which can fairly be called conclusive of Milton's having actually read the Anglo-Saxon poem. It had been published in 1655 at Amsterdam by the Dutch scholar Franciscus Junius just at the time when Milton was beginning the actual composition of his epic. Junius lived in England until 1651, when he received the Caedmon manuscript from Bishop Ussher, and he must, Masson thinks, almost certainly have been an acquaintance of Milton's. There is, on the other hand, evidence that Milton was not well enough versed in Anglo-Saxon to make anything out of the Caedmonian Genesis. In his *History of Britain* (1670) he describes the *Battle of Brunanburgh*, which he had before him in the Anglo-Saxon Chronicle, together with a word-for-word Latin translation, as being quite unintelligible because of its extravagant fancies and metaphors. *Brunanburgh* is much simpler than the Biblical poems; and had Milton been through the latter, with or without Junius as interpreter, it is hard to see how he could have spoken in such perplexity.

An outstanding religious work of the Renaissance, Du Bartas' *La Première Semaine* and *La Seconde Semaine*, translated into English by Joshua Sylvester as *De Bartas His Devine Weekes and Workes* (published in parts, 1592–98; first quarto, 1605), specializes on the creation, with much detailed description of the wonders of the universe and with incidental treatment of the Fall. Du Bartas' poem, like the first two chapters of Ralegh's *History of the World* (1614), belongs in the tradition of hexameral literature which interprets the Biblical account of the creation, intermingling with simple exegesis an immense amount of philosophical and scientific material from various sources.[116] Among the writers of such commentaries were Basil, Augustine, Johannes Scotus, and many other serious theologians who made this their vehicle for discussion of such standard problems as the nature of God, the processes and purposes of creation, the construction of the universe, the angels,

---

[116] Sister Mary Irma Corcoran, *Milton's Paradise with Reference to the Hexameral Background* (Washington, D.C., 1945). See also George W. Whiting, "The Story of Creation," *Milton's Literary Milieu*, pp. 3–25.

man, the animals, etc. Milton knew of Sylvester's translation of Du Bartas, and its influence on his youthful poetic style is well established. The general tone of the work is obviously reproduced in *Paradise Lost,* and many Miltonic scenes, motives, and ideas have their parallels in the earlier epic. G. C. Taylor,[117] who believes that Milton owed more to Sylvester's Du Bartas than to any other work, points out verbal resemblances as well (including one whole line word for word the same). Perhaps, as has been suggested, Milton more or less consciously undertook to outdo Sylvester, as Spenser had undertaken to "overgo" Ariosto.[118] Another poem of Du Bartas, *La Muse Chrétienne,* may also have been known to Milton. Here Urania is, for the first time in literature, hailed as the celestial patroness of divine poetry rather than as the muse of astronomy. This conception became traditional and Milton's invocations are directly referable to it.

RENAISSANCE DRAMATIC VERSIONS OF THE FALL

The story of the Fall and redemption of man was a central subject in medieval religious drama, and Milton's first conception of it as literary material was deeply influenced by this tradition. It is, to be sure, doubtful if he knew any of these plays directly,[119] though he may well have watched as a child the puppet shows of Adam and Eve to which he alludes in *Areopagitica.*[120] But the mysteries were perpetuated in a cultivated and artistic way in the Italian *Sacre Rappresentazione,* and one such drama, the *Adamo* of Giovanni Battista Andreini,[121] published in 1613, may have been known to

---

117 *Milton's Use of Du Bartas.* Dunster (*Considerations on Milton's Early Reading* [London, 1800]) is mainly concerned with the influence on the early poems, but he suggests, without giving details, that *Paradise Lost* was deeply indebted to the same source. Dunster probably assumed that Milton carried the recollection of Du Bartas from his childhood; Taylor, that he continued to read and respect him.

118 On the general indebtedness of Milton to Renaissance epic see Tillyard, *The Miltonic Setting,* pp. 141 ff.

119 See Allan H. Gilbert, "Milton and the Mysteries," *SP,* XVII (1920), 147-69.

120 "A meer artificial *Adam,* such an Adam as he is in the motions" (Yale, *Milton,* II, 527).

121 See Kirkconnell, *The Celestial Cycle,* pp. 227-67.

Milton. It was first mentioned in connection with *Paradise Lost* in 1727 by Voltaire, who said that Milton derived his suggestion for writing the poem from having seen a performance of this play on his Italian journey. The relationship is apparently confirmed by similarities, not so much in *Paradise Lost* itself as in the early dramatic plans in the Cambridge Manuscript, where the allegorical figures of Labor, Famine, Death, etc., which play a prominent part in Andreini, are listed among the *dramatis personae.*

In the change from dramatic to epic form whatever specific traces there may be of the *Adamo* become merged with those of general tradition and are largely obliterated. We may note, however, that the symbolic character of the incidents in Adam's vision of the consequences of his sin may be a survival of the original suggestion from Andreini. Thus, in witnessing the murder of Cain, Adam cries, "And have I then seen Death?" And in the description of the lazar house (XI, 480 ff.) the various curses listed as mutes in the dramatic plans are enumerated and personified:

> . . . Despair
> Tended the sick busiest from Couch to Couch;
> And over them triumphant Death his Dart
> Shook, but delay'd to strike.
>
> (XI, 489–92)

Of the numerous other motifs which this play has in common with *Paradise Lost* the following are most striking: the love of Adam and Eve and the Fall through passion; Lucifer in view of paradise expressing detestation of light; the representations of the passions of pride, revenge, and wretchedness in the infernal council; Lucifer's inspiring leadership; Eve beside a crystal fountain; Adam's dignity and erect condition; the serpent as foretaster of the fruit; Eve's soliloquy on its virtue; the serpent's return as victor with a following revulsion of fear; a conflict of Lucifer with the protecting angels; Adam's bitterness against Eve and their subsequent reconciliation; cherubim as guardians of the gate; Michael as the banishing angel and mouthpiece of God's prophetic comfort. Though no special importance is to be attached to these parallels, since many of the motifs occur elsewhere, they may be used as a check in the attempt to establish Milton's indebtedness to other versions with which his acquaintance is purely hypothetical.

The influence of one other drama on the Fall, the five-act Latin *Adamus Exul* of Hugo Grotius (1601),[122] from which Andreini himself is said to have borrowed, may be regarded as a more probable source. This work was highly praised by such authorities as Scaliger and Causabon, and it ranked as one of the outstanding literary contributions of Renaissance humanism. Edward Phillips in his *Theatrum Poetarum,* a work which is thought to contain reflections of Milton's own critical opinions, mentions its author as one of the most distinguished writers of the age.[123] Milton had been introduced to Grotius himself at Paris, and there is every reason to believe that he was thoroughly familiar with his work. Indeed, the deleted caption, "Adam's Banishment," prefixed to the fourth draft of his plan for *Paradise Lost* in the Cambridge Manuscript sounds like a conscious or unconscious reproduction of Grotius' title.

We may now consider the extent of the traceable influence of the *Adamus* on *Paradise Lost.* Unlike Andreini's *Adamo,* Grotius' play is a unified and coherent tragedy on classical lines. It begins with Satan's arrival in Eden after a flight from hell and the long soliloquy in which he proceeds from despair and defiance to a determination to ruin Adam. In Act II Adam is instructed in the creation of the world and the fall of Satan by an angel, and he holds loving dialogue with Eve. In Act III Satan in his own form tempts Adam and is firmly repulsed. In Act IV he approaches Eve as a serpent, flatters her, and finally persuades her to eat the fruit. Adam enters seeking Eve; he is horrified at her deed but yields to her love and eats. In Act V Satan triumphs in monologue. Adam is tormented by phantoms of despair. Eve endeavors to console him and restrains him from suicide, offering herself as a willing sacrifice to his vengeance. Adam expresses his great love of her. Jehovah, appearing in person, pronounces judgment and summons the cherubim to drive them forth. They enter into exile with expression of sorrow at the loss of Eden. The first four acts are concluded with the angelic chorus.

In general outline this is more remote from Milton's drafts than is the *Adamo.* Milton evidently chose the mystery conception

122 *Ibid.*, pp. 96–220.
123 (London, 1675), II, 74.

of the theme, with its allegorical attendants, as a means of displaying its wider significance in the scheme of human destiny, and this broader plan persists in the completed epic. But Grotius' play stands much nearer to Milton's actual development of the more dramatic part of his material in the coherence of the plot, in the superior handling of the human motives, and in the philosophical and ethical dignity which pervades the whole. It seems probable that Milton moved farther from Andreini and nearer to Grotius as the plan developed in his mind. When he actually undertook the composition of a drama on the Fall, he began not with angelic or allegorical preliminaries, as in Andreini and the preserved drafts, but with a soliloquy of Satan, as in the *Adamus Exul*. In the substance of this soliloquy, as in the whole development of the temptation, fall, repentance, and banishment of Adam and Eve, many of the Miltonic elements are common to both Grotius and Andreini. But the detail is often closer to the Latin than to the Italian treatment. Thus all three poets make much of the brilliant colors and spectacular approach of the serpent; but Milton and Grotius both discard the rabbinical notion of his human face, and in general their descriptions of his labyrinthine antics are more nearly identical. In the account of Satan's procedure in the temptation of Eve, Grotius, like Milton, makes him suggest a fatalistic philosophy, a detail unrepresented in the *Adamo*. The despair of Adam also is less subtly and elaborately developed in Andreini than in the others, and there is no parallel to the proposal of suicide as a way of anticipating the penalty, a proposal which comes in Milton only from Eve but from each in turn in Grotius. Other similar specific resemblances between *Paradise Lost* and *Adamus Exul* are: the geographical description of Eden; Satan's contrast of his own misery with the bliss of Adam and Eve; Adam's hymn of the visible universe as God's handiwork; the angelic ministration to Adam of cosmic instruction and moral warning (Adam's question about the stars, his narrative of the first awakening, the angel's story of Lucifer's rebellion and of the creation, and his emphasis on Adam's superiority to the beasts are all briefly included in the drama). In Milton's use of such motifs as the flattering of Eve by her tempter, his suggestion of God's jealousy as the motive of the prohibition, the reunion of Adam and Eve after their separation, Adam's horror at her deed, the appeal to his love, the changes in nature after the Fall, the reconciliation of the pair after their estrangement, and many others, it is impossible to tell which of his two models he is following more closely.

For the other Renaissance dramas of the Fall which have been alleged as Milton's sources much less can be said. The various Italian plays mentioned by Pearce, Peck, and Todd are comparatively obscure and have no outstanding features in common with Milton's which are not conventional. The much-argued case for the Dutch poet Vondel's *Lucifer* (1654) and his *Adam in Banishment* is less impressive when we consider Vondel's own debt to Grotius, Du Bartas, and other writers whom Milton knew.[124] The *Adam* was printed in 1664, too late in either case to have much affected Milton's original plan. The verbal similarities—when one reads Vondel in the original and not in a Miltonized translation—are inconclusive, and there is the serious question whether Milton in his blindness and with a probably limited knowledge of Dutch could easily have obtained a close familiarity with the work of his contemporary. The significant kinship between *Lucifer* and *Paradise Lost* is that which arises from the independent handling of identical materials by two great poets of similar culture and imaginative inheritance.

ITALIAN ROMANTIC EPIC; SPENSER; THE FLETCHERS;

SHAKESPEARE; MARLOWE

It would naturally be expected that Milton's enthusiasm for the Renaissance masters of romantic narrative, which must have dominated his purpose so long as he continued to cherish the idea of an Arthurian epic, would leave an impress on the poem which he actually did compose, however alien its theme. In form the looser structure of Boiardo, Ariosto, and Spenser was of course repudiated by him. Tasso's *Gerusalemne Liberata* and its critical defense would have fortified in him the conception of a Christian epic severely classical in outline, but with the more authoritative

---

[124] For a critical view of the evidence, see Kirkconnell, *The Celestial Cycle*, pp. 628–31.

models of Virgil and Homer before him he needed no recourse in the matter of epic structure to a derived work. The influence of the Italians is quite traceable, however, in many details of *Paradise Lost*. To mention only the outstanding instances, the humorous and satiric description of the Paradise of Fools in Book III is plainly based on Ariosto's picture of a similar limbo of ecclesiastical vanities on the moon (*Orlando Furioso*, XXXIV, 70 ff.), a passage which Milton had noted in the Commonplace Book before his Italian journey; and the infernal council in Book II, though Milton was familiar with similar scenes from many sources, has much in common with Tasso's account in the fourth canto of the *Gerusalemne*.[125]

To Spenser his debt was more profound. The beginnings of it have already been seen in *Comus*, where the adaptation of myth and allegory to the purpose of earnest philosophical and moral idealism is dominated by the spirit of Milton's great Elizabethan predecessor. To distinguish the Spenserian element in *Paradise Lost* is not so easy, but a suggestion of its importance is afforded by Milton's praise of Spenser in *Areopagitica* as a better teacher than Scotus or Aquinas and by his remark to Dryden that Spenser was his "original." Spenser was a better teacher partly because he was a poet embodying his moral lessons in beautiful imaginative forms and partly because he was a humanist, deriving his philosophy from ancient and not from scholastic thought. As such he stood in Milton's thought as the truest exemplar among his own countrymen of the poetic function and, in spite of differences of temper, theme, and style, was gladly acknowledged as a guide and master. The relationship between *Paradise Lost* and *The Faerie Queene* is accordingly to be sought not in resemblances of incident or phrase but in fundamental community of poetic aim and method. It is pointed out by Edwin Greenlaw in his discussion of his subject[126] that there is a striking analogy between Milton's interpretation of the moral issues involved in Adam's fall and the representation of virtue under trial in the person of Sir Guyon (Book II). The basic

[125] For a discussion of Tasso's influence upon Milton, see F. T. Prince, *The Italian Element in Milton's Verse*.

[126] "A Better Teacher than Aquinas," *SP*, XVI (1917), 196–217, and "Spenser's Influence on *Paradise Lost*."

teaching in each case is that of temperance interpreted according to Platonic ethics as the supremacy of the rational soul over the passionate principle in the soul. For such doctrine in the abstract Milton needed, of course, no source but Plato and the Renaissance tradition generally, but the claim that he found in Spenser an application of Platonic idealism which made a profound impression on his mind and which stimulated and guided his own imaginative activity is one which cannot be denied.

Greenlaw also finds in Spenser's cosmic speculations materials which he believes entered deeply into the substance of Milton's poetic thought. Both poets drew, to be sure, upon the common stock of ancient, medieval, and Renaissance philosophy for their conception of man and nature, and their employment of an identical scheme of the universe is in itself no proof of Milton's indebtedness. But here again we may safely assume that Spenser's poetic embodiment of the cosmic vision in the last two of his *Fowre Hymnes* and elsewhere was an early means of rousing Milton's interest in such matters and of firing his imagination to the height of his tremendous theme. Specifically Spenser's account of the mystic Garden of Adonis furnished detail for Milton's luxuriant Garden of Eden; his expressions regarding Chaos as the womb and grave of the universe and the employment of Demogorgon and Night as personifications of the abyss are echoed in *Paradise Lost,* Book III. Finally there are touches in common[127] between Spenser's story of the attempt of Mutabilitie to regain heaven and Milton's account of the ascent of Satan from hell which appear to show that the later poet felt the analogy between the two episodes and remolded his traditional materials under the influence of the philosophical myth created by his predecessor. Minor reminiscences of Spenserian phrase and idea are, of course, common throughout Milton's poetry. The following parallel, not noted elsewhere, may be given as a signal illustration of the way in which a recollected scene from Spenser might have guided Milton's feeling and poetic expression where one would hardly expect it. King Arthur (I, ix, 15)

[127] Note besides those mentioned by Greenlaw the skeptical suggestion by Mutabilitie that nature is not really dependent upon God (*FQ,* VII, vii, 49; cf. *PL,* V, 720).

tells Redcrosse how he dreamed of the lady of his heart and aspiration, hitherto unseen. Adam, recounting to Raphael his earliest experiences (*PL*, VIII, 452 ff.), describes his vision of Eve in the trance which had been laid upon him during her creation. The high poetic moment in both narratives is when the lovers waken with an intense feeling of loss, and the similarities in expression are enough to suggest the discipleship of one poet to the other; the differences measure the vast distance between them. Spenser gives the whole leisurely stanza to the expression of his idea:

> When I awoke, and found her place devoyd,
> And nought but pressed gras where she had lyen,
> I sorrowed all so much as earst I joyd,
> And washed all her place with watry eyen.
> From that day forth I lov'd that face divyne;
> From that day forth I cast in carefull mynd,
> To seek her out with labor and long tyne,
> And never vowd to rest till her I fynd:
> Nyne monethes I seek in vain, yet ni'll that vow
>   unbynd.

Milton renders Adam's kindred passion in three concentrated lines:

> Shee disappear'd, and left me dark, I wak'd
> To find her, or for ever to deplore
> Her loss, and other pleasures all abjure.
>
> (VIII, 478–80)

The influence of Spenser in coloring Milton's poetic ideas and expression blends with and is often indistinguishable from that of the seventeenth-century Spenserians, particularly Giles and Phineas Fletcher, whose work he had known and had felt the power of from his boyhood. Though Milton owed, perhaps, nothing as fundamental to these two poets as he owed to their original, there are nevertheless clear traces of the influence of their imaginative conceptions on his own. This is most notable in the case of Phineas, whose infernal council in *The Apollyonists* and its Latin counterpart, *Locustae*, includes a representation of Satan as a majestic and defiant being which bears obvious points of resemblance to Milton's. The same author's allegorical figure of Hamartia in *The Purple Island* and of Sin in *The Apollyonists* are the chief imaginative prototypes of the horrible creature whom Satan encounters at hell gate (*PL,* III). The case for Giles Fletcher is more a matter of phraseology. Grosart lists such parallels as this:

> Heav'n wakes with all his eyes,
> Whom to behold but thee, Nature's desire.
> <div align="right">(<i>PL,</i> V, 44–45)</div>
> Heaven awakened all his eyes
> To see another sunne at midnight rise.
> <div align="right">(<i>Christ's Victory,</i> st. 78)</div>

The theme of *Christ's Victory* is the same as that of Book III of *Paradise Lost*, except that Fletcher has preserved the old allegory of the Daughters of God while Milton has put the heavenly debate into the mouth of the Father and the Son. But the provisions in the dramatic plans for a discussion of man's fate by Mercy, Justice, and Wisdom points to *Christ's Victory* as an influence in Milton's elaboration of the scheme of redemption, something which is very scantily represented in Grotius and Andreini. The Fletchers are Milton's most immediate precedents in a kind of poetry which puts a religious subject matter in terms of sensuous imagery. Some critics are inclined to attribute to them a much larger share in furnishing suggestions to Milton's imagination in the actual epic of *Paradise Lost* than to the Continental sources which first led him to project a drama on this theme. Claims in this connection have also been made for the *Davideis*, a Biblical epic published in 1656 by Abraham Cowley.[128]

Of the other English writers to whom Milton owed inspiration Marlowe and Shakespeare are the most conspicuous. Marlowe's style, with its grandiose sweep and its roll of euphonious and exotic proper names, is generally recognized as having assisted in molding Milton's own. This relationship is discussed in Chapter VI. A flash, moreover, of magnificent insight in the elder poet's representation of Mephistopheles,

---

[128] R. Kirsten, *Studien ueber das Verhaeltnis von Cowley und Milton* (Leipzig, 1899).

> Why, this is Hell, nor am I out of it,

apparently finds an echo in Satan's

> Which way I fly is Hell, myself am Hell.

Compare also Faustus' speech in Act II:

> Nay, and this be hell I'll willingly be damned.
> What, sleeping, eating, walking, and disputing?

with Satan's,

> Is this then worst,
> Thus sitting, thus consulting, thus in Arms?
>
> (II, 163–64)

It would be difficult to find other specific parallels.

In the case of Shakespeare the relationship is more complex. Milton's eager reading of the plays is well attested, nor did their profound difference in temperament and Milton's later reservations regarding Shakespeare's art diminish the impression which they left upon his memory. How far Shakespeare permanently determined Milton's modes of conceiving dramatic characters and situations it is hard to say, but we seem to catch in the representation of Satan plotting against Adam and Eve an echo of the similar relations of Iago, Othello, and Desdemona; or in his unrepentant remarks a parallel to the soliloquy of King Claudius. Adam's revulsion against Eve is analogous to that of Antony against Cleopatra, his meditation on the burden and mystery of human life in Book XI to that of Hamlet.[129] The parallels, though suggestive and significant, are intangible, and the case for Shakespeare's influence is largely a matter of specific similarities of phrase. Alwin Thaler[130] has collected a surprising array of such resemblances, and his list, when all allowances are made for accident, remains a testimony to the degree to which Milton's poetic

---

[129] See James Holly Hanford, "The Dramatic Element in *Paradise Lost.*"
[130] "The Shakesperian Element in Milton," *PMLA*, XL (1925), 645–91.

speech was enriched by the fertile imagination of his greatest Elizabethan predecessor.

In general we may say of Milton's echoings of incident, idea, and phrase in *Paradise Lost* and elsewhere that they illustrate the essentially literary character of his inspiration, the wide range of his reading, and the extraordinarily assimilative quality of his mind. A hint which helps account for the manifold reminiscences in his work is given by the anonymous biographer in his account of Milton's occupations during the period when he was composing *Paradise Lost*. "The Evenings hee likewise spent in reading some choice Poets, by way of refreshment after the days toyl, and to store his Fancy against Morning."[131] The cry of plagiarism is, of course, absurd. Milton's own attitude is implied in a statement in *Eikonoklastes:* "Borrowing, if it be not bettered by the borrower, among good authors is accounted plagiarie." He himself certainly leaves nothing as he found it. That is why the resemblances which we have been discussing are in general so shadowy. All is transformed to the substance of his imagination. The Miltonic accent is everywhere, and when the labors of source hunters are done, *Paradise Lost* remains one of the most original works in English or in any literature.

---

[131] Darbishire, *Early Lives,* p. 33.

Chapter 5

PARADISE REGAINED
AND SAMSON AGONISTES

INTRODUCTION

IN 1671 MILTON'S TWO FINAL POEMS APPEARED IN A SINGLE VOLUME
bearing the title, *Paradise Regained. A Poem. In IV Books. To
which is added Samson Agonistes. The Author John Milton.* The
date of entry in the Stationers' Register is September 10, 1670.[1]
The poems had been licensed on July 2 of the same year.[2] No
conclusive evidence of the date or order of their composition is
available. The natural inference is, however, that *Paradise Regained,*
being a kind of sequel to *Paradise Lost,* would have followed that
work directly; this is supported by the account Thomas Ellwood
gives of the part which he played in suggesting it. He had returned
the manuscript of *Paradise Lost* to Milton at Chalfont St. Giles
toward the end of the year 1665 with the following remark: "Thou
hast said much here of *Paradise lost,* but what hast thou to say
of *Paradise found?*"[3] When Ellwood—sometime after his return to
London in 1666—visited the poet again, Milton showed him
Paradise Regained, saying, "This is owing to you: for you put it

[1] J. Milton French, *Life Records,* V, 17.
[2] *Ibid.*
[3] *The History of the Life of Thomas Ellwood,* ed. S. Graveson (London,
1906), p. 199.

into my head, by the question you put to me at Chalfont; which
before I had not thought of."[4] Edward Phillips is uncertain of the
date of *Samson* but says that *Paradise Regained* was "doubtless
. . . begun and finisht and Printed after the other [*Paradise Lost*]
was publisht" (i.e., August, 1667).[5]

Notwithstanding this statement it seems likely that both
poems had been in Milton's mind for some time. In *The Reason
of Church-Government* he had discussed literary forms sanctioned
by classical or Biblical precedent: the long epic, the brief epic
(like the Book of Job), and the drama.[6] *Paradise Lost, Paradise
Regained*, and *Samson Agonistes* fit this classification perfectly. One
need not conclude that Milton definitely planned at this time to
give the public a single specimen of each, but it is clear that he
was considering various forms and models. We may regard it as
significant that, having chosen the classical epic as a pattern for
his first great enterprise, when he came to write again, he should
have wished to experiment with the other types. As to the subjects,
the Cambridge Manuscript notes—written circa 1641—contain the
suggestion of a drama on the life of Christ—"Christus Patiens"—
and several topics from the history of Samson.[7] The theme of
Paradise Regained was in a sense logically necessitated by *Paradise
Lost*; this is not to say that Milton had failed in the earlier poem
to present Christ's part in the theological scheme of salvation, but
he wished to give the actual process in Christ, considered as a

---

[4] *Ibid.*

[5] Darbishire, *Early Lives*, p. 75.

[6] Ed. with preface and notes by Ralph A. Haug, Yale, *Milton*, I, 813 ff.
William R. Parker points out that in this ecclesiastical pamphlet Milton is
partly concerned with vindicating his respect for ancient literary forms by showing that Christian and even Scriptural writers employed them. Job is cited as a
"brief model" of the epic since the Bible obviously contains no "diffuse" model
("On Milton's Early Literary Program"). Parker's observations are just, but
they do not prove that Milton did not consciously or unconsciously accept the
"brief epic" as a formal literary type along with the others and consider its fit-
ness for his present or future purposes. Cf. the more recent and detailed argument by Barbara K. Lewalski, *Milton's Brief Epic*, pp. 3–129.

[7] William R. Parker, "The Trinity Manuscript and Milton's Plans for a
Tragedy," justly questioning the definite statements which have been made in
this book and in others regarding the number of Samson dramas which Milton
lists, goes too far in saying that these early entries reveal no particular concern
with the subject. Samson's marriage choices, his hybris, his various triumphs as
God's champion, all of which are suggested by Milton's titles, touch closely
upon some of Milton's deepest interests.

representative of humanity, of the successful meeting of temptation corresponding to the failure of Adam in a similar situation. The analogy between Adam and Samson had already been noted in *Paradise Lost* (IX, 1059–62), and the Hebrew champion was more than once used in the prose as an instructive symbol.[8]

There is evidence that Milton not only supervised the printing of the 1671 edition with care[9] but perhaps actually made an addition to *Samson Agonistes* while the work was going through the press. Lines 1527–35 appear at the end under the heading "Omissa." The passage in the main body of the text seems coherent without them, and they may well be an afterthought designed to introduce the element of irony into the situation at this point. If so, they suggest the fact that Milton's creative interest in *Samson* was still active at the time of its publication in the last year but three of his life.

PARADISE REGAINED

SOURCES

Paradise Regained follows step by step the incidents of the temptation as given in the Gospel of Luke, except that Milton invents two additional episodes, the banquet scene and the storm.[10] The earlier events of Christ's life are introduced in the thematically significant induction (ll. 1–43), and the later episodes are given largely by implication.[11] The elaboration of detail is largely the work of Milton's own thought and imagination; but Spenser, Giles Fletcher, and the numerous brief epics known as *Christiads* furnished suggestions and provided a tradition of no slight importance. One of Milton's major debts is to the episode of the temptation of Sir Guyon. Spenser, like Milton, makes his demon offer wealth and (in the person of Philotime) worldly power and glory. Mammon

---

[8] See *The Reason of Church-Government*, Yale, *Milton*, I, 858–59; *Areopagitica, ibid.*, II, 557–58.

[9] See Appendix E, "Milton and His Printers."

[10] There is careful exposition of traditional background in Elizabeth Pope, "The Gospel Narrative," *Paradise Regained*, pp. 1–12.

[11] See Northrop Frye's argument, "The Typology of *Paradise Regained*."

tries to reason Sir Guyon into acceptance as Satan tries to reason with Christ. The two moral heroes reject in similar terms the bait held out to them. Guyon's moment of apparent hesitation:

> Me list not (said the Elfin knight) receave
> Thing offred, till I know it be well got
>
> (*FQ*, II, vii, 19)

and his exhaustion after the victory illustrate his humanity and differentiate him from Milton's Christ. Yet even here there are parallels. Thus to Satan's question,

> If Food were now before thee set,
> Would'st thou not eat?
>
> (II, 320–21)

Christ replies,

> Thereafter as I like
> The giver. . . .
>
> (II, 321–22)

And both Guyon and Christ receive physical aid divinely sent. It is evident that Spenser himself is shadowing the temptation of Christ (Mammon's habitation is called a desert [*FQ*, II, vii, 2], and Guyon is said to have been tempted three days [*FQ*, II, vii, 65]).[12] Milton must have perceived this fact and adapted the usable elements in the allegory so that they would contribute to his own interpretation of the Scriptural event. His Christ, therefore, becomes a symbol of temperance—less explicitly, but no less certainly, than Spenser's Sir Guyon.[13]

The influence of Giles Fletcher's *Christ's Victory and Triumph*, because the poem deals directly with the temptation and was certainly known to Milton, is important also, for it is a significant part of the influential *Christiad* tradition. Giles Fletcher's Satan may offer the only other example in the *Christiad* in which the tempter masquerades as an aged, pious hermit. Fletcher's Christ is also tempted with wine and women (in a scene analogous to Milton's banquet episode), and

---

[12] *Ibid.*
[13] See Edwin Greenlaw, "A Better Teacher Than Aquinas," *SP*, XIV (1917), 196–217.

in the temptation of the kingdoms Milton's arrangement of the lures—first the banquet containing the elegant sensual delights, then wealth, then ambition, then glory—follows precisely the order found in Fletcher's allegorical presentation of the kingdom's temptation as the House of Pangloretta, wherein Christ is tempted first by Bacchus and Luxurie, then by Avarice, then by Ambitious Honor, and finally by Pangloretta (Glory) herself.[14]

In its structure the poem is beyond doubt deeply influenced by the Book of Job, which Milton may have regarded as a model of the brief epic. The character of Job is named six times (I: 147, 369, 425; III: 64, 67, 95); the book is quoted twice (I, 33, 368); and there are at least ten other direct allusions to it. Milton parallels the trials of Christ and the trial of Job (I, 146 ff.), and God's address to Job out of the whirlwind parallels the fearsome storm of *Paradise Regained* (IV, 409 ff.). The two works have the common characteristic of proceeding mainly by dialogue which is joined by short introductory, concluding, and linking passages of narrative. The adoption of a certain amount of the technique of classical epic (e.g., the invocation) was inevitable, but there is less such influence in *Paradise Regained* than in *Paradise Lost*. Adornments from ancient poetry and myth are also rare.

In a different way, the poem is filled to an even more remarkable degree than its predecessor with the fruit of Milton's learning. We see, for example, in the description of Imperial Rome, in the resume of the intellectual achievement of Greece, and in the exaltation of Hebrew expression the result of a lifetime of intense and sympathetic study of three literatures. The historical and political knowledge displayed in the account of the situation in the time of Christ bears witness to the close attention which Milton had devoted to these matters in ancient and modern writers. The philosophic meditations on fame and the other objects of human desire, so rich in concrete illustration and so comprehensive in generalization, are eloquent of Milton's familiarity with the detail of recorded human experience and with the pronouncements of all the sages upon its meaning. We can trace in *Paradise Regained* the collection of more than one of the topics which Milton had set down with appropriate

---

[14] Lewalski, *Milton's Brief Epic*, p. 120.

quotation and reference in the Commonplace Book. Thus the remarks on the office and duties of the king have an interesting correspondence with certain passages from Machiavelli and other
authorities which Milton recorded in the Commonplace Book under
the heading "Rex." But all this had been digested and assimilated
until it was part of the substance of Milton's thought and no longer
recognizable as borrowing.

EXPOSITORY OUTLINE

The first seven lines of Book I link the theme of the new poem
with that of *Paradise Lost*. Christ's successful foiling of the tempter
is the logical counterpart of Adam's succumbing to his wiles. The
invocation is made directly to the Divine Spirit and not, as in *Paradise Lost*, to a muse or other epic figure. The action begins when
Satan hears the divine pronouncement at the baptism of Jesus,
"This is my Son belov'd" (1. 85). A new council is summoned in
middle air, and Satan is again appointed to the mission of seduction.
The scene then changes to Heaven, and God predicts to the
assembled angels the victory of the new Adam in the coming conflict, as he had earlier predicted the fall of man. The angels sing a
psalm of triumph. Christ now enters the wilderness and recalls in
self-communion the events of his career which have brought him,
as he supposed, to the moment of the beginning of his ministry.
The intent of God in conducting him to this desert place he does
not yet perceive. After forty days Satan appears disguised as an old
man, proposing, in language almost as bare as that of the Scriptural
account itself, the terms of the first temptation. Christ's rejection
is equally brief and simple. The words "why dost thou then suggest
to me distrust" (1. 355) clearly reveal Milton's interpretation of this
incident. Satan has, to quote the commentary of Calvin on the first
temptation,[15] "made a direct attack on the faith of Christ, in the
hope that, after destroying his faith, he would drive Christ to
unlawful and wicked methods of procuring food."[16] In the succeed-

[15] See Allan H. Gilbert, "The Temptation in *Paradise Regained*," JEGP,
XV (1916), 599–611.
[16] *Ibid.*, pp. 602–03.

ing dialogue Satan, now revealed in his true identity, utters a fawning and hypocritical complaint. Christ pronounces his misery deserved and interposes no objection to the proposal of further conversations. The scene ends with Satan's vanishing and the approach of night.

In Book II Andrew, Simon, and others who have been baptized with Christ experience perplexity and a sense of loss at his disappearance, but they give expression to the hope that God will not allow his promises to be defeated. Mary also accepts in patience the absence of her son. The scene now reverts to middle air, whither Satan returns for further deliberation with his peers. His speech to them is entirely lacking in the high spirit of defiance which had informed his utterance in the first books of *Paradise Lost*. Belial, too, has lost his eloquence, though not his sensuality; his vain suggestion, "set women in his eye," is scornfully rejected. Satan's superior intelligence perceives that the simple allurement which has sufficed for Adam's weakness is here of no avail. He proposes more sophisticated attractions—honor, glory, and popular praise—for his second and more elaborate attempt, but he first prepares an elemental appeal to appetite and natural need. This introductory approach is not a continuation or an inartistic repetition of the first temptation, which has been definitely ended and is marked off by an intervening night and day, and which, besides, represented something quite different from a mere offer of bread. It is rather the first step in the second enticement, which is to comprise, in the Biblical phrase, "the kingdoms of the world and the glory of them." Milton proceeds, as we shall see, through a kind of scale of values, and he appropriately begins with bodily luxury, the lowest and simplest object of worldly attainment. It is proper, therefore, that the offer should take the form of a gorgeous Roman banquet with all the accompanying blandishments of sense.

Christ's preliminary dream of food is parallel to the dream of Eve in Book V of *Paradise Lost*. We are told that now, for the first time, he hungers. Satan asks,

> If Food were now before thee set
> Would'st thou not eat?

(11. 320–21)

and Christ replies,

                         Thereafter as I like
                         The giver. . . .

                                                    (11. 321–22)

The point is that the satisfaction of a fleshly need is not in itself
a sin but may become so when a moral issue is involved. The rich
repast is the offering of Satan and is accordingly rejected. Christ's
victory, here, as later, is a victory of temperance, the triumph of
reason over desire.

    Wealth is next offered as a means to power. Jesus in reply dis-
parages riches without virtue. Material possession is the "wise man's
cumbrance if not snare" (1. 454). As for the scepter which wealth
can buy, true kingship is the sovereignty of man over himself, and
the royal crown, golden in show, is but a wreath of thorns.

    In Book III Satan proceeds without break in the action to
propose the higher object—glory—a fruit of empire as empire had
been of wealth. In a noble passage Christ anatomizes the conception, expressing Milton's scorn of the brutish fame of conquerors
and setting beside it the true fame of heroes who sought it not. The
lines are linked with the digression on the "last infirmity of Noble
mind" in *Lycidas* and the conclusion is the same.

    As an abstract object of ambition, glory is the highest prize
Satan has to offer. He now subtly turns to matters directly connected with the fulfillment of Christ's mission and under guise of
giving him experience toward its accomplishment, he exhibits the
kingdoms of the earth before his eyes. First Parthia, a symbol of
military strength and efficiency, inviting leadership and affording
golden opportunity for the domination of the world. Christ's reply
is that all arms are vanity; his argument postulates the strength of
human weakness. His own weapons are spiritual, and his time is
not yet come. As for the ten tribes of Israel, their deliverance from
bondage is no work of his but is in the hands of God.

    At the beginning of Book IV Satan, with increasing hopeless-
ness, sets the face of his intended victim to the west. Rome in her
glory, present mistress of the world, is at his will. Rome is a type
of grandeur and magnificence and as such is refused, like the vain
ostentation of arms. Technically this concludes the offer of the

kingdoms of the earth, and at this point Satan—futilely, since they have already been rejected—proposes his condition:

> All these
> . . . to thee I give;
>
> .   .   .   .
> . . . if thou wilt fall down
> And worship me. . . .
>
> (11. 162 ff.)

Milton has, however, an important and characteristic addition to make. Christ has completely vindicated his superiority to all the glories which allure the most talented and ambitious men. It has been the public glamor of these things rather than the things themselves on which Satan has relied to appeal to a spirit whom he recognized from the first to be above succumbing to the enticements of sensuality. There remains a type of glory which by its very nature appeals only to a few and can hardly be said to belong to the fleshly kingdoms of the world—the glory of wisdom and intellectual achievement, represented best by ancient Athens.

With new enthusiasm Milton has Satan portray this loftier ideal in all its beauty. The passage is a wonderful resume of the supreme accomplishments of pagan culture—its creation of the great literary forms of epic, drama, lyric; its majestic oratory; its final fruit in philosophy,

> From Heaven descended to the low-rooft house
> Of *Socrates*.
>
> (IV, 273–74)

Here, then, is an attraction which Milton himself felt in fullest measure; when offered to the historical Christ as a means at once congenial to his temper and apparently harmonious with his spiritual aims, it might well be supposed to prove alluring. His reply does not altogether reject it, but exalts above it the inspired literature of the Hebrews, superior at every point in spiritual truth. Without despising the claims of intellectual culture and the arts, Christ avoids the snare of pride, that last infirmity of the noble mind divinely gifted with the capacity of adding to the world's precious heritage of spiritual truth and beauty.

This test concludes the second temptation. Abruptly and in anger Satan proceeds to a final desperate attempt. The new method which he adopts is that of violence—the last resource of those whom the arts of reasoning have failed. Such, at least, is Milton's curious interpretation of the third temptation. Christ is set upon a pinnacle of the temple with the scornful words:

> There stand, if thou wilt stand; to stand upright
> Will ask thee skill. . . .
> . . . If not to stand,
> Cast thy self down.
>
> (11. 551 ff.)

And Satan, with his persistent skepticism, looks to see him fall. The answer is no act of Christ's but a miracle: to the amazement of his enemy he remains divinely supported in his "uneasy station," and it is Satan himself who falls. A throng of angels now bear the Lord from on high to a flowery valley and give him the food which he has refused at Satan's hand; the heavenly choir sing triumph and the founding of a fairer paradise. The poem ends with the quiet return of Jesus to his mother's house.

Although the central conflict of *Paradise Regained* may appear to some to be contrived and devoid of action and tension, and though the central figure may seem more a moral exemplar than a dramatic personage, Arnold Stein and others have effectively argued the opposite.[17] Considering the basic problem of the poem—a hero who must prove himself not by acting but by a special kind of nonaction, a kind of conquering weakness—Stein points out how difficult it is to present weakness *dramatically*. Milton solves the problem, which may be inherent in the material, by shifting much of the dramatic weight onto Satan who plays a dual role as tempter and tempted; ultimately, then, the game he plays is reversed and he becomes the victim. If the reader of the drama focuses on the temptation scenes and upon the dazzling monomania that is Satan, he must soon realize that Christ can only appear tempted by the Satanic devices

---

[17] See Arnold Stein's fine detailed analysis of the action, "*Paradise Regained*."

which do not tempt him at all. Around this ironic imbalance, Christ's quiet mind is constantly alive and active[18] while it disposes of the emptiness which is Satan. The real drama of the poem is internal;[19] what is apparent is the false drama of the poem. In the wilderness Christ lays down the rudiments of the "great warfare" necessary for the ultimate defeat of Satan; during the course of the temptations he defines himself and comes to full knowledge of his threefold mediatorial function. Barbara Lewalski has demonstrated how first as prophet Christ declares the will of the Father and is heavenly teacher; how as king he governs the church by spiritual law; and how as priest he is intercessor for man and ultimate sacrifice. The poem may best be read as the search for, the challenge to, and the definition of these three aspects of Christ's earthly office.[20]

SAMSON AGONISTES

DATE

Since *Samson Agonistes* was published last, following *Paradise Regained*, the general critical and biographical assumption is that it was also written last. Upon this assumption—which has never been proven false—rest the many and varied analogies drawn between Milton and the hero of his drama. It has been argued, for instance, that the poem gains from association with our picture of Milton himself in the last days of his heroic life, blind and alone amid the alien society of the Restoration, confronted with the apparent failure of the cause for which he had battled, but seeking in religious faith the assurance that God

---

[18] Hughes writes that Milton's conception of Christ is to be judged in the light of the epic tradition from Boccaccio and Petrarch. It represents a fusion of the faith of the reformers in a redeemer—the Logos of St. John's Gospel—with the craving of the critics and poets of the later Renaissance for the exemplary epic hero ("The Christ of *Paradise Regained* and the Renaissance Heroic Tradition").

[19] See Louis Martz, *"Paradise Regained:* The Interior Teacher."

[20] *Milton's Brief Epic,* pp. 164–92.

will not long defer
To vindicate the glory of his name
Against all competition, nor will long
Endure it, doubtful whether God be Lord,
Or *Dagon*.

(11. 474–78)

Such an analogue between the poet's own position and that of his
protagonist may have been vividly present in his mind, and into
the representation of Samson he may have put more of himself
than into any other of his imaginative creations. *Samson Agonistes*
indeed may be a work of his old age. But in 1949 William R. Parker
questioned the usual assumptions that are held about *Samson
Agonistes*.[21] He pointed out that Milton himself said nothing about
when the poem was written, that Milton's nephew, Edward Phillips,
who was an amanuensis in Milton's house from 1640 to 1646, says he
does not know when it was written, and that the presence of rhyme
points to a poem that may have a composition date other than the
one usually accepted. Discussing what he calls the "autobiographical
fallacy" about interpretations of the poem, Parker points out that
there were other periods in Milton's life which suggest themselves
as analogous to the situations faced by Samson: a pre-Restoration
situation might suggest similarities between Mary Powell Milton
and Dalila, Harapha and Salmasius, etc. Parker concludes that the
poem was begun in 1646 or 1647, discontinued in April, 1648, when
Milton turned to Psalm translating, and was taken up again in
1652 or 1653 as a form of catharsis. Milton then dropped the subject
when he was forced to go back to work in the pamphlet war.
Although Parker's suppositions are fascinating, they must be regarded as conjectures; they do, however, render suspect the commonly accepted biographical interpretations of the poem. Without
further external evidence scholars may be unable to settle conclusively the matter of the date of *Samson Agonistes*.[22]

[21] "The Date of *Samson Agonistes*." See also the point-by-point rebuttal by
Ernest Sirluck, "Some Recent Changes in the Chronology of Milton's Poems,"
JEGP, LX (1961), 749–85.

[22] John Shawcross' recent edition of Milton's poems (1963), which claims
to follow strict chronological order, prints the poem as if it were begun in 1646;
thus it appears before *Paradise Lost*.

SOURCES

Milton is dependent upon Scripture (Judges, 18–26) for the material of *Samson Agonistes* and in the main on that alone. There is no convincing evidence that he made any extensive use of other literary treatments of his theme. The case for his indebtedness to Vondel's *Samson*, a drama in classical form published in 1660, which, like Milton's, deals with the last day of the hero's life, has been strongly urged by George Edmundson.[23] But it has been attacked with equal vehemence by A. W. Verity and others.[24] The similarities in phrase are not very striking, and the likeness in plot structure is hardly greater than one would expect to result from independent molding of the Biblical materials into the form of ancient tragedy. We have already seen that the specific subject of Samson's death had long been present in Milton's mind. The development of the action by a series of visits to Samson finds no parallel in Vondel. Some minor details are said to have been taken from the history of Samson in the fifth book of Josephus. Verity points to a description of ruins in Gaza called "the theater of Samson" in George Sandys's *Relation of Foreign Travel* as having very probably furnished Milton with hints as to the kind of structure which Samson pulled down on the heads of the Philistines. A *History of Samson* written in 1632 by Francis Quarles has, as George Whiting pointed out,[25] some striking parallels.

Of equal importance with Scriptural influences is that of the "modern" Italian practices mentioned by Milton in his introduction. Speaking of the manner of the choral odes, he indicates that he followed "the Ancients and *Italians*." While F. T. Prince has demonstrated conclusively the influence of Tasso's *Aminta*, Guarini's *Il Pastor Fido*, and Andreini's *L'Adamo* on the structural and rhythmic patterns of Milton's choral odes,[26] Gretchen L. Finney had earlier discussed the wider influence on Milton of the *tragedia per musica* tradition which culminated in the eighteenth-century ora-

[23] *Milton and Vondel* (London, 1885).
[24] *Samson Agonistes* (Cambridge, Eng., 1897), pp. 158–68.
[25] *Milton's Literary Milieu*, pp. 253–64.
[26] *The Italian Element in Milton's Verse*, pp. 145–69, 178–83.

torio.[27] There seems no doubt of Milton's indebtedness to these contemporary Continental examples. The great formative influence on *Samson Agonistes*, however, is classical tragedy; the relation here is important enough to deserve detailed discussion.

RELATIONS TO GREEK DRAMA AND
TO THE CLASSICAL THEORY OF TRAGEDY

On the title page of the first edition of *Samson Agonistes* Milton printed as a motto Aristotle's definition of tragedy (here translated): "the imitation of a serious action, etc., effecting through pity and fear a purification of such emotions." In his introductory note he discusses the crux of this definition, the old question as to what is meant by the catharsis of the emotions. Tragedy converts the emotions to which we are subject from a source of pain to a source of pleasure by artistically embodying them in a dramatic fiction. The pity and fear stirred up in us in the theater are a homeopathic dose, purging the mind of its unwholesome private passions. This idea and purpose were prominently in Milton's consciousness as he wrote the poem. He makes Samson describe his own inner agony in terms which strongly suggest the medical figure used in the introduction, and he has the chorus indicate at the close the calming and ennobling effect which the witnessing of this great event has had on the minds of the spectators.[28]

To be the significant literary form Milton conceived, tragedy must be written in the direct tradition of classical antiquity; it must avoid the sensationalism of the modern stage and behave according to the body of principles laid down by Aristotle in the *Poetics*, elaborated by the critics of the Renaissance, and illustrated by the individual dramas of Aeschylus, Sophocles, and Euripides.[29] *Samson*

---

[27] "Chorus in *Samson Agonistes.*"

[28] See James Holly Hanford, "*Samson Agonistes* and Milton in Old Age."

[29] See Richard C. Jebb, "*Samson Agonistes* and the Hellenic Drama," *Proceedings of the British Academy* (1907-08), pp. 341-48; Paul F. Baum, "*Samson Agonistes* Again," PMLA, XXXVI (1921), 354-71; and W. Brewer, "Two Athenian Models for *Samson Agonistes*," PMLA, XLII (1927), 910-20. E. M. W. Tillyard (*Milton*, pp. 343-44) discusses the use of *peripeteia* in *Samson* and makes the claim that in this matter, as well as in that of catharsis, Milton

Agonistes is offered as a model of what, in these respects, a modern tragedy should be. We are invited not only to read it but to test it by comparison with the greatest of its kind.

The chief points where *Samson Agonistes* stands in obvious contrast with Elizabethan drama and in conformity "with ancient rule and best example" are the following: 1) the limitation of the scope of the action to the final episode in Samson's career; 2) the strict preservation of the unities of time and place; 3) the employment of the chorus and the messenger. The adherence to these and other conventions was not with Milton a mere mechanical or formal matter; it was rather an attempt to secure by their use the artistic effect—the *symmetria prisca*—which he admired in ancient drama and felt the lack of in the modern. He speaks of "verisimilitude and decorum," the two familiar terms in the Aristotelian criticism of the Renaissance, as the objects aimed at. Elsewhere he calls decorum, or artistic propriety, "the grand master peece to observe."[30] These devices were not his masters but his instruments, and his play, as a consequence, is a recreation rather than an imitation of Greek art. The narrowing of the action, the restriction of the number of speaking characters, the limitation of the dramatic time to a single day, and the avoidance of a change of scene enabled him to achieve a certain concentration of effect. The chorus served the purpose at

---

understood Aristotle better than most of his modern commentators. "A *peripeteia* happens, not when there is a mere change of fortune, but when an intention or action brings about the opposite of what was meant. . . . The essence of the plot in *Samson* is that nearly all the actions should lead whither they had not seemed to lead. Jebb pointed out how everything in the plot narrows Samson's prospects into greater and greater chance of ignominy. . . . The *peripeteia* consists in this choice of apparent ignominy inevitably leading to triumph." In thus making his action depend upon *peripeteia*, Tillyard thinks, Milton ranged his plot under the heading of complex, preferred by Aristotle to the simple form. Milton himself in the introductory note says of the plot that the reader may judge whether it is intricate or explicit, "which is nothing indeed but such economy, or disposition of the fable as may stand best with verisimilitude and decorum." J. P. Mahaffy (*What Have the Greeks Done for Modern Civilization?* [New York, 1909], p. 49) finds Milton's development of his theme primarily Euripidean. William R. Parker, on the other hand (*Milton's Debt to Greek Tragedy*), thinks that in the scarcity of characters, the bareness of the plot, and the concentration on a single figure, *Samson* resembles the dramas of Aeschylus.

[30] "Of Education," ed. with preface and notes by Donald C. Dorian, Yale, *Milton*, II, 405.

once of interpreting the emotions appropriate to the successive moments in the action, of clarifying the larger significance of the whole, and of rounding out the story by allusions to Samson's past. The narration of the messenger was a substitute for the actual representation of the catastrophe; this Milton avoided not only because the Greeks had done so, but because verisimilitude, dignity, and the desire to focus attention on the dramatic significance of the event rather than upon the event itself all demanded it.

But Milton was deeply influenced by the content as well as the form of ancient tragedy. He found precedents for his suffering hero in more than one tragic figure of antiquity, and he remolded him to some degree in their great images.[31] Aeschylus' Prometheus is akin to Samson in the grandeur of his woe, but there is something of a parallel with Heracles, a giant of strength like Samson and a performer of incredible labors, but subject also to a spiritual weakness. Like Samson, he becomes enthralled and ultimately brought to destruction by the influence of woman. The specific Heracles drama which here enters into comparison with Milton's is the *Trachiniae* of Sophocles. In other features *Samson Agonistes* is more closely related to the *Oedipus at Colonus;* the direct influence here is apparent. Oedipus, blind and helpless by his own error, is visited by a succession of friends and enemies. He resists the blandishments and threats of Creon as Samson resists those of the Philistines. His former greatness and present misery are remembered in dialogue and chorus. His end is a triumph, though of a different sort. Particularly noticeable as a feature derived from the very essence of Greek tragedy is Milton's attempt to interpret Samson's tragic error as hybris, that overconfidence which leads men to trust too much to their own power and provokes an attack on them by the jealous gods. Milton's conception of Providence rather than Fate

---

[31] Not only have readers sought to determine Samson's predecessors, they have also been tempted to consider Samson a type of the Christ. But although F. Michael Krouse has demonstrated that Samson was part of a tradition which saw him as a Christian saint (*Milton's Samson and the Christian Tradition*), there is not one piece of internal evidence which, when viewed in context, supports the typological contention. William G. Madsen rightfully notes the importance of Samson as an "antitype"; one should "recognize the differences between them [Samson and Christ], for it is essential to the whole doctrine of typology that the type be different from as well as similar to the antitype" ("From Shadowy Types to Truth," *The Lyric and Dramatic Milton*, ed. Joseph Summers [New York, 1965], p. 101).

as the ruling force in the affairs of men prevents him, however, from presenting his hero's struggle in the terms of ancient drama. The principle of hybris is invoked again in the description of the Philistines, and a final chorus applies to them precisely the formula of the Greeks. Offended at their mad pride, God sends to them a spirit of frenzy—the ancient Ate—who impairs their judgments and makes them bring on themselves, by their own acts, an avenging Nemesis.

In the detail of his drama Milton is often reminiscent of the ancients. He employs, though sparingly, stichomythia (a series of alternate speeches of a line length each), and he imitates the riddling question and answer characteristic of Greek tragic dialogue. In the substitution of alternate episode and chorus for the modern act division, and in the distinction between the portions of the play in iambic pentameter and those in lyric measures ("chorus and iambic," as he describes them in *Paradise Regained*), he is also in accord with classic usage. The bitter reflections on the errors brought on mankind by woman are Euripidean, as is the "all is best" formula at the close. The great utterances in which Samson and the chorus recite the tale of human suffering are repetitions, though with a strong accent of individuality, of similar generalizations which pervade Greek drama. And Milton, like the Greeks (particularly Sophocles), makes conscious and consistent use of irony throughout his work.[32]

INTERPRETATION

The outward action of *Samson Agonistes* is summarized by Milton himself in an argument prefixed to the original edition.

[32] The relationship between Milton's *Samson* and ancient drama has been much discussed—most comprehensively by William R. Parker (*Milton's Debt to Greek Tragedy*), who concludes, against Jebb, that Euripides, though Milton's favorite dramatist, is not the predominant influence in *Samson*. Milton was more like Aeschylus in his attitude toward his materials, but it is to Sophocles that he is also indebted. To Parker there is no disparity between the Hellenic form and the Hebraic substance. "*Samson Agonistes* is 'Greek' in the sense that a tragedy written in the days of Aristotle might have been. . . . Because the English poet had intellectual or artistic affinities with each of his three models, he wrote—not as an imitator of one of them, or two—but as a great successor of all three" (pp. 249–50).

Though he does not divide the play into acts, he intimates in his prefatory note that a five-act structure is discernible. William R. Parker, though he declines to call the divisions acts and prefers an analysis of structure based on the practice of the Greeks themselves, recognizes that the play falls into "five distinct parts, each an artistic whole, and all of very nearly the same length." His designation of these parts is substantially the same as the traditional act divisions of the editors:

  I. Samson alone with the Chorus: 1–325
  II. Samson and Manoa: 326–709
  III. Samson and Dalila: 710–1060
  IV. Samson with two instruments of force: 1061–1440
  V. Samson at the feast: 1441–1758[33]

This enumeration of incidents gives no indication of the real dramatic movement, and *Samson Agonistes* has often been said to be deficient in this respect. Samuel Johnson declared that it had a beginning and an end but no middle; to him the various visits were merely episodic, accomplishing nothing in the development of plot and climax. Such a judgment does injustice to the subtlety of Milton's personal interpretation of his theme. The drama is concerned essentially with the fallen Samson's recovery of God's lost favor. This process involves his punishment and repentance, and a sort of probation under new trial, a trial provided by the timidity and lack of faith of Manoa and the chorus, by the attempted seductions of Dalila, and by the threats of Harapha. The spiritual movement is actually much riches than it at first appears.[34]

At the opening Samson is a spectacle of tragic woe. He eloquently laments the misery and debasement of his present state,[35] and the first chorus, unheard by him, echoes and interprets his

---

[33] A *prologos*, 1–114; a *parados* or entering chorus, 115–75; five episodes and five *stasima* in alternation, 176–292, 293–325, 326–651, 652–709, 710–1009, 1010–60, 1061–1267, 1268–99, 1300–1426, 1427–40; an *exodos*, 1441–1758; and a *kommos*, 1660–1758 (*ibid.*, p. 17).

[34] See Ann Gossman, "Milton's Samson as the Tragic Hero Purified by Trial."

[35] See the full-length reading of the passage in Arnold Stein, "*Samson Agonistes*," pp. 137–47.

expression, emphasizing the contrast between what he once was and what he now is.[36] In the ensuing dialogues his attention is diverted to the cause and significance of his suffering. The memory of his fault is more bitter than the punishment wherewith it is visited. He is, however, firm in his conviction, against the intimation of the chorus, that he was, even in his marriage choices, led by God as his chosen instrument, and he replies to their somewhat malicious "Yet *Israel* still serves with all his Sons" (1. 240) by imputing the fault to Israel's governors, who neglected the opportunities which his deeds of strength made for them. The sight of Manoa wakes another "inward grief," and his words are a goad to Samson's bitter remembrance. To his implied doubt of the justice of God's dealings in apparently electing his son as the champion of Israel and then deserting him, Samson again opposes the attitude of faith: God's ways are just. Though he himself, through his own fault, has advanced the cause of Dagon and brought doubt into the feeble hearts of Israel, "propense enough before," he remains unshaken in the belief that God will not long

> Connive, or linger, thus provok'd,
> But will arise and his great name assert.
>
> (11. 466–67)

He has yet no intimation that he is himself to become the instrument of God's purposes, but he instinctively rejects his father's proposal to entreat with the Philistine lords for his release. The end result of the mistaken attempts at comfort has been to sharpen Samson's misery. The scene culminates in a spiritual outburst no longer expressive of the hero's physical suffering but of the agony of the soul which springs from full contemplation of his sins "and sense of Heaven's desertion."

---

[36] Throughout the chorus appears representative of the wisdom of the common man. Collectively they rise to a vision of what it is that inspires or motivates the uncommon man Samson only once (11. 1268 ff.). Before that their refuge is in generalizations drawn from their historical past which usually have little bearing on the present situation. They grow particularly obtuse and static during the course of the poem, counterpointing the heroism and spiritual growth in Samson. For a discussion of this role of the chorus, see Joseph Summers, "The Movements of the Drama," *Lyric and Dramatic Milton*, pp. 153–75.

Henceforth we have recovery. By confronting his own guilt without evasion and by resisting the temptation to doubt that God's ways are just or to fear for the ultimate triumph of his cause, Samson has won the right to be put to proof a second time. His firmness is subjected first to the insidious approaches of Dalila, whose visit, however doubtfully motivated in itself, is essential to the idea of the drama. Her plea is specious, and Samson remains unmoved; the chorus may see something of the significance of his victory:

> Yet beauty, though injurious, hath strange power,
> After offense returning, to regain
> Love once possest, nor can be easily
> Repuls't, without much inward passion felt
> And secret sting of amorous remorse.
>
> (ll. 1003–07)

The chorus also reveals, however, their misunderstanding; Samson has revealed no "inward passion" or "secret sting of amorous remorse" about his rejection of Dalila. Their generality hardly fits the occasion.

Samson next confronts physical force in the person of Harapha, who collapses, like all brute menace, before the champion's indifference to fear, and the chorus, participating for the moment in Samson's strength, sings the great ode,

> O how comely it is and how reviving
> To the Spirits of just men long opprest!
> When God into the hands of thir deliverer
> Puts invincible might
> To quell the mighty of the Earth, th' oppressor,
> The brute and boist'rous force of violent men.
>
> (ll. 1268–73)

They are, of course, like Samson himself, still blind to what is to come, and they go on to sing of patience as the final crown of saints.

The coming of the officer creates a problem. Samson's initial refusal to do his bidding illustrates his uncompromising allegiance to the God of his fathers and his contempt of personal safety. The chorus, unable to sustain the heroic vision of their previous ode, suggests the easier way of yielding, pointing out the fact that he has already served the Philistines (with the old implication that he cannot regard himself as a being set apart). Their reasoning is met with a clear distinction between compromise in things indifferent and the surrender of a point of conscience. Then, as if in answer to this final proof of Samson's single devotedness to God's service, comes again the inner prompting to

> dispose
> To something extraordinary my thoughts.
>
> (ll. 1382–83)

He obeys it unhesitatingly and goes forth under divine guidance as of old. Manoa, meanwhile, is busy with misguided plans for his son's release, the moment of his success ironically coinciding with that of Samson's death. The news of Samson's last destructive act[37] is received by his friends with grief and horror, which turns to satisfaction in the fact that Samson died

> With God not parted from him, as was fear'd,
> But favoring and assisting to the end
>
> (ll. 1719–20)

---

[37] In his final justification of Samson, Milton felt obligated, as St. Augustine and other theologians had, to clear him of the taint of suicide:

> And now li'st victorious
> Among thy slain self-kill'd
> Not willingly, but tangl'd in the fold
> Of dire necessity, whose law in death conjoin'd
> Thee with thy slaughter'd foes.
>
> (ll. 1663–67)

This final act, like his first marriage, was a result of the divine prompting and therefore not subject to the common ethical judgment. (Cf. Augustine, *De Civitate Dei*, I, xxi: *Nec Samson aliter excusatur . . . nisi quia Spiritus latenter hoc iusserat.*) H. J. C. Grierson, who elaborates this point, suggests that Milton might have employed a similar formula in thinking of the crimes of the republican party, when, after the Restoration, all men joined in execrating them: "these acts are not of man but of God and God will vindicate his cause" ("A Note upon the *Samson Agonistes* of John Milton and *Samson* of *Heilige Wraek* by Joost Van Den Vondel," *Extrait des Mélanges Baldensperger* [Paris, 1930]); *Milton and Wordsworth*, pp. 138 ff.

and to exultation in this manifestation of the Almighty's triumph over his enemies.[38]

As thus interpreted *Samson Agonistes* fits closely into the scheme of Milton's major works. It is—in a different sense, of course, from *Paradise Regained*—a counterpart of *Paradise Lost*. Lines 1059–62 of the ninth book of the latter poem show that Milton was conscious of an analogy between the sin of Adam and that of Samson. The last phase of the Hebrew champion's career provides a concrete illustration of the power of a free but erring will to face its sin, maintain itself in obedience, and be restored to grace. The drama, like the epics, is an assertion of eternal Providence and a justification of the ways of God to men.

[38] Cf. with Parker's more detailed exposition (*Milton's Debt to Greek Tragedy*, pp. 30–59). Parker says that Samson's reconciliation to God was not possible until he had proved himself master of his old weakness by rejecting the blandishments of Dalila. Milton is not very successful in representing an emotional conflict in Samson here, if he intended to do so. We have to take it on faith that he was moved to anything but wrath. Obviously this visit, like that of Harapha, rouses him and "determines his will" and, in so doing, advances the action.

8. Frontispiece of 1645 edition of Poems. Milton ridiculed the engraving by William Marshall in the Greek lines below it: "That an unskilful hand had carved this print/You'd say at once, seeing that living face;/But, finding here no jot of me, my friends,/Laugh at the botching artist's mis-attempt." (Masson's translation) (Henry E. Huntington Library)

9. Title page of 1645 edition of Poems. (Henry E. Huntington Library)

0. Contract between John Milton and Samuel Simmons for the printing of *Paradise Lost*, April 27, 1667. Simmons agrees to print not more than 4,500 copies in three impressions of 1,500 copies each, to pay £5 down, a second £5 "at the end of the first impression," a third £5 "at the end of the second impression," and a fourth £5 "at the end of the third impression." Milton's signature was affixed by his amanuensis, Jeremie Picard. *Add. ms.* 5016. (Trustees of the British Museum)

1. Title page of first issue of first edition of *Paradise Lost* (1667). (Henry E. Huntington Library)

2. Milton's signature, November 19, 1651, in the album of Christopher Arnold. The inscription, in John Phillips' hand, is translated as follows: "I am made perfect in weakness. To the very learned Mr. Christopher Arnold, my most obliging friend, I have given this, in memory both of his own worth and of my regard for him. Londini, An.D. 1651. Novem: 19. Joannes Miltonius." There are two errors in the inscription: for αδενία read ἀγθενία and for "sua" read "suæ." "Meoqz" is meant to be read "meoque." Egerton ms. 1324, fol. 85v. (Trustees of the British Museum)

3. Page from John Milton's Bible giving the entries made with his own hand (and that of Jeremie Picard) concerning his birth and those of various members of his family. *Add. ms.* 32310. (Trustees of the British Museum)

4. Milton's monument, sculpted by J. Bacon and apparently erected in 1793, in St. Giles, Cripplegate. The bust was probably derived from a copy of the so-called Pierce-Simon bust now in Christ's College (done either by Edward Pierce or Abraham Simon, around 1651 or even after 1650, from life). Both Milton and his father were buried here; his father was buried on March 15, 1646 (N.S. 1647). (Guildhall Library, London; photo John Freeman)

Melpo mene.   Erato.

IOANNIS MILTONI ANGLI EFFIGIES ANNO ÆTATIS VIGes: Pri:

Urania.   Clio.

Ἀμαθεῖ γεγράφθαι χειρὶ τὴνδε μὲν εἰκόνα
Φαίης τάχ' ἄν, πρὸς εἶδος αὐτοφυὲς βλέπων
Τὸν δ' ἐκτυπωτὸν ᾿κ ἐπιγνόντες φίλοι
Γελᾶτε φαύλ᾿ δυσμίμημα ζωγράφ᾿.

W·M· ſculp:

POEMS

OF

Mr. *John Milton*,

BOTH

ENGLISH and LATIN,
Compos'd at several times.

Printed by his true Copies.

The SONGS were set in Musick by
Mr. HENRY LAWES Gentleman of
the KINGS Chappel, and one
of His MAIESTIES
Private Musick.

—————*Baccare frontem*
Cingite, ne vati noceat mala lingua futuro,
Virgil, Eclog. 7.

Printed and publish'd according to
ORDER.

LONDON,
Printed by *Ruth Raworth* for *Humphrey Moseley*,
and are to be sold at the signe of the Princes
Arms in *Pauls* Church-yard. 1645.

This Presents Made the 27th day of Aprill 1667 Betweene John Milton gent of thone pt
And Samuel Symons Printer of thother pte Wittnesse That the said John Milton in consideracon
of five pounds to him now paid by the said Samll Symons of hwhich the consideracon
menconed hath given graunted and assigned, and by these presents doth give graunt and assigne
vnto the said Samll Symons his executors and assignes All that Booke Copy or
Manuscript of a Poem intituled Paradise lost, or by whatsoever title or name
the same is or shalbe called or distinguished now lately licensed to be printed ...

Sealed and Delivered in the
presence of vs.

John Fisher

Beniamin Greene ser 6 d.
Milton

John Milton

Paradiſe loſt.

A
P O E M

Written in
TEN BOOKS

By *JOHN MILTON.*

Licenſed and Entred according
to Order.

L O N D O N

Printed, and are to be ſold by *Peter Parker*
under *Creed* Church neer *Aldgate* ; And by
Robert Boulter at the *Turks Head* in *Biſhopſgate-ſtreet* ;
And *Matthias Walker*, under St. *Dunſtons* Church
in *Fleet-ſtreet*, 1 6 6 7.

Ἐν ἀθενείᾳ τελειῦμαι

Doctissimo Viro meoq fausori humanissimo,
D. Christophoro Arnoldo dedi hoc, in memo-
riam cum sua virtutis, tum mei erga se studij.
Londini. An: D. 1651 Novem: 19.

              Joannes Miltonius.

John Milton was born the 9th of December 1608 die Veneris half an hower after 6 in the morning

Christofer Milton was born on Friday about a month before Christmass at 5 in the morning 1615

Edward Phillips was 15 year old August 1645
John Phillips is a year younger about October.

My daughter Anne was born July the 29th on the fast at eebning about half an houre after Six 1646

My daughter Mary was born on Wedensday Octob. 25th on the fast day in the morning about 6 a clock 1648.

My son John was born on Sunday March the 16th about half an hower past nine at night 1650

My daughter Deborah was Born the 2d of May Being Sunday Somewhat before 3 of the clock in the morning 1652.

This my wife hir mother dyed about 3 days after. And my son about 6 weeks after his mother

Katherin my daughter by Katherin my second wife, was borne ye 19th of October between 5 and 6 in ye morning and dyed ye 17th of March following 6 weeks after hir mother, who dyed ye 3d of Feb. 1657

14

Chapter 6

STYLE AND VERSIFICATION

DICTION AND SYNTAX

MILTON, AS ALL GREAT ENGLISH WRITERS, IS AN INNOVATOR IN THE matter of expression. His style is unique, forged out of various materials and marked by bold departures from the English literary usage of his own or of any time. Few scholars and critics, however, have been able to agree upon the precise characteristics of what has been termed Milton's "grand style" or upon the degree of its effectiveness. Most agree generally that Milton's style, despite his employment of a verse form identical with that of the Elizabethan dramatists, is totally different from that of Shakespeare and his colleagues. Milton's diction, some claim, has little relish of the speech of men; but after a thorough study of the language of Book VI of *Paradise Lost*, Lalia Phipps Boone has concluded that "the Latinity of Milton's poetic language has been overestimated."[1] The more recent statistical studies of E. M. Clark, which compare the "language at rest" with the "language in motion," reveal that "in motion" Milton's vocabulary is seven percent Anglo-Saxon.[2] But ultimately a statistical count does little to settle the question, and

1 "The Language of Book VI, *Paradise Lost*," p. 127.
2 "Milton's English Poetical Vocabulary," p. 230.

for the particular workings of Milton's various Latinisms, the reader must examine the diction of each passage closely and study the cross-effects in context, for it is true that one unusual word of whatever origin may count more than a dozen typically English words. Helen Darbishire has pointed out how in *Paradise Lost* Latin words are balanced—her term is "retrieved"—by native English ones; in numerous instances a Latin and a native English term are juxtaposed to complement one another and invite the reader to consider the richness evoked by the comparison.[3] A more complete analysis has been made by Christopher Ricks; his chapter on the "enhancing suggestions" of Milton's diction in context is a particularly fine study.[4]

One of the first approaches to a systematic treatment of Milton's style was that of David Masson in the third volume of his edition of the poetical works.[5] The detail of this is too elaborate for presentation here, and much of it is simply a statement of peculiarities of sixteenth- and seventeenth-century usage in general. In 1922 R. D. Havens classified the characteristics of Milton's style which were thought in the eighteenth century to distinguish it from other poetry and which the poets of the period felt obliged to reproduce when they wrote blank verse. Though it does not pretend to be complete or scientifically accurate, this list—when supplemented by Ricks's observations on the syntactical effects gained in individual passages—is a serviceable statement of the obvious differentia of Milton's poetic speech in his blank verse poems. It includes, besides the vaguer items of dignity, stateliness, and the "organ tone," the following concrete characteristics:[6]

1. *Inversion of the natural order of words and phrases:*

> Them thus imploy'd beheld
> With pity Heav'n's high King. . . .
>
> (*PL*, V, 219–20: OVS)

[3] "Milton's Poetic Language," pp. 31–52.
[4] *Milton's Grand Style*, pp. 78–117.
[5] *Works*, III, 3–133.
[6] Raymond D. Havens, *The Influence of Milton on English Poetry*, pp. 80–88; the most recent and comprehensive study of Milton's constructions is Ronald David Emma's *Milton's Grammar*.

> Him the Almighty Power
> Hurl'd headlong flaming from th' Ethereal Sky.
> > (PL, I, 44–45; OSV)
> They looking back, all th' Eastern side beheld
> Of Paradise, so late thir happy seat.
> > (PL, XII, 641–42: SOV)

He calls especial attention to Milton's habit of placing a word between two others which depend on it and on which it depends, e.g. (noun between adjectives), "temperate vapours bland"; (verb between nouns), "Firm peace recovered soon and wonted calm."

2. *The omission of words not necessary to the sense:*

> Extended wide
> In circuit, undetermin'd square or round.
> > (PL, II, 1047–48)

3. *Parenthesis and apposition:*

> Of *Abbana* and *Pharphar*, lucid streams.
> > (PL, I, 469)
> Thir Song was partial, but the harmony
> (What could it less when Spirits immortal sing?)
> Suspended Hell. . . .
> > (PL, II, 552–54)

4. *The use of one part of speech for another: e.g. (verb form as noun),* "the great consult began"; *(adjective form as adverb or as noun)* "grinned horrible," "the palpable obscure," "dark with excessive bright."

5. *Archaisms and Latinisms in vocabulary: e.g.,* "frore," "areed," "wons," "emprise," "nocent," "congratulant," "attrite."

6. *Fondness for collocations of more or less exotic proper names:*

> Of *Cambalu*, seat of *Cathaian Can*,
> And *Samarchand* by *Oxus*, *Temir's* Throne,
> To *Paquin* of *Sinaean* Kings, and thence
> To *Agra* and *Lahor* of great *Mogul*.
> > (PL, XI, 388–91)

7. Unusual and compound epithets analogous to those in Homer: e.g., "night-warbling bird," "three-bolted thunder," "Heaven-banished host," "double-founted streams."

There is perhaps no practice here of which abundant examples could not be found in English literature before Milton. The unique thing is the degree to which they become with him habitual features of style—the warp and woof of his poetical expression. Spenser, of course, used archaisms much more persistently than Milton, with whom the practice is in part at least a survival of the Spenserian tradition in poetry. Marlowe affords the closest English precedent for the magniloquent employment of proper nouns and adjectives, and Milton is indebted to him for this device, though the classics, particularly Aeschylus' *Prometheus*, are also influential. The use of Latinisms and inkhorn terms in general had been a feature of English expression since the beginnings of humanism and was at its height in the early seventeenth century. It was most common in formal prose and was on the whole avoided by the poets. John Donne, to be sure, made free use of the terminology of scholastic philosophy, but neither he nor any other English poet before Milton habitually resorted to a Latinized sentence structure as a means of removing his speech from the sphere of daily life to the lofty and sonorous realms of epic. Such inversions make *Paradise Lost* a difficult poem and the syntax frequently involuted, but as Frank Kermode has suggested, following the syntax is an act analogous to man's devious search for pleasure in a fallen world.[7]

While earlier studies, then, may have overestimated (and therefore wrongly emphasized) Milton's Latinate vocabulary, readers have seldom underestimated or disagreed about the matter of Milton's frequent employment of a Latinate or inflected syntax.[8] C. S. Lewis has stressed the importance of understanding "the Latinism of his constructions,"[9] and R. M. Adams has spoken of the "normally Latin cast" of the syntax.[10] Critics, however, have not always agreed that the frequently employed Latinate syntax is an asset

[7] "Adam Unparadised," p. 95.
[8] Cf. E. M. W. Tillyard's comment, "The main peculiarities or heightenings of Milton's style in *Paradise Lost* are quite unlatin" (*The Miltonic Setting,* p. 124).
[9] *A Preface to "Paradise Lost,"* p. 43.
[10] *Ikon,* p. 103.

to the poem. F. R. Leavis, for instance, maintains that Milton's style was responsible for "the extreme and consistent remoteness of Milton's medium from any English that was ever spoken,"[11] and Donald Davie has also charged the style with poetic ineffectiveness.[12]

This feature of Miltonic style, briefly indicated by Havens under the head of "inversion," has received fuller treatment by a German scholar, Gustav Hubener, in his monograph, *Die Stilistische Spannung in Milton's "Paradise Lost,"*[13] and it never fails to evoke critical comment. Suspension as a trait of style is differentiated from simple suspension as a matter of syntax through its greater artificiality and elaborateness. It is not native to English speech and does not occur in English poetry before the Renaissance, except sporadically and in initial sentences. Nor is it especially characteristic of Spenser. We find it first freely used in Surrey's translation of the *Aeneid*, where it reproduces the periodic structure of the Latin sentence, and it reaches its height in Milton's predecessors of the early seventeenth century—Davies, Donne, the Fletchers, and Cowley. It is to their influence, reinforced by Milton's general penchant toward the classical style in which it originates, that the elaborate periodicity of his construction may be ascribed. Hubener finds less of it in the early poems, but a remarkably Latinized sentence from *Comus* may be cited as an example:

> *Bacchus* that first from out the purple Grape
> Crusht the sweet poison of misused Wine,
> After the *Tuscan* Mariners transform'd,
> Coasting the *Tyrrhene* shore, as the winds listed,
> On *Circe's* Island fell.
>
> (ll. 46–50)

Here the suspension is accomplished by the insertion between subject and predicate of several subordinate elements which retard the completion of the sense. The first clause itself is suspended by the inversion of the verb "crusht" and the adverbial phrase "from out the purple Grape." Finally the sentence includes two bits of Latin

---

[11] "Milton's Verse," p. 51.
[12] "Syntax and Music in *Paradise Lost*," *The Living Milton*, ed. Frank Kermode, pp. 83–84. Cf., however, the favorable views of Stein, Kermode, and Ricks.
[13] (Halle, 1913).

idiom which do not contribute to the suspension, viz., "that first," with "first" probably felt as an adjective (Latin, *qui primus*), and the un-English construction "after the *Tuscan* Mariners transform'd" (Latin, *post nautas mutatos*).

In *Paradise Lost* such suspensions recur at frequent intervals. The opening sentence:

> Of Man's First Disobedience, and the Fruit
> Of that Forbidden Tree, whose mortal taste
> Brought Death into the World, and all our woe,
> With loss of *Eden*, till one greater Man
> Restore us, and regain the blissful Seat,
> Sing Heav'nly Muse. . . .

departs from a natural order, which is especially firmly fixed in imperative sentences, by beginning with the genitive object and inserting between it and the predicate a relative clause with various independent elements. Hubener finds twenty-three elaborate suspensions of one sort or another in the first book; they never occur in succession but alternate with unsuspended passages. The suspensions mark moments of emphatic meanings in the epic narrative; as, for example, the opening of Satan's address to Beelzebub:

> If thou beest hee; But O how fall'n! how chang'd
> From him, who in the happy Realms of Light
> Cloth'd with transcendent brightness didst outshine
> Myriads though bright: If he whom mutual league,
> United thoughts and counsels, equal hope,
> And hazard in the Glorious Enterprise,
> Join'd with me once, now misery hath join'd
> In equal ruin: . . .
>
> (*PL*, I, 84–91)

The structural feature thus described must be accepted as an authentic characteristic of Milton's utterance and one which contributes perhaps more than any other single element to the elevation of his poetic style. But it will not do to treat his sentences as if they were written in accordance with formal grammatical patterns. There is, indeed, a subtle and pervasive defiance of logic in much of his expression which makes such an analysis as Hubener's an only partially adequate representation of the texture of his poetic thought.

The suspension is often more apparent than real. The lines just quoted, for example, can from one point of view be interpreted as a periodic sentence, beginning with a conditional clause: "If thou beest he who, etc. . . . if he whom, etc. . . . now misery hath joined thee with me in equal ruin." In actual effect, however, they are a conglomerate of more or less coordinate ideas expressed in a series of grammatical fragments. It is as if Satan exclaimed first: "Can you be Beelzebub!" then, "How changed you are from your former angelic state," then, "Once we were joined in glorious enterprise, now we are joined in ruin." Clauses formerly subordinate here have a weight which gives them the effect of independent statements. That Milton himself felt the flow of his poetry in a kind of grammatical continuum is often shown by his punctuation. Note the semicolon after "he" and the colon after "bright," where we would use commas and parentheses. Note also the colon after "ruin," where we would perhaps use a period. The next sentence—"And that strife was not inglorious"—thus becomes a continuation of this one. Often a mere comma separates sentences grammatically independent:

> . . . thou hast giv'n me to possess
> Life in myself for ever, by thee I live,
> Though now to Death I yield, and am his due
> All that of me can die, yet that debt paid,
> Thou wilt not leave me in the loathsome grave,
> His prey. . . .
>
> (PL, III, 243–48)

This quotation illustrates a further characteristic element in Milton's thought structure. The use of the comma after "live" leaves the syntax of the next line ambiguous. As we read we inevitably take the clause with the preceding verb—until we come to "yet that debt paid," when we are compelled to readjust our minds and take it with the following. We may, if we wish, clarify the construction with a semicolon, but such ambiguities are too numerous and too effective to warrant this procedure. Similar syntactical ambiguities are illustrated in

> With thee conversing I forget all time,
> All seasons and thir change, all please alike.
>
> (PL, IV, 639–40)

This is another example of what Walter Bagehot called the "haunting atmosphere of enhancing suggestions" in Milton's poetry, suggestions well discussed by Christopher Ricks.[14]

The fact that Milton dictated rather than wrote his mature poetry may have increased his tendency toward a free type of expression characteristic of speech. In any case, his utterance, while pursuing its undeviating larger course and revealing everywhere deliberate purpose, seems like an effect of nature as well as of art and perfectly witnesses the truth of his own account of its inspired origin:

> If answerable style I can obtain
> Of my Celestial Patroness, who deigns
> Her nightly visitation unimplor'd,
> And dictates to me slumb'ring, or inspires
> Easy my unpremeditated Verse.

> (*PL*, IX, 20–24)

ALLUSION AND SIMILE

Another essential quality of Miltonic style is its allusiveness. Insofar as it consists of a rich suggestion of matters of observation in the realm of nature and human experience, this allusiveness is a trait which Milton shares with many poets. In the degree, however, to which his vision is colored by the experience of other men and simple observation modified by knowledge, he is almost unique. The whole treasury of poetry and a vast storehouse of learning are at his command. He assumes that they are also at the command of his reader, and accordingly he loads every rift of his verse with the ore of myth and legend, historical, literary, and scientific fact. Of no other English style is erudition so integral a part. Classical and Biblical allusions are, of course, the most abundant, constituting a kind of current coin of expression.

But Milton writes not only as a literary connoisseur but also as a scholar, appealing in his readers to a love of ordered learning like

[14] *Milton's Grand Style*, pp. 78–117.

his own. Even the echoes of ancient phrase should often be considered not as mere borrowings, conscious or unconscious, but as allusions intended to carry with them the connotations of their original setting. The comprehensiveness and precision of his references and the care he takes to introduce some piece of essential information not really relevant to the purpose of expression are aspects of his general didacticism. The extraordinary thing is the way in which the object is accomplished without a loss of poetic quality. The secret seems to be the degree to which the materials of learning have become associated with sensuous imagery and with moving poetical ideas. Milton is erudite, but all erudition is not for him of equal value. His studies have passed into vital experience and afford him as natural a body of poetical data as birds and flowers.

The scholarly habit of mind seeking order and comprehensiveness is well illustrated by such a passage as the comparison of the Satanic host to various military assemblages of epic legend at the close of Book I (573–87) of *Paradise Lost*:

> . . . For never since created man,
> Met such imbodied force, as nam'd with these
> Could merit more than that small infantry
> Warr'd on by Cranes: though all the Giant brood
> Of *Phlegra* with th' Heroic Race were join'd
> That fought at *Thebes* and *Ilium*, on each side
> Mixt with auxiliar Gods; and what resounds
> In Fable or *Romance* of *Uther's* Son
> Begirt with *British* and *Armoric* Knights;
> And all who since, Baptiz'd or Infidel
> Jousted in *Aspramont* or *Montalban*,
> *Damasco*, or *Marocco*, or *Trebisond*,
> Or whom *Biserta* sent from *Afric* shore
> When *Charlemain* with all his Peerage fell
> By *Fontarabbia*.

The passage is a miniature survey, chronologically arranged, of the great conflicts of heroic legend; a survey, indeed, of the materials of the epic poetry of the past: the wars of the gods and giants (Hesiod); the sieges of Troy and Thebes (Homer, Statius); the battles of Arthur (Geoffrey of Monmouth, etc.); the Crusades and the wars of Charlemagne (Italian chivalric epic). Such comprehensiveness goes beyond the requirements of mere illustration. So, too, does the accurate classification of the two divisions of Celtic chivalry in the phrase, "Begirt with *British* and *Armoric* Knights."

A more elaborate description of ripe humanistic scholarship distilled to an essence and put to the service of poetry is to be found in the descriptive analysis of the culture of ancient Athens offered by Satan as a bait to Christ in *Paradise Regained* (IV, 236 ff.). An outline of this passage would read like the program for a set of lectures on Greek civilization: the physical environment; lyric poetry, Ionian and Doric; Homer and the tragedians; oratory; the schools of philosophy, proceeding from the fountainhead of Socrates—Academics old and new, Peripatetics, Epicureans, Stoics. Everything is compact, orderly, accurate; the essential points and distinctions are indicated with scholarly precision; yet the whole passage, vibrating as it is with Milton's intense enthusiasm for classic culture, is unquestionably poetry. Its phrases—"wielded at will that fierce *Democraty*," "from Heaven descended to the low-rooft house / Of Socrates"—are as concrete in imagery as they are pregnant with suggestion. No other poet has written in precisely this way.

A striking feature of Milton's style in *Paradise Lost* is his use of the epic or expanded simile. In this he follows the model of Homer, Virgil, Statius, Lucan, Spenser, Tasso, etc., and even borrows in some cases similes already employed by these epic predecessors. When he is original, the materials of his comparison are sometimes based on simple observation of nature; oftener he draws from myth and legend, history, travel, science, or the technical arts. These digressions are for him a welcome means of pouring forth the treasures of his mind. When once he is in the vein he does not stop with a single elaborate comparison but proceeds from one to another. Thus the multitude of the Satanic host becomes

> . . . like that Pigmean Race
> Beyond the *Indian* Mount, or Faery Elves,
> Whose midnight Revels, by a Forest side
> Or Fountain some belated Peasant sees,
> Or dreams he sees, while over-head the Moon
> Sits Arbitress, and nearer to the Earth
> Wheels her pale course; they on thir mirth and dance

Intent, with jocund Music charm his ear;
At once with joy and fear his heart rebounds.

(*PL*, I, 780–88)

The alternative comparisons thus offered are usually from widely separated provinces or literatures, particularly from classical mythology and the Bible. Thus Satan's huge bulk is compared first to the ancient giants overthrown by Zeus, then to the Scriptural Leviathan, who, however, promptly becomes the sea beast mistaken for an island in the books of travel. The key to this habit is again, in part at least, Milton's passion for scholarly completeness. He is careful, for example, in describing the Garden of Eden to omit no reference to a parallel happy garden which has been made memorable in song or story. The effect is not pedantic but rich and ornate.

The rhetoric of the Miltonic simile has been exhaustively and quite technically studied by James Whaler.[15] Some of his conclusions as to the characteristic features may here be given. Milton less often than other epic poets uses the simile merely to suspend the narrative and afford relief amid scenes of strife, pain, or crisis. He is generally controlling his expression to some specific logical purpose, whether illustration, aggrandizement, or prolepsis. The second use is particularly important in such a fable as this, and Whaler explains the preference for unusual images over homely ones like Homer's as due to the fact that Milton is seeking to ennoble his narrative rather than merely to illustrate it. The proleptic or anticipatory use of the simile is particularly distinctive of Milton. Thus in *Paradise Lost* (X, 306–11), he likens the construction by Sin and Death of a causeway across Chaos to reach the world and enslave mankind, to the bridge which Xerxes built over the Hellespont; in so doing he not only illustrates the action but to the knowing reader suggestively foreshadows later events. The Persian expedition came to nought, and the same, for all their present ostentatiousness, is to be the history of Sin and Death. Whaler demonstrates, finally, that Milton's similes are organically composed to a degree beyond those of his epic predecessors. A typically complex Miltonic simile directs each detail to some application in the fable, i.e., homologation rather than heterogeneity between terms is the rule. It requires a subtle reader to

15 "The Miltonic Simile"; "Compounding and Distribution of Similes in *Paradise Lost*"; "Animal Simile in *Paradise Lost*." See the more recent article by L. D. Lerner, 'The Miltonic Simile."

catch all the suggested points of the comparison, and the student must be referred for detail to Whaler's elaborate exposition.[16]

We may, however, illustrate what he means by analyzing the simile in *Paradise Lost* (II, 706–11):

> On th' other side
> Incens't with indignation *Satan* stood
> Unterrifi'd, and like a Comet burn'd,
> That fires the length of *Ophiucus* huge
> In th' Artic Sky, and from his horrid hair
> Shakes Pestilence and War.

Satan is like the comet in fiery radiance, in enormousness, in the fact that both are ominous of impending calamity. But there is still more. Satan is a serpent—"Ophiucus" means "holder of serpents"—and hence the comet is appropriately said to fire the length of this particular constellation. Furthermore Satan is always associated with the quarters of the north, for which reason Milton puts Ophiucus in the arctic sky, though only with considerable astronomical freedom.

Even when Milton digresses in his similes it is not as in Homer and other poets, for the sole reason of drawing a diverting picture. There is always some relevant suggestion to be found if one thinks of all the associations. Thus in the celebrated comparison of the shield of Satan to the moon Milton apparently departs from the point to tell of Galileo's telescope and even to mention the place of observation:

> . . . from the top of *Fesole*,
> Or in *Valdarno*.

(PL, I, 289–90)

And he describes what the telescope reveals:

> . . . new Lands,
> Rivers or Mountains in her spotty Globe.

(PL, I, 290–91)

---

[16] Cf., however, the opinions of Waldock and Peter on the Miltonic simile. "The effort to find a continuous relevance in Milton's similes," Waldock writes, "may succeed on occasion, but it is an effort, it seems to me, that can easily overreach itself" (*Paradise Lost and Its Critics*, p. 143). See Peter's A *Critique of Paradise Lost*, pp. 55–58.

But these digressions help. We are invited to see the moon through the eyes of the most quick-sighted and intelligent astronomer of modern times, under ideal atmospheric conditions, under the clear dry sky of Italy. See it thus, "with the daring imagination and furtively proud mind of a scientist"[17] in the days of the Inquisition, and one is prepared to imagine more vividly and with more emotion the shield of Satan. The fact that the moon is not smooth but ridged and channeled intimates the same of Satan's shield and faintly suggests the most superb shield in Homer and in literature, the shield of Achilles.[18] It is, then, in the completeness of its correspondence with the object that the Miltonic simile is most unique and best demonstrates the control which the poet exercised over his artistic imagination.

The characteristics of Milton's expression which come out so clearly in the similes are to be found in a more subtle form in his verse generally. Though little progress has thus been made in analyzing these characteristics, attention may be directed to several exceptionally suggestive stylistic studies, one of which, entitled "Milton and Bentley," is by William Empson.[19] Empson points out in a succession of examples that where Bentley finds fault with Milton he almost invariably does so on a point where eighteenth-century demands for logic, explicitness, and singleness of meaning are violated in the interest of poetic overtones and suggestions characteristic both of Elizabethan and modern verse. Bentley is wrong in his criticisms, certainly, but he writes honestly from the point of view of his age; and such defenders of Milton as Pearce are really no nearer to catching the poet's intention than the heavy-handed classicist whom they ridicule. Thus, for example, neither Bentley nor Pearce recognizes the secret pun which gives poetic richness to the following:

> The Birds thir choir apply; airs, vernal airs,
> Breathing the smell of field and grove, attune
> The trembling leaves. . . .
>
> (*PL*, IV, 264–66)

[17] James Whaler, "The Miltonic Simile," p. 1058.
[18] *Ibid.*
[19] *Some Versions of Pastoral*, pp. 149–91.

Bentley objects that "air" has no plural number in Greek, Latin, or English, where "airs" signifies "tunes." Pearce defends his author on philological grounds, giving authority for taking different airs as different breezes. Both ignore the obvious lead suggested by the word "attune." "The airs attune the leaves," says Empson, "because the air itself is as enlivening as an air: the trees and wild flowers that are smelt on the air match, as if they caused, as if they were caused by, the birds and leaves that are heard on the air; nature, because of a pun, becomes a single organism."[20] It is doubtless possible to be oversubtle in this kind of analysis, but it leads us nearer to the truth than the judgment of T. S. Eliot that the only specifically poetic pleasure that Milton's verse affords is the pleasure of the ear. To complement Empson, one may turn to the suggestions of Christopher Ricks, whose sensitive reading of *Paradise Lost* (Book VIII, 265–66), may be taken as an example of his technique throughout the study. He points out how the line can be infinitely divided, bringing out the "merits of the flowing syntax"; "not that we need to break the verse down like this in reading—its flow keeps us moving. But to do so is instructive, and it confirms Richardson's understanding of the syntax. And the word 'oreflow'd' alerts us to the function of the syntax, itself overflowing."[21] He proceeds to discuss other aspects of Milton's style, including simile and cross-reference. His study is indispensable for the modern student.

It is a curious fact that similes and figurative language generally are not at all evenly distributed in Milton's blank verse poems or even in *Paradise Lost* itself. In Books I and II they are scattered thick as stars. Thereafter they fall off in number, and there are long stretches of the poem—for example, the theological discussion in Book III and the dialogue between Adam and Raphael in Book VIII —in which there are none.

This phenomenon may serve to direct our attention to the fact that Milton really has two styles, corresponding to two different kinds of object or two qualities of poetic inspiration. The one is abundant, highly colored, pictorial, figurative; the other direct, closely woven, and relatively plain. The first is the language of Milton's impassioned visual imagination, the second, of his ethical and intel-

20 *Ibid.*, p. 157.
21 *Milton's Grand Style*, p. 82.

lectual intensity. Many passages, to be sure, show the two modes in combination, and both have the fundamental Miltonic qualities already analyzed. The contrast between them in their purity is, nevertheless, strongly marked. It may already be discerned in *Comus*, but it is clearest in the later poems. In the sonnets, *Paradise Regained*, and *Samson Agonistes*, the barer style predominates—though there are patches of the other, as in the description of the banquet spread for Christ, or the nightly storm followed by a serene dawn, or the choric description of Samson's descent upon the Philistines like an eagle upon tame villatic fowl. In *Paradise Lost* they are balanced fairly evenly. Hell, Chaos, the Garden, Satan lying on the burning lake or standing like Teneriffe or Atlas, visions of cherubim gliding to their stations, the brandished sword of God fierce as a comet, passions of demons, the love of Adam and Eve—these are the objects of a style brilliant with the wealth of Ormus or of Ind. The soberer dialogue in hell, the correlative council in heaven, all exposition of doctrine, Satan's or Adam's self-communion, Raphael's final exhortation—all this is couched in a language relatively plain but full of lofty dignity and capable of both eloquence and passion.

Much has been written regarding the development of Milton's style and its relation to the tendencies of his age. The alterations in the Cambridge Manuscript (see the discussion of the minor poems) show something of the conscious effort which he made to achieve certain definite qualities. C. S. Lewis shows that in a dozen or so of the changes in *Comus*, Milton was deliberately moving away from the dramatic and ebullient in expression and toward the "gnomic" and "poetically chaste." Thus the three lines

> . . . force him to return his purchas back
> Or drag him by the curles and cleave his scalp
> Down to the hips. . . .

become less than two in revision:

> drag him by the curls to a foul death
> Curst as his life. . . .[22]

Other changes tell a different story. Milton often substitutes a fresher and more meaningful epithet for a conventional one, as in

[22] "A Note on *Comus*."

"opening eyelids of the Morn" for "glimmering eyelids," and "westering wheel" for "burnisht wheel." In general the language of *Paradise Lost*, especially of the first two books, is bolder and more striking than that of the minor poems. It is also, however, apt to be more condensed, more difficult, and more severe. Tillyard notes that the tenderness and sensuousness of Milton's youth, while absent from the poem as a whole, are occasionally, as in the close, allowed to have place, as if to reassure us that no powers which he once possessed are lost. He points out also that the remoteness of Milton's mature manner, which has been disliked by some critics, is in conformity with the seventeenth-century theory of propriety in heroic poetry. "The heightened style of *Paradise Lost* was something demanded of him as an epic poet with a rigour against which there was no possible appeal."[23] A similar point is elaborated by Mario Praz, who finds in Milton's style, with its refinement and spiritualization of sixteenth-century sensuousness through the influence of the ideal forms of the classics, a close parallel with the baroque art of Nicolas Poussin.[24]

METRICS

The discussion has inevitably carried us away from the outward features of Milton's literary utterance to the qualities of intellect and emotion which determine them. We may now return to formulate as simply as possible the more obvious facts about his versification. It should be said at the outset that the most complete scientific description of Miltonic prosody would carry us but a little way toward an understanding of the total effect produced by his poetry.[25] Rhythm, vocabulary, sentence structure, and imagery all unite in indistinguishable combination to form the garment of Miltonic

[23] *The Miltonic Setting*, pp. 121–22.
[24] "Milton and Poussin"; see also Roy Daniells, *Milton, Mannerism and Baroque.*
[25] See James Whaler, *Counterpoint and Symbol*, for an attempt to transform the elements of Miltonic prosody into mathematical formulas.

thought and feeling. Thus the "blank verse paragraph" so often mentioned in discussions of Milton's poetry is as much a matter of rhetoric as it is of verse. It is because the sense is suspended through line after line and because Milton is careful to avoid coincidence of the rhetorical pauses with the line ends that we have the continuity of rhythm which is so characteristic a feature of his blank verse.[26]

But even in prosody strictly considered, Milton is an innovator as well as a master, although in this as in stylistic habit his originality lies in his bolder and more individual employment of practices which can be found in earlier English poetry. For instance, William B. Hunter, Jr., has recently argued convincingly that Milton's prosodic practices can be observed in simpler form if one combines various features found in Sylvester's translation of *De Bartas' Devine Weekes and Workes* and in seventeenth-century psalters. Milton's practices, he suggests, are a unique combination of characteristics observed in both sources.[27] Speculating further, Harris Fletcher has offered the possibility that Milton's counterpoint or double rhythm may have been the result of his own intense study of foreign tongues and of his attempt to create in English something like the prosodic forms he found in other languages.[28] The following statement aims at a simple, objective classification which avoids as far as possible controversial questions of metrical theory.

BASIC RHYTHM

The standard of Milton's verse in *Paradise Lost* and *Paradise Regained* and *Samson Agonistes* (except the choruses) may be taken as the line of ten syllables and five accents in rising rhythm (i.e., iambic pentameter unrhymed).[29] Clear examples are found in:

Torments him; round he throws his baleful eyes
(*PL*, I, 56)

[26] Theodore H. Banks, Jr., "Miltonic Rhythm," calculates that forty percent of the full stops in *Paradise Lost* occur medially.

[27] "The Sources of Milton's 'Counterpoint' or Double Rhythm."

[28] "A Possible Origin of Milton's 'Counterpoint' or Double Rhythm."

[29] See F. T. Prince, *The Italian Element in Milton's Verse*, p. 143.

or, better yet, in:

> United thought and counsels, equal hope
>
> (*PL*, I, 88)

As a matter of fact, lines with such even and regular iambic beat are comparatively rare—rarer in Milton's verse than in most English iambic pentameter. Yet probably a majority of his lines approximate it so closely that we are unconscious of the variations. Thus in the line:

> Of that Forbidden Tree, whose mortal taste
>
> (*PL*, I, 2)

most readers would emphasize the second syllable only slightly less than the succeeding ones which bear the metrical accent. And in the line:

> The force of those dire Arms? yet not for those
>
> (*PL*, I, 94)

though the word "dire" is nearly equivalent in weight to "Arms," it does not disturb in any marked way the regularity of beat.

VARIATIONS IN NUMBER OF SYLLABLES

Compared with the eighteenth-century writers of the couplet, Milton is quite free in the admission of syllables above the standard ten. There is, as in most pentameter verse, a considerable number of lines (though not so many as in Shakespeare's later plays) of one or rarely two extra unaccented syllables at the end (weak or feminine ending):

> That durst dislike his reign, and mee preferring
>
> (*PL*, I, 102)

> For solitude sometimes is best society
>
> (*PL*, IX, 249)[30]

[30] According to the tally made by Ants Oras, there are 147 instances of feminine ending in *Paradise Lost* ("Milton's Blank Verse," p. 160).

Extra syllables may also be introduced at any point in the line. This liberty was freely used in later Elizabethan dramatic blank verse. Milton, however, influenced no doubt by classical and Italian practice,[31] apparently admitted extrametrical syllables within the line only when they could be brought under certain rules of elision and contraction. These rules (omitting the elisions and contractions of common speech) were formulated by Robert Bridges in his work *Milton's Prosody*[32] under the following heads:

1. Open vowels; e.g.:

> Above th' *Aonian* Mount, while it pursues
>
> > *(PL, I, 15)*
>
> Strange horror seize th*ee*, and pangs unfelt before
>
> > *(PL, II, 703)*

2. Vowels separated by the liquids *l*, *n*, and *r*:

> As one who long in pop*ulo*us City pent
>
> > *(PL, IX, 445)*
>
> His Temple right against the Temp*le* of God
>
> > *(PL, I, 402)*
>
> A Pill*ar* of State; deep on his Front engraven
>
> > *(PL, II, 302)*

3. Final *en*; e.g., fall'n, ris'n, driv'n, etc.

4. The second personal singular of verbs; e.g., rememberest, thinkst, etc.

The rule of contraction (3 and 4) may be understood to indicate an actual suppression of the contracted syllable in pronunciation, as is clearly indicated by Milton's careful spelling in the first edition. (He prints "Heav'n," "thinkst," etc., as given above.) Not so, however, the elisions. There might be some doubt in the case of "the" before a word beginning with a vowel, where Milton actually prints "th'," but a suppression in the vowel sound in "thee"

> Strange horror seize *thee*, and pangs unfelt before

[31] See F. T. Prince, *The Italian Element in Milton's Verse*, pp. 142–44.
[32] Pp. 3–12.

is unthinkable. Bridges, therefore, concludes that Milton scanned his verse one way (syllabically) and read it another. Yet Milton's elisions are not without practical consequence in the aesthetic consciousness of the modern reader:

> We may say generally that Milton's system in Paradise Lost was an attempt to keep blank verse decasyllabic by means of fictions, or it may be said that he formulated the conditions most common to those syllables which were oftenest and best used for trisyllabic places; and then worked within the lines thus drawn.[33]

Whatever the aesthetic validity or significance of his practice, the facts are interesting as an illustration of the artistic discipline which coexisted with artistic freedom in his work.

In *Paradise Regained* and *Samson Agonistes* Milton admits extra syllables on a somewhat freer basis, but not as freely as in the early poems or in English pentameter verse generally. In his discussion of extrametrical supernumerary syllables (a discussion that remains the best single critical work on the subject), S. Ernest Sprott calculates that less than one percent of the lines in *Paradise Lost* present opportunities for elision, and he concludes that it is

> fairly good evidence that Milton was not, in Paradise Lost at least, much in love with licence. . . . In the face of this, it is difficult not to believe that when, in Paradise Lost as a whole, Milton deliberately prohibited the free use of final extrametrical syllables, he was doing it for the express purpose of ennobling the general style, from which he considered such syllables a detraction.[34]

VARIATION IN THE PLACING OF ACCENT (INVERSION OF RHYTHM)

The iambic succession of unaccented-accented syllables is freely varied, very commonly at the beginning of the line, as in

[33] *Ibid.*, p. 17.
[34] *Milton's Art of Prosody*, pp. 56, 58.

Róse out of *Chaos:* or if *Sion* Hill

(*PL,* I, 10)

This is the easiest and most normal variation of the iambic pattern and is common even with the couplet versifiers of the eighteenth century. According to Sprott's tabulation, first-foot inversion occurs, on the average, in more than fifteen percent of the lines in *Paradise Lost*; third- and fourth-foot inversions occur, on the average, in slightly less than three percent; and second-foot inversions have a frequency count of less than one percent.[35] The following two instances of inversion in the final foot are quite unusual:

Beyond all past example and fú́ture

(*PL,* X, 840)

Which of us who beholds the bright súrface

(*PL,* VI, 472)[36]

VARIATIONS IN NUMBER OF ACCENTS

As we have said above, it is possible to scan most lines in *Paradise Lost* fairly easily as pentameters, allowing for substitution but not doing violence to the prose accent of the words. There are, however, many cases in which it is almost impossible to recognize the normal number of accents in any intelligent reading of the line:

To the Garden of bliss, thy seat prepar'd

(*PL,* VIII, 299)

In the Visions of God: It was a Hill

(*PL,* XI, 377)

Rocks, Caves, Lakes, Fens, Bogs, Dens, and shades of death

(*PL,* II, 621)

Light-arm'd or heavy, sharp, smooth, swift or slow

(*PL,* II, 902)

These are extreme instances in which we feel the rhythm for the moment sharply altered. The normal situation is better represented

[35] *Ibid.,* p. 101.
[36] *Ibid.,* pp. 102–04.

in such a line as the following, where we have a choice of renderings:

And now a stripling Cherub he appears

(*PL*, III, 636)

The question is the degree of stress, if any, one is to put on "he."
Bridges says that there is a "theoretical stress" on such words.
Actually, whatever one may do with his voice, his aesthetic sense is
held by two rhythms simultaneously; and there are enough such
lines almost to establish a four-beat as well as a five-beat pattern.[37]
If one wishes to refine on this, he may consider the line:

Immutable, Immortal, Infinite

(*PL*, III, 373)

as capable of being read three different ways:

Immutable, Immortal, Infinite.
Immutable, Immortal, Infinite.
Immutable, Immortal, Infinite.

Obviously there is opportunity for great variety and subtlety, and of
this opportunity Milton makes the most, the more so because the
rhythm is not marked by stress alone but by other elements as well.
Focusing sharply on what he calls "an equivalence among the verbal
terms and their accents which the terms may not rest back upon,"
Albert Cook[38] has argued that the prosodic uniqueness of *Paradise
Lost* results from this precise rhythmic tension in which all accents
are given almost identical value:

> In Paradise Lost, every accented word stands out when spoken
> as the major one in the line, pulling against the rise of the
> accents, equally strong, which precede and follow. This creates
> a kind of tension analogous to the conflict of physical forces
> found in the structure of a baroque dome.[39]

[37] *Ibid.*, pp. 38–53.
[38] "Milton's Abstract Music."
[39] *Ibid.*, p. 373.

Cook finds the meaning of *Paradise Lost* embodied in its rhythmic tensions—e.g., Adam as general man "can be at once abstract and irrevocably concrete"; Adam's unfallen world is a place "where every aspect of speech and idea gains importance without suppressing the importance of another, just as angels gain rather than lose (as Satan thought) by the preeminence of the Son in Heaven."[40] Cook's effort is a significant attempt to define "Miltonic music" and a quite satisfactory answer to Leavis' comment (one made in rebuttal to T. S. Eliot) that "'Miltonic music' weakens our sense of relevance."[41]

PAUSE

The normal pentameter line tends to divide itself into two balancing parts, but all poets, even the regular versifiers of the eighteenth century, vary the position of the break to avoid monotony. Milton does so more freely than others. Bridges and Sprott show that the metrical pause in Milton, as determined by a grammatical pause, may come at any point in the lines. Extreme instances are:

> Thus with the Year
> Seasons return, but not to me returns
> Day, | or the sweet approach of Ev'n or Morn.
>
> $(1+9)$

> And Bush with frizl'd hair implicit: | last
> Rose as in Dance the stately Trees.
>
> $(9+1)$

There are sometimes two breaks in the line, the "variety and severity" of the breaks being, according to Bridges, a distinction of Milton's verse:

> Hail Son of God, | Saviour of Men, | thy Name
> $(4+4+2)$
> Regions of Sorrow, | doleful shades, | where peace
> $(5+3+2)$

[40] *Ibid.*, pp. 373–74.
[41] *The Common Pursuit* (London, 1952), p. 22.

There may be any number of breaks in the line, as Sprott has demonstrated, from one to seven, and they may occur at any position in the line itself.

Here again the situation is more complex than any statement as simple and definite as the foregoing one can indicate. Pause is a means both of logical expression and of emphasis; it is a factor partly metrical, partly grammatical and rhetorical. The same is true of stress. In the use of both a compromise has to be effected between the demands of prose meaning and of poetic rhythm. We see the problem here particularly clearly at the ends of lines. From the metrical point of view each line is a unit and requires some kind of demarcation at the end. From the grammatical or rhetorical point of view it is often so logically connected with the following line that any break at all is illogical. For instance, in the lines:

> not to me *returns*
> *Day*, or the sweet approach of Ev'n or Morn

readers will differ in what they will do. They may make a slight pause after "returns," or, better, slightly strengthen the metrical stress of the second syllable of the word, or lengthen that syllable, or do both. The eye plays a part, too, making us aware of the line structure, even against a vocal interpretation which does not recognize it at all. There is some external evidence that Milton himself, however much he may have thought in "verse paragraphs," regarded the line as a more or less isolated unit to be indicated as such by some sort of breath, pause, or lingering at the end.[42]

The question of metrical versus grammatical and rhetorical pause applies also to the breaks within the line:

> Regions of Sorrow, | doleful shades, | where peace
> And rest can never dwell.

The two internal breaks would be of equal strength in prose rhetoric, or the second might be greater; but verse rhythm requires the second to be less. Ants Oras has demonstrated statistically that "the

[42] See John S. Diekhoff, "Terminal Pause in Milton's Verse," and Sprott, *Milton's Art of Prosody*, pp. 112–28. Sprott's chapter has an extremely careful tabulation of the breaks and their positions in Milton's verse.

overall trend [in all Milton's work] is towards an increased use of strong pauses. This tendency agrees with Milton's growing preference for briefer clauses and sentences; a technique of prolonged rhetorical and rhythmical suspense seems to be changing into one of more concentration in less space."[43]

Whenever we take a Miltonic verse and scrutinize it in this way, we realize that the sources of its beauty are beyond our powers of analysis and that the reader is called on to exercise a delicacy of artistic judgment like that of a singer or the performer of a piece of instrumental music. Exactly what the author or composer himself would have done, we should be glad to know; but there is no unquestionably right interpretation. Perhaps for this reason Leavis warned that "it is impossible to enforce a judgment about rhythm by written analysis and difficult to do so in any way,"[44] and perhaps for the same reason Christopher Ricks, while commenting upon Arnold Stein's "impressive" but ultimately "worthless" analysis, passes the challenge by.[45] The matter of rhythmical analysis becomes even more complex when we add the factors of pitch, texture or quality, and tempo. The latter point, which has already been touched on, requires much study. English verse has been roughly defined as "speech in which stresses occur at apparently equal intervals of time,"[46] with the explanation that the time intervals are "not exactly equal but only nearly enough equal to seem so to the ear." The analogy with music is very close, the stresses being comparable to the beats in music, and the units of time or feet, to the measures. And verse is perhaps best scanned by using musical notation. Expression in reading, insofar as it involves the time factor, is like rhythmic interpretation in music. Perfectly regular and accurate playing is monotonous and unexpressive. The interpreting musician lengthens one measure or series of measures, quickens others. His beat is constantly changing, yet there is always an approximation of regularity. Such is also the case with the good reader of poetry. Perhaps we might rest our case with Hazlitt's

[43] "Milton's Blank Verse," p. 136.

[44] "Milton's Verse," p. 64.

[45] *Milton's Grand Style,* pp. 24–26.

[46] G. R. Stewart, *The Technique of English Verse* (New York, 1930), p. 2.

comment: "The way to defend Milton against all impugners is to take down the book and read it."[47]

PHRASING

There is, finally, in Milton, as in all poetry, the problem of phrasing or the grouping of syllables into units of pronunciation. Pause, stress, and tempo are all factors here. The phrasal units may sometimes correspond more or less exactly to the metrical feet, as in the monosyllabic line:

And swims | or sinks, | or wades, | or creeps, | or flies.

Oftener they do not. Thus in the line:

Of Man's | First Dis | obe | dience and | the Fruit

"Disobedience" is a unit of pronunciation which occupies parts of three feet. Some students of Milton's verse, impressed by the power and importance of phrasal units, have tried to apply complicated systems of scansion, making use of all the varieties of feet recognized by the Greek and Roman rhetoricians. To do this is to lose sight of the simpler and more regular verse patterns which, though modified, are not destroyed by the irregularities of phrasing. The smallest groups consist of single words like "Disobedience" or of two or three short words like "and the Fruit." But there are larger groupings which embrace the smaller, with varying degrees of pause between them. Again the situation is analogous to that of music. Skill in reading Milton aloud is largely a matter of making the most of the phrasing and of the verse patterns at the same time. As in the case of stress, there is a kind of overlapping of phrasal patterns which is perceived by the mind (Milton's "abstract music") though it cannot be fully rendered by the voice. How, for example, shall we plot the larger phrasal pattern of "Outshone the wealth of Ormus and of Ind"? We have the possibility of saying:

---

[47] *Complete Works of William Hazlitt*, ed. P. P. Howe (London, 1930), V, 61.

> Outshone the wealth | of Ormus and of Ind

and also of saying:

> Outshone the wealth of Ormus | and of Ind

perhaps, even of saying:

> Outshone | the wealth of Ormus and of Ind

and finally of treating the whole line as a unit:

> Outshone the wealth of Ormus and of Ind.

It would certainly be difficult to indicate all this vocally, but the alternative groupings are nevertheless felt. A simpler case is illustrated by the line given as an example of the coincidence of phrasal units with metrical feet:

> And swims or sinks, | or wades, | or creeps, | or flies.

Certainly the impression of monotony is part of the effect wanted, and good reading requires a pause after each verb. But "swims or sinks" go more closely together than the others, a fact emphasized by the omission of the comma in the original edition, and this can be recognized in reading by making the pause briefer after "swims" or by using a slightly different inflection in the voice.

The natural accent in the phrase considered as prose may run counter to the regular beat of the iambic verse. In conspicuous cases we may say that the type of foot is changed. Thus we may say that "Of Man's" is an iamb, but "first Dis-" is an "inverted foot" or a trochee. But the reader feels the iambic beat, and it is an open question how much he is to recognize it in pronunciation. The same is true of the "missing beats" in feet like " | dience and | the Fruit." The phrase "and the Fruit" is a unit with one prose accent. But "and" invites metrical emphasis in the iambic pattern. This brings us back to the subject of five- and four-beat rhythms, already sufficiently discussed. We are thinking here, however, not of two more or less regular patterns but of an entirely irregular prose accent crossing the verse accent. Notable examples are the following:

Prose accent:

$$\text{Bú́rnt áfter them to the bóttomless pít.}$$

Verse accent:

$$\text{Burnt áfter thém to the bóttomless pít.}$$

Prose accent:

$$\text{Sing Héav'nly Múse.}$$

Verse accent:

$$\text{Síng Heav'nly Múse.}$$

RHYMED VERSE: GREEK METERS IN *Samson Agonistes*

We have omitted in this discussion Milton's rhymed verse and the choruses in *Samson Agonistes*. Rhyme has the effect of marking the line end, even where the sense is run on. It is also an ornament which serves to distinguish verse from prose in an obvious and easy way. The stylistic heightening and the bold effects of rhythm in Milton's blank verse are in part due to his supplying the deficiency of rhyme by other means. The choruses of *Samson Agonistes* have irregular line length and sometimes rhyme. The variations from the iambic pattern are so great that one is inclined to abandon the attempt to recognize a theoretical conformity to this English pattern and consider them frankly as a reproduction of Greek and Roman rhythms.

Milton himself has given ground for so doing. He says in the preface:

> The measure of Verse us'd in the Chorus is of all sorts, call'd by the Greeks Monostrophic, or rather Apolelymenon, without regard had to Strophe, Antistrophe, or Epode—which were a kind of Stanzas fram'd only for the Music, then us'd with the Chorus that sung; not essential to the Poem, and therefore not material; or being divided into Stanzas or Pauses, they may be called Allaeostropha.

At first reading this would seem to refer only to the stanzaic arrangement and to warn the reader not to look for the kind of regularity
which he knows to exist in the Greek odes (i.e., identity of strophe
and strophe, antistrophe and antistrophe). But Milton means to
imply also that the individual verses are not in conformity with the
specific patterns found in the ancient odes. And F. T. Prince has
argued recently that Milton's sources were in the relatively recent
Aminta by Tasso and in Guarini's *Il Pastor Fido*.[48] That Milton's
patterns are not "ancient" becomes very clear if we compare the
statement prefixed to the *Ode to Rouse* where the distinction is
made between pattern verses and free verses:

> The ode consists of three strophes, an equal number of anti-
> strophes, and an epode at its close. These divisions, though
> they do not precisely correspond, either in number of verses
> or in sections (cola) that are everywhere unchangeable, we
> have made in the way mentioned above, having in view the
> convenience of the reader, rather than an arrangement by
> which they might be sung according to the ancient measures.
> In other respects this poetic form should perhaps be more
> correctly called monostrophic. The meters in part follow a
> definite scheme, in part are used freely (apolelymenon). The
> Phalaecian verses twice admit a spondee in the third foot, a
> substitution which Catullus makes at will in the second foot.

The inference from this statement is that even when writing
a Latin ode (in 1647), Milton was unwilling to bind himself
invariably to the recognized ancient types, but he knew perfectly
well what some of them (i.e., at least those used by Horace and
Catullus) were, and what liberties were allowed within them. His
own inventions were simply in the way of further modifications
such as the ancients themselves might have made. The Greek
choruses, which must have seemed to him more irregular than they
do to modern metrists, would have given him even stronger precedent than the occasional variations admitted by the Romans. He
would certainly have scanned the verses of the *Ode to Rouse* in the
Greek way; and he perhaps invites the reader to do the same with

---

[48] *The Italian Element in Milton's Verse*, pp. 145–68.

the choruses of *Samson*. The meter would be that of the freest form known to the ancients, the logaoedic, which is a trochaic measure with dactyls and other substitutions.[49] When the lines begin with the upbeat the movement is often very similar to the logaoedic patterns. For example:

> This, | this, | is he;
> Softly | a while,
> Let us | not break | in up | on him;
> O change | beyond | report, | thought, | or belief!
> Can this | be hee, | that he | roic, | that Re | nowned,
> Irres | istible | Samson? | whom | unarmed.

But though these lines begin with trochees, spondees, or dactyls, they seem to end in almost every case with iambs; and from this point on in the choruses the general movement is more clearly iambic, though with occasional lines which definitely suggest the ancient rhythms:

> Useless the | forgery
> Adaman | tean | Proof.

The genius of the language and the traditions of English verse were too strong to admit of Milton's giving us real Greek verse, even in *Samson*, without doing violence to his instincts. He must have considered and rejected the attempts which had been made by Harvey, Sidney, and others to introduce the principles of classic meter consistently into English verse.

---

[49] "Milton has introduced a rhythmic indeterminacy—a sort of multiple possibility of reading which is not only functional, as it was in the iambic-trochaic indeterminacy of *L'Allegro* and *Il Penseroso* . . . but also dramatic. . . . It carries the burden of the drama" (Cook, "Milton's Abstract Music," p. 383).

Chapter 7

MILTON'S FAME AND INFLUENCE

THE SEVENTEENTH CENTURY

THOUGH MILTON LIVED HIS LAST DAYS QUIETLY AND PUBLISHED HIS great poems with no accompaniment of public demonstration, he had at his death already taken his place among the notables of England. As a man of learning, as a Latin and English poet, as the writer of the *Defence against Salmasius,* and as a last survivor of the Commonwealth government, he was naturally an object of public interest. He was visited in his London obscurity by distinguished foreign visitors to England. John Dryden asked his leave to turn *Paradise Lost* into "a Drama in Rhyme: Mr Milton received him civilly, and told him he would give him leave to tagge his Verses."[1] Numerous biographies, by Skinner(?), Aubrey, Wood, Phillips, and Toland, were written and published in the first quarter century after his death.

Though Milton would have acquired no such prompt recognition on the strength of his English poetry alone, and though the taste and temper of the Restoration were all against a proper understanding of his work, there is evidence that *Paradise Lost* was

---

[1] J. Milton French, *Life Records,* V, 46; see also Morris Freedman, "Dryden's 'Memorable Visit' to Milton," *HLQ,* XVIII (1955), 99–108.

both read and admired from the first, not alone by the few men of Milton's own circle who, like Andrew Marvell, shared his moral and political ideas, but even occasionally by the wits of the new age.[2] Havens estimates that some four thousand copies of *Paradise Lost* were in circulation by 1680, enough to supply the "fit audience though few" whom Milton thought he had a right to expect in any age. The leader in critical admiration and the true founder of Milton's literary reputation was John Dryden, who returned to his work again and again in his prose discussions. Eighteenth-century writers, who greatly admired Milton, exaggerated his unpopularity during the Restoration.[3]

It remains true, however, that the changes in moral tone in the nation which attended the Revolution of 1688 made possible a rapid widening of the circle of Milton's admirers. Jacob Tonson, into whose hands the copyright of *Paradise Lost* had fallen, published five successive editions of the poem in the decade from 1688 to 1698, one of them (that of 1695) with a supplement of learned annotations by Patrick Hume. This is the first scholarly edition of Milton, or, indeed, of any English poet. Towards the end of the century there were attempts to translate the poem into German, French, and Latin. And in 1697 and 1698 separate editions of the complete prose works were published. In what should be required reading, William R. Parker has sensitively discussed the matter of Milton's contemporary reputation in the essay which precedes his list of printed seventeenth-century allusions to Milton's work.[4]

---

[2] Richardson has an account of Sir John Denham's enthusiasm for *Paradise Lost*, "Wet from the Press," Darbishire *(Early Lives*, p. 295). He sent it to Dryden, who remarked, "This Man . . . Cuts us All out, and the Ancients too" *(ibid.*, p. 296). See Theodore H. Banks, "Sir John Denham and *Paradise Lost*," *MLN*, XLI (1926), 51–54.

[3] See Raymond Havens, "Seventeenth-Century Notices of Milton," *ES*, XL (1909), 175–86. The popularity of the minor poems is more problematical, but we have the record of Wotton's admiration, and Henry Vaughan, whose early poems are said to show Milton's influence, apparently refers to him in 1655 as one of the irreverent poets who are, nevertheless, among the principal and most learned writers of English verse (see Louise I. Guiney, "Milton and Henry Vaughan," *QR*, CCXX [1914], 353–64). There is also a copy of *Lycidas* bearing the signature of Izaak Walton.

[4] "Milton's Contemporary Reputation," *Reputation*, pp. 1–65.

THE EIGHTEENTH CENTURY

The record of Milton's fame and influence in the eighteenth century is an integral part of the literary and intellectual history of the age. In no other time did he have so many readers or become the occasion of so much discussion. The frequency of editions was increased by leaps and bounds,[5] and the chorus of praise from poets and critics gained continuously in volume. There were editions by Bentley, Hawkey, Newton, Thomas Warton, Todd, and others, and commentaries by the Richardsons, Peck, *et al.*[6] That there were also those who, either on political or on literary grounds (e.g., Dr. Johnson), took a hostile view, is additional proof that Milton in these years was a force to reckon with. The special reasons for this interest are various. On the one hand, there was the fact that Milton was an imitator, however liberal, of the admired ancients. The classical form of *Paradise Lost* invited comparison with Homer and Virgil, and such comparisons were continually made. Milton's puritanism, furthermore, commended itself to an age which had reacted against the spirit of license in Restoration literature; and his general didacticism, far from being felt as a defect, was in entire accord with dominant literary practice. But his appeal was felt primarily on the grounds of the sublimity and

[5] Milton's works were well known also in colonial America. Increase Mather's library contained several volumes of the prose, and seven or eight copies of *Paradise Lost* have been traced as belonging to American collections before 1700, after which time the evidence becomes abundant. The first American edition of the poems was in 1777; it was followed by twenty-eight others before 1815, almost a third as many as were printed in England during the same years. See Leon Howard, "The Influence of Milton on Colonial American Poetry," *HLQ*, IV (1936), 63–89.

[6] See the study of editions and commentary by Ants Oras, *Milton's Editors and Commentators*; see also Nancy Lee Riffe, "Milton in the Eighteenth-Century Periodicals: 'Hail, Wedded Love,'" *N&Q*, XII (1965), 18–19; "Milton's Minor Poetry in British Periodicals Before 1740," *N&Q*, XII (1965), 453–54; "Milton and Eighteenth-Century Whigs," *N&Q*, XI (1964), 337–38.

fervor of his poetic imagination. It was here that he fell in with the underlying current of romanticism which was unsatisfied by the rationalizing poetry of the school of Pope; and as this tendency asserted itself more powerfully, Milton became more and more acclaimed as a champion of the inwardness and freedom of true poetry. Finally Milton's style and versification were fascinating by their very contrast with prevailing literary modes. He was a quarry of poetical phrase for everybody, even for Pope, and a direct model for the vast school of blank versifiers who maintained what might be called the other poetical tradition of the eighteenth century. Taken as a whole, the Miltonism of the eighteenth century is an extraordinarily varied and complex phenomenon. We shall here attempt to set forth only a few of its outstanding phases.

THE EIGHTEENTH-CENTURY ESTIMATE OF MILTON

Critical admiration of Milton was somewhat tempered in the early period by the judgment that his poems failed to conform to the neoclassical rules of poetry. Dryden, in spite of his sense of Milton's greatness, contended that the subject of *Paradise Lost* was "not that of an heroic poem, properly so called. His design is the losing of our happiness; his event is not prosperous like that of all other epic works."[7] Of course, such an opinion would deny the title of "epic" to Homer's *Iliad*. The tendency, however, of Milton devotees among the classicists was to frame a defense which would justify him according to the accepted standards of the school. It was in this spirit that Addison wrote his famous series of eighteen papers on Milton in the *Spectator* in 1712.[8] Both he and Steele had previously, by casual notices and quotations, commended Milton to the public notice. Besides exhibiting its individual beauties in the critique, Addison analyzes *Paradise Lost* according to the ancient theory and dares to compare it on equal terms with the deified works of Homer and Virgil. The effect of this praise from the most respected critic of the time was to enhance the reputation of

[7] "A Discourse Concerning Satire," *Of Dramatic Poesy and Other Critical Essays*, ed. George Watson (London, 1962), II, 84.

[8] The papers may be read in Vols. II and III of Donald Bond's edition of *The Spectator* (Oxford, 1965).

Milton in all quarters. It has been said that Addison's essays created the vogue of *Paradise Lost*, though this appears to be not altogether true. But certainly the papers became at once the piece of standard Milton criticism. They were published separately in 1719 and have been reissued and reread down to the present day. Translated into French (1727),[9] German (1740), and Italian (1742), they became, along with an essay by Voltaire (*Essaie sur la poésie epique*, 1727), the means of introducing Milton's English works widely for the first time to a Continental audience.

Of course, Addison did not claim that Milton's poem was wholly regular; and in one paper (February 9, 1712) he points out its defects, employing the same rules of judgment that he had used in praising him.[10] Thus Milton's fable is defective, being tragic rather than epic. Some of his incidents have not "probability enough for an Epic Poem."[11] His digressions and his allusions to heathen fables in a Christian poem sin against the canon of unity. To other critics even these reservations were unacceptable; they said that Milton was not to be tried by the neoclassical code. He had invented a new type of poem, the divine epic, superior to anything in antiquity. "The fine arts," said Thomas Leland (1740), "have no rules but genius to direct them."

This attitude is in agreement with the increasing tendency to exalt imagination and emotion in poetry above the "correctness" which had been the ideal of the school of Pope. Thus Joseph Warton, in his *Essay on the Writings and Genius of Pope* (1756), places Milton, because of his sublimity and passion, in the first rank of poets with Shakespeare and Spenser and far above the currently accepted writers. As the romantic currents of the eighteenth century became stronger, the feeling that Milton represented the true ideal from which poetry had since declined became increasingly dominant. The new interest in nature, the taste for color and romance, political liberalism, developing humanitarian sentiment,

[9] Although the first French translation of the *Spectator* was completed in 1718, Addison's essays on Milton remained untranslated until 1727, when N. F. Dupre de Saint-Maur included them as a preface to his translation of *Paradise Lost*. The earlier translator had omitted them because of the lack of a current French rendering of the poem.

[10] Bond, *Spectator*, III, 58–64.

[11] *Ibid.*, p. 60.

and finally the movement toward a greater earnestness and spirituality in religion were all favorable to a more generous appreciation of Milton's essential genius.

The most concrete evidences of this are to be found in the warmth and insight which pervade the poetical tributes to his genius scattered thick through the literature of the period. The modern feelings of admiration for Milton's heroic personality and of astonishment at the boldness and sublimity of his imagination find expression much earlier and more completely in verse than in prose. The list of fully sympathetic poetical utterances about Milton is headed by Andrew Marvell's verses prefixed to the 1674 edition of *Paradise Lost*. His praise, though tinged with religious sobriety, sets the style for the more extravagant utterances of later times:

> That Majesty which through thy Work doth Reign
> Draws the Devout, deterring the Profane.
> And things divine thou treat'st of in such state
> As them preserves, and thee, inviolate.
> At once delight and horror on us seize,
> Thou sing'st with so much gravity and ease;
> And above human flight dost soar aloft
> With Plume so strong, so equal, and so soft.
> The Bird nam'd from that Paradise you sing
> So never flags, but always keeps on Wing.

(11. 31–40)

Dryden's famous epigram, which was placed under Milton's portrait in the folio of 1688, goes much further than its author was willing to do in the cooler and more critical medium of prose:

> Three *Poets*, in three distant *Ages* born,
> *Greece*, *Italy*, and *England* did adorn.
> The *First* in loftiness of thought Surpass'd;
> The *Next* in Majesty: in both the *Last*.
> The force of *Nature* cou'd no farther goe:
> To make a *Third* she joynd the former two.[12]

Pope, Addison, and many others expressed their admiration in verse with similar absence of reservation. Milton's blindness is often mentioned in these tributes, especially by those men who inclined to

[12] *Poems*, ed. James Kinsley (Oxford, 1958), II, 540.

make poetic inspiration a quality of the soul, and his own claim to a compensatory inward vision is accepted and elaborated. It remained for Thomas Gray to express this more romantic feeling of his time in language worthy the theme:

> Nor second He, that rode sublime
> Upon the seraph-wings of Extasy,
> The secrets of th' Abyss to spy.
> He pass'd the flaming bounds of Place and Time:
> The living Throne, the sapphire-blaze,
> Where Angels tremble, when they gaze,
> He saw; but blasted with excess of light,
> Clos'd his eyes in endless night.[13]

This widening conception is an index of the acceptance of the whole of Milton's work. His appeal, originally felt almost exclusively in *Paradise Lost*, came gradually to embrace his other works as well; and the minor poems, as we shall see, became part of his direct influence on the history of poetry itself.[14] An odd development of Miltonic enthusiasm of the later eighteenth century was the continuous popularity of *Comus* in various adaptations on the stage.[15]

The general trend met something of opposition in the most important pronouncement on Milton after Addison's critique, namely, that contained in the celebrated biography by Samuel Johnson in the *Lives of the English Poets* (1779–81).[16] Johnson joined the general chorus in praise of *Paradise Lost*, "a poem which, considered with respect to design, may claim the first place, and with respect to performance, the second, among the productions of the human mind."[17] On the whole, however, his treatment of Milton is reactionary: Johnson loathed Milton's politics, and he disparaged his personal character at every point. He was evidently annoyed, also, by the admiration of his contemporaries for the minor poems, and he denied all merit whatsoever to *Lycidas* and

---

[13] *Poetical Works*, ed. A. L. Poole (London, 1926), 11. 95–102. The poem, of course, is the famous *The Progress of Poesy*.

[14] The minor poems were not entirely neglected before 1740; see George Sherburn, "The Early Popularity of Milton's Minor Poems."

[15] There were performances in practically every year from 1738 to 1800. The University of Michigan Library contains nineteen separate editions of either Dalton or Coleman revisions.

[16] Ed. George Birkbeck Hill (Oxford, 1905), I, 84–200.

[17] *Ibid.*, p. 170.

the sonnets. His churlishness provoked a storm of reply from those who accepted Milton's liberalism as completely as they did his art. Cowper, who had a passionate reverence for Milton and once saw him in a vision, expressed the desire to thrash the old Tory till his pension should jingle in his pocket.

One phase of eighteenth-century critical discussion of Milton concerned his versification. The issue as to the respective merits of blank verse and rhyme was one of long standing. Milton himself, in the foreword to *Paradise Lost*, had thrown out a challenge against the prevailing practice of the Restoration poets. But rhyme and regularity had already triumphed, and it was part of the work of eighteenth-century Milton critics to justify his verse on aesthetic grounds. The defense of his subtler harmonies and of the technique by which they were secured was timid at first but finally emphatic enough. An outstanding pronouncement in favor of Miltonic freedom against the tyranny of the couplet was that of Edward Young in his *Conjectures on Original Composition* (1759). Young declared that Pope's rhyming of Homer had "put *Achilles* in petticoats a second time." He continued:

> How much nobler had it been if his numbers had rolled on in full flow, through various modulations of masculine melody, into those grandeurs of solemn sound, which are indispensably demanded by the native dignity of heroick song. . . . Blank verse is verse unfallen, uncurst; verse reclaim'd, reenthron'd in the true language of the gods.[18]

MILTON'S INFLUENCE ON EIGHTEENTH-CENTURY POETRY

The general admiration for Milton which was felt by eighteenth-century writers and the acceptance of *Paradise Lost* as a classic as worthy of imitation as the ancients themselves resulted in far-reaching influence on eighteenth-century poetry. Blank verse was written in large quantities throughout the period, and practically all of it, as Havens has shown, is Miltonic.[19] Except in drama, there

---

[18] Ed. Edith J. Morley (Manchester, 1918), pp. 26–27.
[19] *The Influence of Milton on English Poetry.* This work remains a prime source of information regarding the poetic imitations of Milton.

was, indeed, no other model. And the Miltonic manner, as distinct from his spirit and inspiration, was not difficult to catch. His use of Latinisms, his inversions of natural word order, his collocations of sonorous proper names, and many other conspicuous external traits furnished ready means of stylistic ornamentation which an age largely destitute of poetic originality was all too ready to adopt. These served to cover the bareness of whole acres of descriptive and didactic poetry; they enabled epic poets to conceal their lack of inspiration from themselves. One of the earliest Miltonic imitators was John Phillips in the burlesque poem, *The Splendid Shilling* (1701). Such employment of the high phraseology of *Paradise Lost* on trivial themes to secure an effect of the absurd was very popular. But it was not just the minor men or the parodists who submitted themselves to the spell of Milton. Pope himself, though he used only couplets, plundered the general treasury of phrase to good effect, while Thomson, Young, and Cowper, who maintained in blank verse the more solemn and inward tradition of poetry before its culmination in Wordsworth, were much more profoundly influenced.

Thomson was genuinely stirred by the Miltonic sweep and grandeur. His own imaginative and vaguely religious sense of the majesty of nature found support in the work of his greater predecessor. His style was molded in a remarkable degree out of the Miltonic materials, and sometimes he succeeded in achieving a kindred eloquence. In general, however, the sword of Achilles was far too mighty for him to use successfully, and as a result he fell into all manner of extravagance and absurdity. The grandiose expressions, which were natural and fitting in their application to the remote and lofty matters with which Milton dealt, became a grotesque affectation when employed, as they often were by Thomson and others, as a means of elevating the commonplace. *The Seasons* (1726–30) was the first serious and thoroughgoing attempt to offset the absence of rhyme by the ornamentation of Miltonic phrase, and it set the pattern for much subsequent blank verse. It had also the effect of establishing the artificial diction which is the curse of eighteenth-century poetry generally. Cowper's superior taste enabled him to avoid the excessive Miltonism of Thomson, but his intimate familiarity with, and profound admiration for, *Paradise Lost* left a strong mark on his own blank verse. "One or another feature of Milton's style and diction," wrote Havens, "occurs in almost every paragraph [of _The Task_]."[20]

The discussion of Miltonic imitation has thus far concerned _Paradise Lost_ alone. Of his other works only the lyrics _L'Allegro_ and _Il Penseroso_ exerted any considerable influence on eighteenth-century poetry, and this influence came late. The revival of lyricism after 1740 among men of romantic inclinations took place in part under the influence of these two exquisite companion pieces. Their combination of freshness and poetic enthusiasm with precision of workmanship and restraint of mood made them, as Havens remarked, particularly adapted to a transitional stage between classicism and romanticism. Both Collins and Gray were inspired by them and adopted their personifications, their tone, and, to some extent, their rhythms. A more thoroughgoing imitator was Thomas Warton the younger, whose favorite octosyllabic verse, with its pleasing and mildly romantic descriptions of English rural landscape, reflects the charm of _L'Allegro_ and _Il Penseroso_ and employs their phraseology at every turn. Through these men _L'Allegro_ and _Il Penseroso_ were made widely popular, and their influence was carried on into the great lyric movement of the early nineteenth century. _Il Penseroso_ is sometimes held accountable for the eighteenth-century passion for poetic melancholy. This is hardly true, for the work of the Graveyard School antedated the vogue of Milton's minor poems, and its lugubriousness is of a different type. The tone of _Il Penseroso_ fell in, however, with this sentiment, and devotion to the melancholy Muse is at least in part Miltonic.

MILTON SCHOLARSHIP IN THE EIGHTEENTH CENTURY

The Miltonic activity of the eighteenth century was not confined to poetic imitation and to the attempt to establish his rank according to classic or romantic principles of criticism. The work of scholarly interpretation was also vigorously undertaken by a

[20] _Ibid._, p. 166.

distinguished line of editors and commentators.[21] This activity consisted in: 1) the elaboration of Milton's biography on the basis of earlier records and of the personal material in his prose and poetry; 2) the explanation and illustration of details in the poems; 3) the discovery of sources and analogues for *Paradise Lost* and to a lesser degree for the other poems. These contributions were generally included in one or another of the innumerable editions of Milton's works. They are, of course, closely connected with the critical discussions already mentioned. The learned editorial labors of Patrick Hume in 1695 were followed in 1732 by Richard Bentley's more sensational but less worthy attempt to constitute a critical text of *Paradise Lost* according to the methods which, as a classical scholar, he had been accustomed to apply to ancient authors. Bentley made the undocumented and unwarranted assumption that Milton's work had been corrupted by an editor who, taking advantage of the poet's blindness, had interpolated passages and made minor changes to the detriment of the meter and the meaning. In his attempt to restore the poem to its original form, Bentley, guided solely by his idea of what Milton ought to have said, often exhibited the most extraordinary bad taste and judgment. He was roughly answered in his own time by Pearce and others, and such ineptitudes as his rewriting of the close of *Paradise Lost*:

> They hand in hand with social steps their way
> Through Eden took with Heavenly comfort cheered

have furnished a perennial theme of ridicule for later writers. It remained for William Empson[22] to declare Bentley superior both in sincerity and in discernment to those critics who have found no aesthetic difficulties in Milton's poetry and who praise him for the wrong reason. Of Bentley's vast body of emendations but two have been adopted in the received text, while some five or ten additional ones are held by J. W. Mackail to be all but certain.[23]

The two Jonathan Richardsons, father and son, published in

[21] An elaborate study of the early editions has been made by Ants Oras (*Milton's Editors and Commentators*).

[22] "Milton and Bentley."

[23] "Bentley's Milton," *Studies in Humanism* (London, 1938), pp. 186–209.

1734 *Explanatory Notes and Remarks on Paradise Lost,* including also, as usual, a new life of the poet. The elder Richardson had inherited traditions of the Restoration period and contributed some valuable personal detail regarding Milton. The son, who was a competent classical scholar, contributed useful explanations of the learned allusions. Both were sympathetic and intelligent, and their work became a standard commentary. An elaborate commentary in the complete works, together with a biographical study, was issued in 1740 by Francis Peck under the title *New Memoirs of the Life and Poetical Works of John Milton.* Peck devoted considerable attention to Milton's style and language and to his methods of composition as illustrated by his manuscript corrections. The first variorum edition of *Paradise Lost* was that of Thomas Newton, published with a new life, the best that had been written up to that time, in 1749. This became the basis of a complete variorum of the poetical works by Henry Todd, published in 1801 and revised in 1809. Todd collects in his preliminary account of Milton's life and in his extensive notes to, and discussions of, the poems, the fruits of the scholarly and critical activities of the whole century. He also contributes much material of his own. He adduces a host of literary parallels from classical and modern authors, takes account of the valuable materials afforded by the Cambridge Manuscript, prints the records of the nuncupative will proceedings, and deals extensively with Milton's sources and analogues. His work was not superseded until Masson's three-volume edition, which was first issued in 1874 and then again, in a revised edition, in 1890.

The exploration, often with the implication of plagiarism, of Milton's literary borrowings was a favorite amusement of both eighteenth- and nineteenth-century scholars. The most sensational incident in this connection was William Lauder's claim in his essay on *Milton's Imitations of the Moderns* (1749) to have found the originals of *Paradise Lost* in the Latin drama *Adamus Exul* of Hugo Grotius and in other out-of-the-way neo-Latin poems. It was afterwards shown that the remarkable closeness of Lauder's parallels was due to the fact that he had interpolated among them passages from a Latin translation of Milton's poem by William Hog. If Lauder had contented himself with the *Adamus Exul* as he found it, he would have been on solid ground with Hayley, who, following a suggestion of Voltaire, pointed out the similarities between *Paradise Lost* and the *Adamo* of Andreini, and with Dunster, who brought forward Sylvester's Du Bartas as a primary formative influence on Milton's style. The plausibility of these relationships and of the later claims in favor of Caedmon and Vondel has been discussed in Chapter 4.

THE NINETEENTH CENTURY

There is no evidence of a narrowing of the circle of Milton's readers in the first quarter of the nineteenth century. New editions appeared in increasing numbers, and literary circles continued to pay tribute to his greatness. The discovery, in 1823, of the manuscript of the *Christian Doctrine* was an event of great critical interest. Bishop Sumner was commissioned by the king to translate and publish it, and the text and translation were published in two volumes in 1825. Macaulay's essay, which owed its fame as much to its subject as to its intrinsic brilliancy, was written as a review of Milton's treatise, and the *Christian Doctrine* was made the subject of a popular study by the American Unitarian, William Ellery Channing, in 1826.

It was, however, among the poets who came in the wake of the French Revolution that Milton was the most dynamic force. He was so already in the late eighteenth century to William Blake, in whose image-haunted brain he took his place among the prophets, visiting his waking dreams in person and contributing largely to the materials of his imagination in poetry and art. Over ninety of Blake's paintings and engravings are on Miltonic subjects. His Urizen in the epic poem *Vala* is a wild counterpart of Satan, and Milton himself, standing for the ideal poet, is the titular hero of another work. Blake's own fantastic cosmology and the philosophic ideas embodied in it are indebted, whether by agreement or opposition, to the Miltonic system.[24]

In the *Marriage of Heaven and Hell* Blake says that Satan rep-

[24] See Denis Saurat, *Blake and Milton.*

resents desire and the Messiah, reason, or the restrainer. He then
goes on to invert Milton's ethical code by proclaiming the Messiah
rather than Satan the Evil One, adding in a note that the reason
why Milton wrote in fetters when he wrote of angels and God, and
at liberty when of the Devils and hell, is because he was a true poet
and of the Devil's party without knowing it. This Rousseauistic
proposition represents something new in Miltonic interpretation. It
is really quite different in its implications from Dryden's statement
that Satan is the hero of *Paradise Lost,* for Dryden is thinking in
terms of epic technique, while Blake is declaring that passion and
rebellion, typified in Satan, are the vital motives of Milton's poetic
inspiration. In so doing, he keenly anticipates the trend of a good
deal of subsequent criticism. An identical point of view pervades
Sir Walter Raleigh's brilliant book on Milton, which may fairly be
said to represent the standard opinion of the romantic school. The
theological and moral system under which Milton disciplined himself, its validity no longer felt, was thought to be a contradiction
to his actual experience. Hence the ideals and aims which he
thought he was achieving have been discredited as not representing
the true values of his work, with the inference that Milton's poetry
can no longer be admired as a whole or on his own terms. Matthew
Arnold finds the obsolescence of Milton's theology a barrier to
modern acceptance of *Paradise Lost* and recommends that it be
read in fragments. In general, the dramatic portrayal of Satan in
Books I and II is held to outrank in creative power all the rest of
the poem.

Shelley and Byron, without analyzing the situation as Blake
had done, rejected or ignored Milton's Puritanism, while making
the most of those elements in him which coincided with their own
revolutionary ideas. Thus Shelley found Milton's Satan, as a moral
being, infinitely superior to his God, who bore the familiar earmarks
of the tyrant. His own Prometheus he recognized as a kindred figure
—superior, however, because his activities were directed to man's
good instead of to his destruction. Byron gave a more direct literary
application to the Satan worship of the time by making Lucifer,
in the drama of *Cain,* a champion of man's thirst for intellectual
emancipation. The new age of spiritual rebellion thus adopted
Milton as its ally; its sympathies led it naturally to exalt his personal

career. Thus Shelley ranges him in *Adonais* with the other poet-heroes who have had the world against them.

> He died,
> Who was the Sire of an immortal strain,
> Blind, old, and lonely, when his country's pride,
> The priest, the slave, and the liberticide,
> Trampled and mocked with many a loathed rite
> Of lust and blood; he went, unterrified,
> Into the gulf of death; but his clear Sprite
> Yet reigns o'er the earth; the third among the sons
>   of light.

Wordsworth had a clearer sense of Milton's true quality, and he was profoundly influenced by his spirit and art. His own combination of a temperate love of liberty with an intense moral earnestness was akin to Milton's and predisposed him to admiration. His sonnet, *Milton, thou should'st be living at this hour*, illustrates how deeply he had assimilated the ethical idealism of his master. It was, indeed, the reading of Milton's sonnets which inspired his own masterpieces in this form. There is also a Miltonic quality in Wordsworth's more exalted utterances in blank verse, and though he does not, like Thomson, ape Milton's stylistic peculiarities in an obvious manner, echoes of Miltonic phrase are frequent in his work.

Keats, too, was a Miltonist, but his allegiance was quite different from that of either Shelley or Wordsworth. His feeling for Milton's poetry was primarily aesthetic. The richness of Milton's expression, "poetical luxury" as Keats called it, was naturally attractive to his temperament, but he learned to admire the restraint and dignity which elevated Milton above his own early masters. Keats's enthusiastic study of *Paradise Lost* just after he had written *Endymion* is rightly held to have been of great influence in disciplining and ennobling his work. His *Hyperion* represents an attempt to compose a blank verse epic on the Miltonic plane. In both conception and style the poem owes much to *Paradise Lost*: it was abandoned because Keats felt himself to be doing violence to his genius in adopting a poetical mode which was, after all, alien to his own. Taken as a whole, the romantic period, though its view of Milton was colored by its own emotions, stood close to him in imaginative sympathy and was better equipped than the eighteenth century to value his true poetic quality.

Although later nineteenth-century poets produced nothing comparable to Keats's full-scale imitation of Milton in *Hyperion*, Milton became for the Victorians the poet exemplary of the epithet "sublime": the man whose vision and poetic conception were sublime in "grandeur, largeness, and magnificence."[25] Among Milton's Victorian admirers were numbered Tennyson, Arnold, and Landor; unlike most of the romantics, who were interested in Milton's theology, they were primarily "impressed with his form, style, and metrical skill."[26] In other words, the interests of the audience of *Paradise Lost* had shifted to literary and technical matters and with this shift the audience had naturally narrowed. Perhaps after the publication of Darwin's *Origin of Species* in 1859 readers were less interested in matters of the truth of religious myth and more in the ways religious myths were embodied in verse.

During this latter half of the century, Milton's sonnets began to attract more attention than usual, and the vogue culminated in the fine edition by Mark Pattison published in 1883. His long prefatory essay reflects the age's tremendous interest in the Miltonic sonnet. As James Nelson has shown, nearly everyone agreed upon the excellence of Milton's craft, and all were particularly impressed with the magnificence of the republican furor in the sonnet on the massacre of the Waldenses. Tennyson's *Montenegro* sonnet (1877), in the mood of Milton's outraged cry, is an example of Victorian imitation at its best.[27]

THE TWENTIETH CENTURY

The scholarly study of Milton's life and work has been carried to a point far beyond that reached by the activity of the eighteenth and nineteenth centuries. The collected edition of the poetry and prose

[25] James Nelson, *The Sublime Puritan*, pp. 39–73.
[26] *Ibid.*, p. 126.
[27] *Ibid.*, pp. 20–38.

published by John Mitford in 1851 was for many years the standard collection of the works, while the Bohn edition of the prose, with its translations of the Latin pamphlets, has been the most available means of access to these materials. These were followed by useful editions of the poetry by Moody (1899), Beeching (1900), Wright (1903), and Grierson (1925). The work known as the Columbia Edition, completed in 1938 with a two-volume index published in 1940, still supersedes all others as the official corpus of Milton's poetry, while the Yale Edition of the prose (to be complete in eight volumes) will become the standard edition of Milton's prose works. The best single-volume edition of the complete poems is that edited by Merritt Hughes (1957).

Though the Columbia Edition added a number of hitherto uncollected works, some of them published from manuscript for the first time, and while it contained all that could be wished for in the way of textual apparatus, it did not attempt the heroic task of furnishing complete editorial equipment in the form of annotations and introductions. Under the direction of Don M. Wolfe, the Yale Edition is supplying detailed introductory essays and rich annotations for the prose works; and with Merritt Hughes as general editor, a set of variorum notes and commentary on Milton's poems is being prepared to supplement the Columbia Edition. Hughes is completing the notes for *Paradise Lost*, Walter MacKellar for *Paradise Regained*, John T. Shawcross is completing W. R. Parker's earlier work on *Samson Agonistes*, Douglas Bush is writing notes for the Latin poems, and Hughes is completing the work begun by the late A. S. P. Woodhouse on the minor poems. With the addition of these notes, the Columbia Edition will remain the standard collection of the poetry for an indefinite time. The paraphernalia of Milton study has also been greatly enriched by the publication of dictionaries of his language and of his geographical, historical, and Biblical allusions, and by a concordance of the Latin poems. A new concordance of the poetry has been planned and is scheduled for publication soon. There is still no large-scale allusion book, but William R. Parker's *Milton's Contemporary Reputation* covers the subject to 1674, and the studies of Havens, Good, and Nelson provide a great deal of such material for the eighteenth and nineteenth centuries.

An indispensable bibliographical aid to the study of Milton was provided by Stevens in his *Reference Guide,* which was published in 1930. This, however, includes only materials published since 1800; Fletcher's supplement carries the subject down to 1930. The making of a complete and up-to-date supplement to Stevens and Fletcher was attempted by Calvin Huckabay in 1960. Early editions of the prose works are usually noted and discussed in the lengthy introductions to the selections in the Yale Edition. James Holly Hanford's more recent bibliography (1966) may be supplemented with those compiled in the serials *PMLA, SCN,* and the *Milton Newsletter.*

The modern study of Milton as a man and poet rests on David Masson's monumental seven-volume *Life of Milton in Connection with the History of His Times,* the first volume of which appeared in 1859 and the last (the indispensable index) in 1894. Masson's indefatigable labors in the records and pamphlets of the Puritan period and his minute attention to every detail in the remotest degree related to Milton have made his work, though of oppressive magnitude, the one indispensable body of biographical information. Later biographers, like Mark Pattison, whose brief life of Milton is still among the best, have constructed their interpretations of Milton largely out of the materials furnished by Masson. They have largely ignored the work of Alfred Stern, *Milton und seine Zeit,* which was published in two volumes in 1877–79 and which contains some things not found in its greater English rival. Smaller general biographies continue to be written, and, in the tradition of Belloc, Rose Macaulay, and Dora Raymond, are, most recently, those studies by David Daiches (1957, 1963) and Douglas Bush (1964). To Harris Fletcher's incomplete but prolix study, *The Intellectual Development of John Milton* (2 vols., 1956–   ) we may now add William R. Parker's long-awaited and now published *Milton: A Biography* (2 vols., 1968); this latter study is the single most important biographical work on Milton in our century. Each of Milton's works is carefully dated, placed in biographical context, and then evaluated and discussed critically. The result is a new, scrupulously balanced, and precisely detailed portrait of Milton as man and poet. Readers will stand in awe of Parker's ability to marshal all pertinent data without becoming overwhelmed with the mass of his material.

Controversial in some points (e.g., *Comus*, he argues, is essentially children's entertainment) and always careful to remind us that time itself cannot change conjecture to fact (e.g., *Samson Agonistes* may *not* be a product of Milton's old age), the book will remain a starting point for all students of Milton who wish to begin their studies by distinguishing what we *know* about Milton from what we *think* we know.

For the more advanced student of Milton, the footnotes in Parker's second volume provide a running commentary on Milton scholarship since the seventeenth century. They are a mine of information on critical, scholarly, bibliographical, biographical, and historical information. One finds there the arguments of scholars who disagree with Parker fairly and carefully presented (and fully documented). And there also are the fruits of Parker's research over the years into all the known locations of surviving contemporary editions of Milton's works. His diligent and careful searchings are tabulated so that scholars can consult editions in nearby libraries. And in each instance he evaluates the significance of his findings and of what they tell us of Milton's methods, of seventeenth-century printing, editing, proofreading, and publishing practices, and of Milton's popularity. We might add that the index to the study has the advantage of citing the birth and death dates of all persons listed as well as the dates of their principal publications and revisions of those publications. All readers of Milton will find Parker's book first helpful and then indispensable; it is now the crucial reference for biographical interpretation. Throughout his study Parker has rightfully acknowledged his debt to Joseph Milton French's invaluable documentary research published in his five-volume *The Life Records of John Milton* (1949–58); here the scholar will find listed in chronological order all the known facts of Milton's career.

It is most difficult to make a selection from the category of recent criticism on Milton; there is so much to choose from. Most recently, however, under pressure from Waldock, Broadbent, Empson, and Peter, the more traditional Miltonists have been forced to look at details in Milton's poems more closely than ever before. For instance, a careful arguer must answer Empson's provocative and anti-Christian study that suggests Milton is timely because he is openly critical of God:

The root of his power is that he could accept and express a downright horrible conception of God and yet keep somehow alive, underneath it, all breadth and generosity. . . . Unless you look at the poem like that, so that you are undisturbed by the twentieth-century complaints about its argument, I warmly agree that it feels bad. If you praise it as the neo-Christians do, what you are getting from it is evil.[28]

Discussing the figure of God in the poem, Peter does not argue that Milton's theology is unacceptable, but that Milton himself betrays his uneasiness with the traditional concept of divinity in the very periods, cadences, and rhetorical patterns employed to describe God.[29] Add to this Waldock's charges that in the poem itself Milton's allegations clash discordantly with his demonstrations, Leavis' undervaluing of the "grand style," and T. S. Eliot's earlier attack upon Miltonic "music," and it soon becomes obvious that a new and different kind of criticism is called upon to answer these often perceptive attacks. It seems no longer possible to say that we can understand *Paradise Lost* only by taking an historical perspective on the poem and the rest of Milton's works.

Although the "Miltonoclasts" have not generally evoked a flurry of critical maneuvers in defense of Milton (a notable exception is C. S. Lewis' formidable A *Preface to "Paradise Lost"* [1942]), they have provoked Milton critics into looking more carefully at the texts of the poems themselves. The result has been artful studies by Don Cameron Allen (1954) and Rosemond Tuve (1957) on the minor poems, by B. Rajan (1947), Arnold Stein (1953), Isabel Mac-Caffrey (1959), Joseph Summers (1962), Anne Ferry (1963), and Christopher Ricks (1963) on *Paradise Lost*, and by Arnold Stein (1957) and Barbara Lewalski (1966) on *Paradise Regained*. Supplementing William R. Parker's seminal *Milton's Debt to Greek Tragedy in Samson Agonistes* (1937) is the study of that poem by Arnold Stein in *Heroic Knowledge* (1957). Attempting to answer Milton's critics directly are Christopher Ricks and Bernard Bergonzi; Bergonzi's essay, "Criticism and the Milton Controversy,"[30] admir-

---

[28] *Milton's God* (London, 1965), pp. 276–77.
[29] A *Critique of Paradise Lost*.
[30] *The Living Milton*, ed. Frank Kermode, pp. 162–80.

ably reviews the criticism of the anti-Milton position, while at the same time it makes the point that the charges made by the anti-Miltonists are simply "unanswerable" and "wrong." That is, given the critical grounds upon which the anti-Miltonists argue, it is impossible to answer their arguments, for their assumption is that Milton has written a nineteenth-century novel rather than an epic poem. One can easily see that the merits of *Paradise Lost* are no longer argued in terms of nineteenth-century "sublimity"; rather the twentieth-century concepts of tone, tension, ambiguity, *et al.*, are the current critical preoccupations.

What we are discovering is that Milton is to be understood in various ways: those who enter into and accept at face value both his literary and his religious tradition may offer us a Milton different from the one evoked by those who insist upon the integrity of close textual analysis. Although he is variously understood, few are willing to undervalue his poetic abilities and achievements. In fact, some have suggested that if *Paradise Lost* is judged faulty, the error lies with the ways of fallen man, who, faced with ultimate moral choices in the poem, elects to accept an equivocal position which is an easy escape from responsibility rather than to exercise his will to "see," "judge," and "act" morally, as the poem directs him. There promise to be as many Miltons and as many versions of his poems as there are future readers.

Appendix A

MISCELLANEOUS PROSE ITEMS
OF UNCERTAIN DATE

At some interval of leisure during the Commonwealth or early Protectorate, possibly even as early as the Hammersmith period and surely before his blindness, Milton composed a popular account of Russia[1]—the land, the government, and the people—based on the stories of various explorers which had been printed in Hakluyt's *Voyages*, Purchas' *Pilgrimages* and elsewhere (a list of sources is appended by Milton himself).[2] Such narratives were one of the favorite branches of Milton's reading, and the subject of geography appealed to his curiosity and his imagination. He speaks in his preface as though he had projected a series of descriptions of various countries. As in the *History of Britain* he proposes to give a readable and veracious account in small compass, purged of "long Stories of absurd Superstitions, Ceremonies, quaint Habits, and other petty Circumstances little to the purpose."[3] He condenses and paraphrases his originals, transforming into his own Latinized prose

---

[1] A *Brief History of Moscovia*, ed. George Phillip Krapp, *Works*, X, 327–82. Hereafter this edition will be cited CM. See also John B. Gleason, "The Nature of Milton's *Moscovia*."

[2] *CM*, X, 382.

[3] *Ibid.*, p. 327. See also George B. Parks, "Milton's *Moscovia* Not History."

the plain or florid English of the Elizabethan navigators.[4] The work was published after his death in 1682. The poetic fruits of his study of the voyages had already been garnered in *Paradise Lost*.

Two school textbooks—a Latin grammar and a treatise on logic in Latin—close the list of Milton's original prose works. The first of these, *Accedence Commenc't Grammar, Supply'd with sufficient Rules, For the use of such (Younger or Elder) as are desirous, without more trouble than needs to learn the Latin Tongue*,[5] is a fruit of Milton's interest in pedagogy and of his conviction, expressed in the tractate *Of Education*, that an immense amount of time was wasted by the cumbersome methods of Latin instruction then in vogue. It was published in 1669. The *Artis Logicae Plenior Institutio*,[6] published three years later, is an elaboration in the interest of clarity of Peter Ramus' system, which had been welcomed by the Protestant universities in opposition to the traditional logic of Aristotle, felt to be too much identified with Catholicism.[7] Both works were presumably written in the days when Milton was occupied with the practical work of education.

In 1658 Milton published the first edition of a work on government by Sir Walter Ralegh entitled *The Cabinet Council: containing the Chief arts of Empire and Mysteries of State*. The manuscript, he says in a foreword, had been given to him by a learned man at his death and had been in his hands many years. Milton was keenly interested in the principles and maxims of civic leadership as set forth by the statesmen of the Renaissance (witness his careful study of Machiavelli recorded in the Commonplace Book).

There are other records of Milton's intellectual activities in the form of annotations to volumes which have been preserved from his library, some of them perhaps designed as materials for scholarly editions. We also have his Commonplace Book, consisting of quo-

---

[4] Parallels are given by Prince D. S. Mirsky, *A Brief History of Moscovia* (London, 1929); Allan H. Gilbert's *A Geographical Dictionary of Milton* contains many references to Milton's readings in voyagers and geographers.

[5] Ed. George Phillip Krapp, *CM*, VI, 285–353; see also J. Milton French, "Some Notes on Milton's *Accedence Commenc't Grammar*."

[6] Ed. Allan H. Gilbert, *CM*, XI.

[7] G. C. Moore-Smith notes that the *Logic* must have been written or revised after Milton had abandoned the "orthodox view of the Trinity"; see "A Note on Milton's 'Art of Logic,'" *RES*, XIII (1937), 335–40 (cf. C. A. Patrides, *Christian Tradition*).

tations and references from his reading, chiefly in political and ecclesiastical history, arranged under appropriate headings. These notes were, of course, intended for his use only. The manuscript was discovered in 1874 and published for the Camden Society in 1876.[8] The entries, which range in date from the Hammersmith period to some time after Milton had become blind, are an interesting index of his changing interests and opinions. When arranged chronologically they show him to have been following a consistent program of historical study from the fall of Rome to his own day.[9]

[8] Ed. A. J. Horwood. An edition of the text, with a translation, is included in CM, XVIII, 128–227, and in Yale, *Milton*, I, 344–508 (with preface, translation, and notes by Ruth Mohl).

[9] See James Holly Hanford, "The Chronology of Milton's Private Studies."

Appendix B

MILTON'S "BIOGRAPHIA LITERARIA"

OF THE VARIOUS PASSAGES IN THE PROSE WORKS IN WHICH MILTON pauses to take the reader into his confidence regarding his thoughts and aspirations, two are outstanding autobiographic revelations. The first is a statement in the *Apology* (1642) concerning the development of his ideals of chastity; this document was written in answer to slanderous accusations by Bishop Hall but constitutes an independent record of the successive phases of his emotional life from the beginning of his University career to the close of the Horton period. As a commentary upon his own early poetical work and upon the literary influences under the stimulus of which it was composed, this document is worth volumes of criticism. Milton has analyzed the stages of his inner life as clearly, if not so fully, as Wordsworth did his own in *The Prelude*. The passage is cited here followed by an interpretation[1] of its statements in the light of Milton's youthful poetry:

> I had my time Readers, as others have, who have good learn-
> ing bestow'd upon them, to be sent to those places, where
> the opinion was it might be soonest attain'd: and as the man-

[1] For a fuller analysis see James Holly Hanford, "The Youth of Milton."
Many relevant passages other than those given here are included in John S.
Diekhoff's comprehensive collection of Milton's autobiographic utterances, *Milton on Himself*.

ner is, was not unstudied in those authors which are most commended; whereof some were grave Orators & Historians; whose matter me thought I lov'd indeed, but as my age then was, so I understood them; others were the smooth Elegiack Poets, whereof the Schooles are not scarce. Whom both for the pleasing sound of their numerous writing, which in imitation I found most easie; and most agreeable to natures part in me, and for their matter which what it is, there be few who know not, I was so allur'd to read, that no recreation came to me better welcome. For that it was then those years with me which are excus'd though they be least severe, I may be sav'd the labour to remember ye. Whence having observ'd them to account it the chiefe glory of their wit, in that they were ablest to judge, to praise, and by that could esteeme themselves worthiest to love those high perfections which under one or other name they took to celebrate, I thought with my selfe by every instinct and presage of nature which is not wont to be false, that what imboldn'd them to this task might with such diligence as they us'd imbolden me, and that what judgement, wit, or elegance was my share, would herein best appeare, and best value it selfe, by how much more wisely, and with more love of vertue I should choose (let rude eares be absent) the object of not unlike praises. For albeit these thoughts to some will seeme vertuous and commendable, to others only pardonable, to a third sort perhaps idle, yet the mentioning of them now will end in serious. Nor blame it Readers, in those yeares to propose to themselves such a reward, as the noblest dispositions above other things in this life have sometimes preferr'd. Whereof not to be sensible, when good and faire in one person meet, argues both a grosse and shallow judgement, and withall and ungentle, and swainish brest. For by the firme setling of these perswasions I became, to my best memory, so much a proficient, that if I found those authors any where speaking unworthy things of themselves; or unchaste of those names which before they had extoll'd, this effect it wrought with me, from that time forward their art I still applauded, but the men I deplor'd; and above them all preferr'd the two famous renowners of Beatrice and Laura who never write but honour of them to whom they devote their

verse, displaying sublime and pure thoughts, without transgression. And long it was not after, when I was confirm'd in
this opinion, that he who would not be frustrate of his hope
to write well hereafter in laudable things, ought him selfe to
bee a true Poem, that is, a composition, and patterne of the
best and honourablest things; not presuming to sing high
praises of heroick men, or famous Cities, unlesse he have in
himselfe the experience and the practice of all that which is
praise-worthy. These reasonings, together with a certaine nice-
nesse of nature, an honest haughtinesse, and self-esteem either
of what I was, or what I might be, (which let envie call pride)
and lastly that modesty, whereof though not in the Title page
yet here I may be excus'd to make some beseeming profession,
all these uniting the supply of their naturall aide together, kept
me still above those low descents of minde, beneath which he
must deject and plunge himself, that can agree to salable and
unlawful prostitutions. Next, (for heare me out now Readers)
that I may tell ye whether my younger feet wander'd; I betook
me among those lofty Fables and Romances, which recount
in solemne canto's the deeds of Knighthood founded by our
victorious Kings; & from hence had in renowne over all Chris-
tendome. There I read it in the oath of every Knight, that
he should defend to the expence of his best blood, or of his
life, if it so befell him, the honour and chastity of Virgin or
Matron. From whence even then I learnt what a noble vertue
chastity sure must be, to the defence of which so many worthies
by such a deare adventure of themselves had sworne. And if I
found in the story afterward any of them by word or deed
breaking that oath, I judg'd it the same fault of the Poet, as
that which is attributed to Homer; to have written undecent
things of the gods. Only this my minde gave me that every
free and gentle spirit without that oath ought to be borne a
Knight, nor needed to expect the guilt spurre, or the laying of
a sword upon his shoulder to stirre him up both by his coun-
sell, and his arme to secure and protect the weaknesse of any
attempted chastity. So that even those books which to many
others have bin the fuell of wantonnesse and loose living, I
cannot thinke how unless by divine indulgence prov'd to me
so many incitements as you have heard, to the love and sted-

fast observation of that vertue which abhorres the society of Bordello's. Thus from the Laureat fraternity of Poets, riper yeares, and the ceaselesse round of study and reading led me to the shady spaces of philosophy, but chiefly to the divine volumes of Plato, and his equall Xenophon. Where if I should tell ye what I learnt, of chastity and love, I meane that which is truly so, whose charming cup is only vertue which she bears in her hand to those who are worthy. The rest are cheated with a thick intoxicating potion which a certaine Sorceresse the abuser of loves name carries about; and how the first and chiefest office of love, begins and ends in the soule, producing those happy twins of her divine generation knowledge and vertue, with such abstracted sublimities as these, it might be worth your listning, Readers, as I may one day hope to have ye in a still time, when there shall be no chiding; not in these noises, the adversary as ye know, barking at the doore; or searching for me at the Burdello's where it may be he has lost himselfe, and raps up without pitty the sage and rheumatick old Prelatesse with all her young Corinthian Laity to inquire for such a one. Last of all not in time, but as perfection is last, that care was ever had of me, with my earliest capacity not to be negligently train'd in the precepts of Christian Religion: This that I have hitherto related, hath bin to shew, that though Christianity had bin but slightly taught me, yet a certain reserv'dnesse of naturall disposition, and morall discipline learnt out of the noblest Philosophy was anough to keep me in disdain of farre lesse incontinences than this of the Burdello. But having had the doctrine of holy Scripture unfolding those chaste and high mysteries with timeliest care infus'd that the body is for the Lord and the Lord for the body, thus also I argu'd to my selfe; that if unchastity in a woman whom Saint Paul termes the glory of man, be such a scandall and dishonour, then certainly in a man who is both the image and glory of God, it must, though commonly not so thought, be much more deflouring and dishonourable. In that he sins both against his owne body which is the perfeter sex, and his own glory which is in the woman, and that which is worst, against the image and glory of God which is in himselfe. Nor did I

slumber over that place expressing such high rewards of ever
accompanying the Lambe, with those celestiall songs to others
inapprehensible, but not to those who were not defil'd with
women, which doubtlesse meanes fornication: For mariage must
not be call'd a defilement.[2]

In the first paragraph Milton indicates with some precision the
moment of a new kind of emotional response to the stimulus of
reading characteristic of adolescence. The smooth and glowing
love poetry of Ovid and his fellows has spoken powerfully to his
imagination and has roused in him the impulse of imitation. The
result is clearly written in his own Latin elegies, particularly the
First, Fifth, and Seventh, with their strong accent of sensuous
feeling and their only partly chastened Ovidian tone. The time to
which he refers would be about his nineteenth year. At a later
period he evidently felt the need of regarding the activities of this
epoch with some indulgence. He implies, however, that even then
his zest for the elegists was followed by an idealistic reaction which
soon led to his deserting them for higher objects. Rejecting the
grosser enticements of the flesh, he finds the embodiment of his
new aspirations in the Dantean and Petrarchan exaltation of woman
and in their refinement of the sentiment of love. The Italian sonnets,
closely imitated from Petrarch, may be taken as the immediate fruits
of Milton's second literary discipleship, though their precise date
is uncertain. A more decided advance in point of view is indicated
in the next sentence: "And long it was not after, when I was confirm'd in this opinion, that he who would not be frustrate of his
hope to write well hereafter in laudable things ought him selfe to
bee a true Poem." The key to this is furnished by the Sixth Elegy,
in which Milton abandons the mood of lax indulgence in favor of
an earnest asceticism. The formula given in this work for the
discipline of an epic poet closely parallels that in the *Apology* and
makes it clear that in the quoted passage Milton is looking back to
and thinking in terms of his meditation of 1629. We may assume
that he is recording a more or less definite resolution regarding his
life work, a resolution which we may associate with his coming of

[2] Ed. with preface and notes by Frederick Lovett Taft, Yale, *Milton*, I,
889–93.

age in the same month in which the Latin poem was written. The poem *On the Nativity*, indicative of his earnest devotion to the highest themes, followed immediately after.

Passing over more transient moods and influences which may have intervened, Milton next sets forth his enthusiasm for the literature of chivalry. He probably refers not to his earliest acquaintance with the stories of knighthood in Geoffrey or Malory but to a period of more serious occupation with them as they were interpreted and moralized by the poets of the Renaissance. Above all he is thinking of the "solemn cantos" of the "sage and serious" Spenser, who becomes henceforth a dominant poetic influence. The time is the Hammersmith period or slightly earlier; Milton's interests are leading him toward the selection of an Arthurian subject for his projected epic. The time, however, is not ripe, and he lingers for a while in the easier paths of pastoral poetry. Meanwhile he is adding to his zeal for romantic poetry the study of philosophy. The character of his reference and his bracketing of Plato and Xenophon show very clearly that it is the high doctrine of love and virtue as set forth in the *Symposium* that chiefly attracts him. Such "abstracted sublimities" fit well with the concrete embodiments in Spenser, who had already assimilated them. But in thus turning toward the Renaissance star of Platonic love, Milton also turns to its counterpart of Christian chastity, dwelling especially on the image of the heavenly nuptials of the pure as given in the fourteenth chapter of Revelation. The outcome of these elevated yet fervid imaginings is *Comus*, in which the correlative influences of Spenserian, Platonic, and Apocalyptic allegory are clearly to be traced. The idea of the mystic marriage of the pure soul with God, which is the theme of the Attendant Spirit's Epilogue, is touched on again in *Lycidas* (1637) and, with much sensuous elaboration, in the *Epitaphium Damonis* (1640). The "unexpressive nuptial song" mentioned in the two elegies carries us directly to that place in Scripture (Rev. 14) over which Milton said he did not sleep. In the *Comus* passage the imagery is exclusively Spenserian and Platonic, though the emotion is Christian.

The fervor of Milton's philosophic studies during the Hammersmith period and the degree to which they colored his personal relations and his aspirations as a poet are reflected in the letter to Charles Diodati, quoted in Chapter 1. Here under the aegis of the

Platonic philosophy the emotion of friendship expands to its loftiest significance, fusing itself with the poet's ethical aspirations and with his impassioned dream of fame. The passage prepares us for the outburst four years later in the *Epitaphium Damonis*, and the two utterances together represent the culmination of the glowing idealism of Milton's early manhood.

But precisely what does he mean in 1642, after the return from Italy, when he proposes to entertain his readers with the abstracted sublimities of love and virtue? It is a curious fact that Heavenly Love appears as a character in each of the first three dramatic plans for *Paradise Lost* composed about this time.[3] In the poem itself as Milton finally constructed it some twenty years later, the Platonic raptures have taken on something of a Puritan sobriety. The praise of chastity has become the praise of wedded love; the heavenly marriage finds its counterpart on earth; and the mystic raptures of the Garden of Adonis are transferred to the more human joys of the Garden of Eden. Yet even in *Paradise Lost* we have the strange account of the loves of angels (*PL*, VIII, 611 ff.), and the whole poem may stand as Milton's fulfillment of his promise to write of "that [love] which is truly so," whose "first and chiefest office . . . ends in the soule, producing those [two] happy twins of her divine generation knowledge and vertue."[4]

In writing the passage from the *Apology* Milton's vision is wholly retrospective, and it embraces only one element in his experience; but that element is to be recognized as primary during the period of his youth and dominant in his more intense and personal poetic expression. Meanwhile, however, his cultural interests were broadening, and his purposes in art and life were defining themselves more sharply. The political thought of the ancient orators and historians and the public problems of his own day, though they exercise as yet but little influence in his creative works, are gaining increasing hold on his attention. His conception of virtue is broadening to include justice and morality in the body politic, and the idea of

---

[3] The motive of love and chastity is to be found also in the other dramatic plans, notably in "Sodom Burning," where in an inserted passage Milton outlines a scene in which the angels, pitying the beauty of the Sodomites, "dispute of love and how it differs from lust seeking to win them." At the final destruction of the city the "Angel appears all girt with flame which he saith are the flames of true love."

[4] *Apology*, Yale, *Milton*, I, 891–92.

his own service to his countrymen as one of spiritual and intellectual leadership is acquiring a patriotic and religious fervor. The explicit record of these interests takes the form of a description of the function of the poet in a personal digression in *The Reason of Church-Government* which was written some months earlier than the statement in the *Apology* but better represents the mature aims which are finally to dominate Milton's poetic art. The passage, omitting the beginning, which has already been given, is as follows:

Time servs not now, and perhaps I might seem too profuse to give any certain account of what the mind at home in the spacious circuits of her musing hath liberty to propose to her self, though of highest hope, and hardest attempting, whether that Epick form whereof the two poems of Homer, and those other two of Virgil and Tasso are a diffuse, and the book of Job a brief model: or whether the rules of Aristotle herein are strictly to be kept, or nature to be follow'd, which in them that know art, and use judgement is no transgression, but an inriching of art. And lastly what K. or Knight before the conquest might be chosen in whom to lay the pattern of a Christian Heroe. And as Tasso gave to a Prince of Italy his chois whether he would command him to write of Godfreys expedition against the infidels, or Belisarius against the Gothes, or Charlemain against the Lombards; if to the instinct of nature and the imboldning of art ought may be trusted, and that there be nothing advers in our climat, or the fate of this age, it haply would be no rashnesse from an equal diligence and inclination to present the like offer in our own ancient stories. Or whether those Dramatick constitutions, wherein Sophocles and Euripides raigne shall be found more doctrinal and exemplary to a Nation, the Scripture also affords us a divine pastoral Drama in the Song of Salomon consisting of two persons and a double Chorus, as Origen rightly judges. And the Apocalyps of Saint John is the majestick image of a high and stately Tragedy, shutting up and intermingling her solemn Scenes and Acts with sevenfold Chorus of halleluja's and harping symphonies: and this my opinion the grave autority of Pareus commenting that booke is sufficient to confirm. Or if occasion shall lead to imitat those magnifick Odes and Hymns wherein Pindarus and Callimachus are in most things worthy, some others in their frame judicious, in their matter most an end faulty: But those frequent songs throughout the law and prophets beyond all these, not in their divine argument alone, but in the very critical art of composition may be easily made appear over all the kinds of Lyrick poesy, to be incomparable. These abilities, wheresoever they be found, are the inspired guift of God rarely bestow'd, but yet to some (though most abuse) in every Nation: and are of power beside the office of a pulpit, to imbreed and cherish in a great people the seeds of vertu, and publick civility, to allay the perturbations of the mind, and set the affections in right tune, to celebrate in glorious and lofty Hymns the throne and equipage of Gods Almightinesse, and what he works, and what he suffers to be wrought with high providence in his Church, to sing the victorious agonies of Martyrs and Saints, the deeds and triumphs of just and pious Nations doing valiantly through faith against the enemies of Christ, to deplore the general relapses of Kingdoms and States from justice and Gods true worship. Lastly, whatsoever in religion is holy and sublime, in vertu amiable, or grave, whatsoever hath passion or admiration in all the changes of that which is call'd fortune from without, or the wily suttleties and refluxes of man's thoughts from within, all these things with a solid and treatable smoothnesse to paint out and describe. Teaching over the whole book of sanctity and vertu through all the instances of example with such delight to those especially of soft and delicious temper who will not so much as look upon Truth herselfe, unlesse they see her elegantly drest, that whereas the paths of honesty and good life appear now rugged and difficult, though they be indeed easy and pleasant, they would then appeare to all men both easy and pleasant though they were rugged and difficult indeed. And what a benefit this would be to our youth and gentry, may be soon guest by what we know of the corruption and bane which they suck in dayly from the writings and interludes of libidinous and ignorant Poetasters, who having scars ever heard of that which is the main consistence of a true poem, the choys of such persons as they ought to introduce, and what is morall and decent to each one, doe for the most part lap up vitious principles in sweet pils to be swallow'd down, and make the tast of vertuous documents harsh and sowr. But because the spirit of man cannot demean it selfe lively in this body without some recreating intermission of labour, and serious things, it were happy for the Common wealth, if our Magistrates, as in those famous governments of old, would take into their care, not only the deciding of our contentious Law cases and brauls, but the managing of our publick sports, and festival pastimes, that they might be, not such as were autoriz'd a while since, the provocations of drunkennesse and lust, but such as may inure and harden our bodies by martial exercises to all warlike skil and performance, and may civilize, adorn and make discreet our minds by the learned and affable meeting of frequent Academies, and the procurement of wise and artfull recitations sweetned with eloquent and gracefull inticements to the love and practice of justice, temperance and fortitude, instructing and bettering the Nation at all opportunities, that the call of wisdom and vertu may be heard every where, as Salomon saith, She crieth without, she uttereth her voice in the streets, in the top of high places, in the chief concours, and in the openings of the Gates. Whether this may not be not only in Pulpits, but after another persuasive method, at set and solemn Paneguries, in Theaters, porches, or what other place, or way may win most upon the people to receiv at once both recreation, & instruction, let them in autority consult. The thing which I had to say, and those intentions which have liv'd within me ever since I could conceiv my self any thing worth to my Countrie, I return to crave excuse that urgent reason hath pluckt from me by an abortive and foredated discovery. And the accomplishment of them lies not but in a power above mans to promise; but that none hath by more studious ways endeavour'd, and with more unwearied spirit that none shall, that I dare almost averre of my self, as farre as life and free leasure will extend, and that the Land had once infranchis'd her self from this impertinent yoke of prelaty, under whose inquisitorious and tyrannical duncery no free and splendid wit can flourish. Neither doe I think it shame to covnant with any knowing reader, that for some few yeers yet I may go on trust with him toward the payment of what I am now indebted, as being a work not to be rays'd from the heat of youth, or the vapours of wine, like that which flows at wast from the pen of some vulgar Amorist, or the trencher fury of a riming parasite, nor to be obtain'd by the invocation of Dame Memory and her Siren daughters, but by devout prayer to that eternall Spirit who can enrich with all utterance and knowledge, and sends out his Seraphim with the hallow'd fire of his Altar to touch and purify the lips of whom he pleases: to this must be added industrious and select reading, steddy observation, insight into all seemly and generous arts and affaires, till which in some measure be compast, at mine own peril and cost I refuse not to sustain this expectation from as many as are not loath to hazard so much credulity upon the best pledges that I can give them.[5]

The function which Milton here proposes to himself is essentially a public one, analogous on the one hand to that of the prophets of Israel and on the other to that of the orators and statesmen of Greece and Rome. In the imagination of such a task his ambitions take the form of a loftier enthusiasm than the desire to rival Ovid or Spenser, and though he is still questioning "what K. or Knight before the conquest might be chosen in whom to lay the pattern of a Christian Heroe," it is clear that such a theme will fail to satisfy his more comprehensive purposes. His passion for individual perfection henceforth clothes itself in zeal for public righteousness, and though he still cherishes for himself and for those who can receive it the esoteric doctrine of chastity and true love, his vision is more often directed toward outward objects and events. Both the personal and the public emotions and ideals are embodied in his later writings. Indeed, the two have become largely one.

But though Milton's purposes are already marked and established and the fundamental processes of his development from youth

[5] Ed. with preface and notes by Ralph A. Haug, *ibid.*, pp. 812–21. For a discussion of this passage and for a complete collection of references in Milton's work illustrative of his conception of the poet's function see Ida Langdon, *Milton's Theory of Poetry.*

to maturity seem to be consummated, it required his later experience of life to complete the formation of his poetic mind. His participation in the struggles of the Commonwealth provided him with new materials of art. The disappointment of his hopes and the bitterness of personal affliction deepened in his religious emotions and led him to seek again in the world of imagination the satisfactions which were denied to him in life. His blindness, especially, had an important effect on his inner life and was interpreted by him as an added evidence of the all but sacred character of his inspiration. In this connection we now quote a further prose passage, from the *Second Defence of the English People* (1654). This, set beside the great personal passages in *Paradise Lost*, may stand as the final chapter in Milton's spiritual autobiography. It is in answer to the charge that his affliction was a judgment on him for his sins:

> *Would that it were equally possible to refute this brutish adversary on the subject of my blindness, but it is not possible. Let me bear it then. Not blindness but the inability to endure blindness is a source of misery. Why should I not bear that which every man ought to prepare himself to bear with equanimity, if it befall him—that which I know may humanly befall any mortal and has indeed befallen certain men who are the most eminent and virtuous in all history? Or shall I recall those ancient bards and wise men of the most distant past, whose misfortune the gods, it is said, recompensed with far more potent gifts, and whom men treated with such respect that they preferred to blame the very gods than to impute their blindness to them as a crime? The tradition about the seer Tiresias is well known. Concerning Phineus, Apollonius sang as follows in the Argonautica:*
>
>> Nor did he fear Jupiter himself,
>> Revealing truly to men the divine purpose.
>> Wherefore he gave him a prolonged old age,
>> But deprived him of the sweet light of his eyes.
>
> *But God himself is truth! The more veracious a man is in teaching truth to men, the more like must he be to God and the more acceptable to him. It is impious to believe that God is grudging of truth or does not wish it to be shared with men*

as freely as possible. Because of no offence, therefore, does it seem that this man who was godlike and eager to enlighten the human race was deprived of his eyesight, as were a great number of philosophers. Or should I mention those men of old who were renowned for statecraft and military achievements? First, Timoleon of Corinth, who freed his own city and all Sicily, than whom no age has borne a man greater or more venerated in his state. Next, Appius Claudius, whose vote, nobly expressed in the Senate, delivered Italy from Pyrrhus, her mortal enemy, but not himself from blindness. Thirdly, Caecilius Metellus, the Pontifex, who, while he saved from fire not the city alone but also the Palladium, the symbol of its destiny, and its innermost mysteries, lost his own eyes, although on other occasions certainly God has given proof that he favors such remarkable piety, even among the heathen. Therefore what has befallen such a man should scarcely, I think, be regarded as an evil.

Why should I add to the list other men of later times, such as the famous Doge of Venice, Dandolo, by far the most eminent of all, or Zizka, the brave leader of the Bohemians and the bulwark of the orthodox faith? Why should I add theologians of the highest repute, Hieronymus Zanchius and some others, when it is established that even Isaac the patriarch himself—and no mortal was ever dearer to God—lived in blindness for many years, as did also (for a few years perhaps) Jacob, his son, who was no less beloved by God. When, finally, it is perfectly certain from the divine testimony of Christ our Savior that the man who was healed by Him had been blind from the very womb, through no sin of his own or of his parents.

For my part, I call upon Thee, my God, who knowest my inmost mind and all my thoughts, to witness that (although I have repeatedly examined myself on this point as earnestly as I could, and have searched all the corners of my life) I am conscious of nothing, or of no deed, either recent or remote, whose wickedness could justly occasion or invite upon me this supreme misfortune. As for what I have at any time written (since the royalists think that I am now undergoing this suffering as a penance, and they accordingly rejoice), I likewise call God to witness that I have written nothing of such kind that I was not then and am not now convinced that it was right and true and pleasing to God. And I swear that my conduct was not influenced by ambition, gain, or glory, but solely by considerations of duty, honor, and devotion to my country. I did my utmost not only to free my country, but also to free the church. Hence, when the business of replying to the royal defense had been officially assigned to me, and at that same time I was afflicted at once by ill health and the virtual loss of my remaining eye, and the doctors were making learned predictions that if I should undertake this task, I would shortly lose both eyes, I was not in the least deterred by the warning. I seemed to hear, not the voice of the doctor (even that of Aesculapius, issuing from the shrine at Epidaurus), but the sound of a certain more divine monitor within. And I thought that two lots had now been set before me by a certain command of fate: the one, blindness, the other, duty. Either I must necessarily endure the loss of my eyes, or I must abandon my most solemn duty. And there came into my mind those two fates which, the son of Thetis relates, his mother brought back from Delphi, where she inquired concerning him:

> Two destinies lead me to the end, which is death:
> If staying here I fight around the city of Troy,
> Return is denied me, but immortal will be my fame.
> If homeward I return to my dear native land,
> Lost is fair fame, but long will be my life.

Then I reflected that many men have bought with greater evil smaller good; with death, glory. To me, on the contrary, was offered a greater good at the price of a smaller evil: that I could at the cost of blindness alone fulfill the most honorable requirement of my duty. As duty is of itself more substantial than glory, so it ought to be for every man more desirable and illustrious. I resolved therefore that I must employ this brief use of my eyes while yet I could for the greatest possible benefit to the state. You see what I chose, what I rejected, and why.

Then let those who slander the judgments of God cease to speak evil and invent empty tales about me. Let them be sure that I feel neither regret nor shame for my lot, that I stand unmoved and steady in my resolution, that I neither discern nor endure the anger of God, that in fact I know and recognize in the most momentous affairs his fatherly mercy and kindness towards me, and especially in this fact, that with his consolation strengthening my spirit I bow to his divine will, dwelling more often on what he has bestowed on me than on what he has denied. Finally, let them rest assured that I would not exchange the consciousness of my achievement for any deed of theirs, be it ever so righteous, nor would I be deprived of the recollection of my deeds, ever a source of gratitude and repose.

Finally, as to my blindness, I would rather have mine, if it be necessary, than either theirs, More, or yours. Your blindness, deeply implanted in the inmost faculties, obscures the mind, so that you may see nothing whole or real. Mine, which you make a reproach, merely deprives things of color and superficial appearance. What is true and essential in them is not lost to my intellectual vision. How many things there are, moreover, which I have no desire to see, how many things that I should be glad not to see, how few remain that I should like to see. Nor do I feel pain at being classed with the blind, the afflicted, the suffering, and the weak (although you hold this to be wretched), since there is hope that in this way I may approach more closely the mercy and protection of the Father Almighty. There is a certain road which leads through weakness, as the apostle teaches, to the greatest strength. May I be entirely helpless, provided that in my weakness there may arise all the more powerfully this immortal and more perfect strength; provided that in my shadows the light of the divine countenance may shine forth all the more clearly. For then I shall be at once the weakest and the strongest, at the same time blind and most keen in vision. By this infirmity may I be perfected, by this completed. So in this darkness, may I be clothed in light.

To be sure, we blind men are not the least of God's concerns, for the less able we are to perceive anything other than himself, the more mercifully and graciously does he deign to look upon us: Woe to him who mocks us, woe to him who injures us. He deserves to be cursed with a public malediction. Divine law and divine favor have rendered us not only safe from the injuries of men, but almost sacred, nor do these shadows around us seem to have been created so much by the dullness of our eyes as by the shade of angels' wings. And divine favor not infrequently is wont to lighten these shadows again, once made, by an inner and far more enduring light.[6]

Henceforth Milton was to devote himself to the Heavenly Muse. What are often read as the great personal passages in *Paradise Lost*—the invocation to light in Book III, the prayer to Urania in Book VII, the self-communion regarding his theme and his religious hope of achieving the task to which he has set himself in spite of "cold climate, or years" in Book IX—may be the poetic sublimation of the materials of this prose utterance revealing the abiding inner sources of Milton's inspiration. He has succeeded, after the storm and stress of battle, in reaching on a higher and more serene level the emotional serenity which he had possessed in youth. The images with which his intimate self-revelations may be associated in *Paradise Lost* are identical in character with those which play so large a part in the early poetry.

[6] Ed. with preface and notes by Donald A. Roberts, trans. Helen North, Yale, *Milton*, IV, i, 584–90.

Appendix C

THE MILTON PORTRAITS

Milton's daughter, Deborah Clarke, informed George Vertue in 1721 that the poet's widow had two portraits of her husband, one when a schoolboy, the other at the age of about twenty. The first of these, a well-executed oil painting allegedly by Cornelius Janssen, was purchased by the republican and Milton-lover, Thomas Hollis, from Mrs. Milton's estate and is now in the John Pierpont Morgan Library in New York.* This portrait has been beautifully reproduced in color as the frontispiece of the Columbia Milton. It is a some-what prim but yet engaging half-length representation of the boy Milton, clad in aristocratic Elizabethan doublet, with a countenance expressive of the sweet sobriety of childhood. The face is fair, the hair an unmistakable auburn. The picture is dated 1618 and in-scribed "John Milton. Aetat. 10."

The second picture, referred to by Aubrey (see Chapter 1) as a better likeness than that appearing as frontispieces in his books and said by Mrs. Milton to have been given her by her husband "to show what he was in his youth," was long thought destroyed in the eighteenth century by its owner, Speaker Onslow, because he was annoyed by the requests of visitors to see it. At least one copy had, however, been made and is now at Nuneham.* There are,

* The asterisks on these two pages indicate plates to be found in a group following page 114.

however, other copies, and the original may now hang in the National Portrait Gallery. The original was also used by Vertue for an engraving published in 1731 and frequently reproduced.

A third authentic contemporary likeness of Milton is represented by the engraving prefixed to the first edition of Milton's *History of Britain* (1670).* A Latin inscription declares the engraving to have been done from life by William Faithorne. It gives the deeply lined face of the mature Milton familiar from numerous engravings and busts based upon it. The very similar Bayfordbury drawing (also by William Faithorne and now in the Princeton University Library)* and the Hobart painting are connected with this engraving, and, until recently, it was thought that all three might perhaps be copies from one original. But in tracing the history of the Bayfordbury drawing, John Rupert Martin conjectures "that the picture in Princeton is the original drawing from the life, and that this first conception of Milton was later revised and given a more formal character for the engraving."[1]

Save for the distorted engraving by Marshall prefixed to the 1645 edition of the poems, which Milton himself ridiculed in Greek lines below it,* these four—the Janssen, the Onslow copy, the Faithorne, and the Bayfordbury or Princeton portrait—represent all the unquestionable contemporary likenesses. Catalogues have been published of two considerable collections of Milton prints, portraits, etc., one by George C. Williamson, the other, somewhat more extensive, by Beverly Chew.[2] All the known facts may be found in French's *Life Records.*

---

[1] *The Portrait of John Milton at Princeton,* p. 27.

[2] *Milton Tercentenary: The Portraits, Prints and Writings of John Milton* (Cambridge, Eng., 1908); "Portraits of Milton," *Bibliographer,* II (1903), 92–101.

MILTON'S PRIVATE LIBRARY

MANY REFERENCES IN MILTON'S WORK SHOW HIM TO HAVE BEEN A persistent and enthusiastic book collector, and the building of his private library must be regarded as no insignificant part of his biography. He made expeditions from Hammersmith and Horton to London to buy books. He promises in 1634 to meet his friend Gill "among the booksellers." He asks Diodati in 1637 to send him a copy of Justinian's *History of Venice*. Phillips says that he shipped a parcel of curious and rare books home from Italy, particularly "a chest or two of choice music books." And late in the fifties, long after he could read books with his own eyes, we find him negotiating purchases with his Continental friends.[1] He hesitated to buy the best Bleau Atlas at thirty florins, protesting that "with the present rage for typographical luxury, the furniture of a library costs hardly less than that of a villa." But he did undertake to purchase the stately and expensive volumes of the *Corpus Byzantinae Historiae* as they were issued from the Royal Press at Paris.[2]

Just how extensive Milton's private collection became before it was dissipated is impossible to determine. He had access to the libraries at Cambridge and Oxford, but it seems probable that the

---

[1] See the letters in P. B. Tillyard, *Private Correspondence*.
[2] Epistle XXI to Emeric Bigot, March 24, 1657, *ibid.*, pp. 39–40.

greater part of his wide reading was done at home, and it is safe to say that he owned copies of the authors from whom he cites more or less continuously: the classics, English literature, the church fathers, the standard historians as listed in the Commonplace Book, the Protestant divines, the great Italians. He owned the manuscript of Sir Walter Ralegh's *Cabinet Council,* as we learn from his preface to his edition of that work, and it has recently been shown that he possessed a copy of the *Heptaplomeres* of Jean Bodin, a notoriously heretical work clandestinely circulated in manuscript and very difficult to obtain. If the presence of these rarities is at all characteristic, Milton's library must have been very interesting indeed.

The following books, once owned by Milton, bear his unquestionably genuine autograph:[3]

1. Holy Bible, authorized version, 1612, containing entries of the births and deaths of Milton's family. Now in the British Museum.
2. Euripidis Tragoediae, Gr. et Lat. Beckii, 1602, with autograph and notes. Now in the Bodleian.
3. Lycophronis Alexandra, Geneva, 1601, with autograph and notes. In the library of Mr. and Mrs. Adrian Van Sinderen of Brooklyn, New York.
4. Pindari Olympia, etc., Saumus, 1620, with notes. Now in the library of Harvard University.
5. Arati Phaenomena, etc., Paris, 1559, with autograph and notes. Now in the British Museum.
6. Heraclidis Pontici . . . Allegoriae in Homeri Fabulas de Dijs, Gr. et Lat., Basil, 1544, with autograph. Now in the Library of the University of Illinois.
7. Rime et Prose di Giovanni della Casa, Venice, 1563, with autograph and notes. Now in the New York Public Library.
8. Gildas, De Excidio et Conquestu Britanniae Epistola, 1587,

---

[3] See Patterson, *Works,* XVIII, 557 ff. All the books that have been attributed to Milton's library are discussed there, and the greater part of their marginalia is reproduced. The list errs on the side of inclusiveness. The present writers have omitted all items of whose authenticity they are not personally convinced. It is not intended to deny the claims of others. On the various questions concerning Milton's autographs, see J. Milton French, *Life Records.*

with autograph and notes. Now in the library of Harvard University.

9. Dion Chrysostom's Orations, Paris, 1604.

10. Pvb. Terentii Comoediae . . . , 1635.

The purchase dates of most of these volumes, as written on the flyleaf in Milton's hand, range from 1629 to 1637. Some of them, particularly the Pindar and the Euripides, are heavily annotated by Milton in the most learned fashion and at several periods in his life. A sonnet from another edition has been copied by one of the known amanuenses on a blank page of the della Casa volume. There is an emendation in the text of Lycophron which Milton offers not as a restoration but as an improvement on the original. The line reads "Τρίτωνος ἠμάλαψε κάρχαρος κύων." Milton's comment is "utinam esset κάρχαρόδους hos enim grandior." These are the faint traces of John Milton's keen and passionate interest in his authors during the days at Hammersmith and at Horton and in the quiet intervals of his later life.

There is evidence to show that Milton's library was partly dissipated before his death. The student may choose between the allegation of Elizabeth Fisher (see Chapter 1) that his children made away with some of his books and the statement of Toland that Milton himself contracted his library "because both the heirs he left could not make a right use of it, and that he thought he might sell it more to their advantage than they would be able to do themselves." In any case, however, we have the statement of the anonymous biographer that Milton left "a fair collection." The chances are that this was promptly scattered at his decease. Mrs. Milton retained, at least, the Bible and "two books of paradise," which, together with "some old pictures," "Mr. Milton's pictures and coat of arms," "a tobacco box," etc., are listed in the inventory of her possessions. An unsigned letter in the library of the Marquis of Bath states that Mr. Milton's books "have been looked over by one Mr. Skinner, a scholar and a bold young man, who has culled out what he thought fit." This is Daniel Skinner, Milton's last amanuensis, who had possession of Milton's theological treatise and of his copies of the state letters in manuscript. Edward Phillips, who inherited the notes for the Latin dictionary, may also have had his share of books.

Appendix E

MILTON AND HIS PRINTERS

The text of Milton involves no such difficulties as that of Shakespeare, but it offers problems enough for the amusement and edification of students and the puzzlement of editors. The poet was nothing if not fastidious, and there is plenty of evidence of a struggle on his part to get his work before the public as he wanted it to be, down to the most minute detail—a struggle which was continuously defeated by human perversity and carelessness and by the accident of Milton's being blind. The difficulty of the modern editor of Milton is twofold. He is not sure whether, in a given instance of variation between one edition and another published in the poet's lifetime, he has to do with a Miltonic revision or a printer's error. And he does not know how far Milton himself determined and set store by the minutiae of spelling and punctuation. Perhaps, too, he is uncertain whether these minutiae are worth intruding upon the attention of the modern reader. For these reasons he does not know which edition to follow or how far to normalize the text. Solutions range all the way from facsimile reproductions of this or that edition to complete eclectic modernizations. The question of decision regarding readings is further complicated by the existence of some of Milton's manuscripts, and a study of the situation raises some interesting questions of interpretation and takes us behind the scenes in Milton's literary workshop. Only a few outstanding points can be mentioned here. The interested student may be referred to the introductions to various modern editions, e.g., those of Helen Darbishire, B. A. Wright, and Harris Fletcher, and particularly that of the Columbia Edition.

Milton's first printed English work was the poem *On Shakespeare*, which appeared in the second folio of 1632 (and again in the third folio of 1664) of Shakespeare's plays and (with the initials I. M.) in a 1640 edition of Shakespeare's poems; it was reprinted in the 1645 and 1673 editions of Milton's poems. The variations in the poem in these texts raise the question of whether Milton corrected his proofs and of how far he revised his already printed work. The 1645 and 1673 texts are, except for a few spellings, identical. The 1640 and 1645 texts have more considerable but still minor variations. The title is altered from *An Epitaph on the Admirable Dramaticke Poet W. Shakespear* to *On Shakespear 1630*. This, of course, was determined by Milton himself. So, too, probably, was "needs" for "neede" in line 1 and "need'st" for "needs" in line 6, this last change being a return to the reading of the second folio. Between the second folio and the 1645 edition there are several important variations. "Such dull witness of thy name" becomes "such weak witness of thy name," certainly a Miltonic revision to secure alliteration. In another instance in 1632 the poem read as follows:

Each *part*
Hath from the leaves of thy unvalu'd Book
Those Delphick lines with deep impression took.

In the editions of 1640, 1645, and 1673 the poem reads "each *heart*," etc., and this surely is simply a correction. "Part" must have been a misreading by the compositor due to a resemblance between "h" and "p" in script. We may infer that Milton did not see proof of the poem as it was printed in the second folio, and that he here experienced his first motion of disgust with printers and their ways.[1]

---

[1] The problems raised by the varying texts of the poem are neatly dealt with by H. W. Garrod, "Milton's Lines on Shakespeare," *Essays and Studies by Members of the English Association*, XII (1926), 1–23, where, however, "part" is accepted as representing Milton's original intention. One of the copies of the second folio has "star-ypointed" for "star-ypointing," a more correct form, historically speaking. But Milton probably wrote "star-ypointing." See Robert W. Smith, *The Variant Issues of Shakespeare's Second Folio and Milton's First Published Poem* (Bethlehem, 1928).

The other minor poems offer equally interesting problems.[2] We can here consider only the certain evidence that in the 1673 text a blundering hand attempted to improve Milton's meaning. The poet had furnished the publisher with a printed copy of the 1645 text, in the margins of which he must have written a few corrections and revisions (e.g., "concent," the reading of the manuscript, for "content" in the poem *At a Solemn Music*) and to which he had added many manuscript pages of new material. What must he have thought and said if the following unauthorized alterations ever came to his attention:

> She was pincht and pull'd she sed,
> And he by Friars Lanthorn led
> Tells how the drudging goblin swet.
> > (*L'Allegro*, ed. 1645)
> And by the Friar's Lanthorn led.
> > (*L'Allegro*, ed. 1673)
> To meditate my rural minstrelsie.
> > (*Comus*, ed. 1645)
> To meditate upon my rural minstrelsie.
> > (*Comus*, ed. 1673)
> And hearken, if I may, her business here.
> > (*Comus*, ed. 1645)
> And hearken if I may her business heare.
> > (*Errata*, ed. 1673)

The corrector simply did not understand Miltonic idiom, Latin or English. In the first example, "She" and "he" are "illa" and "ille," meaning "one in the company, a woman," "another in the company, a man." "She was pincht and pull'd, she sed . . . and . . . tells" is grammatically impossible. In the next instance the corrector would have been saved had he remembered *Musam meditare avena* in Virgil. To "meditate the muse" is one thing; to meditate upon it quite another, even if no question of rhythm is involved. The third reading is more open to doubt, but again the corrector apparently could not accept the archaic turn in the transitive use of "hearken." Milton had written the passage in the manuscript precisely as it was printed in 1645. The fact that this change is made in the *Errata* is puzzling enough. Perhaps Milton commissioned Edward Phillips or

---

[2] See Chapter 3 for the discussion of a point of text in *Lycidas*.

Daniel Skinner or some less educated amanuensis to see the edition through the press. The modern editor who wishes to give us Milton's true copy should base his text on the 1645 edition, except for the added material and for occasional readings from the 1673 edition which obviously represent revision.

In the case of *Paradise Lost* the textual problem is a very simple one, unless one wishes to confront the problem of restoring Milton's own spelling and punctuation, in which case it becomes nearly insoluble. The edition of 1667 was very carefully printed. Corrections were made by Milton himself in an errata sheet, and an argument was added in later issues of this edition. The edition of 1674 was set from a printed copy of the 1667, and contains few variations of importance except those made by Milton himself in the process of revision. He divided Books VIII and X into two each, adding a few transitional lines; he distributed the arguments, prefixing them to the various books instead of massing them at the end; and he made some other textual alterations.

The best check we have on Milton's original intentions regarding spelling, punctuation, etc., and on the extent to which they were followed by the printers is the preserved manuscript of Book I, from which the 1667 text was set. (See endpapers.) This is in the hand of an amanuensis. That the poet did care for spelling in certain particulars is proven first by the corrections in the manuscript—as for example "there" to "thir," "voyce" to "voice," "entralls" to "entrails," "Heavn" to "Heav'n," "the" to "th'," "hee" to "he"; secondly by the following items in the *Errata* of the 1667 edition: Book I, 1. 760, for "hundreds" read "hunderds"; II, 414, for "we" read "wee"; VI, 184, for "blessed" read "blest." He evidently was attempting to secure a correct and musical reading of his verse. It was his apparent intention to spell such words as "blessed" with the "ed" when it was to be read as a dissyllable, with "t" when it was to be read as a monosyllable, and to print "th'" for "the" when the syllable count required elision. John Shawcross' more recent investigations into Milton's spelling have revealed, however, that "the assumption that Milton developed a stressed-unstressed principle of spelling of 'be,' the personal pronouns, 'their,' and 'only' is found to be insubstantial. The evidence in manuscript, in prose, and (when all possibilities are examined) in poetry does not bear out this belief, which began with

Richardson."[3] The problem of working out Milton's intentions from the available data has been carefully studied by Helen Darbishire and, more recently, again by Shawcross.[4] Darbishire's conclusion is that the printed page of the first edition is nearer than the manuscript to what Milton would have written. Percy Simpson concurs in this opinion.[5] On Darbishire's evidence, however, it is apparent that Milton did not correct the proofs nearly as carefully as he corrected his fair copy, and that the Miltonic improvements in the 1667 edition are more than counterbalanced by the instances in which the printer deviated from the text in a direction contrary to what we may infer Milton wished. Shawcross' studies have led him to conclude, however, that Darbishire and Wright proceed from certain assumptions which, right or wrong, lead them to see *Paradise Lost* as a primary source of evidence. "It is plain that *Paradise Lost* may offer at best only corroborative evidence of Milton's spelling practices."[6]

Modern editors of Milton either follow the second edition (1674) minutely (as Hughes does), modernize the text throughout, or preserve spellings which they think are characteristic and significant. If they adopt the last-mentioned practice they are largely at the mercy of their own whim. A study of the parts of the Cambridge Manuscript which are in Milton's own hand would give his characteristic spellings for an earlier period of his career, but even these are not consistent. It remains for some editor to make a text based on the manuscript and the 1667 edition but incorporating the clearly Miltonic revisions in the 1674 text and carrying out as consistently as possible all the practices which have been determined as representing Milton's fixed intentions.

Of the individuals with whom Milton had to deal in the publication of his poems the most interesting was Humphrey Moseley, publisher of the edition of 1645. Moseley was a man of genuine taste,

---

[3] "One Aspect of Milton's Spelling: Idle Final 'E'," *PMLA*, LXXVIII (1963), 509; see also Shawcross' unpubl. diss., "Milton's Spelling: Its Biographical and Critical Implications" (New York University, 1958), and his "What Can We Learn from Milton's Spelling?" *HLQ*, XXVI (1963), 351–61.

[4] *The Manuscript of Paradise Lost, Book I* (Oxford, 1931); see also Shawcross' studies mentioned above.

[5] *Proof-Reading in the Sixteenth, Seventeenth, and Eighteenth Centuries* (London, 1931), p. 35.

[6] "One Aspect of Milton's Spelling," p. 510.

who obviously took pride in the character of the books issued under his imprint and who rightly regarded himself as a promoter of excellence in English poetry. "It is the love I have to our language," he wrote in a signed preface to the Milton volume, "that hath made me diligent to collect and set forth such pieces, both in prose and verse, as may renew the wonted honour and esteem of our English tongue." Masson notes his avoidance of controversial literature and lists among the poets whose copy he acquired either by original publication or by subsequent purchase such distinguished names as Donne, Suckling, Crashaw, Carew, Waller, Denham, Davenant, Cowley, and Henry Vaughan. Moseley died in 1661, and the second edition of the poems was printed for Thomas Dring. The first, second, and third editions of *Paradise Lost* were issued by Samuel Simmons; the first of *Paradise Regained* and *Samson Agonistes* by John Starkey. Neither of these men occupies a position comparable to that of Moseley; however, Jacob Tonson, who ultimately acquired the right to publish *Paradise Lost* and made a fortune from it, was a worthy eighteenth-century successor of Milton's first commercial publisher.

The prose works offer fewer textual problems than the poetry, but their printing history is interesting.[7] The first three tracts, *Of Reformation, Of Prelatical Episcopacy*, and *Animadversions*, were published anonymously by Thomas Underhill. The unnamed printers, as Parker has shown,[8] were Richard Oulton and George Dexter. *The Reason of Church-Government* and *An Apology*, which bore Milton's name, were entrusted to another bookseller, John Rothwell, and another printer, Edward Griffin. All five tracts were unlicensed and unregistered, a fact easily explained by the lax administration of the law from the beginning of the Long Parliament until the passing of the Ordinance for Printing, June 14, 1643. When Milton was ready to issue the *Doctrine and Discipline* there was greater difficulty. The book obviously could not be licensed, and Milton was presumably obliged to seek bolder publishers and printers. The imprint bears the initials of Thomas Paine and Matthew Simmons. The latter printed also *The Judgment of Martin Bucer*, a duly licensed

---

[7] See the notes and introductory essays already published in the volumes of Yale, *Milton*.

[8] "Contributions Toward a Milton Bibliography," *The Library*, Fourth Series, XVI (1936), 425–38.

publication, in 1644 and *Eikonoklastes* in 1649. He may have printed *Tetrachordon* and *Colasterion*. By 1650 Milton had deserted him, perhaps because of his carelessness in printing *Eikonoklastes*.[9] Samuel Simmons, to whom seventeen years later Milton gave the copy of *Paradise Lost*, was his successor and perhaps his son.[10]

Of Milton's later prose publications *The History of Britain*, which appeared in 1670, is notable as containing the Faithorne engraving. The text of this edition has been shown to exist in several states, representing successive strata of corrections made while the work was going through the press.[11] Some copies, usually without the portrait, bear the date 1671. It was "printed by J. M." (either John Milton or an unknown printer who happened to have his initials) "for James Allestry." The names of numerous other printers and booksellers occur on the title pages of Milton's various works. His experience with the publishing world as poet, pamphleteer, and official must have been sufficiently varied. We have in a passage in *Areopagitica* the description of "best and diligentest writers" trudging to the printer to make changes in their copy while it is yet in press, "perhaps a dozen times in one book." It is safe to picture Milton himself as often present in the printing houses and thoroughly acquainted with the technique of bookmaking as it was practiced in his day.[12] What editorial assistance he may have had before and especially after his blindness we may never know.

[9] See William R. Parker, "Milton, Rothwell, and Simmons," *The Library*, XVIII (1938), 89–103.

[10] David Masson, *Life*, VI, 509.

[11] See especially Harris Fletcher's, "The First Edition of Milton's *History of Britain*," and Nicholas, "Introduction," *Introduction to Milton's 'History of Britain*,' pp. 5–16.

[12] Authors and correctors apparently read proof in the printing house as the book was going through the press. Sometimes they did so only after some of the sheets had been printed. This partly accounts for the variations in different copies of the same issue of a book (see Simpson, *Proof-Reading*). The variants in the last page of the 1667 *Paradise Lost* are perhaps due to a disturbance of the type.

Appendix F

MILTON IN ITALY

Few episodes in Milton's life are as appealing to the biographer as the tour which he made to the Continent in 1638 and 1639. Its obvious importance prompted Masson to a full treatment of the facts and background, and some additions have been made to our knowledge since his time. There remains, however, much to do before the experience can be appraised for its total effect on the poet's personality and achievement. Even Allodoli's monograph[1] accomplishes less than we might have hoped in view of the author's opportunities for research in Italian libraries. The present essay undertakes only to present some considerations which might well be the object of further study. The cooperative efforts of English and Italian scholarship are required for a really fruitful investigation of this great moment in the cultural relationship between the two nations.

There is little direct evidence why Milton decided at just the time he did to "visit foreign parts and particularly Italy." The tradition of the Continental tour as the capstone of English education was and continued to be strong. But the new travel was different from the old: what Italy now had to offer, while in actuality not so rich, was at least more varied and more accessible to Englishmen than in the earlier Renaissance. Some measure of assimilation and

---

[1] Ettore Allodoli, *Giovanni Milton e l'Italia* (Prato, 1907).

knowledge is necessary before any but the pioneers of culture can make fruitful use of a foreign civilization, and such conditions were not fulfilled in England before the 1600's. The prestige of Italy, long in the making, was still strong enough to prevent the idea of its degeneration and decay from deterring Englishmen from going there for serious study. Addison in the eighteenth century could point triumphantly to the destitution of the Campagna as an example of what an aversion mankind has to arbitrary government and thus help deflect travellers toward France. Milton's earlier remark about the decline of wit with liberty was more than counterbalanced by an interest in and enthusiasm for things Italian. Sandys and others speak frequently of the number of foreigners with whom the streets of Italian cities were "pestered." In many respects Italy was for Englishmen in the seventeenth century what France was to become in the eighteenth: a school of sophistication in all the arts.[2]

The list of outstanding Englishmen who profited by Italy is in itself an indication of what was sought. Inigo Jones studied architecture and drama there for several years and purchased works of art for the Earls of Pembroke and Arundel. Thomas Carew, as secretary to Sir Dudley Carleton from 1613 to 1615, became versed in Italian literature; so also did Suckling and Crashaw at a later time. Sir Kenelm Digby spent two years in Florence from 1622 to 1623. Giovanni Coperario, the teacher of Henry Lawes, received his musical instruction in Italy earlier. Robert Boyle's travels in 1638 closely paralleled Milton's. Another earnest traveller was John Evelyn, who bought "rare tables of veins and nerves" at Padua in 1646. This enumeration omits the mere vacationists, the patrons, the teachers, and the professional writers of travel literature like Moryson, Coryate, Howell, and Sandys.

To return to Milton's personal motivations, we should remember, first, that although he had given up (or all but given up) the church as a career, he was determined not only to be a scholar and a poet but to exercise an influence by his writings parallel with that of the pulpit. The political-religious motive for going to Italy was an important one. Milton, as a prospective statesman of Protestant reform, naturally wanted to see Catholicism in its home—to witness, as Luther had done before him, the magnificence and the corruption

---

[2] Clare Howard, *English Travellers of the Renaissance* (London, New York, and Toronto, 1914), pp. 178–201.

of the Roman church. Once on the scene, he behaved like one of God's spies. He visited a Jesuit college, made the acquaintance of a cardinal, received favors from a future Papal nuncio,[3] allowed himself to be guided by a hermit, and contracted his most lasting Italian friendship with one of the Florentine literati who had remained firmly Catholic in spite of the liberalism of the group. He discussed religion everywhere, but not in such a way as to shut the doors of information. Certainly the church and its workings was one of the great things for an Englishman to witness abroad. He might be expected to return confirmed but no longer naive in his loyalty to the Protestant cause.

The issues were sharpened for Milton by his acquaintance with the Diodati family and their refugee tradition. Perhaps he was looking for vestiges of Italian Protestantism in his trip to Lucca, its place of origin. In any case the visit to Giovanni Diodati at Geneva put him in contact with the freshest memories of this exciting chapter in Reformation history.[4] In this connection one should remember that his English mentor, Henry Wotton, had undertaken to formulate, with Paolo Sarpi and Diodati himself, a Protestant movement in Venice.

To point out this aspect of Milton's interest is not to deny the more obvious cultural objectives.[5] Milton went to Italy, of course, to improve his knowledge of the Italian language and literature, in which he had already made great progress, to see the remains of classical antiquity, and to meet the personalities who, he thought, still carried on the tradition of the Renaissance. Important in this group were the Vatican librarian, Lukas Holste, a humanist of the old school; the learned Florentines of the Svogliati Academy; and the venerable patron of Tasso, Giovanni Battista Manso.

The visit to Galileo was the most dramatic and suggestive of all his contacts. Here, as in the earlier meeting with Grotius, Milton

---

[3] Lukas Holste, himself a convert, represented the Papacy at the conversion of Queen Christina.

[4] See above, Chapter 1.

[5] In the Third Prolusion, Milton suggests a formula for foreign travel: "to let your eyes wander as it were over all the lands depicted on the map, and to behold the places trodden by the heroes of old, to range over the regions made famous by wars, by triumphs, and even by the tales of poets of renown, now to traverse the stormy Adriatic, now to climb unharmed the slopes of fiery Etna, then to spy out the customs of mankind and those states which are well-ordered; next to seek out and explore the nature of all living creatures. . . ."

was seeking membership, not in the conservative older humanistic group nor in the newer body of dilettanti and mere hangers-on of scholarship, but in the seventeenth-century Republic of Letters itself. Milton's allusion to his visit in *Areopagitica* is our sole evidence that it actually took place. He is speaking of the discouragement which restraint of publication brings to learned men, contrasting Italy in this respect with England:

> I could recount what I have seen and heard in other Coun-
> tries, where this kind of inquisition tyrannizes; when I have
> sat among their lerned men, for that honor I had, and bin
> counted happy to be born in such a place of Philosophic free-
> dom, as they suppos'd England was, while themselvs did noth-
> ing but bemoan the servil condition into which lerning amongst
> them was brought; that this was it which had dampt the glory
> of Italian wits; that nothing had bin there writt'n now these
> many years but flattery and fustian. There it was that I found
> and visited the famous Galileo grown old, a prisner to the
> Inquisition, for thinking in Astronomy otherwise then the
> Franciscan and Dominican licencers thought.[6]

This recollection and the later allusions to Galileo's telescope suggest the character and accent of Milton's most important kind of activity in Italy. He went to see people more than things and to discuss with them the interests—cultural, political, religious—which were of the deepest concern to him and them. He took the opportunities which offered themselves to any Englishman qualified to hold converse with the noted scholars and thinkers of the age. But he enjoyed also and made use of special privileges.

The whole subject of Milton's personal relationships on the Continent remains to be worked out. It would be especially revealing to know just how he made his various contacts, what introductions he had, what messages he carried. It was the journeyings and correspondence of men like him that held the widely scattered intellectual group together. We know that Milton carried letters to Lord Scudamore, the English ambassador at Paris, and that he was introduced by Scudamore to Grotius and by Lukas Holste to Cardinal Barberini; the rest is still a matter of guesswork.

It is most tempting to speculate how Milton got access to

[6] Ed. with preface and notes by Ernest Sirluck, Yale, *Milton*, II, 537–38.

Galileo. A real problem exists here, though Liljegren's opinion that such a visit never actually took place has been rejected by Milton and Galileo scholars alike.[7] An interview with the blind philosopher was no ordinary treat for Englishmen at this time. He was restricted to his house, with the provision that he might attend church a block away; and visits by foreigners, especially by heretics, were strictly interdicted. There was, however, clandestine communication with the outside world. Who were the friends who facilitated the meeting? Directly, perhaps, Carlo Dati, who had been Galileo's pupil. But there is a possibility that the Parisian intellectuals who were trying to help Galileo in very practical ways may have directed Milton to him, or even used the poet as a courier. Grotius was one of these, but the principal conspirator against the restrictions of the Inquisition was a person unmentioned by Milton biographers, but whom it is plausible to suppose he knew. This was Elie Diodati, a Parliamentary Advocate at Paris, who had translated some of Galileo's writings into Latin and visited him more than once in Italy.[8] In 1638, the year of Milton's visit, he had translated from the Italian and secured publication of the *Dialogus*. On August 14 of that year Galileo wrote telling him that the Holy Office had learned of certain negotiations between Diodati and the States General of Holland for the purchase of Galileo's invention for the determination of longitude, and he thanked Diodati for having induced their agent, Hortensio, to postpone a journey to see him at Florence. Diodati must have made use of any trustworthy persons to carry messages, and Milton certainly would have been trustworthy. Diodati was related to the English family of that name, being a cousin several times removed of Dr. Theodore, Charles's father, in London, and of Theodore's brother, Giovanni, whom Milton was to meet in Geneva. This refugee clan kept in close touch with one another throughout Europe,

[7] See Marjorie Nicolson, "Milton and the Telescope," *ELH*, II (1935), 1–32.

[8] See G. D. J. Schotel, *Jean Diodati* (Gravenhage, 1844), pp. 106 ff., for an account of Elie Diodati. His relations with Galileo are indicated by J. J. Fahie in *Galileo: His Life and Work* (New York, 1903). The detail of this activity may be followed in the National Edition of Galileo's works. The interrelations of the group of intellectuals to which Galileo and Diodati belonged—Campanella, Gassendi, DuPuy, etc.—are best studied in *Les Correspondants de Peiresc* (ed. Philippe Tamizey de Larroque [Aix, 1881], IV, 338 ff.).

and Milton is not likely to have passed by so conspicuous and congenial a member of it as Elie.[9]

One other contact must be mentioned as associated with an interesting phase of Milton's life in Italy. The minutes of the Svogliati for March 24, 1639, record the reading by Giovanni Battista Doni of a scene from one of his tragedies. At this meeting of the academy Milton was also a performer. He mentions Doni to Lukas Holste in a letter written six days later as being then in Rome but soon to return to Florence as Professor of Greek. This Doni[10] was one of the ablest and most creative persons whom Milton could have met in Italy. A Florentine patrician, born in 1594, he studied literature, philosophy, and mathematics at Rome, jurisprudence in France, and Oriental languages and Hebrew at Pisa, where he became laureate in 1621. The election of Maffeo Barberini as Pope Urban VIII brought him to Rome in close friendship with Cardinal Francesco, whom he accompanied to France and Spain. At the time of Milton's visit he was secretary of the Academy Basiliana founded by Francesco for the study of Greek, but, as we have seen, he had also assumed a professorship of Greek at Florence.[11] He compiled a corpus of ancient inscriptions, projected a great work on libraries, and wrote many treatises on linguistic, literary, and historical subjects.

Most important in the present connection are his distinguished contributions to music and the drama, for here is where Milton's interests would have been keenest. Doni was one of the theorists of the operatic development which took place in the seventeenth century. Following the tradition of a famous earlier group of Florentine scholars and composers, including the father of Galileo, he promoted a revival of what he believed to have been Greek practice,

[9] Actual contact of Elie Diodati with the English family cannot be demonstrated. But both he and they visited Geneva, and Giovanni visited England. Elie Diodati knew Lord Herbert of Cherbury and transmitted copies of his *De Veritate Religionis Christianae* to Gassendi, Peiresc, and Campanella. See Pierre Gassendi, *Opera Omnia* (Florentiae, 1727), III, 337 ff., and Joseph Bougerel, *Vie de Pierre Gassendi* (Paris, 1737). See also de Larroque, *Les Correspondants de Peiresc*.

[10] See Angelo Maria Bandini, *Commentariorvm de Vita et Scriptis Ioannis Bapt. Doni* (Florentiae, 1755).

[11] Masson is confused about Doni, apparently not understanding that he could hold the Florentine professorship while still in residence at Rome. As a matter of fact, it was not until he left Rome in 1646 that he gave it up and was succeeded in 1647 by Dati, who had been his pupil.

advocating a return to ancient simplicity against the virtuosity of the madrigal style. The choruses of Greek tragedy provided a model for the monody sung in *recitativo*, with primary importance given to the words. But it was the belief of the time that all of Greek drama and not only the choruses were sung. The efforts to reproduce these supposed music-dramas of antiquity, influencing and influenced by native Italian developments in musical and dramatic entertainment, resulted in the invention of modern opera.[12] Doni himself set the *Troades* of Seneca to music for performance at the Barberini theater; and Milton, as is well known, was present at the brilliant performance of the pastoral opera, *Chi soffre, speri*, in the same place.[13] The reference to Doni in the letter to Holste makes no mention of his musical theories or of his service to the Barberini, but in view of Milton's deep interest it is hard to believe that the poet did not, either then or later, seek an occasion to talk with him and read his works. The poet's own contribution to the issues between the madrigal and the *recitativo* style is in the sonnet which he addressed to Henry Lawes in 1646. It finds precedence in Campion's comments of the art of "wedding notes and music lovingly together,"[14] and in what other poets were saying about Lawes himself. But the Italians had long been philosophizing on this subject. A sixteenth-century example is Caccini's statement that no value should be placed upon music which makes it impossible to understand the words. Musicians

[12] See Gretchen L. Finney, "Chorus in *Samson Agonistes*."

[13] For the facts about this notable performance see J. Milton French, *Life Records*, I, 391–92. The text was by Giulo Rospigliosi (then a member of Cardinal Francesco's household, afterwards Pope Clement IX), the music by Virgilio Mazzocchi and Marco Marazzuoli, the stage design by Bernini. Of this last Bernini's biographer, Baldinucci, remarks: "Ne vivra sempre la fama nel mondo." Milton calls the entertainment an "ἀκρόαμα . . . Musicum," which would be about the nearest classical word he could get for a musical drama of this kind. According to an eyewitness description, it was Antonio and not Francesco who greeted everybody at the door. Francesco went about from bench to bench. One young man who became noisy was thrown out by Antonio. Milton could not have heard Leonora sing on this occasion, for there were no women at the Barberini entertainments. On the Barberini as patrons of melodrama, see Angelo Solerti, *Le Origini del Melodrama* (Turin, 1903).

[14] *Cf. L'Allegro:*

> Lap me in soft *Lydian* Airs
> Married to immortal verse

(ll. 136–37)

and *At a Solemn Music:*

> Sphere-born harmonious Sisters, Voice and Verse.

who disregard meaning "destroy the unity and meter, sometimes lengthening the syllables, sometimes shortening them in order to suit the counterpoint—a real mangling of the poetry."[15]

Milton's concern with Italian music and his acquaintance with the Italian theater is a subject on which Masson gives us little. The suggestion has been made[16] that Milton was already aware of the new developments before he left England and that *Comus* was written under the influence of the *dramma per musica*. Henry Lawes, the pupil of Coperario, is sure to have communicated what he knew of Italian music to his friend and to have sent him abroad well primed to acquire more. The chests of choice music books which Milton sent home from Venice included, according to Phillips, works by Orazio Vecchi, composer of *Amphiparnaso*, a *commedia harmonica*, not in the *stilo rappresentativo*, but an attempt at conceiving dialogue in madrigal form; Luca Marenzio, who is said to have concentrated on musical expression of the words and to have defended this principle; Gesualdo, a real innovator in harmony, who set poems by Tasso to music; and finally, Monteverdi. Milton's interest in Monteverdi opens up interesting possibilities. He says he spent a whole month in Venice where Monteverdi was director of St. Mark's choir. Two public theaters, the first in Italy, had been established there for the performance of melodramas, and operas of Monteverdi were being given in the year of Milton's visit. The poet was a good enough musician to know the quality of what was set before him, if indeed he had the opportunity to witness such a work as the *Arianna*, and to report his experiences with enthusiasm to his father and to Lawes.

This brings us to the old question of the dramatic plans in the Cambridge Manuscript and their relation to Italian sources. Warburton, writing to Birch,[17] argued against the influence of Andreini, saying that Milton was first inclined to make an opera of the material when Sir John Denham and others contrived to get operas performed after the closing of the theaters. It seems more likely that the

---

[15] Quoted in Enid Welsford, *The Court Masque: A Study in the Relationship between Poetry and the Revels* (Cambridge, Eng., 1927), p. 104.

[16] Gretchen L. Finney, "*Comus, Dramma per Musica*." Mrs. Finney has made a strong case for the specific influence on Milton of *La Catena d'Adone*, a melodrama based on Marino's *Adone*, written by Tronsarelli and Mazzocchi and produced and published (in score) at Rome in 1626.

[17] Henry J. Todd, *Poetical Works*, II, 214.

poet, enamored of what he had seen in Italy and full of enthusiasm for transplanting it to England, wrote out this and the other plans very soon after his return. The program of entertainment to be promoted by the government in *The Reason of Church-Government* (1642), written, certainly, before the closing of the theaters, includes, besides martial exercises, the "learned and affable meeting of frequent Academies" and "set and solemn Paneguries, in Theaters, porches," and other public places. Drama is not specifically mentioned, but "paneguries" is perhaps general enough to include some kinds. Of all the plans the early scenarios of *Paradise Lost* seem most operatic. The subject was common enough in Italy, and there is at least one instance of a full musical treatment.[18] The *Adamo* of Andreini, which still stands as the most plausible Italian influence on Milton's original conception, belonged to the older tradition of the *Sacra Rappresentazione* but was influenced also by contemporary melodrama in the choruses and ballets.[19] We find no evidence that it was produced in Milton's time, but the poet could have bought the book, which had many illustrations taken from actual performance, and easily imagined, on the basis of entertainments he actually had seen, what it would have been like.

Gretchen L. Finney has argued[20] convincingly that *Samson Agonistes* is also in part a fruit of Milton's Italian experience. The chorus had come to be disapproved of in Italy, as in France and England, for strictly literary plays; but its use in melodrama was defended by men like Doni as part of the program of classical revival. The seventeenth century did not, Finney points out, distinguish sharply between pastoral and tragedy. Music-dramas full of triviality reflect classical standards, and even oratorio[21] was felt to be subject

[18] See *The Monthly Magazine*, CXCVIII (1810), 145–47, which prints the Latin text of an oratorio on the Fall, said to have been "copied from an ancient manuscript, found some years ago, in the library of Marquis Scati at Milan," where it was "performed for the first time when Milton was there." There is a succession of brief lyric scenes: Adam contemplating creation; Lucifer rousing his followers; the love of Adam and Eve, with Adam comforting; the temptation and Fall; Satan glorying; Adam and Eve despairing and repentant.

[19] See Winifred Smith, *Italian Actors of the Renaissance* (New York, 1930).

[20] Gretchen L. Finney, "Chorus in *Samson Agonistes*."

[21] For the popularity of oratorio, see Domenico Alaleona, *Studi su la storia dell' Oratorio Musicale in Italia* (Turin, 1908), cited by Mrs. Finney.

to Aristotelian technique. "La Tragedia" appears frequently as the prologue for music-dramas, for example, Rinuccini's *Euridice*. When Milton speaks in the prefatory note to *Samson* of the chorus as still in use among the Italians, it is to melodrama and oratorio that he is referring. At least one oratorio having the Samson story as a theme was in print.[22] One is bound to conclude that the case for Milton's having learned much from those who were contributing to Italy's last great original achievement in the arts is strong, though at present rather intangible.[23]

Of Milton's actual itinerary there is at present little to add to his own statement as interpreted by Masson. It may, however, be pointed out that we are reasonably well informed only about his brief visit to Naples and his life in Florence, four or five months at most out of sixteen. He was in Rome for an equal period, but the record of his experience and contacts there is obviously very incomplete. For the visits to Paris and Geneva there is some data. The period in Venice is a complete blank, except that we know that he must have been there in the spring of 1639. Allowing for the longer residences and for the time consumed in getting from place to place by carriage or on horseback, we have at least three months left to account for, whether in France, Italy, or Switzerland. The possibility

[22] Pietro dell Isola, *Il Sansone, dialogo per musica* (1638). Mrs. Finney describes another Samson (unpublished) by Benedetto Ferrari, who like Monteverdi, was writing for the new Venetian opera houses at the time of Milton's visit.

[23] One wonders whether what Milton learned in Italy may not have had some influence on the future course of theatrical development in England. He must have imparted his ideas and plans to Lawes, perhaps proposing collaboration. Lawes later supplied the music for Sir William Davenant's *The First Days Entertainment at Rutland House* (1657), described on the title page as being "by Declamation and Musick, after the manner of the ancients." The quoted phrase suggests the description of ἀκρόαμα in ancient writers, as well as the theory and practice of the Italians. It says something more than, "this is not a play," to the learned critic who, like Milton, objected to the English stage partly because it had deserted the classical tradition. These ideas were current both inside and outside of Puritan circles, and they carried over to the Restoration. When Dryden asked permission to make an "opera" of *Paradise Lost*, he perhaps knew he was returning to Milton's original idea. Those who recorded the incident presumably did *not* know. Milton is still protesting in *Samson* and in the prefatory note to *Paradise Lost*. He could not, of course, be satisfied with Davenant's and Dryden's reading of the high doctrine of the poet's function which Milton himself had taught in his school out of Aristotle, Horace, and "the Italian commentaries of Castelveltro, Tasso, and Mazzoni, and the others."

of dating his visits to Pisa, Siena, Lucca, Bologna, Ferrara, Verona, Milan, etc., depends on the discovery of Continental records. Count Sforza has suggested that local antiquarianism in Italy might be expected to help in this, even after the destruction wrought by war and flood. Certainly the surviving correspondence of all persons Milton is known to have met and the minutes of the academies he might have been received in should be thoroughly searched. Without such material we can reconstruct his adventures only conjecturally. The general conditions of Italian travel and the customary experiences of Englishmen in the places Milton visited are described in the travel literature of the time. We know, for example, that Milton's trip would have cost him something like £ 400[24] and that much of his journey would have been on horseback. If the account of Moryson is to be trusted, he would have found the tables in the inns of Florence "spread with white cloths, strewed with flowers and fig leaves, with ingestors or glasses of divers colored wines set upon them and delicate fruits which would invite a man to eat and drink who otherwise hath no appetite, being all open to the sight of passengers as they ride by the highway, through their great unglazed windows."

We know also that his luggage would have been ransacked at almost every city for dutiable articles unless he gave the officials a suitable tip. We can imagine him being impressed, as Moryson was, with the condition of the peasantry, "whom the Italians use like oxen and asses for their work," and with the merry life of the courtesans, "feasted at home by their lovers and honored by all men with respectful salutations." Sandys says there were 30,000 of the latter in Naples to a population of 300,000. The remarks which won Milton the reputation among the Italians of being something of a prude may have been directed against this shamelessness.

The guide books tell us, finally, what sights he would have been confronted with in every city and what galleries he would have found open. Thus at Florence there were the Duke's wild beasts, the Pitti Palace, and the Pratolino garden with its water tricks. In Venice he could have visited the Doges' palace and seen the masterworks of Titian and Veronese on the walls. That the echoes of such experiences in Milton's later writings are few proves little. Vallombrosa

[24] See Howard, *English Travellers*, p. 156.

and Fiesole return to furnish beautiful similes in *Paradise Lost*, and there is a casual mention of Italian mountebanks in the *Pro se Defensio*. Marjorie Nicolson has argued plausibly that a visit to the Phlegraean Fields furnished materials for the account of hell and Pandemonium.[25] The description of Imperial Rome in *Paradise Regained*, more visual in its imagery than the parallel portrayal of Athens, perhaps adds reality to Milton's statement that he spent time "viewing the antiquities of that city." But that is about all that remains to attest his interest in the more obvious aspects of Italian travel. However much these things may have impressed him at the time, he did not often store them up for use:

> Me, of these
> Nor skilled nor studious higher argument
> Remains.

His capacity for discarding "tinsel trappings" is illustrated in the reference to his visit to the Viceroy's Palace in Naples, which includes no mention of what so much impressed other English travellers: the "royal and most lovely household stuff," "the large and most sweet gardens and delicate walks paved with divers colored and engraved marbles," the two banqueting houses, the "secret fountains and delicate cages of birds," and the astonishing array of implements of war.

The effects of the Italian journey on Milton's mind were nevertheless extensive and profound, including such significant minutiae as the adopting of the italic "e" in his handwriting and the Roman pronunciation of Latin words. But he seems as well to have gained a new maturity of purpose and a richer conception of the art of poetry.[26] The reasons he gives for returning to England without extending his visit to Sicily and Greece are suggestive of what was happening to him. He had come to feel himself a man and wanted to begin his work. The long period of preparation, which years of study at Hammersmith and Horton would never have completed, was over: he had become an accepted citizen of the world of intellect

[25] Marjorie Nicolson, "Milton's Hell and the Phlegraean Fields," *UTQ*, VII (1938), 500–13.

[26] The influence of Italian poetry on Milton of course antedates the Italian journey, but his interest in and knowledge of recent and contemporary authors must have been greatly extended by his contacts in Italy.

and culture. He had measured the difference between the English tradition and those of other peoples and matched his abilities with those of famous men. He had experienced the stimulation of new and sophisticated ideas in art. It is not surprising that the impediments to action should suddenly have been lifted from his mind.

The great program with which he returned to his native land had two related aspects: he proposed a cultural and spiritual reform of England, in which he as poet and publicist should play a leading part. The literary plans in the Cambridge Manuscript, the exhortation to the magistrates to provide worthy entertainment for the people in *The Reason of Church-Government*, and the actual writing of the first pamphlets show the direction of his mind. And in all this we can clearly trace the influence of his experiences abroad: the theaters and academies, Manso, Doni, Italian literature and literary theory, on the one hand; Grotius, Galileo, Giovanni Diodati, and the traditions of Italian and Genevan Protestantism against the actual background of the Counter-Reformation on the other.

Of the two sets of influence the latter is perhaps the more speculative, but it is certainly not to be neglected. The deepest emotion of Milton's youth was his friendship with Charles Diodati. The most comprehensive political ideal of his maturity was the achievement in Europe of Christian unity under the leadership of Reformed England. In Paris, Italy, and Geneva he had brought home to him the significance of the whole movement which had made the Diodatis exiles,[27] which had governed the political activity of Wotton, which commanded the intellectual energies of Grotius, and which accounted

---

[27] Milton must have been thoroughly acquainted with the saga of the Italian refugees. The various families—Diodati, Calandrini, Burlamaqui, Turrentini—had intermarried, and they all had a rallying point in Geneva, where the continuous tradition of the Italian church shows a succession of pastors from the Lucchese group to 1689. It is now known that Milton's friend Charles Diodati studied theology in this nursery of his clan in 1630 (see Donald Dorian, "Charles Diodati at Geneva," *PMLA*, LIX [1944], 589-91). Elie Diodati was there in that year and again in 1634. Milton's early intimacy with the London family extended beyond Charles himself. See his letter of September 2, 1637. He also knew a Calandrini in London and a Turrentini in Geneva. The Italian girl, Emilia, of the sonnets, has never been identified, and some are still convinced that she must have been of the same background. However much Anglicized or Gallicized the different members of the clan may have become, they could hardly have forgotten or ceased talking about such a burning ancestral experience as that recorded in the family memoirs now in the Geneva library.

for the frustration of Galileo. It was inevitable that his personal loyalties should help motivate and determine his devotion to a public cause. His own peculiar stripe of Protestant theology may owe something to the Italian reformers.[28] Peter Martyr of Vermigli, Bernardino Ochino of Siena, Fausto Socino, Paolo Sarpi, Giacomo Contio (Acontius), Marsiglio Padua, Tremellio of Ferrara, Matteo Gribaldi, Aonio Paleario, and Castellio were familiar names in Reformation history. Some of these men were Christian humanists rather than Lutherans or Calvinists pure and simple; and, generally speaking, Milton was of this tradition. Socinus was the arch heretic of the age, and Milton came nearer to holding with him than with his enemies. Ochino has been claimed as the source of Milton's anti-trinitarian conception. He also wrote a dialogue on polygamy and divorce, which was translated into English in 1567.[29] Acontius undertook in his book of the *Strategems of Satan* to show how few were the essential doctrines of Christianity. This work was revived by the Independents and appeared in English in 1648 with an epistle by John Goodwin and Milton's fellow worker for Protestant unity, John Dury. Lord Falkland with his latitudinarian motto: "in necessariis unitas, in dubiis libertas, in omnibus caritas" was directly or indirectly influenced by him. The Geneva theologians of Italian background were in Milton's time, however, strict Calvinists; and if Milton acquired libertine suggestions there it was by way of reaction to the tradition which had been suppressed.

Perhaps we are going too far afield to suggest a special relationship between Milton and these reformers of Italian origin. They belong to the larger background of his intellectual experience, as Italian music, art, and literature did to his cultural experience. What can be claimed with assurance is that the Continental journey, besides opening up for Milton new avenues of thought and knowledge, confirmed his ambitions as a Protestant humanist and a poet and helped in an important way to determine their direction.[30]

[28] See M. Young, *The Life and Times of Aonio Paleario, or A History of the Italian Reformers in the Sixteenth Century*, 2 vols. (London, 1860).

[29] See L. A. Wood, *The Form and Origin of Milton's Anti-trinitarian Conception* (London, 1911).

[30] The most recent study of Milton's Italian journey is James Holly Hanford's "Milton in Italy"; cf. William R. Parker's account of the Italian journey (*Milton*, I, 169–82).

BIBLIOGRAPHY

BIBLIOGRAPHICAL AND REFERENCE WORKS

Bradshaw, John. *A Concordance to the Poetical Works of John Milton.* London, 1894.

Bush, Douglas. *English Literature in the Earlier Seventeenth Century: 1600–1660.* 2nd rev. ed., Oxford, 1962.

Cooper, Lane. *A Concordance of the Latin, Greek, and Italian Poems of John Milton.* Halle, 1923.

English Association. *The Year's Work in English Studies.* Oxford, 1920– . Milton selections by L. C. Martin, Arnold Davenport, *et al.*

Fletcher, Harris F. *Contributions to a Milton Bibliography, 1800–1930. Being a List of Addenda to Stevens's "Reference Guide to Milton."* Urbana, 1931.

French, J. Milton. *The Life Records of John Milton.* 5 vols., New Brunswick, 1949–58.

Gilbert, Allen H. *A Geographical Dictionary of Milton.* New Haven, 1919.

Huckabay, Calvin. *John Milton: A Bibliographical Supplement, 1929–1957.* Pittsburgh, 1960.

Le Comte, Edward S. *A Milton Dictionary.* New York, 1961.

Lockwood, Laura S. *Lexicon to the English Poetical Works of John Milton.* New York, 1907.

Milton Newsletter, ed. Roy C. Flannagan. Athens [Ohio], 1967– .

Modern Language Association of America. PMLA: Publications of the Modern Language Association of America. Includes annually in May a Milton bibliography in its section on seventeenth century.

Osgood, Charles G. The Classical Mythology of Milton's English Poems. Rev. ed., New York, 1925.

Patterson, Frank Allen, assisted by French R. Fogle. An Index to the Columbia Edition of the Works of John Milton. 2 vols., New York, 1940.

Seventeenth-Century News, ed. J. Max Patrick. New York, 1942–   .

Stevens, David Harrison. Reference Guide to Milton from 1800 to the Present Day. Chicago, 1930.

Thompson, E. N. S. John Milton: Topical Bibliography. New Haven, 1916.

Wells, William, et al. "Recent Literature of the English Renaissance." SP, XIV (1917–   ).

EDITIONS

The Poetical Works of John Milton, ed. Henry J. Todd. 6 vols., London, 1801; 2nd rev. ed., 7 vols., London, 1809.
    Todd's variorum edition is the readiest means of access to the results of eighteenth-century critical and scholarly work on Milton.

The Prose Works of John Milton, ed. J. A. St. John. 5 vols., London, 1848–53.
    Translations of Latin works, including De Doctrina Christiana. Prefaces and notes. To be superseded by the edition now in progress under the general editorship of Don M. Wolfe.

The Works of John Milton in Verse and Prose, ed. John Mitford. 8 vols., London, 1851.
    Complete except for the De Doctrina Christiana and minor items. No translations. Index, no notes.

The Poetical Works of John Milton, ed. David Masson. 3 vols., London, 1874.
    Elaborate introductions, notes, and essays.

Arcades and Comus, Ode on the Morning of Christ's Nativity, etc.; L'Allegro, Il Penseroso, Lycidas, Paradise Lost, Samson Agonistes, ed. A. W. Verity. 11 vols., Cambridge, Eng., 1891–1912. Rev. ed. of Paradise Lost, 1910.
    This edition has elaborate, learned annotations.

The Complete Poetical Works of John Milton, ed. William Vaughan Moody. Boston, 1899. Rev. ed., 1924.
    Brilliant introductions; occasionally inaccurate.

The Poetical Works of John Milton, ed. W. A. Wright. Cambridge, Eng., 1903.
A good modernized text; gives variant readings in full.

The Poems of John Milton, ed. H. J. C. Grierson. London, 1925.
A chronological arrangement.

The Student's Milton, ed. Frank Allen Patterson. New York, 1930.
Complete poems and the bulk of the prose in a single volume. The text of the poems is that of the original editions, with careful collations. A new translation of the Latin poems by Nelson G. McCrea. A revision of this edition appeared in 1933, with annotations to both poetry and prose.

The Works of John Milton, ed. Frank Allen Patterson, *et al.* 18 vols. in 21, New York, 1931–38.
The Columbia Edition, more inclusive than any hitherto. The texts are based on a complete collation of all the manuscripts and early printings. Vol. XVIII contains the hitherto uncollected writings, marginalia, and many items which have been ascribed to Milton on more or less doubtful authority. Additions are to be found in "A First Supplement to the Columbia Milton," T. O. Mabbott and J. Milton French, *N&Q,* CLXXVII (1939), 329–30.

An Index to the Columbia Edition of the Works of John Milton, comp. Frank Allen Patterson, assisted by French R. Fogle. 2 vols., New York, 1940.

The Poems of John Milton, ed. James Holly Hanford. New York, 1936.
Excellent introductions and notes.

The Complete Poetical Works of John Milton, ed. Harris F. Fletcher. Boston, 1941.
A new text.

John Milton's Complete Poetical Works Reproduced in Photographic Facsimile, ed. Harris F. Fletcher. 4 vols., Urbana, 1943–48.

The Poetical Works of John Milton, ed. Helen Darbishire. 2 vols., Oxford, 1952–55.
Unannotated; an attempt to reproduce Milton's intended spelling.

Complete Prose Works of John Milton. Don M. Wolfe, gen. ed. 8 vols., New Haven, 1953– .

John Milton: Poems, ed. B. A. Wright. London and New York, 1956.
Another attempt at reconstruction of Milton's spelling.

John Milton: Complete Poems and Major Prose, ed. Merritt Y. Hughes. New York, 1957.
Excellent annotations; extensive summaries of critical arguments as introductions to the works.

The Complete English Poetry of John Milton, ed. John T. Shawcross. New York, 1963.
Chronologically arranged; careful, accurate, scholarly handling of text.

The Complete Poetical Works of John Milton, ed. Douglas Bush. Boston, 1965.
A modernized text; excellent notes, but without references to secondary studies.

BIOGRAPHIES

Barker, Arthur E. *Milton and the Puritan Dilemma, 1641–1660.* Toronto, 1942. Rptd. 1956.

Belloc, Hilaire. *Milton.* London, 1935.

Bush, Douglas. *John Milton: A Sketch of His Life and Writings.* New York, 1964.

Daiches, David. *Milton.* London and New York, 1957.

Darbishire, Helen, ed. *The Early Lives of Milton.* London, 1932.

Diekhoff, John S. *Milton on Himself: Milton's Utterances Upon Himself and His Works.* New York, 1939. Rptd. 1965.

Fletcher, Harris F. *The Intellectual Development of John Milton.* 2 vols., Urbana, 1956–   .

Garnett, Richard. *Life of John Milton.* London, 1890.

Hanford, James Holly. *John Milton, Englishman.* New York, 1949. Rptd. 1953.

Macaulay, Rose. *Milton.* London, 1934.

Masson, David. *The Life of Milton.* 6 vols., plus index (1894), 1859–80. (Rev. ed. of Vol. I, 1881; rptd. 1946.)

Parker, William Riley. *Milton: A Biography.* 2 vols., London, 1968.

Pattison, Mark. *Milton.* London, 1879.

Raleigh, Sir Walter A. *Milton.* New York, 1900.

Saillens, Emile. *John Milton, Poète combattant.* Paris, 1959.

Stern, Alfred. *Milton und seine Zeit.* 2 vols., Leipzig, 1877–79.

Tillyard, E. M. W. *Milton.* London, 1930.

Tillyard, Phyllis B., trans. *Milton: Private Correspondence and Academic Exercises, Translated from the Latin . . . with an Introduction and Commentary by E. M. W. Tillyard.* Cambridge, Eng., 1932.

Trent, William P. *John Milton: A Short Study of His Life and Works.* New York, 1899.

Wolfe, Don M. *Milton in the Puritan Revolution.* New York, 1941. Rptd. 1963.

BIOGRAPHICAL STUDIES

Allodoli, Ettore. *Giovanni Milton e l'Italia.* Prato, 1907.

Barker, Arthur E. "Milton's Schoolmasters." *MLR*, XXXII (1937), 517–36.

Brennecke, Ernest, Jr. *John Milton the Elder and His Music.* New York, 1938.

Brown, Eleanor. *Milton's Blindness.* New York, 1934.

Bush, Douglas. "The Critical Significance of Biographical Evidence: John Milton." *English Institute Essays: 1946*, pp. 5–19.

Clark, Donald L. *John Milton at St. Paul's School: A Study of Ancient Rhetoric in English Renaissance Education.* New York, 1948.

Clavering, Rose, and John T. Shawcross. "Milton's European Itinerary and His Return Home." *SEL*, V (1965), 49–59.

Dobree, Bonamy. "Milton and Dryden: A Comparison and Contrast in Poetic Ideas and Poetic Method." *ELH*, III (1936), 83–100.

Dorian, Donald C. *The English Diodatis: A History of Charles Diodati's Family and His Friendship with Milton.* New Brunswick, 1950.

Elton, William. "New Light on Milton's Amanuensis." *HLQ*, XXVI (1963), 383–84.

Evans, Willa M. *Henry Lawes: Musician and Friend of Poets.* New York, 1941.

French, J. Milton. "The Autographs of John Milton." *ELH*, IV (1937), 301–30.

———. "Milton's Annotated Copy of Gildas." *Harvard Studies and Notes*, XX (1938), 76–80.

———. *Milton in Chancery: New Chapters in the Lives of the Poet and His Father.* New York, 1939.

———. "The Reliability of Anthony Wood and Milton's Oxford M.A." *PMLA*, LXXV (1960), 22–30.

Hanford, James Holly. "The Chronology of Milton's Private Studies." *PMLA*, XXXVI (1921), 251–314. Rptd. *John Milton: Poet and Humanist.* Cleveland, 1966, pp. 75–125.

———. "The Youth of Milton: An Interpretation of His Early Development." *Studies in Shakespeare, Milton, and Donne.* New York, 1925, pp. 89–163. Rptd. *John Milton: Poet and Humanist.* Cleveland, 1966, pp. 1–74.

———. "Milton in Italy." *AnM*, V (1964), 49–63.

Hone, Ralph E. "New Light on the Milton-Phillips Family Relationship." *HLQ*, XXII (1958), 63–75.

Hunter, Joseph. *Milton. A Sheaf of Gleanings after His Biographers and Annotators: I. Genealogical Investigation; II. Notes on Some of His Poems.* London, 1850.

Hunter, William B., Jr., "Some Speculations on the Nature of Milton's Blindness." *JHM*, XVII (1962), 333–41.

Liljegren, S. B. *Studies in Milton.* Lund [Sweden], 1918.

Martin, Burns. "The Date of Milton's First Marriage." *SP*, XXV (1928), 475–62.

Martin, John Rupert. *The Portrait of John Milton at Princeton, and Its Place in Milton Iconography*. Princeton, 1961.

————. "The Milton Portrait: Some Addenda." *PULC*, XXIV (1963), 168–73.

Morand, Paul P. *De Comus à Satan, l'ouvre poétique de John Milton expliquée par sa vie*. Paris, 1939.

————. *The Effects of His Political Life upon John Milton*. Paris, 1939.

Parker, William Riley. "On Milton's Early Literary Program." *MP*, XXXIII (1935), 49–53.

————. "The Trinity Manuscript and Milton's Plans for a Tragedy." *JEGP*, XXXIV (1935), 225–32.

————. *Milton's Contemporary Reputation, an Essay, together with A Tentative List of Printed Allusions to Milton, 1614–1674*. Columbus, 1940.

————. "Milton's Last Sonnet." *RES*, XXI (1945), 235–38.

————. "Wood's Life of Milton: Its Sources and Significance." *PBSA*, LII (1958), 1–22.

Rand, E. K. "Milton in Rustication." *SP*, XIX (1922), 109–35.

Saurat, Denis. *Milton: Man and Thinker*. 2nd rev. ed., New York, 1944.

Shawcross, John T. "Speculations on the Dating of the Trinity MS. of Milton's Poems." *MLN*, LXXV (1960), 11–17.

————. "The Chronology of Milton's Major Poems." *PMLA*, LXXVI (1961), 345–58.

————. "Milton's Decision to Become a Poet." *MLQ*, XXIV (1963), 21–30.

Sirluck, Ernest. "Milton's Idle Right Hand." *JEGP*, LX (1961), 749–85.

Sotheby, Samuel Leigh. *Ramblings in the Elucidation of the Autograph of Milton*. London, 1861.

Thompson, E. N. S. "Milton's Part in *Theatrum Poetarum*." *MLN*, XXXVI (1921), 18–21.

Wright, B. A. "Milton's First Marriage." *MLR*, XXVI (1931), 383–400; XXVII (1932), 6–23.

THE PROSE WORKS

Barker, Arthur E. "Christian Liberty in Milton's Divorce Pamphlets." *MLR*, XXXV (1940), 153–61.

Cawley, Robert R. *Milton's Literary Craftsmanship: A Study of "A*

Brief History of Moscovia": With an Edition of the Text. Princeton, 1941.

Ekfelt, Fred E. "The Graphic Diction of Milton's English Prose." *PQ,* XXV (1946), 46–69.

———. "Latinate Diction in Milton's English Prose." *PQ,* XXVIII (1949), 53–71.

Fink, Zera S. "The Theory of the Mixed State and the Development of Milton's Political Thought." *PMLA,* LVII (1942), 705–36.

Fletcher, Harris F. *The Use of the Bible in Milton's Prose.* Urbana, 1929.

———. "The First Edition of Milton's *History of Britain.*" *JEGP,* XXXV (1936), 405–14.

French, J. Milton. "Milton as a Historian." *PMLA,* L (1935), 469–79.

———. "Milton as Satirist." *PMLA,* LI (1936), 414–29.

———. "Some Notes on Milton's *Accedence Commenc't Grammar.*" *JEGP,* LX (1961), 641–50.

Gilman, Wilbur E. *Milton's Rhetoric: Studies in His Defense of Liberty. University of Missouri Studies,* XIV, Columbia, 1939.

Gleason, John B. "The Nature of Milton's *Moscovia.*" *SP,* LXI (1964), 640–49.

Haller, William, ed. *Tracts on Liberty in the Puritan Revolution, 1638–1647.* 3 vols., New York, 1934.

———. *The Rise of Puritanism: or, The Way to the New Jerusalem as Set Forth in Pulpit and Press from Thomas Cartwright to John Lilburne and John Milton, 1570–1643.* New York, 1938.

———. *Liberty and Reformation in the Puritan Revolution.* New York, 1955.

Hanford, James Holly. "The Date of Milton's *De Doctrina Christiana.*" *SP,* XVII (1920), 309–19.

Hughes, Merritt Y. 'The Historical Setting of Milton's *Observations* on the *Articles of Peace.*" *PMLA,* LXIV (1949), 1049–73.

———. "Milton's Treatment of Reformation History in *The Tenure of Kings and Magistrates," The Seventeenth Century.* Stanford, 1951, pp. 247–63.

———. "New Evidence on the Charge that Milton Forged the Pamela Prayer in the *Eikon Basilike.*" *RES,* n.s. III (1952), 130–40.

Kelley, Maurice. "Milton's Debt to Wolleb's *Compendium Theologiae Christianae.*" *PMLA,* L (1935), 156–65.

———. *This Great Argument: A Study of Milton's De Doctrina Christiana as a Gloss upon Paradise Lost.* Princeton, 1941.

Le Comte, Edward S. "Milton's Attitude Towards Women in the *History of Britain.*" *PMLA,* LXII (1947), 977–83.

Lewalski, Barbara K. "Milton: Political Beliefs and Polemical Methods, 1659–60." *PMLA*, LXXIV (1959), 191–202.

Lowenhaupt, Warren H. "The Writing of Milton's *Eikonoklastes.*" *SP*, XX (1923), 29–51.

Neumann, J. H. "Milton's Prose Vocabulary." *PMLA*, LX (1945), 102–20.

Nicholas, Constance, comp. *Introduction and Notes to Milton's 'History of Britain', Designed to be Used with Volume X, Columbia Edition, The Works of Milton. Illinois Studies in Language and Literature*, XLIV, Urbana, 1957.

Parker, William Riley. "Education: Milton's Ideas and Ours." *CE*, XXIV (1962), 1–14.

Parks, George B. "The Occasion of Milton's *Moscovia.*" *SP*, XL (1943), 399–404.

———. "Milton's *Moscovia* Not History." *PQ*, XXXI (1952), 281–21.

Sewell, Arthur. "Milton's *De Doctrina Christiana.*" *E&S*, XIX (1934), 40–65.

———. *A Study in Milton's Christian Doctrine.* London, 1939.

Siebert, F. S. "Control of the Press During the Puritan Revolution, 1640–1660." *Freedom of the Press in England, 1476–1776: The Rise and Decline of Government Controls.* Urbana, 1952, pp. 165–233.

Sirluck, Ernest. "Milton's Political Thought: The First Cycle." *MP*, LXI (1964), 209–24.

Svendsen, Kester. "Science and Structure in Milton's *Doctrine of Divorce.*" *PMLA*, LXVII (1952), 435–45.

———. "Milton's *Pro Se Defensio* and Alexander More." *TSLL*, I (1959), 11–29.

———. "Milton and Alexander More: New Documents." *JEGP*, LX (1961), 796–807.

Thompson, E. N. S. "Milton's Prose Style." *PQ*, XIV (1935), 1–15.

Whiting, George W. "The Sources of *Eikonoklastes*: A Resurvey." *SP*, XXXII (1935), 74–102.

MISCELLANEOUS MINOR POEMS

Allen, Don Cameron. "The Search for the Prophetic Strain: *L'Allegro* and *Il Penseroso.*" *The Harmonious Vision: Studies in Milton's Poetry.* Baltimore, 1954, pp. 3–25.

Babb, Lawrence. "The Background of 'Il Penseroso.' " *SP*, XXXVII (1940), 257–73.

Baldwin, Edward Chauncey. "Milton and the Psalms." *MP*, XVII (1919), 457–63.

Barker, Arthur E. "The Pattern of Milton's *Nativity Ode.*" *UTQ*, X (1941), 167–81.

Broadbent, J. B. "The Nativity Ode." *The Living Milton: Essays by Various Hands*, ed. Frank Kermode. London, 1960, pp. 12–31.

Brooks, Cleanth. "The Light Symbolism in 'L'Allegro'–'Il Penseroso.' " *The Well Wrought Urn: Studies in the Structure of Poetry*. New York, 1947, pp. 47–61.

———, and J. E. Hardy, eds. *Poems of Mr. John Milton: The 1645 Edition with Essays in Analysis*. New York, 1951.

Bush, Douglas. "The Date of Milton's *Ad Patrem*." MP, LXI (1964), 204–08.

Carpenter, Nan Cooke. "The Place of Music in *L'Allegro* and *Il Penseroso*." UTQ, XXII (1953), 354–67.

Cope, Jackson I. "Fortunate Falls as Form in Milton's 'Fair Infant.' " JEGP, LXIII (1964), 660–74.

Evans, G. Blakemore. "Milton and the Hobson Poems." MLQ, IV (1943), 281–90.

Hardison, O. B., Jr. "Milton's 'On Time' and Its Scholastic Background." TSLL, III (1961), 107–22.

Hunter, William B. "Milton Translates the Psalms." PQ, XL (1961), 485–94.

Leishman, J. B. " 'L'Allegro' and 'Il Penseroso' in their Relation to Seventeenth-Century Poetry." E&S, n.s., IV (1951), 1–36.

Maclean, Hugh N. "Milton's *Fair Infant*." ELH, XXIV (1957), 296–305.

Maddison, Carol. *Apollo and the Nine: A History of the Ode*. Baltimore, 1960.

Nelson, Lowry. *Baroque Lyric Poetry*. New Haven, 1961.

Parker, William Riley. "Milton's Hobson Poems: Some Neglected Early Texts." MLR, XXXI (1936), 395–402.

———. "Notes on the Chronology of Milton's Latin Poems." *A Tribute to George Coffin Taylor: Studies and Essays, Chiefly Elizabethan, by His Students and Friends*, ed. Arnold Williams. Chapel Hill, 1952, pp. 113–31.

Ross, Malcolm M. "Milton and the Protestant Aesthetic: the Early Poems." UTQ, XVII (1948), 346–60.

Shawcross, John T. "The Manuscript of 'Arcades.' " N&Q, n.s., VI (1959), 359–64.

Studley, Marian H. "Milton and His Paraphrases of the Psalms." PQ, IV (1925), 364–72.

Tate, Eleanor. "Milton's 'L'Allegro' and 'Il Penseroso'—Balance, Progression, or Dichotomy?" MLN, LXXVI (1961), 585–90.

Tillyard, E. M. W. " 'L'Allegro' and 'Il Penseroso.' " *The Miltonic Setting: Past and Present*. Cambridge, Eng., 1938, pp. 1–28.

Tuve, Rosemond. "Structural Figures of *L'Allegro* and *Il Penseroso*."

Images & Themes in Five Poems by Milton. Cambridge, Mass., 1957, pp. 15–36.

———. "The Hymn on the Morning of Christ's Nativity." *Images & Themes in Five Poems by Milton.* Cambridge, Mass., 1957, pp. 37–52.

Wallace, John Malcolm. "Milton's *Arcades.*" *JEGP,* LVIII (1959), 627–36.

Wright, William Aldis, ed. *Fascimile of the Manuscript of Milton's Minor Poems.* Cambridge, Eng., 1899.

COMUS

Allen, Don Cameron. "The Higher Compromise: *On the Morning of Christ's Nativity* and *A Mask.*" *The Harmonious Vision: Studies in Milton's Poetry.* Baltimore, 1954, pp. 24–40.

Arthos, John. *On "A Mask Presented at Ludlow-Castle."* Ann Arbor, 1954.

———. "The Realms of Being in the Epilogue of *Comus.*" *MLN,* LXXVI (1961), 321–24.

Barber, C. L. "*A Mask Presented at Ludlow Castle:* The Masque as a Masque." *The Lyric and Dramatic Milton,* ed. Joseph Summers. New York, 1965, pp. 35–63.

Diekhoff, John S. "The Text of *Comus,* 1634 to 1645." *PMLA,* LII (1937), 705–27.

———, ed. *A Maske at Ludlow: Essays on Milton's "Comus."* Cleveland, 1968.

Dyson, A. E. "The Interpretation of *Comus.*" *E&S,* n.s., VIII (1955), 89–114.

Egerton, Lady Alix. *Milton's "Comus," Being the Bridgewater Manuscript, With Notes and a Short Family Memoir.* London, 1910.

Finney, Gretchen L. "*Comus, Dramma per Musica.*" *SP,* XXXVII (1940), 482–500.

Haun, Eugene. "An Inquiry into the Genre of *Comus.*" *Essays in Honor of Walter Clyde Curry.* Nashville, 1954, pp. 221–39.

Jayne, Sears. "The Subject of Milton's Ludlow *Mask.*" *PMLA,* LXXIV (1959), 533–43.

Klein, Joan Larson. "Some Spenserian Influences on Milton's *Comus.*" *AnM,* V (1964), 27–47.

Lewis, C. S. "A Note on *Comus.*" *RES,* VIII (1932), 170–76.

Shawcross, John T. "Henry Lawes's Setting of Songs for Milton's *Comus.*" *JRUL,* XXVIII (1964), 22–28.

Steadman, John M. "Milton's *Haemony:* Etymology and Allegory." *PMLA,* LXXVII (1962), 200–07.

Tillyard, E. M. W. "The Action of *Comus.*" *Studies in Milton.* London, 1951, pp. 82–99.

Tuve, Rosemond. "Image, Form, and Theme in A *Mask.*" *Images & Themes in Five Poems by Milton.* Cambridge, Mass., 1957, pp. 112–61.

Visiak, E. H., ed. *The Mask of Comus, with Airs.* London, 1937.

Welsford, Enid. *The Court Masque: A Study in the Relationship Between Poetry and the Revels.* Cambridge, Eng., 1927.

Woodhouse, A. S. P. "The Argument of Milton's *Comus.*" *UTQ*, XI (1941), 46–71.

————. "*Comus* Once More." *UTQ*, XIX (1950), 218–23.

LYCIDAS

Abrams, M. H. "Five Ways of Reading *Lycidas.*" *Varieties of Literary Experience: Eighteen Essays in World Literature*, ed. Stanley Burnshaw. New York, 1962, pp. 1–29. This essay first appeared in Patrides, see below.

Adams, Richard P. "The Archetypal Pattern of Death and Rebirth in Milton's *Lycidas.*" *PMLA*, LXIV (1949), 183–88.

Allen, Don Cameron. "The Translation of the Myth: The Epicedia and *Lycidas.*" *The Harmonious Vision: Studies in Milton's Poetry.* Baltimore, 1954, pp. 41–70.

Battestin, Martin C. "John Crowe Ransom and *Lycidas*: A Reappraisal." *CE*, XVII (1956), 223–28.

Daiches, David. *A Study of Literature for Readers and Critics.* Ithaca, 1948, pp. 170–95.

Daniells, Roy. "*Comus* and *Lycidas.*" *Milton, Mannerism and Baroque.* Toronto, 1963, pp. 19–50.

Elledge, Scott, ed. *Milton's "Lycidas": Edited to Serve as an Introduction to Criticism.* New York, 1966.

Hanford, James Holly. "The Pastoral Elegy and Milton's *Lycidas.*" *PMLA*, XXV (1910), 403–47. Rptd. in Patrides, pp. 27–55, see below, and in *John Milton, Poet and Humanist, Essays by James Holly Hanford*, ed. John Diekhoff (Cleveland, 1966), pp. 126–60.

Harrison, Thomas Perrin, Jr. *The Pastoral Elegy: An Anthology* (with translations by Harry Joshua Leon). Austin, 1939.

MacCaffrey, Isabel. "*Lycidas*: The Poet in a Landscape." *The Lyric and Dramatic Milton*, ed. Joseph Summers. New York, 1965, pp. 65–92.

Mayerson, Caroline. "The Orpheus Image in *Lycidas.*" *PMLA*, LXIV (1949), 189–207.

Mossner, Ernest C., ed. *Justa Edovardo King*. The Facsimile Text Society, No. 45, New York, 1939.

Oras, Ants. "Milton's Early Rhyme Schemes and the Structure of *Lycidas*." *MP*, LII (1954), 12–22.

Patrides, C. A., ed. *Milton's "Lycidas": The Tradition and the Poem*. New York, 1961.

Prince, F. T. "*Lycidas*." *The Italian Element in Milton's Verse*. Oxford, 1954, pp. 71–88.

Ransom, John Crowe. "A Poem Nearly Anonymous." *American Review*, I (1933), 179–203, 444–67. Rptd. in *The World's Body* (New York, 1938), pp. 1–28, and in Patrides, see above.

Rinehart, Keith. "A Note on the First Fourteen Lines of Milton's *Lycidas*." *N&Q*, CXCVIII (1953), 103.

Shumaker, Wayne. "Flowerets and Sounding Seas: A Study in the Affective Structure of *Lycidas*." *PMLA*, LXVI (1951), 485–94. Rptd. in Patrides, see above.

Tuve, Rosemond. "Theme, Pattern and Imagery in *Lycidas*." *Images & Themes in Five Poems by Milton*. Cambridge, Mass., 1957, pp. 73–111. Rptd. in Patrides, see above.

Wallerstein, Ruth. "Iusta Edouardo King." *Studies in Seventeenth Century Poetic*. Madison, 1950, pp. 96–114.

Woodhouse, A. S. P. "Milton's Pastoral Monodies." *Studies in Honour of Gilbert Norwood*, ed. M. E. White. Toronto, 1952, pp. 261–78.

THE SONNETS

Carey, John. "The Date of Milton's Italian Poems." *RES*, n.s., XIV (1963), 383–86.

Hanford, James Holly. "The Arrangement and Dates of Milton's Sonnets." *MP*, XVIII (1921), 475–83.

Honigmann, E. A. J., ed. *Milton's Sonnets*. London and New York, 1966.

Parker, William Riley. "Milton's Last Sonnet." *RES*, XXI (1945), 235–38.

———. "Milton's Last Sonnet Again." *RES*, n.s., II (1951), 147–52.

———. "The Dates of Milton's Sonnets on Blindness." *PMLA*, LXXIII (1958), 196–200.

Pattison, Mark, ed. *The Sonnets of John Milton*. London, 1883.

Prince, F. T. "Della Casa and the Heroic Sonnet." *The Italian Element in Milton's Verse*. Oxford, 1954, pp. 14–33.

———. "Milton's Sonnets." *The Italian Element in Milton's Verse.* Oxford, 1954, pp. 89–107.

Shawcross, John T. "Of Chronology and the Dates of Milton's Translation from Horace and the *New Forcers of Conscience.*" *SEL,* III (1963), 77–84.

Slakey, Roger L. "Milton's Sonnet 'On His Blindness.' " *ELH,* XXVII (1960), 122–30.

Smart, John S., ed. *The Sonnets of Milton.* Glasgow, 1921. Rptd. 1966.

Stevens, David H. "The Order of Milton's Sonnets." *MP,* XVII (1919), 25–33.

Stoehr, Taylor. "Syntax and Poetic Form in Milton's Sonnets." *ES,* XLV (1964), 289–301.

Svendsen, Kester. "Milton's Sonnet on the Massacre in Piedmont." *Shakespeare Association Bulletin,* XX (1945), 147–55.

Woodhouse, A. S. P. "Notes on Milton's Early Development." *UTQ,* XIII (1943), 66–101.

PARADISE LOST

Allen, Don Cameron. "Description as Cosmos: The Visual Image in *Paradise Lost.*" *The Harmonious Vision: Studies in Milton's Poetry.* Baltimore, 1954, pp. 95–109.

———. "Milton and the Love of Angels." *MLN,* LXXVI (1961), 489–90.

Barker, Arthur E. "Structural Pattern in *Paradise Lost.*" *PQ,* XXVIII (1949), 16–30.

Bell, Millicent. "The Fallacy of the Fall in *Paradise Lost.*" *PMLA,* LXVIII (1953), 863–83.

Blondel, Jaques. *Milton, poète de la Bible dans le Paradis perdu.* Paris, 1959.

Broadbent, J. B. *Some Graver Subject: An Essay on Paradise Lost.* London, 1960.

Brooks, Cleanth. "Eve's Awakening." *Essays in Honor of Walter Clyde Curry.* Nashville, 1954, pp. 281–98.

Bush, Douglas. *"Paradise Lost" In Our Time: Some Comments.* Ithaca, 1945.

Butler, A. Z. "The Pathetic Fallacy in *Paradise Lost.*" *Essays in Honor of Walter Clyde Curry.* Nashville, 1954, pp. 269–79.

Cirillo, Albert R. "Noon-Midnight and the Temporal Structure of *Paradise Lost.*" *ELH,* XXIX (1962), 372–95.

Colie, Rosalie L. "Time and Eternity: Paradox and Structure in *Paradise Lost.*" *JWCI,* XXIII (1960), 127–38.

Condee, Ralph W. *Milton's Theories Concerning Epic Poetry: Their Sources and Their Influence upon "Paradise Lost."* Urbana, 1949.

Conklin, George N. *Biblical Criticism and Heresy in Milton.* New York, 1949.

Cope, Jackson I. *The Metaphoric Structure of "Paradise Lost."* Baltimore, 1962.

Curry, Walter Clyde. *Milton's Ontology, Cosmogony, and Physics.* Lexington, 1957.

Daiches, David. 'The Opening of *Paradise Lost.*" *The Living Milton: Essays by Various Hands*, ed. Frank Kermode. London, 1960, pp. 55–69.

Darbishire, Helen, ed. *The Manuscript of Milton's "Paradise Lost": Book I.* Oxford, 1931.

Diekhoff, John S. *Milton's "Paradise Lost": A Commentary on the Argument.* New York, 1946. Rptd. 1958.

Empson, William. "Milton and Bentley." *Some Versions of Pastoral.* London, 1935, pp. 149–91.

———. "Emotions in Words Again." *KR*, X (1948), 579–601. Rptd. in *The Structure of Complex Words.* London, 1951, pp. 101–04.

———. *Milton's God.* 2nd ed., London, 1965.

Ferry, Anne. *Milton's Epic Voice: The Narrator in "Paradise Lost."* Cambridge, Mass., 1963.

Fish, Stanley. *Surprised by Sin: The Reader in "Paradise Lost."* London and New York, 1967.

Fox, Robert C. "The Character of Mammon in *Paradise Lost.*" *RES*, n.s., XIII (1962), 30–39.

———. "The Character of Moloc in *Paradise Lost.*" *Die neueren Sprachen*, XI (1962), 389–95.

Gardner, Helen. "Milton's Satan and the Theme of Damnation in Elizabethan Tragedy." *E&S*, n.s., I (1948), 46–66.

Gilbert, Allan H. *On The Composition of "Paradise Lost": A Study of the Ordering and Insertion of Material.* Chapel Hill, 1947.

Greenlaw, Edwin. "Spenser's Influence on *Paradise Lost.*" *SP*, XVII (1920), 320–59.

Hanford, James Holly. "The Dramatic Element in *Paradise Lost.*" *SP*, XIV (1917), 178–95.

———. "Milton and the Art of War." *SP*, XVIII (1921), 232–66.

Harding, Davis P. *The Club of Hercules: Studies in the Classical Background of "Paradise Lost." Illinois Studies in Language and Literature*, L, Urbana, 1962.

Hart, Jeffrey. "*Paradise Lost* and Order." *CE*, XXV (1964), 576–82.

Hughes, Merritt Y. *Ten Perspectives on Milton.* New Haven and London, 1965.

Hunter, William B., Jr. "Prophetic Dreams and Visions in *Paradise Lost.*" *MLQ*, IX (1948), 277–85.

———. "The Meaning of 'Holy Light' in *Paradise Lost* III." *MLN*, LXXIV (1959), 589–92.

———. "Milton's Urania." *SEL*, IV (1964), 35–42.

Kermode, Frank. "Adam Unparadised." *The Living Milton: Essays by Various Hands,* ed. Frank Kermode. London, 1960, pp. 85–123.

Kirkconnell, Watson. *The Celestial Cycle: The Theme of "Paradise Lost" in World Literature with Translations of the Major Analogues.* Toronto, 1952.

Kranidas, Thomas. *The Fierce Equation: A Study of Milton's Decorum.* The Hague, 1965.

Lewalski, Barbara K. "*Paradise Lost* 'Introduced' and 'Structured in Space.'" *MP*, LXI (1963), 122–26.

———. "Structure and the Symbolism of Vision in Michael's Prophecy, *Paradise Lost,* Books XI–XII." *PQ*, XLII (1963), 25–35.

Lewis, C. S. *A Preface to "Paradise Lost."* London, 1942.

Lovejoy, Arthur O. "Milton and the Paradox of the Fortunate Fall." *ELH*, IV (1937), 161–79. Rptd. in *Essays in the History of Ideas.* Baltimore, 1948, pp. 277–95.

MacCaffrey, Isabel G. *Paradise Lost as "Myth."* Cambridge, Mass, 1959.

Madsen, William G. *From Shadowy Types to Truth: Studies in Milton's Symbolism.* New Haven and London, 1968.

Martz, Louis. "*Paradise Lost:* The Journey of the Mind." *The Paradise Within: Studies in Vaughan, Traherne, and Milton.* New Haven and London, 1964, pp. 103–67.

McColley, Grant. *"Paradise Lost": An Account of Its Growth and Major Origins, With a Discussion of Milton's Use of Sources and Literary Patterns.* Chicago, 1940.

Nicolson, Marjorie Hope. *The Breaking of the Circle: Studies in the Effect of the "New Science" upon Seventeenth-Century Poetry.* Rev. ed., New York, 1960.

Patrides, C. A. "*Paradise Lost* and the Theory of Accommodation." *TSLL*, V (1963), 58–63.

———. *Milton and the Christian Tradition.* Oxford, 1966.

Peter, John. *A Critique of Paradise Lost.* London, 1960.

Prince, F. T. "On the Last Two Books of *Paradise Lost.*" *E&S*, XI (1958), 38–52.

Rajan, B. *Paradise Lost and the Seventeenth Century Reader.* 2nd rev. ed., London, 1962.

Samuel, Irene. "The Dialogue in Heaven: A Reconsideration of *Paradise Lost*, III, 1–417." PMLA, LXXII (1957), 601–11.

——. *Dante and Milton: The Commedia and Paradise Lost.* Ithaca, 1966.

Shumaker, Wayne. "The Fallacy of the Fall in *Paradise Lost*." PMLA, LXX (1955), 1185–87.

Sims, James H. *The Bible in Milton's Epics.* Gainesville, 1962.

Steadman, John M. "Adam and the Prophesied Redeemer (*Paradise Lost*, XII, 359–623)." SP, LVI (1959), 214–25.

——. "Archangel to Devil: The Background of Satan's Metamorphosis." MLQ, XXI (1960), 321–35.

——. "Mimesis and Idea: *Paradise Lost* and the Seventeenth-Century World-View." EUQ, XX (1964), 67–80.

——. "Pandaemonium and Deliberative Oratory." Neophil., XLVIII (1964), 159–75.

Stein, Arnold. *Answerable Style: Essays on Paradise Lost.* Minneapolis, 1953.

Summers, Joseph. *The Muse's Method: An Introduction to Paradise Lost.* Cambridge, Mass., 1962.

Svendsen, Kester. *Milton and Science.* Cambridge, Mass., 1956.

Taylor, George C. *Milton's Use of Du Bartas.* Cambridge, Mass., 1934.

Tillyard, E. M. W. *Studies in Milton.* London, 1951.

Waldock, A. J. A. *Paradise Lost and Its Critics.* Cambridge, Eng., 1947.

Woodhouse, A. S. P. "Pattern in *Paradise Lost*." UTQ, XXII (1953), 109–27.

Wright, B. A. *Milton's Paradise Lost.* London and New York, 1962.

PARADISE REGAINED

Allen, Don Cameron. "Realization as Climax: *Paradise Regained*." *The Harmonious Vision: Studies in Milton's Poetry.* Baltimore, 1954, pp. 110–24.

Barker, Arthur E. "Structural and Doctrinal Pattern in Milton's Later Poems." *Essays in English Literature from the Renaissance to the Victorian Age Presented to A. S. P. Woodhouse*, ed. Millar MacLure and F. W. Watt. Toronto, 1964, pp. 169–94.

Blondel, Jacques. *Le paradis reconquis.* Paris, 1955.

Frye, Northrop. "The Typology of *Paradise Regained*." MP, LIII (1956), 227–38.

Hughes, Merritt Y. "The Christ of *Paradise Regained* and the Renaissance Heroic Tradition." *SP*, XXXV (1938), 254–77.

Kermode, Frank. "Milton's Hero." *RES*, n.s., IV (1953), 317–30.

Lewalski, Barbara K. *Milton's Brief Epic: The Genre, Meaning, and Art of Paradise Regained.* Providence, 1966.

Martz, Louis. "*Paradise Regained:* The Meditative Combat." *ELH*, XXVII (1960), 223–47.

―――. "*Paradise Regained:* The Interior Teacher." *The Paradise Within: Studies in Vaughan, Traherne, and Milton.* New Haven and London, 1964, pp. 171–201.

Pope, Elizabeth. *Paradise Regained: The Tradition and the Poem.* Baltimore, 1947.

Sackton, Alexander. "Architectonic Structure in *Paradise Regained.*" *UTSE*, XXXIII (1954), 37–39.

Samuel, Irene. "Milton on Learning and Wisdom." *PMLA*, LXIV (1949), 708–23.

Schultz, Howard. "Christ and Antichrist in *Paradise Regained.*" *PMLA*, LXVII (1952), 790–808.

Steadman, John M. 'The 'Tree of Life' Symbolism in *Paradise Regain'd.*" *RES*, n.s., XI (1960), 384–91.

―――. "*Paradise Regained:* Moral Dialectic and the Pattern of Rejection." *UTQ*, XXXI (1962), 416–30.

Stein, Arnold. "*Paradise Regained.*" *Heroic Knowledge: An Interpretation of Paradise Regained and Samson Agonistes.* Minneapolis, 1957, pp. 3–134.

Woodhouse, A. S. P. "Theme and Pattern in *Paradise Regained.*" *UTQ*, XXV (1956), 167–82.

SAMSON AGONISTES

Allen, Don Cameron. "The Idea as Pattern: Despair and *Samson Agonistes.*" *The Harmonious Vision: Studies in Milton's Poetry.* Baltimore, 1954, pp. 71–94.

Beum, Robert. "The Rhyme in *Samson Agonistes.*" *TSLL*, IV (1962), 177–82.

Boughner, Daniel C. "Milton's Harapha and Renaissance Comedy." *ELH*, XI (1944), 297–306.

Finney, Gretchen L. "Chorus in *Samson Agonistes.*" *PMLA*, LVIII (1943), 649–64.

Gossman, Anne. "Milton's Samson as the Tragic Hero Purified by Trial." *JEGP*, LXI (1962), 528–41.

Hanford, James Holly. "*Samson Agonistes* and Milton in Old Age." *Studies in Shakespeare, Milton, and Donne*. New York, 1925, pp. 167–89. Rptd. in *John Milton: Poet and Humanist*. Cleveland, 1966, pp. 264–86.

Krouse, F. Michael. *Milton's Samson and the Christian Tradition*. Princeton [for Cincinnati], 1949.

Miriam Clare, Sister. *Samson Agonistes: A Study in Contrast*. New York, 1964.

Parker, William Riley. "The Trinity Manuscript and Milton's Plans for a Tragedy." *JEGP*, XXXIV (1935), 225–32.

———. *Milton's Debt to Greek Tragedy in Samson Agonistes*. Baltimore, 1937.

———. "The Date of *Samson Agonistes*." *PQ*, XVIII (1949), 145–66.

———. "Notes on the Text of *Samson Agonistes*." *JEGP*, LX (1961), 688–98.

Prince, F. T., ed. *Samson Agonistes*. London, 1957.

Sellin, Paul R. "Milton's Epithet *Agonistes*." *SEL*, IV (1964), 137–62.

Stein, Arnold. "*Samson Agonistes*." *Heroic Knowledge: An Interpretation of Paradise Regained and Samson Agonistes*. Minneapolis, 1957, pp. 137–202.

Wilkenfeld, Roger B. "Act and Emblem: The Conclusion of *Samson Agonistes*." *ELH*, XXXII (1965), 160–68.

Wilkes, G. A. "The Interpretation of *Samson Agonistes*." *HLQ*, XXVI (1963), 363–79.

Woodhouse, A. S. P. "Tragic Effect in *Samson Agonistes*." *UTQ*, XXVIII (1959), 205–22.

MILTON'S STYLE AND VERSIFICATION

Arthos, John. *Dante, Michelangelo, and Milton*. London, 1963.

Banks, Theodore H., Jr. "Miltonic Rhythm: A Study of the Relation of the Full Stops to the Rhythm of *Paradise Lost*." *PMLA*, XLII (1927), 140–45.

Boone, Lalia Phipps. "The Language of Book VI, *Paradise Lost*." *SAMLA Studies in Milton: Essays on John Milton and His Works*, ed. J. Max Patrick. Gainesville, 1953, pp. 114–27.

Bridges, Robert. *Milton's Prosody*. Oxford, 1893. Rptd. 1901.

Broadbent, J. B. "Milton's Rhetoric." *MP*, LVI (1959), 224–42.

Clark, Evert M. "Milton's English Poetical Vocabulary." *SP*, LIII (1956), 220–38.

Cook, Albert. "Milton's Abstract Music." *UTQ*, XXIX (1960), 370–85.

Daniells, Roy. *Milton, Mannerism and Baroque.* Toronto, 1963.

Darbishire, Helen. "Milton's Poetic Language." *E&S,* X (1957), 31–52.

———. "Milton's Prosody in the Poems of the Trinity Manuscript." *PMLA,* LIV (1939), 153–83.

Diekhoff, John S. "Rhyme in *Paradise Lost.*" *PMLA,* XLIX (1934), 539–43.

———. "Terminal Pause in Milton's Verse." *SP,* XXXII (1935), 235–39.

Ekfelt, F. E. "The Graphic Diction of Milton's English Prose." *PQ,* XXV (1946), 46–69.

Emma, Ronald David. *Milton's Grammar.* The Hague, 1964.

Fletcher, Harris F. "A Possible Origin of Milton's 'Counterpoint' or Double Rhythm." *JEGP,* LIV (1955), 521–25.

Hunter, William B., Jr. "The Sources of Milton's Prosody." *PQ,* XXVIII (1949), 125–44.

Kellog, George A. "Bridges' *Milton's Prosody* and Renaissance Metrical Theory." *PMLA,* LXVIII (1953), 268–85.

Leavis, F. R. "Milton's Verse." *Revaluation: Tradition and Development in English Poetry.* London, 1936, pp. 42–67.

Lerner, L. D. "The Miltonic Simile." *EC,* IV (1954), 297–308.

Miles, Josephine. *The Continuity of Poetic Language: Studies in English Poetry from the 1540's to the 1940's.* Berkeley, 1951.

Oras, Ants. "Milton's Blank Verse and the Chronology of His Major Poems." *SAMLA, Studies in Milton: Essays on John Milton and His Works,* ed. J. Max Patrick. Gainesville, 1953, pp. 128–97.

Prince, F. T. *The Italian Element in Milton's Verse.* Oxford, 1954.

Ricks, Christopher. *Milton's Grand Style.* Oxford, 1963.

Sprott, S. Ernest. *Milton's Art of Prosody.* Oxford, 1953.

Tuve, Rosemond. *Elizabethan and Metaphysical Imagery: Renaissance Poetic and Twentieth-Century Critics.* Chicago, 1947.

Watkins, W. B. C. *An Anatomy of Milton's Verse.* Baton Rouge, 1955.

Whaler, James. "Compounding and Distribution of Similes in *Paradise Lost.*" *MP,* XXVIII (1931), 313–27.

———. "Animal Simile in *Paradise Lost.*" *PMLA,* XLVII (1932), 534–53.

———. "The Miltonic Simile." *PMLA,* XLVI (1931), 1034–74.

———. *Counterpoint and Symbol: An Inquiry into the Rhythm of Milton's Epic Style.* Copenhagen, 1956.

Widmer, Kingsley. "The Iconography of Renunciation: The Miltonic Simile." *ELH,* XXV (1958), 258–69.

FAME AND INFLUENCE

Adams, Robert M. *Ikon: John Milton and the Modern Critics*. Ithaca, 1955.

Barker, Arthur E. "'. . . And on His Crest Sat Horror': Eighteenth Century Interpretations of Milton's Sublimity and His Satan." *UTQ*, XI (1942), 421–36.

Bergonzi, Bernard. "Criticism and the Milton Controversy." *The Living Milton: Essays by Various Hands*, ed. Frank Kermode. London, 1960, pp. 162–80.

Blondel, Jaques. "Sur dix années de critique miltonienne." *EA*, XVI (1963), 38–53.

Brooks, Cleanth. "Milton and Critical Re-Estimates." *PMLA*, LXVI (1951), 1045–54.

———. "Milton and the New Criticism." *SR*, LIX (1951), 1–22.

Collins, John Churton. "Miltonic Myths and Their Authors." *Studies in Poetry and Criticism*. London, 1905, pp. 167–203.

Dalton, John. *Comus, A Mask: (Now Adapted to the Stage) As Altered from Milton's Mask at Ludlow Castle*. London, 1738.

Dryden, John. *The State of Innocence, and Fall of Man: An Opera Written in Heroic Verse*. London, 1677.

Empson, William. "Milton and Bentley." *Some Versions of Pastoral*. London, 1935, pp. 149–91.

Gilbert, Allan H. "Some Critical Opinions on Milton." *SP*, XXXIII (1936), 523–33.

Good, John Walter. *Studies in the Milton Tradition*. Urbana, 1915.

Gordon, R. K. "Keats and Milton." *MLR*, XLII (1947), 434–46.

Havens, Raymond D. *The Influence of Milton on English Poetry*. Cambridge, Mass., 1922.

Jenny, Gustav. *Miltons Verlorenes Paradies in der deutschen Literatur des 18. Jahrhunderts.* Sankt Gallen [Germany], 1890.

Martin, Leonard Cyril. "Thomas Warton and the Early Poems of Milton." *Proceedings of the Bibliographical Association*, XX (1934), 24–43.

Myers, Robert Manson. *Handel, Dryden, and Milton: Being a Series of Observations on the Poems of Dryden and Milton, as Alter'd and Adapted by Various Hands, and Set to Musick by Mr. Handel, to Which are Added, Authentick Texts of Several of Mr. Handel's Oratorios*. London, 1956.

Nelson, James G. *The Sublime Puritan: Milton and the Victorians*. Madison, 1963.

Oras, Ants. *Milton's Editors and Commentators from Patrick Hume to Henry John Todd (1695–1801): A Study in Critical Views and Methods.* London and Tartu, Estonia, 1931.

Parker, William Riley. *Milton's Contemporary Reputation, an Essay, Together with a Tentative List of Printed Allusions to Milton, 1641–1674, and Facsimile Reproductions of Five Contemporary Pamphlets Written in Answer to Milton.* Columbus, 1940.

Pommer, Henry F. *Milton and Melville.* Pittsburgh, 1950.

Samuel, Irene. *Plato and Milton.* Ithaca, 1947.

Saurat, Denis. *Blake and Milton.* Bordeaux, 1920.

Scherpbier, H. *Milton in Holland: A Study in the Literary Relations of England and Holland before 1730.* Amsterdam, 1933.

Sensabaugh, George F. *That Grand Whig, Milton.* Stanford, 1952.

———. *Milton in Early America.* Princeton, 1964.

Sherburn, George. "The Early Popularity of Milton's Minor Poems." *MP,* XVII (1919–20), 259–78, 515–40.

Stanton, Robert. "*Typee* and Milton: Paradise Well Lost." *MLN,* LXXIV (1959), 407–11.

Telleen, John Martin. *Milton dans la Littérature française.* Paris, 1904.

Thaler, Alwin. "Milton in the Theatre." *SP,* XVII (1920), 269–308.

Woodhouse, A. S. P. "The Historical Criticism of Milton." *PMLA,* LXVI (1951), 1033–44.

GENERAL CRITICISM AND INTERPRETATION

Arnold, Matthew. "Milton." *Essays in Criticism, Second Series.* London and New York, 1888.

Brinkley, Roberta F. *Arthurian Legend in the Seventeenth Century.* Baltimore, 1932.

Bush, Douglas. *English Literature in the Earlier Seventeenth Century: 1600–1660.* 2nd rev. ed., Oxford, 1962.

———. *Mythology and the Renaissance Tradition in English Poetry.* 2nd rev. ed., New York, 1963.

Clark, Sir George Norman. *The Seventeenth Century.* 2nd rev. ed., Oxford, 1947.

Davies, Godfrey. *The Early Stuarts, 1603–1660.* 2nd rev. ed., Oxford, 1959.

Diekhoff, John S. "Critical Activity of the Poetic Mind: John Milton." *PMLA,* LV (1940), 748–72.

Eliot, T. S. "A Note on the Verse of John Milton." *E&S,* XXI (1935), 32–40.

Emerson, Ralph Waldo. "Milton." *North American Review,* XLVII (1838), 56–73.

Frye, Northrup. *The Return of Eden: Five Essays on Milton's Epics.* Toronto, 1965.

Grierson, H. J. C. *Cross Currents in English Literature of the XVIIth Century; or, The World, The Flesh, and the Spirit: Their Actions and Reactions.* London, 1929.

————. *Milton and Wordsworth: Poets and Prophets. A Study of Their Reactions to Political Events.* New York, 1937.

Hanford, James Holly. "Milton and the Return to Humanism." *SP*, XVI (1919), 126–47.

Knight, G. Wilson. *Chariot of Wrath: The Message of John Milton to Democracy at War.* London, 1942.

Langdon, Ida. *Milton's Theory of Poetry and Fine Art.* New Haven, 1924.

Le Comte, Edward S. *Yet Once More: Verbal and Psychological Pattern in Milton.* New York, 1953.

Macaulay, Thomas B. "Milton." *Edinburgh Review*, LXXXIV (1825), 304–46.

Mahood, M. M. *Poetry and Humanism.* New Haven and London, 1950.

Nicolson, Marjorie Hope. *John Milton: A Reader's Guide to His Poetry.* New York, 1963.

Praz, Mario. "Milton and Poussin." *Seventeenth-Century Studies Presented to Sir Herbert Grierson.* Oxford, 1938, pp. 192–210.

Ross, Malcolm M. *Milton's Royalism: A Study of the Conflict of Symbol and Idea in the Poems.* Ithaca, 1943.

Sayce, Richard Anthony. *The French Biblical Epic in the Seventeenth Century.* Oxford, 1955.

Schultz, Howard. *Milton and Forbidden Knowledge.* New York, 1955.

Smith, Logan Pearsall. *Milton and His Modern Critics.* London, 1940.

Spingarn, J. E., ed. *Critical Essays of the Seventeenth Century.* 3 vols., Oxford, 1908–09. Rptd., Bloomington, 1957.

Swardson, Howard Roland. *Poetry and the Fountain of Light: Observations on the Conflict Between Christian and Classical Traditions in Seventeenth-Century Poetry.* London, 1962.

Thompson, E. N. S. *Essays on Milton.* New Haven, 1914.

Thorpe, James E., Jr., ed. *Milton Criticism: Selections from Four Centuries.* New York, 1950.

Tillyard, E. M. W. *The Metaphysicals and Milton.* London, 1956.

Trevelyan, G. M. *England Under the Stuarts.* 2nd rev. ed., London, 1947.

Whiting, George W. *Milton's Literary Milieu.* Chapel Hill, 1939.

Willey, Basil. *The Seventeenth Century Background.* London, 1934.

INDEX